The Exclusive Economic Zone

Charles Quince

Series in Law

VERNON PRESS

www.vernonpress.com

In the Americas:
Vernon Press
1000 N West Street,
Suite 1200, Wilmington,
Delaware 19801
United States

In the rest of the world:
Vernon Press
C/Sancti Espiritu 17,
Malaga, 29006
Spain

Series in Law

Library of Congress Control Number: 2018964969

ISBN: 978-1-62273-535-8

Table of contents

Chapter 1

Introduction

The UN has not only been influential in maintaining global peace and security but also in implementing legal mechanism that controls the seas. The role it plays in the progressive development of the law of the sea is, without a doubt, significant. The highlight of this important work comes under the guidance of the Third UN Convention of the Law of the Sea (UNCLOS), which essentially defines the two-hundred-mile limits of the Exclusive Economic Zone (EEZ).

The background of the two-hundred-mile EEZ can be found in the unilateral actions that South American nations implemented to protect exclusive claims to natural resources off their shoreline.[1] These claims covered not only the underlying seabed, but also pertinent natural resources in the seabed as well. The concept of the EEZ was further shaped by UNCLOS III and Articles 45–61 of the Informal Single Negotiating Text (ISNT) appended to the Second Substantive Session of UNCLOS III.[2] The revised Single Negotiating Text associated with the 1976 New York sessions clarified and reformulated the provisions set forth in Articles 45–61 of the ISNT.[3] The standards associated with the EEZ were reproduced in the informal composite negotiating text (ICNT), the 198 Draft Convention, and in the Law of the Sea (LOS) Convention.[4]

---

[1] Gabriel González-Videla, "Chilean Presidential Declaration Concerning the Continental Shelf," June 23, 1947; Eduardo Ferrero, "El Nuevo Derecho del Mar: El Perú y las 200 Millas," Peruvian Decree No. 781, August 1, 1947; Winston Conrad Extavour, *The Exclusive Economic Zone: A Study of the Evolution and Progressive Development of International Law of the Sea* (Geneva: Institut Universitaire de Haute Etudes Internationales, 1979), 73.

[2] John R. Stevenson and Bernard H. Oxman, "The Third United Nations Conference on the Law of the Sea: The 1975 Geneva Session," *AJIL* 69, no. 4 (1975): 763.

[3] The third substantive session of UNCLOS III was held between March 15 and May 7 of 1976 in New York and the fourth session was held between August 2 and September 10 of 1976. Bernard H. Oxman, "The Third United Nations Conference on the Law of the Sea: The 1976 New York Sessions," *AJIL* 71, no. 2 (1977): 248.

[4] "Informal Composite Negotiating Text," UN Doc. A/Conf. 62/WP.10, July 10, 1977, http://legal.un.org/docs/?path=../diplomaticconferences/1973_los/docs/english/vol_8/a_conf62_wp10.pdf&lang=E; "Draft Convention on the Law of the Sea," UN Doc. A/Conf. 62/L. 78, August 28, *Official Records* 15 (1981), http://legal.un.org/diplomaticconferences/1973_los/vol14.shtml, 172; Stevenson and Oxman. "The Third United Nations Conference on the Law of the Sea: The 1975 Geneva Session," Articles 55–75.

Generically, the EEZ concept gives coastal states the exclusive right to develop a maritime zone beyond and adjacent to the territorial sea extending two hundred miles from their baselines. As numerated in the UNCLOS III, these states have sovereign rights to natural resources and other collateral activities relating to economic exploration and exploitation in their respective maritime zones. As defined by the LOS Convention, coastal states enjoy jurisdictional rights pertaining to the erection of artificial islands, structures, and installations; marine scientific research (MSR); and preservation of the sea environment. In addition, developing states also enjoy traditional rights that other states enjoy when it comes to overflight, cable, and pipeline laying, and the right of navigation.[5]

One of the most outstanding features of the EEZ concept is that state practice seems to play a defining role in its development prior to the conclusion of UNCLOS III in 1982. During the initial stages of the conference, only a minimum number of states with fishery jurisdictional claims went beyond the 12 miles limit.[6] However, by the late 1970s, the number of states with these fishery claims increased to well over ninety, including almost fifty states developing their own EEZ.[7] State legislative and treaty formulation reflected the ongoing negotiation process associated with UNCLOS and the rules finalized in the negotiating text and in the Draft Convention. In this framework, one commentator noted,

> The provisions of the Negotiating Texts and of the Draft Convention elaborated by the Third U.N. Conference on the Law of the Sea and the consensus which emerged at the Conference, have had ... a constitutive or generating legal effect, serving as the focal point for and the authoritative guide to a consistent and uniform practice of states.[8]

Implementing the EEZ provisions, as defined by the guidelines of UNCLOS III, continued after the LOS Convention came into force. Globally, states con-

---

[5] This, of course, is a general description concerning the rights of states, as expressed in Article 56 and 58 of the LOS Convention. For more detailed information on the rights of states, see Clive Parry, John P. Grant, Anthony Perry, and Arthur D. Watts, eds., *Encyclopedic Dictionary of International Law* (New York: Oceana, 1986), 122.

[6] Robert B. Krueger and Myron H. Nordquist, "The Evolution of the 200 Mile Exclusive Economic Zone: State Practice in the Pacific Basin," *VJIL* 19, no. 2 (1979): 324–25.

[7] *Ibid.*

[8] Jimeneze D'Arechaga, "Case Concerning the Continental Shelf (Tunisia v. Libyan Arab Jamahiriya)," *ICJ Rep* Sep. Op. (1982): 115, para. 54; Felipe H. Paolillo, "The Exclusive Economic Zone in Latin American Practice and Legislation," *ODIL* 26, no. 2 (1995): 106.

tinue to apply various aspects of this Convention,[9] although implementation reflects the policy goals of each state.

This book attempts to present a comprehensive study of the EEZ concept as it relates to the LOS Convention and state practice. Although coastal states may have the right to develop a two-hundred-mile EEZ and this right is an integral part of contemporary international relations, it is also true that the EEZ concept is shrouded in legal ambiguities. As noted by one legal expert, "though there is general agreement that the EEZ is already or is fast becoming an accepted doctrine in international law there are differences in terms of exactly what this acceptance entails and what specific rights and duties it encompasses."[10] In essence, the EEZ concept needs a thorough analysis to decipher the rights and duties of the states that develop their EEZ according to international norms.

This work will systematically examine the LOS Convention's EEZ guidelines in the context of the development of UNCLOS III, and analyze evolving state practice in the context of national proclamations and legislative action to identify which provisions (if any) are taken in state practice and which provisions do not correlate with the guidelines of the LOS Convention. The scope of the EEZ rule will be examined to determine what rights nonparty states have under the LOS Convention.

To ensure that a comprehensive analysis emerges on the subject, this work is divided into five chapters. Chapter one gives an overview of the rules, under international law, pertaining to the living resources of the sea's water column before the convening of the First Substantive Negotiating Session of UNCLOS in 1974. This background information will clarify the development of the EEZ regime that was given at UNCLOS.

Chapter two analyzes the nature and breadth of coastal states' rights and the corresponding duties in the EEZ under the LOS Convention. Although the hypothesis associated with the EEZ was largely accepted at UNCLOS III, the imprecise wording of the negotiation history created ambiguities that lead to problems. Thus, an examination of the LOS Convention's EEZ provisions relating to coastal states' rights is helpful. Because coastal states' rights in the EEZ have

---

[9] UN Division for Ocean Affairs and the Law of the Sea, *Law of the Sea Bulletin,* no. 23 (1993): 15; UN Division for Ocean Affairs and the Law of the Sea, *Practice of States at the Time of Entry into Force of the United Nations Convention on the Law of the Sea* (New York: United Nations, 1994), 9–18, 35–40, 70–75, and 176–91.

[10] Lawrence Juda, "The Exclusive Economic Zone: Compatibility of National Claims and the UN Convention on the Law of the Sea," *ODIL* 16 (1986): 2.

come under the aegis of various judicial terms in the LOS Convention, chapter two is divided into two sections: one relates to coastal states' rights pertaining to economic uses of the EEZ and the other focuses on coastal states' rights and duties pertaining to the noneconomic uses of the EEZ.

In chapter three, I will examine the rights and correlating duties of third (developing) state users of the EEZ, as these responsibilities were defined at UNCLOS and formulated in the provisions of Part V of the LOS Convention. These responsibilities are divided into two distinct sections: the noneconomic users of the EEZ and those related to the living resources of the EEZ. In the category of noneconomic users, an intense analysis focuses on the navigational and nonnavigational military uses of the EEZ in the context of UNCLOS negotiations and related provisions of the LOS Convention. The rights that the LOS Convention does not expressly give to coastal or other states are also examined. In regard to the second category of responsibilities, I will examine whether the provisions pertaining to access of the EEZ's living resources give priority of access to any specific group of states.

The fourth chapter involves the study of how states implement the provisions of the EEZ between the years 1975 to the present. As a central point, the various two-hundred-mile claim zones are highlighted, along with the trend of states when it comes to extending their jurisdictional zones. I will further examine the LOS Convention to ascertain whether the validity of these claims is supported by the provisions contained in the Convention.

The fifth chapter centers on an examination of the EEZ as it relates to contemporary times and the relationship between the EEZ and customary international law. I will analyze the prerequisites for establishing international custom and how these requirements are applied to the two-hundred-mile EEZ. I will further examine the scope of customary international law as it pertains to EEZ concept to see if the LOS Convention can be applied by or against third states.

The methodical approach that helps facilitate this study involves the historical legal and positivist approach. Legal development related to the rights of coastal states' control over living resources adjacent to the sea's water column are analyzed and divided into three primary stages: The pre-UNCLOS III stage, the UNCLOS III negotiating stage, and the post-UNCLOS III stage (with special attention given to the last two stages). This requirement is needed to clarify the exact scope of the rights of coastal states under contemporary international law.

I. The Concept of Freedom of the Seas and Access to Living Resources of the Sea's Water Column

To gain clarity on how access to fisheries beyond the territorial sea developed in the confines of international law before the First Substantive Session of UNCLOS III, it is important to examine the high seas regime as it applies to the living resources of the sea's water column. This analysis will be bolstered by a concise historical account of the development of the coastal states' jurisdiction over fisheries, particularly under the auspices of the Truman Proclamations of 1945 and through the failure of the world community to come to an agreement regarding fishery limits at the 1958 and 1960 Geneva Conferences and the First Substantive Session of UNCLOS III in Caracas in the early 1970s.

The concept of "freedom of the sea" was developed and facilitated by the legal expert Hugo Grotius' seminal work *Mare Liberum.*[11] In this work, Grotius argued that his client, the Dutch East India Company, theoretically had the right to freely navigate the Indian Ocean and other bodies of water that the Spanish and the Portuguese had monopolized economically.[12] Although Grotius highlighted the economic and political domination that Spain and Portugal held over the seas, the freedoms associated with navigational travel and fishing played a prominent role in this thought process: "The sea is common to all, because it is so limitless that it cannot become a possession of any one, and because it is adapted for the use of all, whether we consider it from the point of view of navigation or fishing."[13]

Although Grotius' theory about the application of the law of the sea was influential, his assertions provoked widespread disagreement among other scholars.[14] His insistence that nations should enjoy open and free fishing on the high seas directly challenged the interests of a number of powerful maritime states, especially England.[15] England, along with other powerful European nations, was not prepared to accept the notion of total freedom of the seas. The Dutch, a fierce maritime rival of English, used their herring-fishing success along the British coastline to increase their financial viability and their global power. To curtail such exploitation of its fisheries, the British asserted sovereign authority over undefined English water through the implementa-

[11] Hugo Grotius, *The Freedom of the Seas, or the Right Which Belongs to the Dutch to Take Part in the Eastern Indian Trade* (Indianapolis, IN: Library Fund, 2004).
[12] Thomas Wemyss Fulton, *The Sovereignty of the Seas* (London: William Blackwood and Sons, 1911), 338–39.
[13] Grotius, *The Freedom of the Seas,* 28.
[14] Fulton, *The Sovereignty of the Seas,* 349–77.
[15] *Ibid.,* 351.

tion of progressive tax policies by King James over all foreign fishing activities.[16] A Scottish lawyer, William Welwood, directly confronted Grotius' assertions regarding the freedom of the seas by suggesting that coastal states has the right to exploit fishery resources germane to their region. He argued that coastal states had a legal duty to protect and preserve fisheries in the waters off their coasts and those fishers from foreign countries should not be permitted to fish in those waters.[17] Welwood used Biblical scripture and a broad interpretation of Roman law to strengthen his argument.[18] Under his interpretation of Roman law, Welwood argued that the freedom-of-the-sea concept only applied to native Roman citizens, not to fisherman of other nations.[19] He also believed that a hundred-mile nautical limit should be the set limit for coastal states' sovereignty.[20]

Perhaps the most coherent and direct reply to Grotius' concept of the freedom of the sea came from John Selden's work *Mare Clausum.* In *Mare Clausum,* Selden asserts that natural law decrees that mankind should control the sea.[21] He used ancient traditions and Biblical guidelines to support his theory. Using Genesis verses "And the fear of you and the dread of you shall be upon ... all the fishes of the sea," Selden argued that man was divinely ordained to dominate the seas.[22] He also suggested that the Biblical verse "Replenish the Earth and Subdue it" indicated man's dominion over the fish of the sea.[23]

Selden used customs and traditions of ancient and contemporary countries to support his argument. He notes that these customs and traditions justified the acquisitions of the sea's resources.[24] On its face, Selden's assertions directly confronted Grotius' view that custom disproves any appropriation of the sea or its resources.

The arguments present by Welwood and Selden concerning the freedom of the seas ultimately prevailed. For over two-hundred years, Selden's theory

---

16 *Ibid.*

17 William Welwood, *An Abridgement of All Sea-Lawes,* 1613, cited by Leslie M. MacRae, "Customary International Law and the United Nations Law of the Sea Treaty," *California Western International Law Journal* 13 (1983): 192.

18 *Ibid.*

19 *Ibid.*

20 *Ibid.*

21 John Selden, *Of the Dominion or Ownership of the Sea,* trans. Marchamont Nedham (1652; repr., New York: Arno, 1972), 18–20.

22 Genesis 9:2, cited by *ibid.,* 28.

23 *Ibid.*

24 *Ibid.,* 42.

was considered the leading authority on maritime law in England and on the European continent, which put the concept of freedom of the sea under a cloud of ambiguity.[25] The notion of freedom of the seas became accepted in Europe only after England had attained the status of a global maritime power during the early nineteenth century.[26] British naval forces provided foundational support for the doctrine. The Industrial Revolution also played a key role in the adoption of the freedom-of-the-seas doctrine by European nations. The decline of Dutch fisheries during this time period, coupled with England's rise in this industry, helped facilitate the widespread acceptance of the doctrine on the European continent.[27] In essence, by the early nineteenth century, the doctrine of freedom of the seas had become a basic principle of the Law of the Sea.

As far as fisheries outside the confines of the territorial sea were concerned, states could not implement actions that would restrict the freedom of the seas.[28] Upholding fishing activities, an integral part of the concept of the freedoms of the seas, meant that no nation could legally claim jurisdiction over fishing activities that took place beyond the territorial sea limits. Various courts on domestic and international levels accepted the concept of freedom on the high seas. The English Admiralty Court expressed this sentiment when it stated:

> All nations being equal, all have an equal right to the unappropriated parts of the ocean for their navigation, in places where no local authority exists. Where the subject of all States meet upon a footing of entire equality and independence, no one state, or any of its subjects, has a right to assume or exercise authority over the subject of another.[29]

Fisheries resources beyond the territorial sea came under the authority of the law of possession: title to them was vested in the nation that claimed them as possession.[30] The Behring Sea Fur Seals Arbitration of 1893 solidified this rule.[31] The arbitration came from attempts to uphold conservation measures on the

---

[25] Fulton, *The Sovereignty of the Seas*, 9–10, and 374.

[26] Albert W. Koers, *International Regulation of Marine Fisheries: A Study of Regional Fisheries Organizations* (London: Eyre & Spottiswoode, 1973), 16.

[27] Fulton, *The Sovereignty of the Seas*, 334.

[28] Emmerich de Vattel, *The Law of Nations or the Principles of Natural Law*, vol. 1, trans. C. G. Fenwild (Washington: Carnegie Institution, 1916), 84–85.

[29] "Le Louis," Dods (Great Britain) 2 (1817): 210.

[30] Koers, *International Regulation of Marine Fisheries*, 19.

[31] "Behring Sea Fur Seals Arbitration (Great Britain v. United States of America), 1893," *Moore Digest* 1 (1898): 755.

high seas. The United States had strongly objected to the atrocities of British fishers toward the fur seals of the Behring Sea. The Tribunal ruled that activities outside of the scope of the territorial sea were a legitimate exercise of the principle of freedom of the seas and that the United States did not have jurisdiction over the fur seals when they were outside the three-mile territorial sea.[32]

Since the late nineteenth century, fishing technology and techniques have vastly impacted the fishing industry.[33] The development of trawler fishing, coupled with the advent of sonar to help locate fish, as well as the substitution of steam vessels for the sailing smacks, has revolutionized the fishing industry.[34] One of the most important aspects of these developments centers on the emergence of distant-water fishing activities.[35] Fishers from powerful maritime nations gained the capability to operate efficiently for extended periods of time over vast water distances far from their home shores.[36] In addition, increased capabilities by these fishers allowed them to exploit the traditional fishing grounds of less developed coastal states.[37] The results of these increased capabilities of fishers have led to overexploitation of the world's fishing stocks.[38]

As seen above, the traditional notion that the sea is an inexhaustible source of supply for the world's needs is completely invalid. The response of the law of the sea to these technological developments and their impact on state actions is analyzed in the next section.

II. The Exclusive Fishing Rights of Coastal States

Undeniably, the international law of the sea has been attentive to the technological changes of fishing techniques that threatens fishery industries by facilitating the depletion of fishery resources.[39] Because of this potential deterioration to fishery resources, the international law of the sea has placed limitations on fishing activities on the high seas.

---

32 *Ibid.*, 948.

33 Koers, *International Regulation of Marine Fisheries*, 27–28.

34 *Ibid.*

35 Ram P. Anand, "The Politics of a New Legal Order for Fisheries," *ODIL* 11 (1982): 270.

36 Wilbert M. Chapman, "Fishery Resources in Offshore Waters," in *The Law of the Sea: Offshore Boundaries and Zones*, ed. Louis M. Alexander (Columbus: Ohio State University Press, 1967), 92.

37 Anand, "The Politics of a New Legal Order for Fisheries."

38 Koers, *International Regulation of Marine Fisheries*, 28.

39 *Ibid.*

The Territorial Sea

The territorial sea represents the waterway that is adjacent to the coastline of a state, extending beyond its land territory and internal waters, over which the state has sovereignty.[40] The protection of coastal states' territory and its citizens is one of the primary reasons the territorial sea was established.[41]

In essence, the first limitation placed on freedom of fishing in the seas resulted from the notion that not all waterways are covered by the regime of the high seas.[42] By definition, the high seas are that body of water that is not included in the territorial sea or in the vicinity of a state's internal waters.[43] Thus, the freedom of fishing activities does not extend to the sea areas included in the internal waters and territorial sea of coastal states.

Although the development of the territorial sea has resulted from the need to initiate navigational and domestic security, coastal states' exclusive jurisdiction over adjacent fisheries corresponds to the width of the territorial sea. Coastal states that rejected the concept of a narrow territorial sea have often argued that a narrow territorial sea is not complemented by acknowledgement of the coastal state's jurisdiction in a zone that lies beyond the fishing activities of the territorial sea, and that no definitive purpose could be served by creating a narrow limit for the territorial sea.[44] These states believed that a narrow territorial sea strip does not provide adequate protection for their fishing activities.

The assumption that exclusive fisheries jurisdiction was independent of the concept of the territorial sea gained momentum after the First Codification Conference of 1930.[45] The failure to establish a territorial sea maximum width at the 1930 Conference facilitated the rise of a series of claims to adjacent resources of the high seas, either by the extension of the territorial sea or by the extension of exclusive fishing rights.

---

[40] Ian Brownlie, *Principles of Public International Law*, 4th ed. (Oxford: Clarendon Press, 1990), 83–84.

[41] Ivan Anthony Shearer, ed., *Starke's International Law*, 11th ed. (Boston: Butterworths, 1994), 220.

[42] Koers, *International Regulation of Marine Fisheries*, 17–18.

[43] "Convention on the High Seas, Geneva, April 29, 1958," *UNTS* 450 (1963): 82, Article 1.

[44] Myres S. McDougal and William T. Burke, *The Public Order of the Oceans* (New Haven, CT: Yale University Press, 1987), 453–82.

[45] Jesse S. Reeves, "The Codification of the Law of Territorial Waters," *AJIL* 24, no. 3 (1930): 492–93.

Post-1930 Claims to High Seas Resources

The extension of state jurisdiction over large parts of the high seas started early in Latin America. These national claims developed prior to World War II and were centered on the need for security.[46] Since World War II, coastal states claims to fishing rights in waters adjacent to the territorial sea have continually risen, leading to limitations on the traditional concept of freedom of fishing on the open seas. The period following World War II has been marked by an increase toward extending national jurisdiction over the waters adjacent to the territorial sea to give coastal states more economic control over the exploitation of living resources in such waters.[47] The initiation of these claims emerged for two reasons: first, a need existed to develop the most effective regime to help facilitate conservation of the living resources; second, a need existed for coastal states to achieve control over the primary economic resources germane to these waters.[48]

The Truman Proclamation of 1945 on the seabed and coastal fisheries started these unilateral extensions.[49] One proclamation to which Truman affixed his signature sought to protect the Alaskan salmon fisheries from exploitation by Japanese fishers.[50] Waters that were traditionally fished by U.S. citizens or expected to be fished by U.S. citizens would be controlled by the United States, whereas waters that were jointly exploited by citizens of different nations should be regulated by agreements between the two competing nations.

The other Truman proclamation asserted U.S. jurisdiction and control over the natural resources of the subsoil and the seabed of the continental

---

[46] On October 3, 1939, Declaration of Panama created a security buffer zone that extended three hundred to twelve hundred miles from the shoreline and included all the countries of the American Continent except Canada. International Conference of American States in Panama, "Declaration of Panama," *AJIL* 34, Suppl. 1 (1940): 17.

[47] Andrzej Straburzyński, "Exclusive Fishery Zones: International and Polish Practice," *PYIL* 29 (1970): 257.

[48] Malgorzata Fitzmaurice-Lachs, "The Legal Regime of the Baltic Sea Fisheries," *NILR* 29, No. 2 (1982): 200.

[49] Presidential Proclamation No. 2667, Concerning the Policy of the United States with Respect to the Natural Resources of the Subsoil and Seabed of the Continental Shelf, September 28, 1945, in ST/LEG/SER. B/1 (1951): 38; Presidential Proclamation No. 2668, Concerning the Policy of the United States with Respect to Coastal Fisheries in Certain Areas of the High Seas, September 28, 1945.

[50] Carolyn Hudson, "Fishery and Economic Zones as Customary International Law," *SDLR* 17, no. 3 (1980): 661–66.

shelf continuous to its coasts[51] to solidify the investment climate for U.S. oil companies.[52] The proclamation emphasized that the waters above the continental shelf would not be affected and would remain open for freedom of navigation. Although the proclamation outlined no specific boundary, a later public statement by the presidential staff indicated that one-hundred fathoms would represent the maximum outer limit.[53] This, in essence, meant that the United States used this proclamation to lay claim to the natural resources that were germane to the continental shelf.[54] The Truman proclamations did not generate wholesale protests from other states, mainly because no states believed the proclamations violated their rights. In reality, instead of generating protests, other states began making the same types of claims,[55] which ultimately led to the development of the concept of coastal state jurisdiction over the continental shelf.

Some Latin American states asserted a much wider jurisdiction that not only included the continental shelf, but also the waters above it.[56] A little over a month after Truman issued his proclamation on the continental shelf, Mexico announced that the continental shelf adjacent to its coasts would be incorporated into its national territory,[57] with Panama taking similar actions in March of 1946.[58] Unlike the Truman proclamation, these two South American declarations extended the coastal state's jurisdiction over the entire continental shelf. President Peron of Argentina announced, in October 1946, that not only was the continental shelf adjacent to Argentina considered sovereign territory, but also the *epicontinental sea* that covered that shelf was also under Argentinian control.

---

51 Presidential Proclamation No. 2668.

52 Hudson, "Fishery and Economic Zones as Customary International Law," 664.

53 A fathom is a unit of measurement of the depth of water equal to 1.8 meters.

54 Hudson, "Fishery and Economic Zones as Customary International Law," 664–68.

55 For additional information on these claims, see Martinus Willem Mouton, *The Continental Shelf* (The Hague: Martinus Nijhoff, 1952).

56 For more information on these claims, see United States Department of State, Bureau of Intelligence and Research, Geographer, *International Boundary Study, Series A: Limits in the Seas, National Claims to Maritime Jurisdiction* No. 36 (1973); F. V. García Amador, "Latin America and the Law of the Sea," Law of the Sea Institute, Occasional Paper No. 14, July 1972; Louis B. Sohn and Kristen Gustafson, *The Law of the Sea in a Nutshell* (St. Paul, MN: West Group, 1984), 116.

57 Presidential Declaration with Respect to the Continental Shelf, October 29, 1945, in ST/LEG/SER. B/1 (1951): 13.

58 Political Constitution of Panama. March 1, 1946, in ST/LEG/SER. B/1 (1951): 15 Article 209.

Following this lead, Chile declared sovereign control over both the continental shelf and its resources. On June 23, 1947, Chile proclaimed "its national sovereignty over the seas adjacent to its coasts whatever may be their depths, and within those limits necessary in order to reserve, protect, preserve, and exploit the natural resources ... found on, within, and below the said seas."[59] The declaration fixed the area concerned at two-hundred miles and provided for the free navigation of third and developing countries.[60] Chile used the October, 1939, Panamanian declaration as precedent to support its claim and the principle of unilateralism associated with the Truman proclamations.[61] The primary objectives of establishing this zone involved security, preservation, and exploitation of the zone's resources, which seems to indicate that the Chilean declaration sought to establish a maritime zone based on the notion of limited sovereignty over the territorial sea, rather than full control over the area.

Peru, to enhance its anchovy fishery industry, proclaimed Peruvian sovereignty and jurisdiction over adjacent waters up to a distance of two hundred miles. In its proclamation, Peru allowed freedom of navigation to vessels of all nations in its declared zone.[62] Because the Peruvian continental shelf is narrower than that of Chile, it has to rely on a two-hundred-mile distance to assert its authority.[63] The incompatibility between the traditional concept of the territorial sea, as expressed in the 1958 Convention, and a provision in Peruvian Supreme Decree No. 781 that protects the notion of freedom of navigation, combined with the preambular considerations of the Peruvian Supreme Decree, implies that the claim centered on limited functional sovereignty rather than a claim to a full territorial sea maritime zone.

The declaration made by Costa Rica in 1949 placed emphasis on the notion that the continental shelf was subject to national sovereignty "at whatever depth

---

59 Chilean Presidential Declaration Concerning the Continental Shelf, in ST/LEG/SER. B/1 (1951): 6.

60 *Ibid.*

61 The Declaration was adopted in the form of a resolution of the first Consultative Meeting of the Ministers of Foreign Affairs of the American Republics, Panama 23, September 23 to October 3, 1939, in Chapman, "Fishery Resources in Offshore Waters"; Ann L. Hollick, "The Origins of the 200-mile Offshore Zones," *AJIL* 71 (1977): 495.

62 Theodore A. Garaioca, "The Continental Shelf and the Extension of the Territorial Sea," *U. Miami L. Rev* 10 (1956): 493–94.

63 Krueger and Nordquist, "The Evolution of the 200 Mile Exclusive Economic Zone," 324–25.

it is found."[64] However, the Costa Rican legislation seems insufficient when expressing exactly what rights were valid. The legislation proclaimed that Costa Rica's rights and interests were expressed in accordance with "maritime fishing and hunting" that was "carried on in said area" and that these activities would be "under the surveillance of the government of" Costa Rica.[65] In essence, Costa Rica initiated a more comprehensive protective shield over a zone of two-hundred miles than the other South American nations.

Ecuador has a narrow continental shelf that contains abundant fishing opportunities off its coastline. In a 1950 proclamation, it stated that the continental shelf up to the two-hundred-meter isobaths belonged to Ecuador, and that Ecuador had the authority to exert control over that part of the shelf as well as overfishing areas adjacent to the shelf.[66]

The 1950 Constitution of El Salvador stated that the territory of the nation includes "the adjacent seas to a distance of two hundred miles from the low waterline and the corresponding airspace, subsoil, and continental shelf."[67] In short, El Salvador supported the notion of freedom of navigation but not the freedom of overflight.

The Constitution placed the two-hundred-mile area, along with the corresponding subsoil, sea, and airspace, under the territorial authority of El Salvador. This is one of the definitive features of the territorial-sea framework. In addition, though freedom of navigation was maintained, reference to it was not made to cover freedom of overflight. Forbidding overflight in the zone is another chief feature associated with the regime of the territorial sea. Consequently, this claim seems to be a claim to the territorial sea in the strictest sense.

In 1950, Honduras enacted Legislative Decree No. 102, which defined the continental shelf and "the waters which cover it, in both the Atlantic and Pacific Oceans, at whatever depth it may be found and whatever its extent may be" as it relates to the national territory.[68] Honduras claimed "full" and "inalienable" dominion over all resources found in the area.[69] In addition, Honduran Congressional Decree No. 104, issued on March 7, 1950, amended Article 621 of the Civil Code to read, "The sovereignty of the state shall extend

---

64 Decree No. 190 Concerning Fishing and Hunting. September 28, 1949, in ST/LEG/SER. B/1 (1951): 6–7.

65 *Ibid.*

66 Decree Concerning the Limits of the Territorial Sea. November 6, 1950, and Legislative Decree of February 21, 1951, in ST/LEG/SER. B/8 (1959): 9.

67 ST/LEG/SER. B/1 (1951): 30; Article 7.

68 *Ibid.*, 11; Article 4.

69 *Ibid.*, 23.

to submarine platform, as continental and insular shelf and the overlaying waters, at whatever may be its extent, without prejudice to the right of free navigation in accordance with international law."[70]

The terminology that Honduras used in its legislative action is revealing. The terms "dominion," "sovereignty," and "part of the national territory" are key words used to denote a state's authority over a specific geographical area. This interpretation is bolstered by the notion that Congressional Decree No. 21, issued on December 21, 1957, asserts that the sea and airspace above the continental shelf comes under the authority of the Honduran government and is subject to its laws and control.[71]

In August 1952, Chile, Peru, and Ecuador met at a conference that became known as the Declaration of Santiago. This tripartite conference developed a policy centered on a "200 mile maritime zone."[72] The parties maintained that their respective governments were "bound to ensure for their people access to necessary food supplies and to furnishing them with the means of developing their economy." These South American countries stated that "as a principle of their international maritime policy … each of them possess sole sovereignty and jurisdiction over the area of the sea adjacent to the coast of its own country and extending not less than two hundred nautical miles from the said coast."[73]

Two salient points align with this declaration that must be highlighted. The first relates to the economic and social reasoning of the Proclamation. The wording emphasizes economic development and the conservation and safeguarding of natural resources.[74] The second feature centers on the notion that the declaration concerns a maritime zone that aims for specific objectives rather than the notion of the territorial sea in the strictest sense of the concept.[75] The reason is that the declaration refrained from using the label "territorial sea" when referring to the area, although it did use the terms "sovereignty" and "jurisdiction" in its text. Also, although the text of the declaration spoke of sovereignty, it implicitly acknowledged the concept of freedom of navigation.[76] The declaration quickly gained traction in the Inter-American system, garnering

---

[70] ST/LEG/SER. B/6 (1957): 21–22.

[71] *Ibid.*, 23.

[72] The Declaration on the Maritime Zone. August 18, 1952, in ST/LEG/SER. B/6 (1957): 723–24.

[73] *Ibid.*, para. 2.

[74] *Ibid.*, Preamble, para. 1 and 2.

[75] F. V. García Amador, *The Exploitation and Conservation of the Resources of the Sea* (Leiden, Netherlands: A. W. Sijthoff, 1973), 78–86.

[76] Amador, "The Latin American Contribution," 33.

strong support from such influential organizations as the Inter-American Congress of International Law and the Tenth Inter-American Conference.

In assessing the actions taken by the South American countries, it seems apparent that early Latin American state claims to resources beyond the territorial sea were not uniform in language or content. As some commentators have noted, no unified Latin American position existed on the law of the sea regarding the exploitation and conservation of natural resources of the sea.[77] Because these Latin American claims stayed within the confines of the continental shelf, no states raised any objections to them. The primary objections that came from other states involved those claims that sought to extend not only the coastal states' exclusive rights to natural resources that lay within the shelf, but also the living resources that were above the shelf.[78] These objections focused on the argument that they were incompatible with the principles of the freedom of the seas and breached the principles of freedom of fishing.

In the court case, *The North Sea Continental Shelf,* the International Court of Justice (ICJ) asserted that for a rule to properly develop into customary law, "state practice, including that of states whose interests are specifically affected, should have been both extensive and virtually uniform."[79] The Court also reasoned that a state objection to a rule during the formative stages of a norm can prevent it from becoming binding on it.[80] The quantitative element of state practice that the ICJ expressed is a feature on which many scholars have commented.[81]

---

77 *Ibid.,* 37.

78 D. P. O'Connell, *The International Law of the Sea,* vol. 1, ed. I. A. Shearer (Oxford: Clarendon Press, 1982), 31; Barbara Kwiatkowska, "New Soviet Legislation on the 200-Mile Economic Zone and Certain Problems of Evolution of Customary Law," *NILR* 33 (1986): 44; Tullio Treves, "Codification du Droit International et Pratique des Etats dans le Droit de la Mer," RCADI 223 (1990/4): 85.

79 "North Sea Continental Shelf Cases (Federal Republic of Germany v. Denmark; Federal Republic of Germany v. Netherlands)," *ICJ Rep* (1969): 42–43; see also Michael Akehurst, "Custom as a Source of International Law," *British Yearbook of International Law* 42 (1975): 16–17.

80 North Sea Continental Shelf Cases, para. 101.

81 See C. Quince, *The Persistent Objector and Customary International Law* (Denver, CO: Outskirts Press, 2010), 48–49.

UNCLOS I (1958), UNCLOS II, and Exclusive Fishing Rights

To bring some type of coherence to the chaotic situation that defined the decades of the 1940s and 1950s, the UN convened the First Conference on the Law of the Sea in Geneva in 1958. The backdrop of this conference centered on the need to systematically develop and codify the law of the sea. The conference used draft conventions produced by the International Law Commission along with statements developed by various nations on the competing issues surrounding the law of the sea as focal points of discussions. Four conventions were concluded that reasserted the historical notion of freedom of the seas, including freedom of fishing.[82]

UNCLOS addressed the issue of fisheries by connecting it with the high-seas regime and with the breadth of the territorial sea. Regarding the high seas regime, the central points of debate involved which state may exercise conservation control over fishing activities on the high seas. The results of these discussions were ultimately preserved in the Convention on Fishing and Conservation of the Living Resources of the High Seas.[83] This convention was adopted to protect the living resources of the high seas from overexploitation as well as to curtail coastal states' assertions of exclusive fishing rights in waters adjacent to the high seas.[84] The premise behind this lay in the belief that because the convention assures coastal states that implementing conservation measures was a key necessity, these states would abandon their need to make extensive claims.[85]

The finer points of the convention did not involve dictating such specific measures as closed fishing seasons or the size and type of fish that could be taken. What the convention did do was enact guidelines states could follow in conservation matters and specified the circumstances and conditions under which these conservation measures could be applied to foreign fishing vessels in areas of the high seas. Article 6 confirmed the traditional principle of freedom of fishing on the high seas. However, it acknowledged that the conserva-

---

[82] The four Geneva Conventions were developed in April, 1958, and consisted of the "Convention on the Territorial Sea and the Contiguous Zone," *UNTS* 516 (1964): 205–24; "Convention on the High Seas," 82–102; "Convention on the Continental Shelf," *UNTS* 499 (1964): 311–20; "Convention on Fishing and Conservation of Living Resources of the High Seas," *UNTS* 599 (1966): 286–300.

[83] "Convention on Fishing and Conservation of Living Resources of the High Seas."

[84] Derek W. Bowett, *The Law of the Sea* (Manchester: Manchester University Press, 1967), 11.

[85] D. J. Attard, *The Exclusive Economic Zone in International Law* (Oxford: Clarendon Press, 1987), 12.

tion of the living resources of the high seas was a priority. The convention required that all states have a duty to cooperate with other states in implementing pertinent conservation initiatives.[86] The convention defined conservation as "the aggregate of the measures rendering possible the optimum sustainable yield from those resources so as to secure a maximum supply of food and other marine products."[87]

The most salient point is that, from the perspective of the coastal states, the exercise of the freedom of fishing by other nations was subject to the interests and rights of coastal states, as defined by the guidelines of the convention.[88] The interests and rights that apply to coastal states beyond the territorial sea are highlighted in Articles 6 and 7. Article 6, para. 1 explicitly acknowledges the coastal states' need to maintain the productivity of the living resources in any area of the high seas adjacent to its territorial sea and the need to initiate measures that would enhance conservation. Article 7 gives a broad definition of exactly what this entails. It states that regulation of fisheries would center on mutual agreements and when this element was not possible, any coastal state may deploy unilateral conservation actions that are appropriate to any stock of fish in any area of the high seas adjacent to its territorial sea. But such measures would be valid only under the following circumstances:

1. calls for an urgent application of conservation measures in light of existing knowledge of the fisheries;
2. the measures adopted are compatible with scientific findings;
3. if measure adopted are not compatible with scientific finding in their entirety, they discriminate against foreign fishers. However, if other states refuse to accept these measures, any one of them may invoke the compulsory arbitration procedure outlined in Articles 9–12.[89]

---

[86] "Convention on Fishing and Conservation of Living Resources of the High Seas," Article 1.
[87] *Ibid.*, Article 2.
[88] *Ibid.*, Article 1, para. 1.
[89] For a more extensive examination of this convention, see W. W. Bishop, "The 1958 Geneva Convention on Fishing and Conservation of the Living Resources of the High Seas," *Cornell Law Review* 62 (1982): 1206–29; Patricia W. Birnie, "The Law of the Sea before and after UNCLOS I and UNCLOS II," in *The Maritime Dimensions*, ed. Ronald Peter Barston and Patricia W. Birnie (London: George Allen and Unwin, 1980), 19–20.

The hallmark of this convention lay in the notion that it did not allow any preferential rights for coastal states to fisheries in waters beyond their territorial sea. The matrix of this convention involves the application of conservation measures without discrimination and ensures an optimum supply of marine products that could be used as food. This measure also upheld the rule of freedom of the high seas under which ships need only observe the laws associated with their flag state. Although a coastal state has the authority to develop conservation measures that are compatible with offshore fisheries, they are not empowered to exert direct control over citizens from foreign states.

For the question of fisheries as they relate to the breadth of the territorial sea, the most glaring issue centers on whether coastal states should be given exclusive fishing rights in the high seas adjacent to and beyond the territorial sea. During this time period, it was believed that if the only way a coastal state could secure recognition of its rights to exclusive fishing areas outside the territorial sea was to expand the territorial sea itself, the recognition of this right in a continuous zone would secure a narrow territorial sea and nullify the state's desire to extend its territorial jurisdiction.[90] The United States used this assessment to propose a three-mile territorial-sea limit coupled with a six-mile limit for exclusive fishing under the guideline that traditional fishing rights would not be excluded for a ten-year period.[91] The ten-year requirement the United States proposed was eventually reduced to five years. Following the lead of the United States, Canada suggested a three-mile territorial sea limit and granted recognition of exclusive fishing to coastal states with a continuous zone of twelve miles.[92] The Canadian proposal was later modified to be compatible with the U.S. proposal and gained the support of Mexico and India.[93]

Although this compromise received wide support, it did not gain the required two-thirds votes needed to pass. Other well-intended measures also failed to gain the necessary votes to pass. One particular measure that stands out is the Icelandic proposal that aimed to grant coastal states preferential rights when citizens are "overwhelmingly" dependent on coastal fisheries for their economic livelihood and where the "coastal population depends primarily on coastal fisheries."[94] As benevolent as this proposal seemed to be, it did not achieve its goal of granting preferential rights to coastal states. In the

---

90 A. H. Dean, "The Geneva Conference on the Law of the Sea: What Was Accomplished," AJIL 52 (1958): 607–28.

91 UN Doc. A/Conf. 13/C. 1/L. 159, *Official Records* 3 (1958): 253.

92 UN Doc. A/Conf. 13/C. 1/L. 77, Rev. 1, 2, 3, *Official Records* 3 (1958): 232.

93 Revision 2 of the proposal, *ibid.*, 232.

94 UN Doc. A/Conf. 13/C. 1/L. 131, *Official Records* 3 (1958): 269.

final analysis, the conference eventually rejected any and all proposals regarding the territorial sea limit and the coastal state's rights to exclusive fishing zones. These two prominent issues had to be addressed at UNCLOS II.

In essence, another attempt to address the issues surrounding the breadth of the territorial sea and fisheries delimitation was discussed at UNCLOS II. The U.S.–Canadian "six plus six" formula, where coastal states would enjoy preferential fishing rights in any area of the high seas beyond the exclusive fishing zone under specific conditions, was put to vote at UNCLOS II but ultimately failed.[95] Although no agreement was reached regarding the convention, it was acknowledged that the extent of the territorial sea was closely tied to fishing activities and that the primary reason coastal states wanted to extend their territorial-sea jurisdiction involved the need to acquire exclusive fishing rights over living resources.

Post-Geneva and the Geographical Scope of Coastal States' Exclusive Fishing Rights

Lack of success to achieve an agreement on the issue of the breadth of the territorial sea and recognizing any special rights of exclusive access to fisheries on the part of coastal states in adjacent waters beyond the territorial sea fundamentally influenced the behavior of coastal states during post-Geneva discussions. This failure to achieve any type of lasting agreement largely compelled the coastal states to take it upon themselves to address issues concerning the territorial sea. Consequently, the fourteen years that highlighted the post-Geneva period, 1960–1974, saw an increase in global claims to exclusive fishery zones (EFZ) by competing coastal states.

Nations had an overarching inclination toward two positions during this time period. The first trend that emerged was initiated by Western European and Scandinavian countries.[96] These states seemed to make their claims more compatible with the general consensus revealed at UNCLOS II, asserting a twelve-mile exclusive fishing zone.[97] These claims closely aligned with restricting the geographic latitude of coastal states' exclusive fishing rights to a distance that would not exceed twelve miles, while simultaneously limiting the breadth of the territorial sea to a much shorter distance.

---

[95] The U.S.–Canadian proposal failed by a vote of 30 in favor to 21 against with 18 abstentions. The result: the two-thirds majority was not met.

[96] Straburzyński, "Exclusive Fishery Zones," 57–71.

[97] "Fisheries Jurisdiction Case (United Kingdom v. Iceland), Merits, Judgment July 25, 1974," *ICJ Rep* 1974, 23.

Coastal states employed bilateral and multilateral methods to achieve these objectives. Bilaterally, Scandinavian and Western European countries and other nations signed various agreements that contained the twelve-mile exclusive fishing zone.[98] These bilateral agreements represented the mutual interests of the respective parties in developing such zones and worked out arrangements between parties in continuing the fishing rights of those who were not party to the agreements when the twelve-mile zone was established.[99] Most of these agreements included guidelines to consider when foreign fishing activities ceased and made provisions for the future. Straburzyński touched on this agreement when he wrote, "The temporary right of foreign fishers to continue to fish in the fishery zone of a given coastal state is almost universally recognized in the contemporary international practice."[100]

The purpose behind traditional fishing rights involves providing a protective shield to fishers of noncoastal states, as well as to those fishers who fish in distant waters, from being arbitrarily excluded from areas where they traditionally fished. Any exclusion of foreign fishers would come under a gradual "phrase out" period, giving these fishers ample time to cease fishing in the coastal state's fishery zone and relocate to a new fishing area without incurring undue economic hardship.[101]

On the multilateral level, the development of the twelve-mile exclusive fishing zone crystalized under the European Fisheries Convention (EFC) of 1964.[102] The EFC was the first global instrument to grant recognition to exclu-

---

[98] A very good example of this is "United Kingdom and Denmark Agreement Regarding the Fisheries Zone Around the Faroe Islands, 1959," *RGDIP* 67 (1963): 621; "Iceland-Federal Republic of Germany Exchange of Notes Constituting an Agreement Concerning the Fishery Zone Around Iceland, Reykjavik, July 19, 1961," *UNTS* 409, 47; Norway and USSR Fisheries Agreement, 1964.

[99] Straburzyński, "Exclusive Fishery Zones," 261–62; Shigeru Oda, "International Law of the Resources of the Sea," *RCADI* (1986): 394–95.

[100] Straburzyński, "Exclusive Fishery Zones," 265; A. E. Gotlieb, "The Canadian Contribution to the Concept of a Fishing Zone in International Law," *CYIL* 2 (1964): 55.

[101] Jacques-Yvan Morin, "La Zone de Pêche Exclusive du Canada," *CYIL* 2 (1964): 104; Douglas M. Johnston, *The International Law of Fisheries: A Framework for Policy-Oriented Inquiries* (New Haven, CT: Yale University Press, 1965), 445.

[102] The European Fisheries Convention was concluded on March 9, 1964 and came into force on March 15, 1966. It signatories included Austria, Belgium, Denmark, France, the Federal Republic of Germany, Ireland, Italy, Luxembourg, the Netherlands, Portugal, Spain, Sweden, and the United Kingdom. For the text of the convention see "European Fisheries Convention, and Agreements on Transitional Rights (Fishing Limits; Settlement of Disputes)," *ILM* 3 (1964): 469.

sive fishery zones.[103] One of the most important factors concerning the EFC is that it was developed by a conglomerate of states that had historically opposed all attempts by others states to expand their fisheries jurisdiction beyond the territorial sea limit.

Under the guidelines of the EFC, each state could develop a fishery zone. This zone, according to the provisions of the convention, has two sections that consist of two six-mile belts, under different regimes. The first section extended six miles from the baseline, with the coastal states given exclusive right to fish. The coastal states also maintained exclusive jurisdiction in fishery matters. Section two created a belt that measured between six and twelve miles from the baseline. In the latter section, coastal states retained the exclusive right to fish along with other parties who had traditionally fished in that particular belt between January 1, 1953, and December 31, 1962.[104]

Several states were not party to the EFC when it acknowledged the right to develop such a zone. Shortly after the EFC came into force, the United Kingdom implemented a policy that established a twelve-mile fishery zone.[105] The assertions made by the British were largely determined by the interests of British coastal fishers' anxiety concerning the growing competition that the fishing vessels of Belgium, France, Poland, and the Soviet Union presented off its coastline.[106] Poland acknowledged this fishery zone, a country which at the time did not officially claim any exclusive fishing rights beyond the three-mile territorial sea limit.[107] This recognition followed the provisions of the September 26, 1964 agreement that permitted Polish fishers the temporary right to fish for herring in certain areas within six and twelve miles, and permitted use of the British fishery zone for minor fishing expeditions outside the territorial sea and no fishing in the belt between three and six miles from the British coast's baselines.[108]

The Soviet Union recognized the right of the coastal state to create a twelve-mile fishery zone under the auspices of the September 30, 1964 Exchange of Notes with the United Kingdom.[109] In addition, the German Democratic Republic, Japan, the United States, New Zealand, and South Korea also acknowl-

---

103 Fitzmaurice-Lachs, "The Legal Regime of the Baltic Sea Fisheries," 200–202.
104 UN Doc. A/Conf. 13/C. 1/L. 77, Rev. 1, 2, 3 Article 3.
105 "European Fisheries Convention," 1067.
106 Jean De Brencker, "La Convention de Londres sur la Pêche du 9 Mars 1964," *RBDI* 1 (1966): 144–45.
107 Straburzyński, "Exclusive Fishery Zones," 265.
108 "Poland and United Kingdom: Fisheries agreement," *ILM* 4 (1965): 168–69.
109 "U.S.S.R. and United Kingdom: Fisheries Agreement," *ILM* 4 (1965): 174–75.

edged this zone as the general acceptable right of coastal states to extend their jurisdiction up to the twelve-mile limit without reservations.[110]

Furthermore, Finland recognized the twelve-mile fishery zone by supporting the Canadian–U.S. proposal of an exclusive fishery zone of six miles adjacent to the six-mile territorial sea discussed at UNCLOS.[111]

The nations of Latin America, Africa, and Asia mainly led the second trend. During the 1960s and into the 1970s, these states sought to attract political support (on the regional and global level) for their respective two-hundred-mile exclusive fishing and economic zones. Uruguay, after declaring their sovereign rights over a two-hundred-mile maritime zone that included airspace, seabed, and subsoil in 1969, initiated a meeting with Latin American nations in March 1970 to clarify competing positions on maritime policies.[112] The formal meeting between these Latin American nations became known as the Declaration of Montevideo on the Law of the Sea.[113]

Two main events led to the formation of the Montevideo Conference. The first involved attempts by the United States and Soviet Union to resolve the issue of a territorial sea limit through international conference[114] and second, the UN Resolution asking member states about their views concerning the convening of a new conference on the law of the sea.[115] The Montevideo Conference mentioned the geoeconomic ties that bound the sea and the men who use it, giving the coastal state the right to benefit from the natural resources found in territorial waters. Emphasizing the binding nature of these ties, the resulting Declaration acknowledged the coastal state's right to exercise control over the natural resources adjacent to their coasts "in order to achieve the maximum development of their economy and to raise the living standards of their people."[116] The limit of this control was "in accordance with their geographical and geological

---

110 Fitzmaurice-Lachs, "The Legal Regime of the Baltic Sea Fisheries," 202.

111 *Ibid.*

112 "Uruguay: Decree Extending Territorial Waters," *ILM* 8 (1969): 1067; A. Szekely, *Latin America and the Development of the Law of the Sea* (Dobbs Ferry, NY: Oceana, 1979); K. Hjertonson, *The New Law of the Sea: Influence of the Latin American States on Recent Development of the Law of the Sea* (Leiden, Netherlands: A. W. Sijthoff, 1973), 68.

113 This meeting consisted of Argentina, Brazil, Chile, Ecuador, El Salvador, Panama, Peru, Nicaragua, and Uruguay. "The Declaration of Montevideo on Law of the Sea," *ILM* 9 (1970): 1081.

114 Branford M. Taitt, "The Exclusive Economic Zone: A Caribbean Community Perspective, Part I, Evolution of a Concept," *WILJ* 7 (1983): 43.

115 Hjertonson, *The New Law of the Sea*, 68.

116 "The Declaration of Montevideo," para. 1.

characteristics and with factors governing the existence of marine resources and the need for their national utilization."[117]

Because only countries with two-hundred-mile territorial limits were invited to the conference, a two-hundred-mile spatial limit was not the central factor of the Declaration and this spatial limit is only mentioned in its preamble. In all likelihood, this was a move to encourage those Latin American nations that did not have a two-hundred-mile territorial sea limit to support the Declaration. The Declaration maintained that maritime sovereignty and jurisdiction should be exercised "without prejudice to freedom of navigation by ships and overflight by aircraft of any flag."[118] Because third states can assert rights in maritime zones and this right is a central feature of the high-seas regime, one could argue that the establishment of these rights was created mainly to ensure proper jurisdiction over a state's territorial waters. However, upon closer examination of the statements of the delegates participating in the conference, participating states seemed to want to take different approaches to the issues surrounding the two-hundred-mile zone.[119] For example, the statements made by Brazil, Panama, and Nicaragua equated the freedom of navigating with that of innocent passage.

The representatives of the Montevideo Conference also agreed to hold another conference, at Lima, pertaining to important issues surrounding the law of the sea.[120] This meeting would involve all states of Latin America and Caribbean regions with the goal of establishing common grounds and positions relating to the coastal states' rights in adjacent seas.[121] Twenty states attended the August 1970 conference.[122] To garner wider support, observers from Canada, India, Iceland, Egypt, Senegal, the Republic of South Korea, Yugoslavia, and the UN were invited to attend.[123] The conference agreed to adopt the Declaration of the Latin American States on the Law of the Sea.[124]

---

117 *Ibid.*, para. 2.

118 *Ibid.*, para. 6.

119 L. D. M. Nelson, "The Patrimonial Sea," *ICLQ* 22 (1973): 676; Taitt, "The Exclusive Economic Zone," 43.

120 Resolution No. 3 taken at the Montevideo Conference adopted the proposal of Peru to convoke all Latin American states at Lima in August 1970.

121 "The Declaration of Montevideo on the Law of the Sea," 1081–83.

122 The participating states were Argentina, Barbados, Paraguay, Peru, the Dominican Republic, Trinidad and Tobago, Uruguay, and Venezuela.

123 Attard, *The Exclusive Economic Zone in International Law,* 19.

124 The Declaration was adopted by only fourteen states. See Taitt, "The Exclusive Economic Zone," 44.

The principles associated with this Declaration bear similar qualities to those enumerated in the Montevideo Declaration.[125] However, no guidelines regarding the two-hundred-mile territorial limit were discussed. Each contracting state was given wide latitude to establish maritime limits, considering geographical, geological, and biological concerns as well as how the state would make use of the resources.[126] A majority of the states who signed this Declaration did not acknowledge Principle 3, which highlighted the freedom of navigation and overflight requirements.[127] This action on the part of the states, coupled with the fact that a total of six states refused to be party to the Declaration, suggests a lack of unity among Latin American states when it came to creating a legal regime that would govern the various uses of the two-hundred-mile zone.

Over a year and a half later, a specialized Conference of the Caribbean States on Problems of the Sea was convened at Santo Domingo in the Dominican Republic. The objective of this conference was to resolve common problems associated with the laws of the sea and harmonize their efforts to solidify their responses to the issue of the coastal states' exclusive fishing rights beyond the territorial sea.[128] Fifteen nations from the subregion participated in this conference as full members.[129] Other Caribbean states were free to attend as observers.[130]

The Declaration of Santo Domingo[131] was a direct result of the conference as well as the establishment of certain principles pertaining to the law of the sea and the patrimonial sea. The concept of *sui generis* defines exactly what the

---

125 The most significant provision contained in this declaration centers on Principle 5, scientific research activities in the zone: "The right of the coastal state to authorize, supervise, and participate in all scientific research activities which may be carried out in the maritime zone subject to its sovereignty or jurisdiction and to be informed of the findings and the results of such research."

126 The Declaration of the Latin American States on the Law of the Sea (Lima, 1970), para. 2.

127 Attard, *The Exclusive Economic Zone in International Law*, 19.

128 The Conference convened at Santo Domingo, capital of the Dominican Republic, June 6–9, 1972. See Extavour, *The Exclusive Economic Zone*, 148–50.

129 These states include Barbados, Colombia, Costa Rica, the Dominican Republic, Guatemala, Haiti, Honduras, Jamaica, Mexico, Nicaragua, Panama, Trinidad and Tobago, Venezuela, El Salvador, and Guyana. UN Doc. A/AC. 138/SR, *Official Records* 78 (1972): 11.

130 Hjertonson, *The New Law of the Sea*, 73.

131 "Specialized Conference on the Caribbean Countries on the Problems of the Law of the Sea: Declaration of Santo Domingo," *AJIL* 66 (1972), 918.

patrimonial sea is in the Declaration: "The coastal state has sovereign rights over the renewable and nonrenewable natural resources, which are found in the waters, sea-bed and in the subsoil of an area adjacent to the territorial sea called the patrimonial sea."[132]

The right to authorize and regulate MSR, along with preventing pollution in the zone, lies within the jurisdictional domain of the coastal state.[133] In its entirety, the breadth of the zone would be subject to international agreements and provisions of the UN Charter. In this context, the area that comprises the territorial sea and the patrimonial sea should not exceed the set limit of two hundred miles in breadth.[134] Problems associated with the delimitation of the zone that may arise between two or more states would be remedied by the procedural guidelines outlined in the UN Charter.[135] The concept of freedom of navigation and overflight in and over the patrimonial sea also received protection.[136]

Thus, the concept of the patrimonial sea correlates with the sovereignty principles set forth in the Montevideo and Lima Declarations that gives coastal states jurisdiction over all resources adjacent to the sea without permitting control over navigation and overflight beyond the territorial sea. However, some creative ideas developed from this process. One of the most prominent ones involves the proposal of a twelve-mile territorial sea that emphasizes the coastal states' economic jurisdiction over the area. This proposal took precedent over all other jurisdictional matters, including matters pertaining to security. This feature separated the principles associated with the territorial sea from those associated with the patrimonial sea.[137]

Few African states were established before the final conclusion of the 1958 Geneva Convention.[138] In addition, the territorial sea and fisheries limits that were enforceable in most independent states were observed by the major maritime powers of the world. During the period between the end of UNCLOS I and the beginning of UNCLOS III, African practices concerning fishing

---

[132] *Ibid.*, Patrimonial Sea, para. 1.

[133] *Ibid.*, para. 2.

[134] *Ibid.*, para. 3.

[135] *Ibid.*, para. 4.

[136] *Ibid.*, para. 5.

[137] Jorge Castañeda, "The Concept of the Patrimonial Sea in International Law," *IJIL* 12 (1972): 538.

[138] Before UNCLOS I was convened, only seven African states were independent. See Nasila S. Rembe, *Africa and the International Law of the Sea: A Study of the Constitution of the African States to the Third United Conference on the Law of the Sea* (Leiden, Netherlands: Sijthoff and Noordhoff, 1980), 236, Appendix IV.

limits indicated that no regional limit was initiated. In the post-Geneva period, fifteen African states claimed a territorial sea of twelve miles without making specific claims regarding fishing limits.[139] These states included Algeria, Benin, Ethiopia, Kenya, Libya, Madagascar, Nigeria, Togo, Somalia, Sudan, and Sierra-Leone.[140] A prime example involves the Kenya Proclamation issued on June 6, 1969.[141] This proclamation set the breadth of the territorial sea at twelve miles, but did not address the issue of fisheries. Like the Kenyan Proclamation, the Malgash Decree No. 66.007 likewise established a territorial sea with a twelve-mile breadth.[142] For these states, fishery limits seem to correspond with the limits of the territorial sea.

Various African states chose a territorial-sea limit less than twelve miles in breadth with a twelve-mile fishery zone.[143] The Ivory Coast's claim of 1967 represents this type of action by setting the territorial sea limit at six miles.[144] This decree also created a contiguous zone of six miles and extended the fishery limit up to twelve miles. In this additional fishing zone, fishing activities were reserved only for Ivory Coast nationals and the decree was completely silent on the rights of fishers from other states who traditionally fished the area. Other African countries established a twelve-mile territorial sea limit with a contiguous fishery zone that went beyond this point. For instance, the Moroccan law pushed their claims beyond the territorial sea and fishery limits.[145]

By the close of the 1960s, African states, on the regional level, showed a strong tendency toward developing the law of the sea along the same lines as the Latin American states. In other words, they sought to extend the geo-

---

[139] Douglas M. Johnston and Edgar Gold, "Extended Jurisdiction: The Impact of UNCLOS III on Coastal State Practice," in *The Law of the Sea: State Practice in Zones of Special Jurisdiction, Proceedings of the Thirteenth Annual Conference October 15–18, 1979,* ed. Thomas A. Clingan (Honolulu: Law of the Sea Institute, University of Hawaii, 1982), 27–49.

[140] *Ibid.*

[141] Presidential Proclamation, June 6, 1969, in ST/LEG/SER. B/15 (1970): 95–96.

[142] S. Houston Lay, Robin Rolf Churchill, and Myron H. Nordquist, (eds.), *New Directions in the Law of the Sea,* vol. 1 (Dobbs Ferry, NY: Oceana, 1973), 250.

[143] These states included Cape Verde, Tunisia, and Senegal. Johnston and Gold, "Extended Jurisdiction," 27–49.

[144] Lay, Churchill, and Nordquist, *New Directions in the Law of the Sea* 250.

[145] Abdelkader Lahlou, *Le Maroc et le Droit des Pêches Maritimes* (Paris: Librairie Générale de Droit et de Jurisprudence, 1983), 254–55; Congo decided to establish a 12-mile territorial sea with a fishery zone of 15 miles, while Cameroon and Gambia respectively established 18- and 50-mile territorial seas. Johnston and Gold, "Extended Jurisdiction," 39–43.

graphical limit of the coastal state's exclusive fishing rights up to a maximum distance of two-hundred miles.[146] The reasons behind this move varied. First, over forty African nations came under the umbrella of "independent members" in the international community at the conclusion of UNCLOS I and were not participants in the 1958 Geneva conventions. These independent African states believed that the Geneva conventions only protected the interests of major maritime states.[147] These states wanted a law that would reflect their maritime interests; specifically, a law that would facilitate their social and economic development and close the inequality gap that existed between the developed and developing nations.

Second, new advancements in fishing technology gave the powerful maritime states the capacity to extend their fishing activities on the high seas, which threatened the fishing resources of less developed states. Major maritime states, namely Japan and the Soviet Union, developed and increased their global fishing fleets to include "factory ships" that had the capability to catch, clean, fillet, and freeze great quantities of fish without entering the ports of adjacent coastal states.[148] Such mass-producing fishing fleets invariably harmed the fishing opportunities of less developed states and caused the states of Africa to become alarmed at the possible long-term effects of such large-scale fishing operations.[149] To achieve their maritime objectives, the African states decided to take joint action. In 1971, the Organization of African Unity Council of Ministers approved two important resolutions: one pertaining to fisheries and the other relating to the African states' jurisdictional rights over their natural resources.[150] Regarding fishing, the African states "confirmed the inalienable rights of the African countries over the fishery resources of the continental shelf surrounding Africa."[151] The African states also affirmed that the exploitation of natural resources in each country would correspond with the national laws and regulations of African states.[152]

---

146 Rembe, *Africa and the International Law of the Sea*, 234.

147 *Ibid.*, 122.

148 *Ibid.*, 148; Anand, "The Politics of a New Legal Order for Fisheries." 273.

149 Anand, "The Politics of a New Legal Order for Fisheries." 272–73; Dean, "The Geneva Conference on the Law of the Sea," 762–64.

150 OAU Resolution on Permanent Sovereignty of African Countries over their Natural Resources (CM/Res. 245) and OAU Resolution on Fisheries (CM/Res. 250), in Shigeru Oda, *The International Law of the Ocean Development: Basic Documents* (Leiden, Netherlands: Sijthoff, 1972), 27, 28.

151 Resolution on Fisheries, in *ibid.*, para. 1.

152 Resolution on Permanent Sovereignty, in *ibid.*, para. 1.

Additionally, an assemblage of sixteen African countries held a seminar at Yaoundé, Cameroon, during June of 1972 to discuss issues pertaining to the law of the sea. The seminar endorsed a number of recommendations.[153] On issues relating to natural resources, the seminar suggested that African states had the authority to establish an economic zone beyond the territorial sea limit. These African states would have "exclusive jurisdiction for the purpose of control, regulation, and national exploitation of the resources of the sea and their reservation for the primary benefit of their peoples and their respective economies."[154] Another incentive for creating the EEZ involved the prevention and control of environmental pollution.[155] The protection of the traditional rights of freedom of navigation, overflight, and the freedom to lay submarine cable and pipelines were major tenets of these recommendations.[156]

Concerning the external limits of the EEZ, no maximum limit was recommended, but it was suggested that any limit agreed upon should be in nautical miles. The seminar further determined that any such limits should be "in accordance with regional considerations, taking duly into account the resources of the region and the rights and interests of the land-locked states (LLS) without prejudice to limits already adopted by some states within the region."[157] Recommendations II suggested the continental shelf should be part of the economic zone, which meant that the zone could ultimately be extended hundreds of miles from the coastline.

In regard to LLS access to the resources of the EEZ, the seminar recommended that the exploitation of the living resources should be accessible to both land-locked and geographical challenged African states.[158] The only qualifying factor was that any operation by LLS should come under the control of African capitals and personnel.[159] The latter proposal seems to suggest a unified, joint venture between LLS and African coastal states with the stipulation that the exploration and exploitation of the EEZ's resources would come under the jurisdictional domain of African states.

The creation of such economic zones became a topic of discussion in other venues. It was given detailed attention at the Asian–African Legal Consultative

---

153 "African States: Conclusions of the Regional Seminar on the Law of the Sea," *ILM* 12 (1973): 210.

154 *Ibid.*, Recommendations I(a)(3).

155 *Ibid.*

156 *Ibid.*

157 *Ibid.*

158 *Ibid.*, Recommendations II.

159 *Ibid.*

Organization (AALCO) committee meeting[160] held at Colombo (1971), Lagos (1972), and New Delhi (1973).[161] During the Lagos session, a Kenya representative presented a working paper entitled "The Exclusive Economic Zone Concept." The theoretical framework of this paper centered on the use of the zone as a protective shield for coastal states' economic interests.[162] Article 2 discussed the right of all states to create an economic zone beyond the territorial sea limit of two-hundred miles where states would have complete jurisdiction over the natural resources for the expressed purpose of exploring and exploiting them. However, all other states would be able to enjoy the traditional freedoms of the sea with the exception of the freedom of fishing. Article 6 addressed the rights of LLS. This Article allowed neighboring developing LLS to exploit the living resources in regional economic zones. Similar to the provisions agreed upon at the regional seminar held at Yaoundé, the Kenya proposition attempted to restrict LLS participation in EEZ resources by providing that those states' activities come under the control of their government and personnel.[163] This proposition was even more restricted in nature because many developing LLS did not have the financial viability or the technical training to engage in extended activities. Thus, many LLS would be excluded de facto from participating in the exploitation of the EEZ's resources.

The issues surrounding the development of the EEZ became a central topic at the 1974 Twenty-First and Twenty-Third Ordinary Sessions of the Organisation of African Unity (OAU). This proclamation came under the Declaration of the OAU on the Issues of the Law of the Sea.[164] This proclamation was also the result of the Twenty-First Ordinary Session that recognized African states' authority to

---

[160] The AALCC, originally known as the Asian Legal Consultative Committee was established on November 15, 1956 by the governments of Burma, Ceylon, India, Indonesia, Iraq, Japan, and Syria as an advising body of legal experts to deal with problems that came to it., and to help facilitate the exchange of ideas and information on issues that were of common interest among participating countries. After April 19, 1958, the name was officially changed to the Asian–African Legal Consultative Committee when African countries joined the Committee.

[161] For a more detailed discussion held at the Colombo session (Twelfth Session) between January 18–27, 1971 see, Report of the Twelfth Session of the AALCC, 203–4; for more information on the Thirteenth Session (Lagos) held during the time period January 18–25, 1972 see Report of the Thirteenth Session, 155–60; and for additional information pertaining to the Fourteenth Session (New Delhi) held between January 10–18, 1973 see Report of the Fourteenth Session, 61–63.

[162] Draft Articles on the Exclusive Economic Zone Concept, in "African States," 210.

[163] *Ibid.*, Article 6.

[164] "Organization of African Unity: Declaration on African Cooperation, Development, and Economic Independence," *ILM* 12 (1973): 996–1013.

create an EEZ with a two-hundred-mile limit.[165] The guidelines associated with this declaration were similar in tone to those proposed at the AALCO committee meeting. The text included references to the sovereign rights of coastal states over mineral and biological resources in the zone,[166] coastal states duty to prevent and control pollution, safety measures that uphold legitimate uses of the area,[167] and recognition of the right of LLS and similar geographically disadvantaged states to share in the exploitation of living resources of regional EEZs.[168] This right originated from the concept of African solidarity.[169] The Fourth Summit conference of Non-Aligned Countries Meeting in Algiers, held between September 5 and 9 of 1973, gave further support to the concept of the EEZ.[170]

In essence, the dawning of the 1970s witnessed developing countries giving some type of support to the idea of a two-hundred-mile zone for economic purposes. The chief reason coastal states sought to develop a zone involved the protection of resources adjacent to their coastline from overexploitation by other states, particularly from states that engaged in distant water fishing.[171] During this time period, many developing states sought participation in the new international economic order.[172] One of the chief ways economic

---

165 *Ibid.*, para. C.

166 *Ibid.*

167 *Ibid.*

168 *Ibid.*

169 *Ibid.* It must be noted that the declaration referred to the development of the two-hundred-mile EEZ that were set forth in the preambular clauses. These considerations included a need to reinforce the principle of coastal state sovereignty over natural resources, supported by the OAU and the UN General Assembly in various resolutions; the right of African countries to exploit the resources of the sea surrounding their continent for the benefit of their peoples; the nonparticipation of African states at UNCLOS I and UNCLOS II; and the imbalance between the developed and developing states in their capacity to access and enjoy the resources of the sea.

170 Resolution Concerning the Law of the Sea, September 9, 1974, in Oda, *The International Law of the Ocean Development*, 4.

171 A. Mpazi Singela, "Land-Locked States' Rights in the Exclusive Economic Zone from the Perspective of the UN Convention on the Law of the Sea: An Historical Evaluation," *ODIL* 20, no. 1 (1989): 65.

172 "Declaration on the Establishment of a New International Economic Order, Adopted by the UN General Assembly at its Sixth Special Session. GA. Res. 3201," UNGAOR, Suppl. No. 1 UN. Doc. A/9559, 1974; "Program of Action on the Establishment of a New International Economic Order, Adopted by the UN General Assembly at its Sixth Special Session, GA. Res. 3202," UNGAOR, Suppl. No. 1, UN Doc. A/9559, 1974; "Charter of Economic Rights and Duties of States, GA. Res. 3281," UNGAOR 29 Suppl. No. 31, 50, UN Doc. A/9631, 1974.

equity could be achieved was through the exclusive appropriation and use of resources that lay adjacent to the territorial sea. This area of the sea possessed the most valuable fishing resources.[173]

As indicated by the activities above, African, Asian, and Latin American countries helped solidify the two-hundred-mile exclusive fishing limit in the concept of the law of the sea. However, during the time frame of the early 1970s, these states relied on collaborative efforts to garner political support for the two-hundred-mile zone on the international level, at a time when the concept of the two-hundred-mile zone was still a regional matter. In fact, the majority of states during this time period limited their fisheries jurisdiction to twelve miles. As the 1970s drew to a close, the ratio of states claiming exclusive fisheries rights within twelve miles to those states that wanted a much wider maritime breadth were 91 to 18.[174]

Additionally, these claims lacked uniformity in their entirety. The dissimilarity of the rights claimed by these states in maritime zones is worth noting. Three preeminent claims highlight the diversity of these claims. The first involves the claim by Latin American and African states. These states sought to extend sovereignty over adjacent high-seas waters and the natural resources therein under an extended territorial sea that contained breadths that ranged between thirty and two-hundred miles.[175] The second involves the promotion of claims under the pretense of conserving the living resources in specific maritime areas. These claims can be exemplified by the Indian claims of 1956[176] and 1957.[177] In form and nature, these claims differ greatly from earlier ones because foreign activities that take place in those zones would not be completely eliminated, but rather limited only as a way to preserve the living resources in the zone. Some experts expounded pointedly on these circumstances. One noted commentator stated, it should be pointed that we

---

[173] Ram P. Anand, *Legal Regime of the Seabed and the Developing Countries* (Delhi, India: Thomson Press, 1975), 43; Louis Henkin, "Old Politics and New Directions," in *New Directions in the Law of the Sea,* vol. 1, ed. S. Houston Lay, Robin Rolf Churchill, and Myron H. Nordquist (Dobbs Ferry, NY: Oceana, 1973), 3.

[174] Straburzyński, "Exclusive Fishery Zones," 269–70.

[175] A prime example is the case of Brazil. In May 1970, this state extended its territorial sea up to two hundred miles; "Brazil: Decree-Law Extending Territorial Sea to 200 Miles No. 1098 of May 15, 1970," *ILM* 10 (1971): 1224–25. Ecuador made a similar move in 1969 by amending Article 633 of its Civil Code; Decree No. 1542 on November 10, 1966, in ST/LEG/SER. B/15 (1970): 78.

[176] Presidential Proclamation of 29 November 1956, in ST/LEG/SER. B/15 (1970): 49.

[177] Proclamation of Governor-General of December 20, 1957, in ST/LEG/SER. B/15 (1970): 107.

ought to differentiate claims to exclusive fishery zones from claims to conservation zones, since the latter does not deprive foreigners of the right of fishing but only limits that right in order to preserve the living resources of the sea. In other words, the conservation zone does not exclude the application of the freedom of fishing but only limits it, firstly but not exclusively, in the interest of the coastal state, but at any rate the establishment of such a zone also indirectly serves the interests of all states in the maintenance of the productivity of the living resources of the sea.[178]

The third type concerns exclusive fishery or economic zones established for the expressed purpose of jurisdictional control over fisheries.

Generally, the numerical ratio shown above suggested states limited the breadth of the belt in which they claimed exclusive rights for their nationals fishing up to the twelve-mile limit correlated with the rights associated with the 91 to 18 ratio. In addition, states that supported a twelve-mile exclusive fishing zone came from a wide geographical area. Such practice seems to suggest a "general practice" among states and supports the ICJ's reasoning that the extension of the fishery zone up to twelve miles from the baseline was generally accepted by the majority of states.[179]

Did customary international law allow coastal states to extend their exclusive fishing rights beyond the twelve-mile limit during this time frame? No, because very few developing coastal states asserted such rights during this period and the guidelines of UNCLOS I gave coastal states sovereign rights over resources of the continental shelf but only preferential rights for coastal fisheries.[180] Thus, coastal states did not have exclusive regulation over their coastal fisheries, although they did have jurisdictional preference for fishing the waters.[181] In addition, the ICJ, in ruling in the Fisheries Jurisdiction case, stated that two concepts have crystalized as customary law in recent years arising out of the general consensus revealed at [the 1960] Conference. The first is the concept of the fishery zone. ... The second is the concept of prefer-

---

178 Straburzyński, "Exclusive Fishery Zones," 269.

179 "Fisheries Jurisdiction Case (United Kingdom v. Iceland)," 3; "Fisheries Jurisdiction Case (Federal Republic of Germany v. Iceland), Merits, Judgment of July 25, 1974," *ICJ Rep* (1974): 175.

180 "Convention on the Continental Shelf" and Resolution on Special Situations Relating to Coastal Fisheries, adopted on April 26, 1958.

181 Robin Rolf Churchill, "The Fisheries Jurisdiction Cases: The Contribution of the International Court of Justice to the Debate of Coastal State's Fisheries Rights," *ICLQ* 24 (1975): 87–88; Carl August Fleischer, "The New Regime of the Maritime Fisheries," *RCADI* (1988/2), 122–23.

ential rights of fishing in adjacent waters in favor of the coastal state in a situation of special dependence on its coastal fisheries.[182]

The ICJ further elaborated:

> State practice on the subject of fisheries reveals an increasing and widespread acceptance of the concept of preferential rights for coastal states, particularly in favor of countries or territories in a situation of special dependence on coastal fisheries. ... After these Conferences, the preferential rights of the coastal state were recognized in various bilateral and multilateral international agreements.[183]

This observation by the ICJ indicates that the waters beyond the twelve-mile limit was an integral part of the high seas because preferential rights "in fact" generally excludes a state's right to an exclusive fishing zone.

---

[182] "Fisheries Jurisdiction Case (United Kingdom v. Iceland)," 23.
[183] *Ibid.*, 26.

Chapter 2

The Coastal State and the EEZ

One of the most conspicuous differences between the EEZ concept and the traditional notion of the law of the sea is the EEZ's viability and functional capability within the two-hundred-mile territorial limit. This difference is all the more noticeable when compared to the capabilities assigned to the contiguous zone and the continental shelf.[1] In the case of the contiguous zone and the continental shelf, coastal states have well-defined rights that correlate to the rights approved by the global community. The EEZ concept, expressed in the text of the LOS Convention, takes a different approach. In the confines of the Convention, the rights and duties of coastal states regarding the EEZ are explicitly stated along with the rights of third states.

Although coastal states enjoy a comprehensive list of rights in their EEZ, they also have specific duties they must perform. The coastal states' rights over economic activities in the zone generally comeunder the umbrella of "sovereign rights," whereas rights pertaining to other areas has been framed by the concept of jurisdiction. This wide range of rights, and the differences that separate them, indicates that these rights are not applied in the same manner. Thus, an examination of the nature and scope of these rights is in order, as they pertain to general rights over the EEZ's economic activities, the coastal state's jurisdiction over the living resources of the superjacent waters of the EEZ, and the nature of the coastal state's rights over nonliving resources.

The Coastal State's Rights over the EEZ's Economic Activities

Part V of the LOS Convention enumerates the specific rights of the coastal state in its EEZ. The central feature of Part V is Article 56, which gives coastal states sovereign rights in the EEZ for exploiting, exploring, conserving, and managing the natural resources of the superjacent waters. During the negotiating stages at UNCLOS III, most proposals pertaining to the establishment of an EEZ came from African and Latin American countries. These proposals supported coastal

---

[1] "Convention on the Continental Shelf," Articles 2–3; "Convention on the Territorial Sea and the Contiguous Zone," Article 24.

states' sovereign rights over the EEZ's natural resources.[2] The relationship between coastal states' sovereign rights and the natural resources of the EEZ became a focal point during the negotiating stages of UNCLOS III.[3]

In technical and professional terms, sovereign rights are those a state alone possesses that enable it to carry out its proper functions.[4] Article 56(1)(a) of the LOS Convention gives coastal states *sovereign rights* in exploring, exploiting, conserving, and managing the living and nonliving resources of the seabed and subsoil. The purposes specified under the coastal states' sovereign rights are similar in tone to those expressed in the 1958 Convention on the Continental Shelf.[5] The term "for the purpose of" contained in Article 56 not only grants sovereign rights to coastal states, but also denotes certain limits and restrictions in economic activities. In essence, Article 56 does not grant coastal states unabridged sovereignty, but only specific sovereign rights that would enable them to achieve their economic goals. The terminology used suggests the coastal states' sovereign rights only pertain to the natural resources of the zone rather than to the zone itself. One prominent scholar elaborated on this feature, stating,

> The term [sovereign rights], conveys the idea of a functional approach. The coastal state does not have full sovereignty as on its land or in its territorial sea but a right of jurisdiction that is related to certain purposes. Beyond the jurisdiction so defined, there is no special basis for coastal state rights, and the traditional rules developed for the high seas will continue to apply.[6]

---

[2] Mohamed Dahmani, *The Fisheries Regime of the Exclusive Economic Zone* (Boston: Martinus Nijhoff, 1987), 39.

[3] Stevenson and Oxman. "The Third United Nations Conference on the Law of the Sea: The 1975 Geneva Session," 775.

[4] Henry Campbell Black, Joseph R. Nolan, and Jacqueline M. Nolan-Haley, *Black's Law Dictionary,* 6th ed. (St. Paul, MN; West, 1990), 1396; Carl August Fleischer, "The Exclusive Economic Zone under the Convention Regime and in State Practice," in *The 1982 Convention on the Law of the Sea, Proceedings of the Seventeenth Annual Conference, July 12–16, 1983,* ed. Albert W. Koers and Bernard H. Oxman (Honolulu: Law of the Sea Institute, University of Hawaii, 1984), 253; Bruce E. Alexander, "The Territorial Sea of the United States: Is it Twelve Miles or Not?" *JMLC* 20 (1989): 458.

[5] "Convention on the Continental Shelf," Article 2; "The Law of the Sea Convention," *ILM* 21 (1982): Article 7(1)–(3).

[6] Fleischer, "The New Regime of the Maritime Fisheries," 149.

This interpretation corresponds with the numerous proposals submitted to the UN Seabed Committee.[7] The reasoning for this limitation lies in the belief that coastal states may use any acknowledgement of rights over the seabed and superjacent waters as a focal point to further extend their jurisdictional powers that would jeopardize the traditional concept of freedom of navigation.[8]

Whether coastal states' sovereign rights in the EEZ exist *ipso facto* is determined by the comparative analysis between the continental shelf and the EEZ, as these concepts are expressed in the LOS Convention. Part VI covers the concept of the continental shelf, incorporating Article 2 of the 1958 Continental Shelf Convention. According to Article 77(2) provision, if the coastal state does not exercise its enumerated sovereign rights over the continental shelf, no other nation can take the initiative and exercise control over it. In addition to this, Article 77(3) states that the rights over the continental shelf do not depend on any formal declaration or expressed occupation of the continental shelf.[9]

Regarding the EEZ, the language of Articles 55 and 56 indicates that the coastal state's EEZ rights exist *ipso facto,* closely resembling rights to the continental shelf. According to Article 55, the EEZ is "an area beyond and adjacent to the territorial sea, subject to the specific legal regime established" in Part V. Article 56 further elaborates that "in the exclusive economic zone, the coastal state has" certain rights in the maritime area known as the EEZ. In short, upon reading the two articles as one joint statement, one may have the impression that the Convention either supposes that each coastal state party to it would eventually claim an EEZ or that the Convention obligates every coastal state to claim an EEZ. However, upon closer examination, both interpretations seem illogical. On one hand, no logical explanation exists for the Convention to compel a coastal state to establish an EEZ if that state refuses to do so.[10] On the other hand, Article 57 explicitly states that the EEZ shall not extend two hundred miles beyond the baseline, the point from which the territorial sea is measured. This provision suggests the coastal state is the final arbiter in establishing the breadth of zones. Thus, the final decision of whether a state should have an EEZ rests entirely with the state.[11] In addition to

[7] "Report of the Committee on the Peaceful Uses of the Seabed and Ocean Floor beyond the Limits of National Jurisdiction," UNGAOR 28th Sess., Suppl. No. 21, UN Doc. A/9021 (1969).

[8] B. Obinna Okere, "Nigeria's Exclusive Economic Zone," *NLJ* 12 (1984): 69.

[9] "Convention on the Continental Shelf," Article 77(3).

[10] Carl August Fleischer, "The Right to a 200 Miles Exclusive Economic Zone or a Special Fishery Zone," *SDLR* 14 (1977): 551.

[11] Rudolf Bernhardt, "Custom and Treaty in the Law of the Sea," *RCADI* 205 (1987): 295.

these two reasons, the LOS Convention expressly states that the rights of coastal states are not predicated on occupation or proclamation and no such provision pertaining to the EEZ exists in Part V.

Taking the above into consideration, it seems the drafters' central aim involved making the EEZ more of a concessive zone rather than a preemptory one.[12] Nor does it seem compulsory when the breadth is set at two hundred miles[13] with geography limiting some claims[14] and choices.[15] Isolated rock foundations that cannot possibly sustain human habitation or economic life cannot create a continental shelf or EEZ, but islands with similar conditions can.[16] A prime example of this can be found in the case *Greenland/Jan Mayen Case (Denmark v. Norway).* In this case, the Court was prepared to accept the notion that the island of Jan Mayen, with its extreme weather climate and sparse population, could qualify for an EEZ under Article 121 para. 3 of the LOS Convention.[17]

The Content of the Coastal State's Jurisdiction on the Living Resources of the EEZ

One of the chief focal points of the EEZ concept is fishing rights.[18] Coastal states' rights and responsibilities pertaining to EEZ fisheries are explicitly defined in Article 56 1(a) and further highlighted in Articles 61 and 62. With sovereign rights as the centerpiece, Articles 61 and 62 grant coastal states far-reaching authority in EEZ fisheries. These extensive powers pertain to the allocation of EEZ fisheries, the establishment of laws and regulations relating to fishing in the EEZ, the authority to enforce fisheries laws and regulation in the EEZ, and the development of regulations aimed at addressing important issues for specific species in the EEZ.

The Coastal States' Authority and the Allocation of EEZ Fisheries

The LOS Convention definitively gives coastal states extensive powers in the allocation of fisheries in the EEZ. The prescription for the allocation of EEZ

---

[12] O'Connell, *The International Law of the Sea,* 371–72.

[13] Juda, "The Exclusive Economic Zone," 2.

[14] Kuan-Ming Sun, "Policy of the Republic of China toward the South China Sea," *MP* 19 (1995): 401.

[15] Bernhardt, "Custom and Treaty in the Law of the Sea," 295.

[16] "The Law of the Sea Convention," Article 121, paras. 2 and 3.

[17] "Case Concerning Maritime Delimitation in the Area between Greenland and Jan Mayen (Denmark v. Norway)," ICJ Rep (1993): 73–74.

[18] Bernhardt, "Custom and Treaty in the Law of the Sea," 296.

fisheries is preserved in the following provisions: Article 61 para. 1—"The coastal state shall determine the allowable catch of the living resources in its exclusive economic zone"; Article 62 para. 2—"The coastal state shall determine its capacity to harvest the living resources of its economic zone"; and Article 62 para. 2—"It shall ... give other states access to the surplus of the allowable catch."[19]

The Authority to Determine the Allowable Catch

The concept of giving coastal states the power to determine the acceptable catch (AC) of living resources in the EEZ originated from the Six Eastern European Nation's proposal of August 5, 1974,[20] which specifies that the yearly AC should be determined for each species of fish or other living resource, with the exception of highly migratory species (HMS).[21] The initial draft, proposed at UNCLOS III[22] in 1975, eliminated the phrase "for each species" while simultaneously adding a more detailed provision that stated "the coastal state shall determine the allowable catch of the living resources in its economic zone and shall ensure through proper conservation and management measures that ensures that the maintenance of the living resources in the exclusive economic zone is not endangered by over exploitation."[23]

The abovementioned provision definitively gives coastal states the right and duty to determine the AC. Although the LOS Convention does not define the term *allowable catch,* it is the determination of the AC that creates the system of allocation and access for third states, especially when these states depend on surplus resources to survive. Some organizations have addressed the issue of AC in their policy framework. The Department of Fisheries of the Food and Agriculture Organization of the UN defines AC as "that catch which, if taken

19 Fitzmaurice-Lachs, "The Legal Regime of the Baltic Sea Fisheries," 233.

20 Bulgaria, Byelorussian SSR, German Democratic Republic, Poland, Ukrainian SSR, and USSR: "Draft Articles on the Economic Zone," UN Doc. A/Conf. 62/C. 2/L. 38, August 5, 1974, *Official Records* 3 (1975): 214–15. It is noteworthy that the name of Byelorussian SSR officially became the Republic of Belarus on Sept. 19, 1991. See "Status of the United Nations Convention on the Law of the Sea," *Law of the Sea Bulletin,* no. 19 (1991): 1, note d.

21 "Draft Articles on the Economic Zone," Article 12.

22 "Informal Single Negotiating Text," UN Doc. A/Conf. 62/WP. 8/pt. II, *Official Records* 4 (1975): 152.

23 "The Law of the Sea Convention," Article 61 paras. 1 and 2.

in any one year, will best enable the objectives of fisheries management (i.e., optimum long-term yield) to be achieved."[24]

According to Article 61(2), the guidelines for determining the AC should include "the best scientific evidence" in order to prevent overexploitation of the EEZ's living resources.[25] Upon closer examination, determining the AC seems to be a discretionary choice on the part of the coastal state. Although the LOS Convention definitively addresses this process, it also contains specific qualifications that the coastal state must follow when determining the AC.

The first enumerated qualification is located in Article 61(2), which compels coastal states to employ "the best scientific" evidence available. However, this requirement highlights a number of problems. In the first instance, *best* implies the coastal state must only find the best information it can gather from its own sources; not the most accurate scientific evidence when gathering data related to catch statistics from other coastal states in the region.[26] This interpretation is supported by the phrase "available to it," suggesting that coastal states are not obliged to actively conduct scientific investigations to obtain the most valuable scientific evidence for taking the required measures, but can employ these measures based on the scientific evidence it can access.[27]

Similar to a majority of the international fisheries conventions,[28] the LOS Convention has a maximum sustained yield[29] provision that calls for the

---

24 Department of Fisheries of Food and Agriculture Organization of the UN, mimeographed document submitted to UNCLOS III, Geneva Session of 1975, Doc. GE. 75-64093.

25 It is worth noting that the process of developing measures to prevent overexploitation must also be based upon the best scientific evidence available to the coastal state. Article 61 para. 2.

26 Alfred H. A. Soons, "Regulation of Marine Scientific Research by the European Community and Its Member States," *ODIL* 23 (1992): 259–60; S. Kwame B. Mfodwo, Ben Martine Tsamenyi, and Sam K. N. Blay, "The Exclusive Economic Zone: State Practice in the African Atlantic Region," *ODIL* 20 (1989): 452.

27 However, the lack of compulsion in this Article is offset by the requirement in para. 5, which calls for the contribution and exchange of any relevant information through international organizations.

28 For example, see Convention on Fishing and Conservation of the Living Resources of the High Seas, April 29, 1958, Article 2; Agreement for the Implementation of the Provisions of the United Nations Convention on the Law of the Sea of December 10, 1982, Relating to the Conservation and Management of Straddling Fish Stocks and Highly Migratory Fish Stocks, United Nations, Doc. A/Conf. 164/37, September 8, 1995, Article 5(b).

coastal state to establish fisheries conservation objections when exercising its fishery authority in the EEZ. Article 61(2) provides that coastal states "shall ensure through proper conservation and management measures that the maintenance of the living resources is not endangered by overexploitation." The same Article further states, in para. 3, that "such measures shall be designed to maintain or restore populations of harvested species at levels which can produce the maximum sustainable yield as qualified by relevant environmental and economic factors, including the economic needs of the coastal fishing communities and the special requirement of developing countries."

Many fishery experts believe the concept of maximum sustainable yield (MSY) is inadequate.[30] Such imprecise qualifiers as relevant "environmental and economic" factors imply that the coastal state may use any number of statements to qualify its determination of the MSY. Such factors as the economic needs of the coastal fishing communities, special requirements of developing states, current fishing patterns, and the independence of stocks support this interpretation. With this in mind, a coastal state can adjust its MSY according to the needs of the fishing community. This implies that the language of the LOS Convention allows for discretionary action on the part of a coastal state in implementing the MSY.

The Authority to Determine Harvesting Capacity

In accordance with the sovereign rights, coastal states enjoy in the EEZ, Article 62(2) gives additional powers to the coastal state to establish its harvesting capacity (HC). If, as in some instances, the harvesting capacity (HC) of the coastal state is equal to or greater than the AC, only the coastal state would be permitted to fish in its EEZ. However, a coastal state also has the authority to allow other states to conduct fishing activities in its zone even if the HC is equal to the AC; however, this authority is predicated on the coastal state's

---

[29] The term *maximum sustainable yield* (MSY) refers to a constant amount of catch produced by a fish stock during fishing activities. John P. Harville, "Multidisciplinary Aspects of Optimum Sustainable Yield," in *Optimum Sustainable Yield as a Concept in Fisheries Management,* ed. P. M. Roedel (Lawrence, TX: Allen Press, 1975), 51–64. See also Sohn and Gustafson. *The Law of the Sea in a Nutshell,* 124.

[30] William T. Burke, "The Law of the Sea Convention Provisions on Conditions of Access to Fisheries Subject to National Jurisdiction," *OLR* 63 (1984): 78; P. A. Larkin, "An Epitaph for the Concept of Maximum Sustainable Yield," *Trans AFS,* 1 (1977): 3–7; S. P. Balasubramanian, "Fisheries Provisions of the ICNT—Part II," *MP* 6 (1982): 27–28; John M. MacDonald, "Appreciating the Precautionary Principle as an Ethical Evolution in Ocean Management," *ODIL* 26, no. 3 (1995): 273.

determination of its HC amounts. To facilitate this authority, the coastal state should establish an HC that is open to interpretation.

Some commentators have suggested that the guidelines spelled out in Article 62(2) relate to the domestic HC of the coastal state.[31] This restrictive interpretation of the coastal state's HC seems problematic, because the coastal state should have broad capacity to fish and use foreign capital and fishing vessels.[32] The reasoning behind this premise is simple. First, no guidelines exist in the LOS Convention obligating a coastal state to harvest the catch only through its own citizens or through other self-supporting mechanisms. Second, developing countries advanced the notion of an EEZ to level the economic playing field. Many of these states lack the technological capacity to implement fishing activities that would satisfy the consumption needs of their populations. A restriction in the HC of their domestic fishing vessels translates to a reduction in the economic benefit that comes from fishing activities.

In essence, that the LOS Convention does not contain a guiding provision concerning the development of the HC seems to imply that a coastal state has wide discretion when addressing this issue. The mandatory dispute-settlement procedure contained in Part XV, Section 2, Article 297(3)(a) that excludes guidelines for a coastal state's development of the HC further supports the notion that the coastal state has broad discretion when confronting this issue.

The Authority to Determine the Surplus Catch and to Allow Access to Third States

Under Article 62(1), coastal states have the duty to promote optimum use of the living resources in its EEZ. This obligation includes two levels of exploitation before the surplus can be determined. The first level involves the AC of fish in the EEZ and the second is the coastal state's HC.[33] If the AC and the HC are the same, the coastal state is under no obligation to allow foreign fishing vessels access to its zone. However, if a surplus exists, the coastal state should allow other states access to the surplus through agreements or some other

---

[31] William T. Burke, "U.S. Fishery Management and the New Law of the Sea," *AJIL* 76 (1982): 33; Sohn and Gustafson. *The Law of the Sea in a Nutshell,* 124.

[32] Shigeru Oda, "Fisheries under the United Nations Convention on the Law of the Sea," *AJIL* 77 (1983): 744.

[33] "The Law of the Sea Convention," Article 61(1) and 62(2).

arrangements.[34] Instead of leaving the surplus closed to fishing activities, these agreements would facilitate optimum use of the living resources. If a coastal state announced a surplus in the zone, it would seem like a correspondingly weak obligation to grant access to it. Article 297(3)(b) states that some type of obligation exists and that compulsory measures may be initiated where a coastal state has "arbitrarily refused to allocate to any state ... the whole or part of the surplus it has declared to exist." But upon closer examination, the exclusion of this area from the compulsory dispute-settlement mechanism suggests this obligation has very little force. Additionally, it is not an obligation to allow routine access to the area,[35] but one based on agreement only and then only in accordance with the expressed terms and conditions of the agreement. The stipulations in Article 62(2) pertaining to the accessibility of third states are, therefore, virtually powerless. As one noted expert commented, the requirement in Article 62(2) "places no meaningful obligation upon the coastal state."[36] Although the surplus concept plays a prominent role in facilitating access to the living resources of the EEZ, the concept itself is a "slippery"[37] one, based upon a "culmination of very complex operations"[38] that combines scientific and nonscientific deliberations.

Even in circumstances where coastal states have limited HC, ecological situations in which no surplus exists or in which the declaration of the surplus would be detrimental to the interests of the coastal state may exist.[39] Consequently, the issue of whether the coastal state has an obligation to declare a surplus is important because the answer centers on the third states' accessibility to the surplus, as directed by the guidelines of the LOS Convention.

---

34 It was at the First Session of the Enlarged Seabed Committee in 1971 that Mexico first advanced the basic principles that evolved into the surplus concept stating that the share of offshore resources of a coastal state that should be reserved for its nationals should be commensurate with the state's fishing capacity at a given time. The surplus could then be made available to other states. For additional information on this topic, see Jean F. Carroz, "Le Nouveau Droit des Pêches et la Notion d'Excédent," 24 *AFDI* 24 (1978): 851–65.

35 Jean F. Carroz and Michel Savini, "The Practice of Coastal States Regarding Foreign Access to Fishery Resources: An Analysis of the Bilateral Agreements," in *FAO Fisheries Report No. 293* (Rome: FAO, 1983), 47.

36 Burke, "U.S. Fishery Management and the New Law of the Sea," 90.

37 J. A. Gulland, "Conditions of Access to Fisheries: Some Resource Considerations," in *FAO Fisheries Report No. 293* (Rome: FAO, 1983), 86.

38 Carroz and Savini. "The Practice of Coastal States Regarding Foreign Access to Fishery Resources," 47.

39 Gulland, "Conditions of Access to Fisheries: Some Resource Considerations," 82–86.

On a more practical level, the procedural guidelines available to a coastal state gives it the authority to set HC levels at a level equal to that of the AC, or set an AC level below its HC level. Although this premise is feasible, questions of legality surround this issue. When a coastal state arbitrarily refuses to determine the allowable catch of the living resources in its EEZ after a foreign state has shown interest in fishing in the zone, the foreign state can compel the coastal state to establish the AC of the living resources.[40] In essence, a coastal state's irrational response to a request by a foreign state regarding the AC can result in a direct challenge of the coastal state's action. This may mitigate the situation in favor of the foreign state, but the action on the foreign state's request rests on two central points: the difficulty of establishing whether such act by the coastal state was indeed arbitrary, and whether the foreign state can compel the coastal state to mitigate the situation rather than agreeing to a mutual settlement that may alter the actions of the coastal state.[41]

Another way to examine the situation is to consider whether the failure of the coastal state to establish an AC of a surplus could be challenged on the basis of abuse of power.[42] Although the agreement addresses and confronts the issue of arbitrary actions and abuse of power, it does not seem to have much impact on a third state that has been denied access. If those states used the abuse-of-power defense, they invariably will find it harder to prove their claims than the coastal state's claim of faithfully exercising it rights. As noted by the International Law Association,

> It may be accepted that the principle of good faith is a universally recognized principle of law, but its legal counterpart ... the doctrine of abuse of rights ... is an invalidating ground likely to be invoked only with great reluctance by an International Tribunal, and in very flagrant cases. Where, as in the situation presently under study, the contest is likely to be between two states arguing about a delicate balance of rights and duties affecting vital aspects of national sovereignty, the is-

---

40 "The Law of the Sea Convention," Article 297(3)(b)(ii).

41 This further absence of mandatory dispute settlement is interpreted by Burke as the confirmation of a coastal state's exclusive competences. Burke, "U.S. Fishery Management and the New Law of the Sea," 79.

42 Article 300 of the LOS Convention indicates that states that are party to it should, in good faith, fulfill the obligations of the Convention, and "exercise the right, jurisdiction, and freedoms recognized in this Convention in a manner which would not constitute an abuse of rights."

> sue is unlikely to be presented in terms such as to invite application of the doctrine of abuse rights.[43]

In essence, at the very least, a coast state must allocate a surplus when it has designated one and when a foreign fishing state has requested it.

The Coastal State's Powers, the Prescription of Laws, and Fishing Regulations in the EEZ

According to Article 62(4), coastal states have the authority to implement legislative measures and develop pertinent regulations for fishery activities in its EEZ. The central point of this provision seems to focus on the various types of regulatory authority of a coastal state on foreign fishing activities. This Article may address the notion that coastal states are likely to exercise proper legislative and administrative authority over areas that are widely used by its nationals.[44]

When it comes to its nationals, a coastal state is empowered to develop laws and regulations that complement its national objectives (such as laws that increase employment or economic efficiency of its fishing industry). However, in exercising such authority, a coastal state should follow the guidelines expressed in Article 61 pertaining to the conservation of the EEZ's living resources.

Article 62(4) defines the limits of the coastal state's regulatory powers. These regulatory powers are not limited by the provisions of the LOS Convention, mainly because of the ubiquitous expression *inter alia* that precedes the listings. As expressed by one expert, "What one must necessarily emphasize here is that this enumeration of the regulatory powers of the coastal state is in no way exhaustive, since the word 'notament' clearly indicates that enumeration at best is an example of the application of general power."[45] Thus, the list sought to highlight the importance of the various developing coastal states at UNCLOS III and their input in the development of the rights of foreigners to fish in their EEZs.[46]

---

[43] *Report of the Committee on Land-Locked States, Belgrade Conference, 1980* (London: International Law Association, 1980), 11.

[44] Dahmani, *The Fisheries Regime of the Exclusive Economic Zone*, 81–82.

[45] Jean Maurice Arbour, "L'Affaire du Chalutier-Usine 'La Bretagne' ou les Droits de l'État Côtier dans sa Zone Économique Exclusive," *CYIL* 24 (1986): 70. Text translated by author.

[46] A good example is the statement of the representative of Sri-Lanka made at the First Substantive Session of UNCLOS III, Caracas, June 20–August 29, 1974, in III Official Reports, 1975, 186.

Article 62(4) considers two sets of regulatory powers. The first addresses the implementation of conservation and management measures that apply to all fishers, including citizens of the coastal state. Under the first subparagraphs (b), (c), (d), (e), and (f), the coastal state has the authority to develop laws and legislation concerning fishing quotas, fishing seasons, fishing areas, and the physical sizes of the fish that may be caught. The second set of subparagraphs, (a), (g), (h), (i), and (j), formulates specific terms and conditions regarding access to fisheries. The terms and conditions expressed in these subparagraphs include guidelines for obtaining licenses, setting fees, designating landing places, training, and joint ventures. In this context, a coastal state can rely on a variety of terms and conditions it can reference when implementing its authority. These conditions also highlight the notion that coastal states enjoy immense control over access to their zones.

In implementing its regulatory powers, a coastal state's laws and regulations "shall be consistent with" those provided for in the LOS Convention.[47] Nonetheless, Article 297(3)(a) of Part XV (provision pertaining to dispute settlements) states that coastal states "shall not be obliged to accept the submission to such settlement of any disputes relating to its sovereign rights with respect to the living resources in the EEZ or their exercise, including its discretionary powers for … the terms and conditions established in its conservation and management laws and regulations." This provision suggests that a coastal state's capacity in this matter is exclusive.

The Coastal State's Authority and the Enforcement of Conservation and Management Measures

On the most basic level, the term *enforcement* relates to "the process" that compels a state to adhere to established rules and regulations.[48] For fisheries, enforcement means fishers will comply with the legislative initiatives enacted by the coastal state or similar international fisheries organization. The guidelines of the LOS Convention grant coastal states the power to take all necessary enforcement steps to ensure the protection of fisheries in their EEZ. Article 73 of the Convention is the principal source of this entitlement. This

---

[47] "The Law of the Sea Convention," Article 62(4).

[48] Albert W. Koers, "Enforcement of Fisheries Agreements in the High Seas: A Comparative Analysis of International State Practice," Law of the Sea Institute, University of Rhode Island, Occasional Paper No. 6, June 1970, 2.

specific provision regarding these rights of the coastal state has been unaltered since the time they first appeared in the ISNT during the mid-1970s.[49]

The enumerated fishery-enforcement rights consolidated proposals made by various African coastal states[50] and the United States.[51] Other proposals suggested by the European economic community (EEC),[52] the territorial states,[53] and the Soviet Union[54] did not become a part of the LOS Convention.

Article 73 of the LOS Convention is the seminal provision that grants a coastal state the right to take all enforcement measures needed to ensure compliance with its fisheries laws and regulations in its EEZ. This enforcement process involves preventive measures that include surveillance, stopping, boarding, and inspecting vessels.[55] Surveillance entails observing fishing activities performed by fishing vessels in the EEZ. Stopping and boarding the vessels is necessary to confirm any suspected violations detected by surveillance operations or to conduct a hands-on inspection. Generally, appointed officials carry out inspection activities, boarding fishing vessels to ensure personnel are complying with fisheries regulations.

---

[49] "Informal Single Negotiating Text," Article 61.

[50] See, UN Doc. A/Conf. 62/C. 2/L. 82, of August 26, 1974, in R. Platzoder (ed.), *Third United Nations Conference on the Law of the Sea: Documents of the Caracas Session* (Hamburg: United Nations, 1975), 186–88. The central point of this proposal not only covered fisheries but also all activities within the zone of the coastal state. The coastal state has the exclusive right to make and enforce regulations pertaining to licensing vessels and gear; fishing seasons; the type, size, and amount of fishing gear; and the types and sizes of the vessels used for the fishing activity.

[51] UN Doc. A/Conf. 62/C. 2/L. 47 of August 8, 1974, in Platzoder, *Third United Nations Conference on the Law of the Sea,* 155–62. The aspects of the U.S. proposal retained in the LOS Convention are those relating to release of arrested personnel and vessels upon the posting of a bond, as well as the prohibition against corporal punishment.

[52] UN Doc. A/Conf. 62/C. 2/ L. 40 of August 5, 1974, in Platzoder, *Third United Nations Conference on the Law of the Sea,* 145–52.

[53] UN Doc. A/AC. 138/SC. II/L. 27 of July 13, 1973, in Shigeru Oda, *The Law of the Sea in Our Time—II: The United Nations Seabed Committee, 1969–1973* (The Hague, Netherlands: Sijthoff Publications on Ocean Development, 1977), 243. This proposal, suggested by Peru, Ecuador, and Panama, envisaged full territorial sea powers of enforcement out to two hundred miles.

[54] UN Doc. A/AC. 138/SC. II/L. 6 of July 18, 1972, in Oda, *The Law of the Sea in Our Time,* 213–14. This proposal gave a coastal state the right to stop and inspect foreign vessels with reasonable cause, but only permitted the coastal state to present a statement of violations to the flag state. Additional action was left to the discretion of the flag state, which would notify the coastal state of the action taken.

[55] "The Law of the Sea Convention," Article 73(1).

A remedy for violations of enforcement measures is one of the chief issues highlighted. The means to punish violations includes detentions or arrest of the vessel and bringing its personnel before judicial proceedings along with issuing penalties after the adjudication process.[56] Hence, violations of the coastal state's laws and regulations by a national or a foreign citizen may result in arrest and punishment by a court of law.[57]

Even though Article 73 is entitled "enforcement of laws and regulations of the coastal states," it really only pertains to measures taken to address violations of the laws and regulations initiated by a coastal state to protect its sovereignty over the living resources in the EEZ. Paragraphs 1 and 3 highlight this point, referencing fisheries laws and regulations. However, it seems these protective measures can be applied to all seafaring vessels; not only those that have violated the regulations and laws of the coastal state. Although Articles 73(1) and (3) expressly concern fisheries laws and regulations, pares. 2 and 4 of Article 73 covers not only fishing vessels, but every vessel. Thus, a scientific vessel doing research on how weather patterns affect the ocean is subject to the coastal state's enforcement powers, like a fishing vessel.

Although Article 73 bestows on the coastal state the right to enforce its laws and regulations pertaining to its EEZ, these enforcement powers are limited. These limitations involve the kind of punishment issued and the prompt release of the vessel and its personnel once bond has been posted.[58] Regarding limits on punishment, Article 73(3) states, "coastal state penalties ... may not include imprisonment in the absence of agreements to the contrary by the states concerned."[59] In accordance with this provision, a coastal state's judicial remedy for vessels that violate its laws and regulations is limited to financial penalties only. However, because no set standard imposes such financial penalties, the imposition of these penalties seems to fall within the domestic jurisdiction of the coastal state.

Article 73(2) states that vessels and crews that come under arrest "shall be promptly release upon the posting of reasonable bond or other security." However, upon closer examination, the Convention does not explicitly define

---

[56] *Ibid.*, paras. 2, 3, and 4; see also William T. Burke, Richard Legatski, and William W. Woodhead, *National and International Enforcement in the Ocean* (Seattle, WA: University of Washington Press, 1975), 1.

[57] Oda, "Fisheries under the United Nations Convention on the Law of the Sea," 747.

[58] "The Law of the Sea Convention," Article 73, paras. 2 and 3.

[59] This exclusion of imprisonment as a form of penalty seems to apply to violations of fisheries laws and does not extend to cases of fishing without a license. See Oda, "Fisheries under the United Nations Convention on the Law of the Sea," 747.

what represents "reasonable bond or other security." Some experts suggest that the bond and security requirement cannot be issued objectively.[60] In essence, the amount of bond and or security is a subjective matter left entirely up to the coastal state. However, if the release of the vessel and personnel is unjustly delayed, the states involved in the matter can address their grievances with the International Tribunal for the Law of the Sea.

Provisions for Specific Species

As mentioned earlier, Article 56 "is an establishment clause" that definitively delineates the rights of coastal states[61] in their EEZ. Sovereign rights are the guiding principles of the rights of coastal states and the living resources of the EEZ. Articles 61 and 62 provide additional details relating to a coastal state's authority and the living resources of the EEZ. Part V of the LOS Convention contains specific provisions that cover the category of certain fishes. The seminal issue regarding these specific provisions pertains to the sovereign rights of a coastal state.

The Regime for Resources Located in Multiple Zones

The law of the sea acknowledges that fishes do not respect coastal boundaries, but habitually migrate across EEZs of neighboring states and across boundaries in areas of the high seas. The law of the sea obligates states to act cooperatively in conserving and overseeing the exploitation of transboundary fish stocks. Article 63 of the LOS Convention is the vehicle that obligates coastal states to cooperate, either directly or through an international organization, with other states when fishes from the same straddling stocks cross various EEZs. States must collaborate to establish appropriate conservation and management initiatives. Regarding shared stocks (stocks that occur in the EEZs of multiple coastal states), Article 63(1) compels coastal states to "seek to agree," either unilaterally or through regional or subregional organizations, to cooperative measures that would ensure the conservation and develop-

---

[60] *Ibid.*, 749.

[61] Bernard H. Oxman, "An Analysis of the EEZ as Formulated in the Informal Composite Negotiating Text," in *The Law of the Sea: State Practice in Zones of Special Jurisdiction, Proceedings of the Thirteenth Annual Conference, October 15–18, 1979,* ed. Thomas A. Clingan, (Honolulu: Law of the Sea Institute, University of Hawaii, 1982), 27–49.

ment of shared stocks.[62] Some international law experts[63] suggest that the obligation expressed in this provision obligates coastal states to work collaborate in conserving and managing shared living resources; however, this view is unsound because the underlying objective is to seek an agreement. A coastal state is only obligated to enter negotiations and pursue efforts as far as possible with the view of forming a viable agreement.[64]

Additionally, measures agreed by coastal states must conform to the other provisions of Part V of the LOS Convention on the EEZ. This suggests that the provisions established in Article 63(1) complement rather than replace the general provisions of Part V of the LOS Convention. Thus, each coastal state still maintains its sovereign rights afforded by Article 56(1)(a) over the shared stock species found in their EEZs, but is bound by the conservation and use obligations explicitly stated in Articles 61 and 62 of the LOS Convention.

Resources Straddling the High Seas and the EEZ

Article 63(2) of the LOS Convention states that straddling fish stocks are stocks located in the EEZ and in the area adjacent to the high seas.[65] Pollock, one of the better known straddling fish stocks of the Pacific Ocean, are fished in two areas of the high seas: the *Donut Hole* located in the Bering Sea, and the *Peanut Hole* located in the Okhotsk Sea.[66] In the Northeast Atlantic, migratory fish are represented by such stocks as cod, haddock, and halibut from Greenland.[67] The Northwest Atlantic contains such mobile stocks as American plaice, yellowtail tuna, and redfish, which are found in the EEZs of Canada,

---

62 "The Law of the Sea Convention," Article 63(1). For further analysis regarding Article 63 and its applicability to transboundary marine fisheries between EEZs; see Ellen Hey, *The Regime for the Exploitation of Transboundary Marine Fisheries Resources* (Dordrecht: Martinus Nijhoff, 1989), Chapter 5.

63 For instance, see Gary H. Knight, "Effect of a Law of the Sea Treaty on the Fishery Conservation and Management Act of 1976," in *Report to the Gulf of Mexico Fishery Management Council* (Tampa: Gulf of Mexico Fishery Management Council, 1977), 13.

64 Burke, "The Law of the Sea Convention Provisions," 106.

65 See J. F. Caddy, "Some Considerations Relevant to the Definition of Shared Stocks and their Allocation between Adjacent Economic Zones," in FAO Fisheries Circular No. 1749, July 1982, 29–30; *Food and Agriculture Organization of the United Nations Report of the Technical Consultation on High Seas Fishing*, Doc. A/Conf. 164/INF/2, 1993.

66 "World Review of Highly Migratory Species and Straddling Stocks," *Food and Agriculture Organization of the United Nations Fisheries Technical Paper No 337* (Rome: Food and Agriculture Organization of the United Nations, 1994), 50–54.

67 *Ibid.*, 58–60.

Greenland, and member states of the EEC.[68] These stocks of fishes are generally exploited by coastal states when they migrate into their EEZs, as well as by vessels from foreign states fishing on the adjacent high seas. In the region of the Atlantic Southwest, squid, hake, and southern blue whiting comprise the majority of fish stocks.[69]

Straddling fish stocks represent a very good example of the correlation between the high seas and the EEZ. Article 63(3) of the LOS Convention acknowledges this relationship. This article asserts that where the same stock species are located in the EEZ and in an area that extends beyond and adjacent to the zone, coastal states and their foreign counterparts who fish these areas "shall seek, either directly or through appropriate subregional or regional organization, to agree upon the measures necessary for the conservation of these stocks in the adjacent area." In essence, this provision explicitly states that, in instances where the same stock of species occurs in an EEZ and in areas frequented by fishers from foreign states, the states concerned are obligated to seek an agreement on conservation and management measures for the entire stock, including the areas that lie in the high seas. However, this obligation seems to be ineffective because states are not compelled to establish joint measures or collaborative actions, but only to "seek" agreement on such measures. If the motion to "seek an agreement" fails, the coastal state is authorized to adopt conservation and management measures that apply only to that portion that lies in its EEZ. According to the standards set by the principles of international law, if the coastal state goes beyond the two-hundred-mile limit, it would not be able to unilaterally confront foreign fishing activities, even in instances where this activity creates detrimental effects on the living resources in the coastal state's EEZ.[70]

Since the LOS Convention has come into force, new issues have emerged on the conservation and management of straddling stocks.[71] A vast number of valuable fish stocks are accessible outside the EEZ two-hundred-mile limit, and in contemporary times, foreign fishing activities have steadily extended beyond the EEZ's outer limits exponentially.[72] The harvesting cycle occurring

---

[68] *Ibid.*, 54–58.

[69] *Ibid.*, 61–63.

[70] Ted L. McDorman, "Stateless Fishing Vessels, International Law and the UN High Seas Fisheries Conference," *JMLC* 25 (1994): 546–47.

[71] Francisco Orrego Vicuña, "Towards an Effective Management of High Seas Fisheries and the Settlement of the Pending Issues of the Law of the Sea," *ODIL* 24 (1993): 84.

[72] Rögnvaldur Hannesson, "Fishing on the High Seas: Cooperation or Competition," *MP* 19, no. 5 (1995): 371.

in the same ecosystem as that of the EEZ, coupled with the lack of unified conservation measures, easily could result in overexploitation of the living resources.[73] Many coastal states regard this as potentially dangerous to the stock species that lie in their EEZs as well as to fisheries-management regimes that have developed since the creation of the two-hundred-mile zone.[74]

At the Conference on Conservation and Management of High Seas Living Resources held in Newfoundland in 1990, some states voiced concerns over this underlying issue.[75] During this meeting, a number of measures were emphasized to stem adverse effects of high seas fisheries and living resources in the EEZ. These measures were coupled with the notion that conservation and management of straddling stocks on the high seas should be compatible with measures applied by a coastal state in the EEZ. This issue was also the main topic of discussion at the UN Conference on Environment and Development held in Rio de Janeiro during the early 1990s,[76] which also suggested that a UN Conference on highly migratory stocks and straddling fish stocks be convened.[77]

Between 1993 and 1995 the UN General Assembly, upon the advice of the officials at the UN Conference on Environment and Development,[78] established an intergovernmental forum under the title *The United Nations Conference on Straddling Fish Stocks and Highly Migratory Fish Stocks,*[79] to facilitate the implementation of the LOS Convention's provisions. The chief aim of the Conference involved identifying and assessing vital issues pertaining to the conservation and management of fish stocks and to develop means to improve cooperative efforts among states for fisheries. Additionally, the Conference sought to ensure its objectives were consistent with the guidelines ex-

---

[73] *Ibid.*

[74] *Ibid.*

[75] Conference on the Conservation and Management of the Living Resources of the High Seas, St. John, Newfoundland, September 5–7, 1990.

[76] "Conservation and Management of Living Resources of the High Seas: Proposal Submitted to the Third Session of the Preparatory Committee for the United Nations Conference on the Environment and Development, Geneva, August 12–September 4, 1991," *Law of the Sea Bulletin,* no. 19 (1991): 42–44. Cosponsors: Argentina, Barbados, Canada, Cape Verde, Chile, Fiji, Guinea-Bissau, Iceland, Kiribati, New Zealand, Peru, Western Samoa, Senegal, Solomon Islands, and Vanuatu.

[77] See UN Doc. A/Conf. 151/4 (Part II), *Official Records* (1992): chap. 17 paras. 17–52.

[78] UN General Assembly Resolution 47/192, 1992.

[79] Citation is in the text of the Conference's document.

pressed in the LOS Convention, specifically for rights and obligations of coastal states and the states fishing on the high seas.[80]

The Conference included five individual Substantive Sessions.[81] At the Fifth Substantive Session, held in New York between July 24 and August 4, 1995, the Conference finalized its work by concluding the *Agreement for the Implementation of the Provisions of the United Nations Convention on the Law of the Sea of 10 December 1982 Relating to the Conservation and Management of Straddling Fish Stocks and Highly Migratory Fish Stocks.*[82] One of the central features of this agreement centered on the need to ensure that the biological uniformity of the straddling fish stock are compatible with the conservation and management initiatives adopted on the high seas and in areas within the national jurisdiction of the parties.[83] Although consistency with the provisions of the LOS Convention and application to straddling stocks are the chief features of the instrument, coastal states have a duty to promote the conservation and management of fish stocks in the areas of the sea that falls in their jurisdiction.[84]

To ensure compatibility between the measures adopted on the high seas and in national jurisdictions, as well as with Article 63(2) of the LOS Convention, coastal states and states whose citizens fish for stocks in adjacent high seas are obligated to establish a cooperative relationship. In determining the compatibility of conservation and management measures, the states involved in the process must consider (a) the conservation measures adopted and implemented in accordance with Article 61 of the LOS Convention with respect to the same stock fished by the coastal state in the areas under national jurisdiction; (b) previously agreed measures that apply to the high seas, enumerated in the LOS Convention as they pertain to relevant coastal states and states fishing on the high seas; (c) previously agreed measures established and applied for the same stocks by a subregional or regional fisheries-management organization; (d) the biological unity and other biological char-

---

80 Frida María Armas Pfirter, "Straddling Stocks and Highly Migratory Stocks in Latin American Practice and Legislation: New Perspectives in Light of Current International Negotiations," *ODIL* 26 (1995): 138.

81 The Proceedings of the second, third, and fourth sessions of the conference are summarized in *Earth Negotiations Bulletin*, vol. 7, no. 30, April 4, 1994; no. 39, August 29, 1994; and no. 43, April 14, 1995.

82 UN Doc. A/Conf. 164/37, September 8, 1995. According to Article 37, the Agreement shall be open for signature and remain open for signature at the United Nations headquarters for twelve months from the 4th of December 1995.

83 *Ibid.*, Article 7 para. 2.

84 *Ibid.*, Article 3 para. 1.

acteristics that represent the stocks; and (e) the dependence of coastal states and states fishing on the high seas concerning the targeted fish stocks.[85]

The Agreement also implemented specific general principles aimed at clarifying the nature and objectives of the conservation and management measures, precautionary measures, and how consistently these measures would be applied by the coastal state in its EEZ and by the coastal state and other states that fished the areas beyond the EEZ outer limit.[86] Furthermore, a coastal state and other states concerned have a duty to work toward making the conservation measures as compatible as possible within a reasonable time frame.[87] Although the details are being worked out, the states concerned must establish provisional arrangements.[88] When all avenues to cooperative efforts have been exhausted, any participating state may implement the settlement-dispute procedure outlined in Part VIII of the Agreement.[89]

Compliance and enforcement of conservation and management measures are a vital part of the agreement and obligate states to seek cooperative ventures to ensure compliance with and enforcement of conservation and management measures for straddling fish stocks.[90] In this context, when a coastal state believes a vessel has been involved in unauthorized fishing activities in its jurisdiction, the coastal state can request the vessel's flag state to initiate an investigation into the questionable activities.[91] In addition, the vessel's flag state must cooperate with the coastal state in whose jurisdiction the violations occurred, take appropriate enforcement and corrective actions, and may authorize officials from the coastal state to board and conduct an inspection of the vessel.[92] Moreover, the agreement gives states that are party to a subregional or regional fisheries organization the power to board and inspect vessels flying the flag of other states when they are found in any high seas areas under the jurisdiction of that particular organization.[93]

If clear and present violations of the conservation and management measures are found, the inspecting state must gather all pertinent evidence and immedi-

---

85 *Ibid.*, Article 7 para. 2.
86 *Ibid.*, Article 5.
87 *Ibid.*, Article 7 para. 3.
88 *Ibid.*, para. 5.
89 *Ibid.*
90 *Ibid.*, see Part VI and Article 20 para. 1.
91 *Ibid.*, para. 6.
92 *Ibid.*
93 *Ibid.*, Article 21 para. 1.

ately notify the flag state about all alleged violations.[94] The flag state should follow the notification of the violations with a full investigation into the matter and take proper actions if evidence indicates the coastal state's laws have been broken.[95] In addition, port states have the authority to inspect documents, fishing equipment, and the catch on board fishing vessels when such vessels dock voluntarily in their ports or at their offshore terminals.[96]

Port states also have the authority to implement legislative measures that prohibit landings and transshipments when the catch results from violating a coastal state's conservation measures.[97] In dispute settlements that concern the interpretation of a specific agreement, Article 27 contains guidelines that resemble the provisions located in Article 33(1) of the UN Charter. Article 27 obligates parties to seek a viable solution to disputes through peaceful means. The mechanisms for dispute resolution include negotiation, inquiry, mediation, arbitration, and adjudication. It is also clear that finding peaceful avenues to a dispute is always the chief objective.[98]

Regulation of Highly Migratory Species

The term *highly migratory species* refers to a specific type of fish that migrates wide distances and spends a great portion of its life cycle outside the two-hundred-mile limit.[99] Annex I of the LOS Convention gives a detailed listing of designated migratory species. The list includes nine tuna species, twelve marlin species, four saury species, and cetaceans. The chief characteristic of these species is their mobility; they can travel great distances, which creates a wide area of distribution in and outside the two-hundred-mile limits of the EEZ. In the North Pacific, such species as bluefin tuna and albacore may travel across the Pacific Ocean in a very short period of time. They may be exploited in the coastal waters of the United States, then, in a little less than a year, travel to the

---

[94] *Ibid.*, para. 5.

[95] *Ibid.*, para. 6(a).

[96] *Ibid.*, Article 23 para. 2.

[97] *Ibid.*, para. 3.

[98] *Ibid.* It is worth noting that Article 30 concerning the procedures for the settlement of disputes provides "that provisions relating to the settlement of disputes set out in Part XV of the LOS Convention apply *mutatis mutandis* to any dispute between states parties to" the Agreement concerning the interpretation or application of the Application, whether or not they are also parties to the LOS Convention.

[99] Stephen R. Katz, "Consequences of the Economic Zone for Catch Opportunities of Fishing Nations," *Marit. Stud. Mgmt.* 2 (1975): 149.

coastal waters of Japan.[100] Southern bluefin tuna, generally located in the waters of the southern hemisphere, journey from their spawning areas in Australia to such areas as the Atlantic, Pacific, and Indian Oceans.[101] However, the scientific accuracy of the LOS Convention's data can be undetermined because the Convention's list contains fish species that has a limited migratory range.[102]

From a commercial-value standpoint, the various species of tuna are some of the most important fish species among HMS, and a large percentage of global initiatives concern this species.[103] Article 64 of the LOS Convention directly addresses the issue of HMS. The first paragraph of this article mandates that coastal states and other states whose nationals fish for HMS must develop cooperative efforts to ensure conservation and promotion of optimum use of such species throughout the region that lies in and beyond the EEZ. This provision originated in the ISNT[104] and has been virtually unchanged since it became transfixed to the texts of UNCLOS III. These provisions are expressed in the part addressing primarily the EEZ, applied "in addition to other provisions" of Part V of the LOS Convention.[105] Therefore, a coastal state enjoys sovereignty over HMS in its EEZ, as dictated in Article 56 of the LOS Convention. As one international law expert succinctly put it, the effect of the provisions that are included in paragraph 1 of Article 64 is "to place limitations upon the exercise of these sovereign rights by requiring the coastal state to co-operate with other states in the region."[106]

In the beginning, the United States refused to recognize a coastal state's jurisdiction over tuna. The United States firmly held the view that tuna, in accordance with Article 64 of the LOS Convention, did not come under the general jurisdiction of a coastal state when they were present in its EEZ. Instead, the freedom of fishing on the high seas extended when it came to such fish species, and the conservation, management, and optimum use of these species could only be affected by prior international arrangements between the

---

100 Camillus Narokobi, "The Tuna Issue, The South Pacific, and the United States," in *Consensus and Confrontation: The United States and the Law of the Sea Convention,* ed. John M. Van Dyke (Honolulu: Law of the Sea Institute, University of Hawaii, 1985), 370–75.

101 *Ibid.*

102 For instance, skipjak or yellowfin tuna.

103 Pfirter, "Straddling Stocks and Highly Migratory Stocks in Latin American Practice and Legislation," 134.

104 "The Law of the Sea Convention," Article 53.

105 *Ibid.,* Article 64 para. 2.

106 Edward D. Brown, *The International Law of the Sea: Introductory Manual* (Brookfield, VT: Dartmouth, 1994), 229.

coastal state and other fishing states in the region.[107] Costa Rica, Panama,[108] and the Bahamas[109] supported the position of the United States.

Although the U.S. view on this issue remained somewhat isolated, most international law experts took a distinctive opposing view on this issue.[110] Using an argument that is central to the LOS Convention, these experts suggest that Article 64(2) explicitly states that the provisions contained in paragraph 1 of Article 64 will be applied "in addition to the other provisions" of Part V. In their opinion, this provision acknowledges and affirms the tenets of Article 56, which supports the premise that highly migratory tuna falls under the authority of the coastal state.[111] Additionally, all other distant water fishing states opposed the view espoused by the United States.[112] In this context, Australia made a resounding statement, indicating that U.S. views on this issue were "inconsistent" with the standards of international law.[113] Moreover, overwhelming state practice supports the notion that a coastal state has jurisdiction over highly migratory tuna throughout the EEZ.[114] The combination of these factors eventually compelled the United States to alter its views on migratory tuna, thereby rendering its practice consistent with global state practice subsequent to the enactment of the LOS Convention.[115]

Thus, HMS represent the close interactions that take place between the EEZ and the high seas. The LOS Convention affirms this interrelationship in Article 64, delineating a relationship that calls for cooperative efforts. Also,

---

107 See President Reagan's statement on the two-hundred-mile EEZ, reproduced in *VJIL* 23 (1983): 598–601; Christopher J. Healey, "United States Tuna Management Policy," *ASIL* 5 (1981): 84–85.

108 See Costa Rica, Panama, and the United States. Agreement on Tuna Fishing and Protocol, April 12, 1983, cited by Vicuña, "Towards an Effective Management of High Seas Fisheries," 85.

109 The Bahamas Fisheries Resources Act, 1977, in ST/LEG/SER. B/19 (1980): 18–19.

110 See, for instance, William T. Burke, "Highly Migratory Species in the New Law of the Sea," *ODIL* 14 (1983): 273–314; Hugo Caminos, "The Regime of Fisheries in the Exclusive Economic Zone," in *The Exclusive Economic Zone: A Latin American Perspective*, ed. Francisco Orrego Vicuña (Boulder, CO: Westview Press, 1984), 149.

111 Fleischer, "The New Regime of the Maritime Fisheries," 256.

112 Deborah Cass, "The Quiet Revolution: The Development of the Exclusive Economic Zone and Implications for Foreign Fishing Access in the Pacific," *MULR* 16 (1987): 95.

113 *Australian Foreign Affairs Record* 56, Sept. (1985): 824, cited by *ibid.*

114 See Aide-Memoire concerning Amendments to the Magnuson Fishery Conservation and Management Act: Amendment to Include Highly Migratory Tuna and Species of fish under United States Jurisdiction, 22 May 1991: "Legal Information Relevant to the United Nations Convention on the Law of the Sea," *Law of the Sea Bulletin*, no. 19, 1991, 21.

115 *Ibid.*, para. 2.

such acknowledgement is confirmed in the *United Nations Conventions on the Law of the Sea of 10 December 1982 Relating to the Conservation and Management of Straddling Fish Stocks and Highly Migratory Fish Stocks.*[116] Article 3 applies the provision of the above Agreement in relationship to the straddling stocks of HMS.

Conservation and Protection of Marine Mammals

Whales, seals, porpoises, and other cetaceans represent the main species that fall under the topic of "Marine Mammals."[117] A coastal state has sovereign rights over these species, as expressed in Article 56 of the LOS Convention. Moreover, some marine mammals, such as dolphins, are listed in Annex I as HMS and thus come under the authority of Article 64 of the LOS Convention.

There is not a high reproduction rate among marine mammals and this can result in depletion of the species in a relatively short period of time. The LOS Convention seems to address this issue concerning marine mammals: Article 65 contains a specific provision relating to this species. Under Article 65, a coastal state or some equally authorized international organization is empowered to limit or prohibit the exploitation of these resources more strictly than other living resources. This particular provision is compatible with the sovereign rights of the coastal state.[118] Some legal experts[119] suggest states have no duty to establish an allowable catch ratio for these species or a need to ensure their optimum use as a harvested resource. States must establish some type of cooperative venture to conserve various species and must work through the appropriate international organization such as the International Whaling Commission to enhance conservation and management activities. The LOS Convention, through the provisions contained in Article 120, dictates that the same duties be performed on the high seas. However, the interpretation that would exclude the concept of optimum use is not self-evident be-

---

[116] UN Doc. A/Conf. 164/37.

[117] Cynthia E. Carlson, "The International Regulation of Small Cetaceans," *SDLR* 21 (1984): 577–623.

[118] Jean F. Carroz, "Les Problèmes de la Pêche a la Conférence sur le Droit de la Mer et dans la Pratique des Etats," *RGDIP* 84 (1980): 721.

[119] Burke, "U.S. Fishery Management and the New Law of the Sea," 115; Robin Rolf Churchill and Alan Vaughan Lowe, *The Law of the Sea,* 3rd ed. (Manchester, England: Manchester University Press, 1988), 238.

cause cetaceans and dolphins are considered HMS in Annex I of the LOS Convention and are subject to the optimum use requirement.[120]

Conservation of Anadromous Species

The term *anadromous species* refers to migratory fishes that hatch in fresh water, migrate to the sea to grow, and then return to fresh water to spawn.[121] From the standpoint of commercial value, salmon is one of the most important fish among anadromous species[122] and a large percentage of international agreements address this particular fish.[123]

Provisions aimed specifically at anadromous fish species were included in the LOS Convention through Article 66. Article 66 states that the state of origin of anadromous stocks (i.e., rivers that lie in the jurisdiction of a particular state) has "primary interest and responsibility for such stocks."[124] This provision was included in the first negotiating text of UNCLOS III.[125] As a result of this provision, anadromous species can only be fished in the jurisdictional waters of the state from which they originated.[126] This also means that anadromous species are subject to the sovereign rights of the state from which they originated.

Article 66(1) explains certain exceptions to this general rule for anadromous species. According to this provision, fishing for anadromous stocks could be conducted on the high seas when fishing for such stocks in the jurisdictional waters of the state of origin might result in economic distress for a state other than a state of origin. If such problems do arise, the states

---

[120] W. T. Burke suggests that this inclusion in Annex I is a technical error arising from the fact that Articles 64 and 65 were once one article in the Informal Negotiating Text. In his opinion, Article 64 should not be regarded as applicable to cetaceans, optimum use not being required in this case by virtue of Article 65 being read together with Article 61(4). Burke, "U.S. Fishery Management and the New Law of the Sea," 115.

[121] This definition is taken from the Canadian working paper "The Special Case of Salmon: The Most Important Anadromous Species," submitted to UNCLOS III, Caracas Session, 1974, UN Doc. A/Conf. 62/C. 2/L. 81, August 23, 1974, in Platzoder, *Third United Nations Conference on the Law of the Sea*, 185–86.

[122] Sturgeon and Shad are other examples of anadromous species.

[123] "Convention for the Conservation of Salmon in the North Atlantic Ocean, 1982," *OJEC* L378 (1982): 24; "Convention for the Conservation of Anadromous Stocks in the North Pacific Ocean of 1992," *Law of the Sea Bulletin*, No. 22 (1993): 21.

[124] "The Law of the Sea Convention," Article 66(1).

[125] *Ibid.*, Article 54.

[126] "The Law of the Sea Convention," Article 66(3)(a).

involved are advised to mediate the problems to determine the best measures to remedy the situation.[127]

In addition, the state of origin can (because of its primary responsibility for such stocks), according to the guidelines of Article 66(2), develop a total allowable catch for stocks originating from its rivers. However, this feature is allowed only through prior consultation with other states that fish these stocks. The duty to consult other states when establishing a total allowable catch ratio applies not only to anadromous species that are to be fished beyond the outer limits of the EEZ,[128] but also to the anadromous species that migrate into or through the EEZs of states other than the state of origin.[129] The established total allowable catch must be observed in the high seas as well as in the EEZs of other nations.[130] This particular statement highlights the universal nature of the rights and responsibilities of the state of origin.

The Management of Catadromous Species

The term *catadromous species* refers to fish species that live in fresh water but migrate to the sea to spawn.[131] Eels and mullets are prime examples of catadromous species. Unlike Article 66, which focuses on anadromous species, Article 67 covers catadromous species and contains general provisions about these species. Anadromous stocks generate more interest from states than catadromous stocks.[132]

In some ways, the provisions of Article 67 have similarities to Article 66. One central principle they share is that the state in whose waters catadromous species spend the majority of their life cycle in is responsible for the management of these species.[133] The direct result of this principle is that these species will be fished solely in the sea areas that lie landward of the outer limits of the EEZ.[134] Fishing for catadromous species on the high seas is not allowed.

Furthermore, if the catadromous species migrates through the EEZ of a state other than the state from which it originated, the states involved must

---

127 *Ibid.*

128 *Ibid.*

129 *Ibid.*, para. 4.

130 Fleischer, "The Exclusive Economic Zone under the Convention Regime and in State Practice," 278.

131 David Ponsonby and Georges Dussart, *The Anatomy of the Sea* (San Francisco: Chronicle Books, 2005), 278.

132 Attard, *The Exclusive Economic Zone in International Law*, 189.

133 "The Law of the Sea Convention," Article 67(1).

134 *Ibid.*, para. 2.

develop cooperative ventures aimed at enacting management measures through mutual agreement.[135] This coordinating agreement must be built on the reasonable management of the species and should highlight the responsibilities of the management state in maintaining the species.[136] In essence, even though other coastal states may have an interest in the species, they do not have full autonomy over the species in their zones.

When considering the above analysis, under the EEZ fisheries regime contained in Part V of the LOS Convention, the coastal state enjoys far-reaching rights in the management and use of the EEZ's fisheries. In exercising these rights, the coastal state has a number of obligations. These duties include the coastal state's proper use of conservation and management measures to protect the living resources of the EEZ and the coastal state's duty to promote the optimum use of the EEZ's living resources, including implementing provisions that control foreign fishers' access to the zone. However, the coastal state has much flexibility in establishing the allowable catch ratio and the capacity to harvest the resource. A decision concerning giving foreign states access to the zone must consider the economy of the coastal state as well as other detrimental effects this access may have on the coastal state's community. The dispute-settlement mechanism established by the LOS Convention and an integral part of Article 297(3)(a) prohibits any review of the coastal state's decisions on these issues. In short, the LOS Convention grants coastal states extensive decision-making powers based on their interests in what species get fished, how much of the species gets fished, and who may fish the species in the EEZ.

Sedentary Species and Nonliving Resources of the EEZ

Sedentary species and the nonliving resources of the subsoil and seabed of the EEZ are highly discussed topics when it comes to the law of the sea. The subjects fall under the sovereign rights of the coastal state by virtue of Article 56 of Part V of the LOS Convention.[137] However, the coastal state's authority over fish is expressed in Part VI of the LOS Convention, under two cross-references from Article 68 in the EEZ for sedentary species and under Article 56(3) for nonliving resources of the EEZ.

---

[135] *Ibid.*, para. 3.

[136] *Ibid.*

[137] These two subjects also fall under the sovereign right of the coastal state under Article 77(4) of Part VI (Continental Shelf).

Sedentary Species

Background concerning sedentary species can be found during the formative stage of the 1958 Geneva conventions. The International Law Commission included sedentary species in its definition of natural resources during its meeting in 1953.[138] The final definition of the term evolved from an extensive debate and compromise between states that wanted to exclude living resources altogether and those that wanted to include bottom fish.[139] The final definition of the term sedentary species was adopted in the Geneva Convention on the Continental Shelf, Article 2(4), and has remained the same in the informal composite negotiating text. Sedentary species are immobile or species that are under the seabed at their harvesting stage, and are unable to move except when they are in constant physical contact with the seabed or subsoil.[140] Sponges, corals, oysters, lobsters, and mussels represent sedentary species.[141]

Some commentators have noted that this definition of sedentary species lacks clarity.[142] The lack of a uniform list of sedentary species seems to support this argument. The fishing states, in practice, have adopted various lists based on their fishing interests that either includes or excludes certain sedentary species.[143] In essence, whether or not a specific species falls in the category of sedentary species remains a subjective decision made solely by the coastal state.

As mentioned earlier, Article 68 of Part V definitively excludes sedentary species from the application of this part. Article 77(1) of Part VI, the section addressing the continental shelf, states that the coastal state enjoys jurisdiction over the continental shelf specifically for the purpose of exploring and exploiting its natural resources. The rights given to coastal states under the latter provision are invariably the same rights coastal states enjoy under the Geneva Convention on the Continental Shelf, Articles 2 and 3, and under customary international law.[144] These rights are not qualified by a state's occupation or by any official proclamation. They are exclusive in the sense that if the coastal state does not choose to exploit its resources, no other state may

---

138 Bowett, *The Law of the Sea*, 35.

139 Ebere Osicke, "The Contribution of States from the Third World to the Development of the Law on the Continental Shelf and the Concept of the Economic Zone," *IJIL* 15 (1975): 321–22.

140 "The Law of the Sea Convention," Article 77 para. 4.

141 Bowett, *The Law of the Sea*, 35; Martin Dixon, *Textbook on International Law* (London: Blackstone Press, 1995), 177.

142 Oda, "International Law of the Resources of the Sea," 427.

143 *Ibid.*

144 "North Sea Continental Shelf Cases," 39.

not exploit the resources without the express consent of the coastal state.[145] The coastal state can either grant permission or withhold permission without giving any reasonable explanation. This subjective treatment of sedentary species located in the EEZ implies that a coastal state is not obligated to implement management or conservation measures, nor is it obligated to accommodate foreign fishers.[146] In Article 77, the coastal state's sovereign rights main purposes are predicated on exploring and exploiting, thereby omitting the conservation and management element. When this omission is connected with the injunction in Article 68 that no provisions in Part V are to apply to sedentary species expressed in Article 77(4), it is quite clear that the previous discussions involving obligatory conservation and management measures are not required by the coastal state. The other provisions that involve declaring and providing access to a surplus, safeguarding associated or dependent species, initiating arrangements for the economically dislocated, geographically disadvantaged, or land-locked states would also be excluded, as would the Article 73 requirement regarding imprisonment, and release on bond.[147]

The Nonliving Resources of the EEZ

One element of the LOS Convention is that it gives coastal states exclusive rights to explore, exploit, conserve, and manage nonliving resources in the EEZ.[148] With the exception of the guidelines pertaining to "conserving and managing" and "superjacent water," the rights enjoyed by a coastal state are similar to the rights it enjoys in seabed resources under the 1958 Convention on the Continental Shelf and in customary international law.[149] All who have had the opportunity to exercise jurisdiction over their continental shelves have done so.[150] Coastal states' dealings with nonliving resources focus primarily on exploration and exploitation, whereas coastal states' relationship with living resources addresses conservation management.[151]

Because the continental shelf sometimes extends within the two-hundred-mile limit of the EEZ for these specific resources, one central issue that had to be resolved at the negotiation sessions of UNCLOS III involved which of the

---

145 *Ibid.*, 36.

146 Dixon, *Textbook on International Law*, 183.

147 Rama Puri, "The Legal Regime of Marine Fisheries," *IJIL* 22 (1982): 249.

148 "The Law of the Sea Convention," Article 56(1)(a).

149 Churchill and Lowe, *The Law of the Sea*, 137.

150 Jonathan I. Charney, "The Exclusive Economic Zone and Public International Law," *ODIL* 15 (1985): 244.

151 Churchill and Lowe, *The Law of the Sea*.

two regimes should prevail. Two compelling trends emerged at the negotiation sessions of UNCLOS III when discussing this issue. The first trend appeared during the initial stages of UNCLOS III and involved the notion that the continental-shelf regime should be assimilated into the EEZ's two-hundred-mile limit.[152] Many African and Latin American countries, as well as some LLS, supported this notion.[153] These nations put forth a number of strong arguments to support their position. The representative from Zaire seems to capture the spirit of these arguments:

> The principle of the common heritage of mankind was of great importance to his delegation. Any application of the exploitability criterion would leave for the common heritage merely those areas that were unexploitable and therefore of little value. The only criterion should be that of distance. It was logical for the limits of the continental shelf and the economic zone to coincide. Consequently, the shelf as a separate entity would disappear. These states that claimed acquired rights over the continental shelf were doing so under the 1958 Convention that was now being reviewed.[154]

However, for states with extended continental shelves (i.e., the United States, Australia, Canada, the Soviet Union, and Argentina[155]), these arguments were not too convincing, particularly because they omitted the notion that broad-shelf states enjoy sovereign rights beyond the proposed two-hundred-mile limits under the 1958 Convention on the Continental Shelf.[156] These states believed that absorbing the continental shelf regime into the two-hundred-mile limits of the EEZ would irretrievably damage the rights that they already enjoy.[157]

The broad-shelf states were in the majority in discussions at UNCLOS III. However, because their arguments had validity, and because the textual wording of Article 1 of the 1958 Convention on the Continental Shelf included the

---

[152] Jean-François Pulvenis, "Zone Économique et Plateau Continental: Unité ou Dualité," *RIRI* 12 (1978): 107–10.

[153] *Ibid.*, 107–8.

[154] *Official Records* 2 (1974): 176; see also Pulvenis, "Zone Économique et Plateau Continental," 109.

[155] Pulvenis, "Zone Économique et Plateau Continental," 112.

[156] *Ibid.*

[157] See, for instance, the statement of the Canadian representative at UNCLOS III, Caracas Session, 1974, *Official Records* 2 (1974): 146–47.

principle of *natural prolongation*[158] concerning land mass, the positions espoused by these states certainly could not be ignored. UNCLOS III, therefore, had to seek an alternative solution to this issue. Articles 76, 82, and 56 of the LOS Convention reflects this compromise, with the former Article allowing coastal states the right to extend their continental shelf beyond the two-hundred-mile limit.[159] This position correlates with the principles of international law and was supported by a great number of states. In contrast, a percentage of the products that came from the exploitation of continental-shelf mineral resources found beyond the two-hundred-mile limit was made payable to the international seabed authority, which distributed the resources between the states who were party to the LOS Convention.[160] This concession made to those states conformed with the guidelines of the first trend.

Just as importantly, under Article 56(1) and 57 of Part V, entitled "Exclusive Economic Zone," coastal states have jurisdiction in exploring and exploiting, conserving, and managing the natural resources of the seabed and subsoil up to two hundred miles. Article 77(1) of Part VI on the Continental Shelf grants coastal states virtually the same rights. In addition, under a cross-reference from Article 56(3), coastal states' authority over seabed and subsoil resources can be exercised in accordance with Part VI on the Continental Shelf. This cross-reference calls into question whether the EEZ regime merges with that of the continental shelf.

For all intents and purposes, the provisions preserved in Article 56(3) seem to acknowledge the autonomy of both institutions. This assessment finds support in the parallel provisions located in Part V and Part VI that cover such matters as coastal states' sovereign rights over the resources that lie in the seabed and subsoil, sedentary species, and artificial islands.[161] In both parts, two related but independent regimes develop. Thus, Judge Gros was correct when he pointed out in the *Continental Shelf (Libyan Arab Jamahiriya v. Malta) Case 1984,* that "comparison of Articles 56–62 and 73–74 (zone) with 76, 77, 78, 81, and 83 (continental shelf) seems to leave only this alternative: either two legal regimes or chaos."[162]

This EEZ and continental-shelf complementary system becomes problematic in delimitation, especially between states with opposite coasts. If the distance between two states with opposite coasts exceeds four hundred miles and there

---

[158] This was a principle introduced by the ICJ in "North Sea Continental Shelf Cases," 31.
[159] "The Law of the Sea Convention," Article 76(b).
[160] *Ibid.*, Article 82.
[161] *Ibid.*, Articles 68 and 56(1)(b)(i), respectively.
[162] *ICJ Rep* (1984): 21.

is a continental shelf that lies between them, the delimitation issue that may arise can be resolved by applying the provisions contained in Article 83(1),[163] namely through an mutual assured agreement[164] that is compatible with the standards of international law[165] and results in an equitable resolution.[166] If the distances between these states are less than four hundred miles, the situation becomes more problematic. If the two states have claimed an EEZ, and both have agreed to disregard the continental shelf altogether, a viable resolution would be difficult to achieve. However, assuming that one of the state's continental shelf extends beyond the median line of the two opposite coasts, can that particular state still maintain sovereign rights over that specific portion of the continental shelf, expressed in Article 77(1) of the LOS Convention?

Because the regime of the continental shelf was developed earlier than that of the EEZ, and given that, under the 1958 Convention on the Continental Shelf and the LOS Convention, the rights of a coastal state are not predicated on occupation or any expressed proclamation, it seems highly improbable that a coastal state would abandon its claim to its continental shelf beyond the median line of the two states with opposite coasts. However, by virtue of the guidelines contained in Article 56(1), a coastal state enjoys, within the boundaries of its EEZ, expressed sovereign rights for exploring and exploiting the nonliving resources of the seabed and subsoil. In essence, it seems very unlikely that a state would allow an opposing state to claim the continental shelf underlying its EEZ.

---

[163] The principles outlined in Article 83(1) are the same as those in Article 74(1) regarding the delimitation of the EEZ.

[164] In the "North Sea Continental Shelf Cases," the ICJ noted that, according to the basic tenets of law and of opinion juris, delimitation is to be affected by agreement between the parties concerned. See also "Case Concerning Delimitation of the Maritime Boundary in the Gulf of Maine Area (Canada v. United States)," *ICJ Rep* (1984): 299–300, para. 112.

[165] Articles 74(1) and 83(1) state that the delimitation of the EEZ and the continental shelf shall be affected by agreement on the basis of international law, as referenced in Article 38 of the Statute of the International Court of Justice. Neither the LOS Convention nor Article 38 of the ICJ explain exactly what norms should be considered by parties in the process of delimitation. However, several norms were highlighted, such as that delimitation should be deployed according to equitable principles. See *ibid.*, 295; "Case Concerning the Continental Shelf (Libyan Arab Jamahiriya v. Malta)," *ICJ Reports* (1985): 33; Janusz Symonides, "Delimitation of Maritime Areas between the States with Opposite or Adjacent Coasts," *PYIL* 13 (1984): 36–44.

[166] See "Delimitation of Maritime Areas between Canada and the French Republic, Decision of Arbitration dated 10 June 1992," *ILM* 31 (1992): 1163 para. 38; also Janusz Symonides, "Delimitation of Maritime Areas between the States with Opposite or Adjacent Coasts," 44–46.

One way to resolve this issue involves absorbing the continental-shelf regime (when it is within the two-hundred-mile limit) into the EEZ. One commentator noted that if the distance between two states with opposite coasts is less than four hundred miles, the EEZ should be delimited, regardless of the continental shelf between these states.[167]

However, an opposite state with a broad shelf would likely disagree with this view. Under such situations, it would be possible for this state not to claim an EEZ and base its assertions solely on continental-shelf theory. In addition, even if a state does claim an EEZ, it can assert its authority over a continental shelf based purely on the principles of customary international law. A prime example of this involves the Socialist Republic of Vietnam. This nation, in May 1977, made a statement that the economic zone should be extended two hundred miles from its baselines.[168] This country further stated that "The continental shelf of the Socialist Republic of Vietnam comprises the seabed and subsoil of the submarine areas that extends beyond the Vietnamese Territorial Sea throughout the natural prolongation of the Vietnamese land territory to the outer edge of the continental margin."[169]

Another solution is the establishment of two different maritime boundary lines, one for the EEZ and another for the continental shelf. Regarding this issue, Libya, during the hearing on the *Continental Shelf (Tunisia v Libyan Arab Jamahiriya) Case,* put forth this view:

> Libya considers that, as between states with opposite or adjacent coasts, the delimitation of their respective continental shelf areas and of their economic zones ought not, in the majority of cases, to be different. Nevertheless, there may be factors relevant to fishing, such as established practices, which have no relevance to shelf resources; and conversely, there may be factors relevant to shelf resources such as geological features controlling the extent of a natural prolongation of no relevance to fishing. It therefore follows that the two boundaries need not necessarily coincide.[170]

---

167 Shigeru Oda, *International Law of the Resources of the Sea* (Germantown, MD: Sijthoff and Noordhoff, 1979), 93.

168 Statement on the economic zone, May 20, 1977, in Robert W. Smith (ed.), *Exclusive Economic Zone Claims: An Analysis and Primary Documents* (Boston: Martinus Nijhoff, 1986), 481.

169 *Ibid.*, para. 4.

170 D'Arechaga, "Case Concerning the Continental Shelf," 232.

Not all states have the use of a maritime boundary line to delimit the two zones. However, a large percentage of coastal states have developed a single maritime boundary with the aim of delimiting the EEZ and the continental shelf in various parts of the world.[171] Furthermore, only a small percentage of states have agreed to establish two different maritime boundary lines for different purposes. For instance, the agreement between Australia and France pertaining to maritime boundaries separating the Heard and Kerguelen Islands located in the South Indian Ocean and the Australian mainland and New Caledonia, concluded on January 4, 1982, with the two nations agreeing to establish two different maritime boundary lines for different purposes.[172] On a similar basis, concerning the agreement between Australia and Papua New Guinea concluded on December 18, 1978, the fisheries jurisdictional boundary line does not correspond to the boundary line of the continental shelf.[173]

When analyzing the information presented above, only one conclusion can result: the rights of a coastal state over the EEZ's nonliving resources of the seabed and subsoil are dictated by the law of the continental shelf. This chief feature of the continental-shelf regime develops from the cross-reference contained in Article 56(3) to Part VI on the Continental Shelf. Thus, it follows that such rights that coastal states have over the EEZ's seabed and subsoil are similar to the rights that coastal states have over the resources of the continental shelf. These rights are functional in nature. In short, their main purposes are explicitly defined and exclusive. In spite of this, the EEZ and the continental shelf remain legally autonomous, even though within the two-hundred-mile limit they virtually operate with respect to the same geographical area and similar nonliving resources. These two concepts have a contradictory structure and very different origins.[174] This, in some instances, can justify the development of two different boundaries.

The Coastal State's Rights over other Economic Resources of the EEZ

Article 56(1)(a) asserts that the coastal state's sovereign rights may be applied to "other activities for the economic exploitation and exploration of the zone, such as the production of energy from the water, currents, and winds." Under

---

171 See UN Division for Ocean Affairs and the Law of the Sea. *Practice of States*, 14.

172 J. R. V. Prescott, "Maritime Boundaries and Issues in the Southwest Pacific Ocean," in *Ocean Boundary Making: Regional Issues and Developments*, ed. Douglas M. Johnston and P. M. Saunders (London: Croom Helm, 1988), 288–90.

173 *Ibid.*, 289.

174 Edward D. Brown, "The Continental Shelf and the Exclusive Economic Zone: The Problem of Delimitation at UNCLOS III," *Marit. Pol. Mgmt.* 4 (1976): 402.

the revised single negotiating text, Part II Article 44(1)(c), the coastal state has "exclusive jurisdiction" in other activities for the economic exploration and exploitation of the EEZ. In other words, the coastal state alone has the authority to legislate and implement all necessary enforcement measures in the zone with respect to these activities.[175]

The terms "exclusive jurisdiction" were later replaced in the ICNT of 1977 with the terms "sovereign rights" during the revision process of the EEZ's provisions to emphasize the economic nature of the EEZ.[176] In the above provision, three types of economic activities are highlighted regarding the EEZ: activities concerning the production of energy from water, currents, and winds. This list is somewhat allegorical because the comprehensive expression "other activities for economic exploitation and exploration of the zone" seems to suggest that coastal states have management and control responsibilities over all economic activities in the EEZ and because the words "such as" highlight the point that few activities mentioned in that provision are meant to be illustrative and not conclusive.

Thus, coastal states' rights over the economic uses of the EEZ go beyond those activities associated with the production of energy from water, currents, and winds, and extend to include all other economically related activities that will be made accessible by technological advancements. It is noteworthy that prior to the convening of UNCLOS III, customary international law had not granted coastal states these rights. Although the territorial sea regime includes coastal states' sovereignty over economic activities related to the exploitation and exploration of the territorial sea,[177] none of the contiguous zone, exclusive fishing zones, or continental shelf regimes were overly concerned with such activities. Under each of these regimes, third states retained the right to make such uses of the sea as was a reasonable use of the high seas.

Coastal States' Noneconomic Rights in the EEZ

Additional coastal states' rights in the EEZ pertain to artificial islands, installations and structures, MSR, and preservation of the zone's marine environment. Regarding these features, Article 56(1)(b) stipulates that in the EEZ, coastal states have jurisdiction, as provided in the provision of the LOS Convention regarding the following:

---

[175] Extavour, *The Exclusive Economic Zone,* 48.

[176] Attard, *The Exclusive Economic Zone in International Law,* 48.

[177] "Convention on the Territorial Sea and the Contiguous Zone," Article 1.

1. The establishment and use of artificial islands, installations, and structures;
2. MSR; and
3. The protection and preservation of the marine environment.

Unlike the economic rights granted to the coastal states, which are framed in terms of "sovereign rights," the rights enumerated in this provision are expressed in terms of "jurisdiction." Although this term relates more to the adjudication authority associated with the courts, it has a broader meaning in the context of international law. Jurisdiction essentially means that the state has the authority to enforce a rule of law;[178] thus, the state has the authority to exercise certain powers. The jurisdiction of a state grants validity to its legislative and judicial actions. As one legal expert puts it, "the sovereign cannot confer jurisdiction on his courts or his legislature when he has no such jurisdiction according to the principles of international law."[179] Certain limits may exist in the scope of jurisdiction. For instance, a state may assert jurisdiction over all individuals in a specific geographical location and for all purposes, or it may limit the extent of the jurisdiction exercised according to the type of person, area, or purpose.[180]

Coastal States' Jurisdiction over Artificial Islands, Installations, and Structures

Article 56(1)(b) gives coastal states jurisdiction over artificial islands, installations, and structures. In the first text[181] of UNCLOS III, the words "exclusive rights" and "jurisdiction" reflected this, but were later changed to the text displayed in Article 56(1)(b). This change in textual semantics is not significant because Article 60 of the LOS Convention states that coastal states should be granted exclusive rights in constructing, authorizing, regulating the construction and operation of artificial islands, installations, and structures on the one hand, and the use of these objects on the other hand.

When Article 60 of the LOS Convention addresses the issue of artificial islands, installations, and structures in the EEZ, it distinguishes between artificial islands and installations and structures, but clarifies none of these

---

178 Dixon, *Textbook on International Law,* 115.

179 Joseph H. Beale, "Jurisdiction of a Sovereign State," *Harvard LR* 36 (1923): 243.

180 Linda A. Malone, *International Law* (New York: Aspen, 1995), 66–67.

181 See "Informal Single Negotiating Text," Article 45(1)(b).

terms.[182] Article 60(1)(a) gives coastal states exclusive jurisdiction to construct, authorize, and regulate the construction, operation, and use of artificial islands, regardless of their intended purposes. This suggests that third states are prohibited from building or operating such islands for military or other purposes without the express consent of the coastal state.

In contrast, regarding installations and structures, Article 60(1)(b) grants coastal states exclusive jurisdiction and the authority to construct and regulate the construction, operation, and use of such objects only if they are for resources, MSR, or economic and environmental purposes. This specific provision exemplifies the compromise that took place between the two approaches at UNCLOS III. The first approach supports the premise that all artificial islands, installations, and structures should come under the authority of the coastal state; the second approach supports the notion that coastal states should have jurisdiction over artificial islands, installations, and structures when these objects serve a specific economic purpose.[183]

In interpreting maritime powers, the latter provision suggests that third states have a right to establish installations and structures in the EEZ that do not have an economic objective, except when they are detrimental to the rights of the coastal state in the EEZ. The difference between artificial islands used for any purpose and installations and structures used for limited purposes is unclear,[184] but because the LOS Convention does not define these groups of objects, it must be inferred that they do not overlap.[185] Nonetheless, coastal states' position seems to be bolstered by its ability to assert that a foreign structure or installation inhibits it right to exercise jurisdiction in the EEZ; a claim that would be hard to challenge.

Coastal states have certain limitations when they do decide to establish these objects. The qualifications of these limitations include requiring the coastal

---

[182] Bouchez, Jaenicke, and Jennings define the term artificial islands as a "man-made structure or area of land surrounded by water and physically connected with the seabed, always above water at high-tide, intended to be permanent, and which cannot be removed without losing its identity." L. Bouchez, G. Jaenicke, and R. Y. Jennings, "Feasibility Study on the Development of Industrial Islands in the North Sea," *International Law Aspects* 4 (1974): 2. Concerning the definition of "structure," see Alfred H. A. Soons, *Marine Scientific Research and the Law of the Sea* (Deventer: Kluwer Law and Taxation, 1982), 233.

[183] Rüdiger Wolfrum, "The Emerging Customary Law of Marine Zones: State Practice and the Convention on the Law of the Sea," *NYIL* 18 (1987): 137.

[184] Churchill and Lowe, *The Law of the Sea*, 138–39.

[185] *Ibid.*, 139.

state to provide notice of their construction of these objects, give warning of their presence, and remove these objects once they are no longer in use.[186] The construction of these objects should never hinder or impede the activities associated with the "recognized sealanes essential to international navigation."[187]

In conclusion, the right that coastal states have regarding artificial islands, installations, and structures in its EEZ are similar to the powers granted to coastal states under Article 5 of the 1958 Convention on the Continental Shelf[188] with respect to structures built to exploit the resources of the continental shelf. However, the range of these rights has been extended when the purposes of these objects have expanded.

Coastal States' Rights regarding Marine Research in the EEZ

Before UNCLOS I was convened, no specific provisions addressed marine research. Thus, ocean scientists had the freedom to conduct MSR without constraint.[189] Even for the research that took place in the territorial sea, permission was rarely asked and when it was asked, was often just a formality.[190]

At UNCLOS I, new guidelines related to the conduct of MSR that took place beyond the territorial sea. Article 2 of the 1958 Convention on the High Seas specifies that the high seas are open to all nations and "no state may validly purport to subject any part of them to its sovereignty." It further asserts that this freedom includes, *inter alia*, the freedom of navigation, freedom to fish, freedom to lay submarine cables and pipelines, freedom of overflight, and all other freedoms that correlate with the general principles of international law.

Some legal experts have suggested that because the freedom to conduct MSR on the high seas is not expressly mentioned in this article, this could not be considered as a freedom of the high seas.[191] However, inherent problems align with this view. First, the expressions "*inter alia*" and "others which are recognized by the general principles of international law" suggest that the lists of the

---

186 "The Law of the Sea Convention," Article 60(3).

187 *Ibid.*, para. 7.

188 It is worth mentioning that Article 80 of the LOS Convention stipulates that "Article 60 applies *mutatis mutantis* to artificial islands, installations and structures on the continental shelf."

189 O'Connell, *The International Law of the Sea*, 1026.

190 Richard J. McLaughlin, "Confidential Classification of Multi-Beam Bathymetric Mapping of the U.S. EEZ: Is a New U.S. Marine Scientific Research Policy in Order?" *ODIL* 19 (1988), 12.

191 See, for example, the statement of the Yugoslavian delegate made at UNCLOS III, Caracas Session, 1974, in II Official Records, 1974, 348 para. 19.

freedoms defined in Article 2 are not exhaustive; and second, the historical development of this provision does not support this view. In fact, the International Law Commission explicitly stated, in its commentary concerning Article 27 of its Draft Articles relating to the law of the sea, that the carrying out of MSR on the high seas is a principle freedom of the high seas.[192] Therefore, under the 1958 Geneva Convention on the High Seas, the authority to conduct MSR, at least in the water column of the sea beyond the territorial sea, seems to suggest that freedom of the high seas does not require prior consent.

Similar provisions of the 1958 Geneva Convention on the Continental Shelf are an integral part of Article 5. Article 5(1) dictates noninterference "with fundamental oceanographic or other scientific research carried out with the intention of open publication," but suggests, in a subsequent paragraph, that the "consent of the coastal state shall be obtained in respect of any research concerning the continental shelf and undertaken there." However, the coastal state should try to honor any request submitted by a qualified institution that wishes to conduct scientific research on the ecological characteristics of the continental shelf, subject to the provision that grants the coastal state the right to partake in the research, along with making the results available to the coastal state. But these provisions are imprecise at best. The lack of distinction between "pure scientific research" and exploration[193] gives the coastal state a good basis to deny a request for scientific research. In short, this Convention helped develop a precedent for the coastal state's authority over research in the area outside the territorial sea and grants the coastal state the power to place conditions on the research activities, such as the right of the coastal state to participate in the research and to have access to the results of the research.

The issue concerning just how much authority a coastal state has over research in areas beyond the territorial sea was a central point of discussion in the Third Committee of UNCLOS III.[194] The consent regime developed from a compromise resolution between two competing interests: the industrialized states wanted complete freedom to conduct research in all nonterritorial waters, and the developing states advocated for establishing protection

---

192 See the statement of the Japanese delegate made at UNCLOS III, Caracas Session, 1974, *Official Records* 2 (1974): 353.

193 For a detailed examination of the international legal regime of MSR under the 1958 Geneva Conventions; see Soons, *Marine Scientific Research and the Law of the Sea* 5–8 and 118–25.

194 John R. Stevenson and Bernard H. Oxman, "The Third United Nations Conference on the Law of the Sea: The 1974 Caracas Session," *AJIL* 69 (1975): 27–28.

against economic exploitation and threats to their national security.[195] Initial proposals submitted for negotiations ranged from the requirement that a coastal state should only be notified in advance and comply with the standards of international law[196] to the requirement that there must be absolute consent from the coastal state.

An important proposal, submitted at the Second Substantive Session of UNCLOS III in 1975, suggested that research pertaining to the exploration and exploitation of natural resources be subject to the absolute consent of the coastal state, whereas other scientific research projects would require only notification to the coastal states along with adherence to other specified responsibilities.[197] Such leeway given to fundamental research activities drew criticism from developing states.[198] This criticism led to the creation of a regime that required consent for all research conducted in the EEZ, based on adherence to all specified conditions.

Article 56 of the LOS Convention asserts that the coastal state has "jurisdiction as provided for in the relevant provisions of this Convention" in regards to MSR. The relevant provisions are clarified in Part XIII of the LOS Convention, specifically Articles 246–54. Article 246(1) states that coastal states have the right to "regulate, authorize, and conduct marine scientific research" in the EEZ. This Article also stipulates, in paragraph 2, that "marine scientific research in the exclusive economic zone ... shall be conducted with the consent of the coastal state." In other words, any research conducted without the express consent of the coastal state would be in violation of the coastal state's jurisdiction. However, the coastal state is obligated to give consent for all other MSR under "normal circumstances."[199] But, what exactly constitutes

---

195 Milenko Milić, "The Third United Nations Conference on the Law of the Sea," *Case Western Reserve Journal of International Law* 8, no. 1 (1976): 183, 184. The same issue became a topic during the formative stages of the Stockholm Conference and the Rio Declaration when the global community sought to address the problems associated with international environmental awareness.

196 See the Draft Articles on MSR submitted to UNCLOS III, at the Caracas Sessions, 1974, by Belgium, Austria, and fifteen other states, UN Doc. A/Conf. 62/C.3 /L. 19, August 23, 1974, *Official Records* (1974): 307; Abdulqawi A. Yusuf, "Towards a New Legal Framework for Marine Research: Coastal State Consent and International Coordination," *VJIL* 19 (1979): 413–15.

197 UN Doc. A/Conf. 62/ S. R. 26, April 3, 1975, *Official Records* 3 (1975): 252.

198 Extavour, *The Exclusive Economic Zone*, 208–9.

199 "The Law of the Sea Convention," Article 246(3).

"normal circumstances" is unclear and seems to be left to the subjective opinion of the coastal state.[200]

Given that sometimes normal circumstances do arise, a coastal state may still withhold its consent if the situation dictates, such as when the project "is of direct significance for the exploration and exploitation of natural resources,"[201] which is sometimes a fundamental part of MSR. The coastal state has the authority to suspend or halt research activities if they are not conducted in accordance with the agreement or if a major change has occurred that would inherently affect the consent previously granted.[202]

Coastal states need not give consent directly. The consent of the coastal state may be implied under two circumstances: when the coastal state has not reacted to the query within four months after receiving the request concerning the research (i.e., request for consent),[203] or when the research project will be carried out or preformed under the auspices of an international organization of which the coastal state is a member. In the latter case, the research in question must have been previously approved by the coastal state when the decision was taken by the organization to carry out the project, and the coastal state did not expressly object to this action within the four-month time period of notification.[204]

When a state intends to perform MSR in the EEZ or on the continental shelf of a coastal state, the coastal state must be given specific information regarding the research activities six months prior to the commencement of the research project. This obligation is regarded as a request for consent from the coastal state.[205] The state conducting the research must comply with a number of specified conditions. One of the most important conditions involves giving the coastal state an opportunity to take part, or at least be represented in the research activities, and have access to the results of the research. This access includes data and samples collected, assisting in assessing or inter-

---

200 Yusuf, "Towards a New Legal Framework for Marine Research," 418.

201 "The Law of the Sea Convention," Article 246(5)(6).

202 In relation to this, O'Connell states, "the line between pure marine scientific research and the gathering of information which is significant for the exploration and exploitation is one difficult to maintain"; O'Connell, *The International Law of the Sea,* 1028. Singela asserted, "All marine scientific research bears some direct significance to the exploration and the exploitation of the marine resources"; A. Mpazi Singela, *Land-Locked States and the UNCLOS Regime* (New York: Ocean Publications, 1983), 324.

203 "The Law of the Sea Convention," Article 253(1)(a) and (b).

204 *Ibid.,* Article 252.

205 *Ibid.,* Article 247.

preting the data, samples, and research results, and the removal of installations and equipment used once the research activities are finished.[206]

Finally, a dispute may arise when a coastal state exercises its right to deny consent for MSR or when it issues an order for all research activities to cease. such a case is exempted from the compulsory binding-dispute settlement system.[207] Nonetheless, these disputes are still subject to the LOS Convention's compulsory conciliation procedures.[208] Any additional disputes involving MSR must be settled in accordance with the procedures detailed in binding decisions.[209]

In conclusion, LOS Convention's guidelines concerning research activities in the EEZ extend the consent regime of the 1958 Convention on the Continental Shelf to the water column above the shelf. This is highlighted by the fact that a coastal state's consent is an important prerequisite for foreign access to MSR in the EEZ. Although the coastal state must give its consent to research conducted by third states in its EEZ under "normal circumstances," this qualification is unclear and does not constitute a definitive obligation that compels the coastal state to act. Additionally, even if normal circumstances do exist, access to MSR in the EEZ is still subject to certain conditions expressed in Article 246(5). The inclusion of imprecise terms under these circumstances gives the coastal state the prerogative to grant or withhold consent. The coastal state's choice in this matter appears to be highlighted by the fact that the decision to prohibit foreign scientific research in its EEZ is expressly exempted from the compulsory third-party dispute-settlement mechanism found in the text of the LOS Convention.[210]

Coastal States' Rights regarding the Protection and Preservation of the EEZ's Marine Environment

From the very beginning, supporters of the EEZ concept suggested the EEZ regime should include coastal states' rights to protect and preserve the EEZ's marine environment.[211] At the height of the negotiations session at UNCLOS III, supporters of the EEZ concept maintained that a close relationship exists between jurisdiction over resources and jurisdiction regarding the protection of these resources from the devastating effects of marine pollution. A July 16,

---

206 *Ibid.*, Article 248.
207 *Ibid.*, Articles 248 and 249.
208 *Ibid.*, Articles 297 para. 2(i) and (ii).
209 See Jonathan I. Charney, "Entry into Force of the 1982 Convention on the Law of the Sea," *VJIL* 35 (1995): 390, note 53.
210 "The Law of the Sea Convention," Article 264 and Part XV.
211 *Ibid.*, Article 297(2)(a) and (b).

1974 statement by the Canadian delegate in the Third Committee at the Caracas Sessions of UNCLOS III pointed out this specific relationship: "What had to be emphasized was that the economic zone was not simply a contiguous resource zone ... but involved the function and inter-relationship between resource jurisdiction and the prevention of pollution."[212]

Nonetheless, the issue remained of exactly what degree a state would be able to exercise this right during the discussions at UNCLOS III.[213] The maritime states' central argument has been that any exercise of jurisdiction in this manner should be based on internationally agreed pollution standards, because if coastal states could impose their own standards when it came to shipping design and construction, the concept of freedom of navigation would be seriously impeded. The compromise to this underlying issue was adopted by UNCLOS III, stipulated in Articles 56(1)(b)(iii), 208, 210, 211, 214, 216, and 220 of the LOS Convention.

On the most basic level, the LOS Convention obligates all state parties to "protect and prevent" ecological damage to the marine environment,[214] and to implement all measures, consistent with the treaty, that prevent, reduce, and control pollution of the marine environment, regardless of the source of the pollution.[215]

As it relates to the EEZ, Article 56(1)(b)(iii) explicitly states that coastal states have authority in the EEZ to protect and preserve the marine environment. The relevant provisions that address this subject are contained in Articles 210 and 216, addressing the dumping of waste matter; Articles 208 and 214 pertaining to pollution from seabed activities; and Articles 211, 220, and 234 related to pollution from vessels.

Dumping in the EEZ

Dumping is defined as any deliberate disposal of waste matter from aircraft, platforms, and vessels, as well as any deliberate disposal of aircraft, platforms, vessels, or other human-made structure at sea.[216] Article 210(5) of the LOS Convention states that dumping in the territorial sea or the EEZ, or onto the

---

212 See "Specialized Conference on the Caribbean Countries," Subsection entitled the "Patrimonial Sea," principle 2.

213 Doc. A/Conf. 62/ C.3/ SR.4, *Official Records* 2 (1974): 318.

214 Stevenson and Oxman. "The Third United Nations Conference on the Law of the Sea: The 1974 Caracas Session," 783–89.

215 "The Law of the Sea Convention," Article 192.

216 *Ibid.*, Article 194(1).

continental shelf, "shall not be carried out without the express prior approval of the coastal state." These guidelines made it clear that the freedom of states to dump is qualified by consent requirements when states desire to dump into the EEZ of other countries.[217]

In addition, coastal states are empowered to implement laws and regulations concerning dumping in their EEZ "after due considerations of the matter with other states which by reason of their geographical situation may be adversely affected thereby." Although this right is prescriptive in nature, it is not discretionary, because coastal states must legislate in accordance with the standards of international rules, established through competent international organizations of diplomatic conferences.

For enforcement, Article 216(1)(a) states that the laws and regulations implemented in accordance with the LOS Convention and applicable international rules and standards for the prevention, reduction, and control of dumping shall be enforced "by the coastal state with regard to dumping within its ... exclusive economic zone." This means that enforcing the laws and regulations designed to prevent and reduce dumping in the EEZ is the sole domain of the coastal state. Regarding this matter, one legal expert stated that this extension of jurisdiction is important to the preservation and protection of the resources over which the coastal state has sovereign rights.[218]

Pollution from Seabed Activities

The LOS Convention grants environmental powers and responsibilities to those states that have jurisdiction over a particular activity. In this context, Article 208 states that "coastal states shall adopt laws and regulations to prevent, reduce, and control pollution of the marine environment arising from or in connection with seabed activities subject to their jurisdiction." Hence, in the jurisdictional zones of states, such as internal waters, territorial waters, the EEZ, and the continental shelf, confronting activities that result in pollution in the seabed comes under the authority of the coastal state. The competence that empowers the coastal state seems to correlate with those powers that the coastal state enjoys under the continental-shelf regime,[219] including the implementation of laws and regulations and their enforcement.[220] Regard-

---

[217] *Ibid.*, Article 1.

[218] MacDonald, "Appreciating the Precautionary Principle as an Ethical Evolution in Ocean Management," 273.

[219] Claude Douay, "Le Droit de la Mer et la Préservation du Milieu Marin," *RGDIP* 84 (1980): 206–7.

[220] Churchill and Lowe, *The Law of the Sea*, 140.

ing the former, the coastal state has the authority to establish legislative measures aimed at preventing, reducing, and controlling pollution from seabed activities under its jurisdiction.[221] Implementing such laws and regulations "shall be no less effective than international rules, standards, and recommended practices."[222] This means that the coastal state has the authority to develop laws and regulations that are effective and rigid.

As far as enforcing these laws goes, Article 214 asserts that "states shall enforce their laws and regulations adopted in accordance with Article 208 and shall adopt laws and regulations and take other measures necessary to implement applicable international rules and standards" to protect the marine environment from pollution that arises from seabed activities under their jurisdiction. As a side point, the coastal state is the only state that has the capacity to enforce norms aimed at preventing and reducing pollution from seabed activities that take place in the EEZ.

Pollution from Vessels

Regarding pollution from vessels[223] in the EEZ, the approach of the LOS Convention is different from that adopted to address pollution that results from dumping and seabed activities. The Convention acknowledges the authority of the coastal state regarding the marine environment when it comes to this issue, but also considers the interests of other states when it comes to navigation.[224] Laws and regulations that pertain to pollution from vessels must, according to Article 211(5), conform and give effect to "generally accepted international rules an standards established through competent international organizations or general diplomatic conferences."[225] This is essential for maritime states because a universal two-hundred-mile economic zone would encompass some of the most vital shipping routes in the world.[226] In instances where such international rules and standards are considered inadequate to

---

221 "The Law of the Sea Convention," Article 214.

222 *Ibid.*, Article 208 paras. 1 and 2; and Articles 193 and 194 para. 2.

223 *Ibid.*, Article 208(3).

224 For an overview of the development of international law for the prevention and control of pollution from vessels, see Jan Schneider, "Prevention and Control of Marine Pollution: Pollution from Vessels," in *The Environmental Law of the Sea*, ed. Douglas M. Johnston (Gland, Switzerland: International Union for Conservation of Nature and Natural Resources, 1981); Lawrence Juda, "IMCO and the Control of Pollution from Ships," *ICLQ* 26 (1977): 558–84.

225 Alan E. Boyle, "Marine Pollution under the Law of the Sea Convention," *AJIL* 79 (1985): 360–61.

226 "The Law of the Sea Convention," Article 211(5).

meet special circumstances in clearly defining the areas of a state's EEZ,[227] the competent international maritime organization, in all likelihood the Intergovernmental Maritime Consultative Organization (IMCO),[228] should be consulted and within a year, if that international organization agrees, the coastal state for that particular area may "adopt laws and regulations for the prevention, reduction, and control of pollution from vessels implementing such international rules and standards or navigational practices as are made applicable, through the organization, for special areas."[229]

Additionally, the LOS Convention further states, in Article 211(6)(c), that:

> if the coastal state intend to adopt additional laws and regulations for the same area for the prevention, reduction, and control of pollution from vessels, they shall when submitting the aforesaid communication, at the same time notify the organization thereof. Such additional laws and regulations may relate to discharge or navigational practices but shall not require foreign vessels to observe design, construction, manning, or equipment standards other than generally accepted international rules and standards; they shall become applicable to foreign vessels 15 months after the submission of the communication to the organization, provided that the organization agreed within 12 months after the submission of the communication.

These provisions grant coastal states the power to enact additional rules for certain areas of the EEZ, and for the pollution, reduction, and control of pollution from ships. Nonetheless, in exercising this additional enactment competence, a coastal state must satisfy specific conditions where such competence can be exercised when it rests on technical reasons linked to the oceanographic and ecological aspects of the zone, the use and nature of seaborne traffic, and all scientific and technical justifications provided by the coastal state itself. Furthermore, the coastal state does not determine whether an area of the EEZ has special circumstances. Rather, the competent interna-

---

[227] J. C. Philips, "The Economic Resources Zone and the South West Pacific," *Int. L.* 16 (1982): 273.

[228] The existence of special circumstances may be justified by the presence of oceanographic particularities of the area such as rising tides, currents, and winds; ecological factors include alternating temperatures and salting.

[229] It is interesting to note that UNCLOS III likely meant that the competent international organization should be the IMCO. Jose Luis Vallarta, "Protection and Preservation of the Maritime Environment and Marine Scientific Research at the Third United Nations Conference on the Law of the Sea," *LCP* 46, no. 2 (1983): 151.

tional organization (most likely the IMCO) makes this decision. In addition to the above, any regulation issued by the coastal state cannot enter into force and become binding on other nations until the regulations receive official approval from the IMCO.

The reasoning behind these precautions has to do with avoiding any unjustified interference with the freedom of navigation in certain parts of the EEZ. It also involves subordinating the exercise of state competence to IMCO monitoring of any motives that lie behind the implementation of national regulation. The IMCO's main responsibility is to ensure that coastal states' rules and regulations conform and are compatible with international law standards. In the final analysis, a coastal state's competency regarding this field is predicated more on international principles than on the individual discretion of the coastal state.

Regarding enforcement of relevant international rules or global legislative initiatives and regulatory provisions that correlate with them, jurisdiction is a shared mechanism by the flag state, port state, and coastal state when violations are committed in the EEZ.[230] With respect to this specific domain, the coastal state has little or no authority.[231] However, the first of two exceptions is when enforcement action could be implemented by the coastal state when the vessel accused of committing a violation of internal and or international rules in a port or offshore terminal of a coastal state;[232] In the second instance, action could be taken when evidence accrues indicating that a foreign vessel committed violations in the EEZ that resulted in major damage or the potential for major damage to the coastline or related interests of the coastal state or to it resources in the EEZ.[233]

In addition, even where evidential proof emerges that a vessel operating in a coastal state's EEZ or its territorial sea committed a violation of the applicable rules for the prevention, reduction, and control of pollution from vessels, the coastal state's enforcement actions still has limitations. First, any adjudicated action against the offending vessel should be suspended until any corresponding charges brought by the flag state are clarified or

---

230 "The Law of the Sea Convention," Article 211(6)(a).

231 *Ibid.*, Articles 211, 217, 218, and 220. The flag state has a prominent role in enforcement of the relevant measures regarding vessels that fly its flag or that are registered in its territory, *ibid.*, Article 216.

232 Charney, "The Exclusive Economic Zone and Public International Law," 253.

233 "The Law of the Sea Convention," Article 220(1).

implemented.[234] Second, only monetary damages may be imposed on foreign vessels that commit violations.[235]

When it comes to the protection of the marine environment in the EEZ, coastal states' authority has increased greatly. Coastal states' competence to protect and preserve the marine environment takes priority over all other matters related to the EEZ and continental-shelf resources. However, although coastal states have, in their EEZ, the authority to protect and preserve the marine environment, and this authority may also be applied to foreign vessels that navigate its EEZ, this authority is a shared authority and is not exclusively left to the coastal state.

---

[234] *Ibid.*, para. 6; see also Francisco Orrego Vicuña, *The Exclusive Economic Zone: Regime and Legal Nature under International Law* (Cambridge: Cambridge University Press, 1989), 87–88.
[235] "The Law of the Sea Convention," Articles 220(2) and 228(1).

Chapter 3

Third States and the Exclusive Economic Zone

The high seas are "all parts of the sea that are not included in the territorial sea or the internal waters of a nation."[1] All nations have access to the high seas, and no state may validly subject any part of them to its sovereignty.[2] In addition to this, Article 2 of the Convention on the High Seas states that the freedom of the high seas comprises, *inter alia,* the freedom of navigation, freedom of fishing, freedom to lay submarine cables and pipelines, freedom of overflight, and other freedoms that are compatible with the general principles of international law.

In contemporary times and as a result of the guidelines established by the LOS Convention, the high seas *stricto sensu* begins only at the outer limits of the EEZ.[3] This supposition grants coastal states the power to explore, exploit, conserve, and manage all natural resources found in the water column, seabed, and its subsoil up to two hundred miles from its baselines.[4] It also gives coastal states sovereign rights regarding the establishment and use of artificial islands, installations, and structures; marine scientific research; and the protection of the marine environment.[5] However, third states also have certain rights in the EEZ. These rights fall under two distinct classifications: rights pertaining to noneconomic uses and rights related to access to the living resources of the EEZ. Article 58(1) states that in the EEZ, all nations

---

1 "Convention on the High Seas, Geneva," 82–103, Article 1. The Preamble of this Convention stipulates that the states that are parties to this convention, "desiring to codify the rules of international law relating to the high seas ... adopted the following provisions as generally declaratory of established principles of international law."

2 *Ibid.,* Article 2.

3 "The Law of the Sea Convention," Articles 55 and 56. See also, Edward D. Brown, "The Significance of a Possible EC EEZ for the Law Relating to Artificial Islands, Installations and Structures, and to Cables and Pipelines, in the Exclusive Economic Zone," *ODIL* 23 (1992): 119.

4 "The Law of the Sea Convention," Articles 56(1)(a) and 57.

5 *Ibid.,* Articles 56(1)(b)(i), (ii), and (iii).

> enjoy, subject to the relevant provisions of this Convention, the freedoms referred to in Article 87 [the article defining high seas freedoms], of navigation and overflight and of the laying of submarine cables and pipelines and other internationally uses of the sea related to these freedoms, such as those associated with operations of ships, aircrafts, and submarine cables and pipelines, and compatible with the other provisions

of the LOS Convention. The issue that becomes a central point of discussion is whether the freedoms granted to third states in the EEZ are of the same magnitude as traditional high-sea freedoms?

Regarding the right to access living resources, two specific provisions of Article 62 dictate which states will be granted access to EEZ fisheries. Paragraph 2 obligates the coastal state to grant access and also singles out LLS and graphically disadvantaged states (GDS) for "particular regard." Paragraph 3 requires the coastal state to "take into account all relevant factors" and further highlights four different categories of states: the coastal state; LLS[6] and GDS;[7] developing states in the region or subregion; and states which that made significant efforts to research and identify fish stocks. Upon closer examination, these provisions on access are somewhat unclear.[8] The ambiguity surrounding these provisions is partly because the LOS Convention does not state whether the relevant factors referenced in paragraph 3 are to be considered in the order listed.

The Rights of Third States and the Noneconomic Uses of the EEZ

According to the guidelines of customary international law and the LOS Convention adopted in 1958, ships and airplanes have rights of freedom of navigation, fishing, overflight, laying of submarine cables and pipelines, and other rights dictated by the principles of international law. *Reasonable use* defines the overriding criteria to which states must abide when implementing these freedoms.[9]

During the developmental stages of the EEZ, protecting the right of communication became a central point of the discussions. At the height of the pre-UNCLOS III sessions, Latin American and African States' extensive claims over vast portions of the high seas, along with promoting the preser-

---

6 *Ibid.*, Article 69.

7 *Ibid.*, Article 70.

8 Balasubramanian, "Fisheries Provisions of the ICNT—Part II," 40.

9 Juda, "The Exclusive Economic Zone," 31.

vation of the freedom of navigation over asserted zones, became a definitive theme during the negotiations.[10] In addition to this, during the discussions at UNCLOS III (particularly at the 1974 Caracas Sessions), emphasis rested on the need to preserve the freedoms of navigation, overflight, and the laying of submarine cables and pipelines in the EEZ. In this context, the Chilean delegate stated, "The economic zone could be defined legally as a jurisdictional zone over which the coastal state exercised sovereign rights of a primary economic nature, without prejudice to the freedoms of navigation and overflight, up to 200 miles."[11]

Because of these discussions, provisions that were part of the negotiating texts of UNCLOS III preserved those freedoms in the EEZ, and they eventually became an influential part of Article 58(1); as well as being compatible with similar provisions of the LOS Conventions. Hence, noneconomic rights of third states in the EEZ falls under two distinct categories: freedom of navigation, overflight, and laying of submarine cables and pipelines; and other lawful international uses of the sea that corresponds to the first category.

Freedom of Navigation

In the 1893 *Behring Sea Fur Seals Arbitration (Great Britain v. the United States),* Britain asserted the right of freedom of navigation as "the right to come and go on the high seas without" undue hindrance.[12] In this context, Gidel supported this assertion, stating that the idea essentially contained in the freedom of navigation on the high seas is the idea of prohibiting the interference of navigational travel.[13]

Hence, the right to navigate freely on the high seas is a fundamental freedom that emanates from the general principle of the freedom of the high seas.[14] This freedom includes the general rule that each nation, during peacetime, has exclusive jurisdiction only over all ships that are entitled to fly their flag on the

---

[10] See, for instance, "The Declaration of Montevideo on Law of the Sea," Principle 6; "Organization of African Unity: Declaration on African Cooperation, Development, and Economic Independence," Article 7.

[11] *Official Records* 2 (1974): 203, para. 8; also the statements of the delegates of Mauritania and Switzerland, *Official Records* 2 (1974): 178 and 180.

[12] "Behring Sea Fur Seals Arbitration," 948.

[13] *Yearbook of the International Law Commission* 2 (1950): 69. Translation by the author.

[14] R. Galindo Pohl, "The Exclusive Economic Zone in the Light of Negotiations of the Third United Nations Conference on the Law of the Sea," in *The Exclusive Economic Zone: A Latin American Perspective,* ed. Francisco Orrego Vicuña (Boulder, CO: Westview Press, 1984), 55.

high seas.[15] The concept of freedom of navigation is not an absolute rule. In the *Fisheries Jurisdiction Case (United Kingdom v. Iceland),* the ICJ noted that, in the exercise of the freedom of the high seas, all states must have "reasonable regard to the interests of other states."[16] Other restrictions describe the exercise of freedom of navigation. These acts include prohibitions of states from allowing their flagships to engage in piracy or slave trading, the right of approach of warships, and fisheries conservation.[17] The LOS Convention restricts unauthorized broadcasting and the engagement in illegal drug trafficking.[18]

In contemporary times, and as a direct result of UNCLOS III negotiations, certain practical rights were granted to coastal states in the EEZ that extend up to 188 miles from the outer limit of the territorial sea; an area that historically considered part of the high seas. Furthermore third states, regardless of their geographical location, are given the right of freedom of navigation, dictated by the guidelines of Article 87, which establishes the freedoms of the high seas. However, the exercise of freedom of navigation is conditional, qualified by the relevant provisions of the LOS Convention. Some commentators have questioned whether navigation in the EEZ has adequate protection against the invasive actions of the coastal state. In a letter to the President of the United States, a U.S. Congressman stated that the LOS Convention fails "to offer clear" and convincing "protection for navigation rights in the new 200 miles exclusive economic zone."[19]

However, upon further examination, this viewpoint seems unsubstantiated. On the contrary, the general provisions of the LOS Convention and the specific regime of the EEZ clearly indicates concern for safeguarding the freedom of navigation in the EEZ. This is logical because protecting the freedom of navi-

---

[15] Georg Schwarzenberger and Edward D. Brown, *A Manual of International Law* (Milton, Oxon, England: Professional Books, 1976), 109.

[16] "Fisheries Jurisdiction Case (United Kingdom v. Iceland),"22.

[17] Brownlie, *Principles of Public International Law,* 238–49.

[18] "The Law of the Sea Convention," Articles 108 and 109.

[19] See letter of Congressman John Breaux, December 10, 1980, cosigned by 13 other members of the U.S. House of Representatives, addressed to President-elect Ronald Reagan, in U.S. Senate Committee on Arms Control, Oceans, International Operations and Environment, 97th Congress, 1st Session, 144–45. Also, Alam asserted that the freedoms accorded to third states in the EEZ are not identical to those enjoyed on the high seas. Shah Alam, "The Problem of the Legal Status of the Exclusive Economic Zone," *IJIL* 24 (1984): 485.

gation is a traditional part of the freedom of the high seas and is an integral part of the rules governing conventional and customary international law.[20]

In fact, Article 58(1) of the LOS Convention asserts that in the EEZ, all nations enjoy "the freedoms referred to in Article 87 of navigation and overflight and of the laying of submarine cables and pipelines." This direct reference to Article 87, which indexes the major freedoms of the high seas, clearly states that the freedom of navigation granted to third states in the EEZ is similar to that enjoyed on the high seas. Regarding this issue, the U.S. delegate to UNCLOS III, Bernard Oxman, noted,

> As to the qualitative nature of the freedom of navigation, overflight, and laying of submarine cables and pipelines, the adjectival clause "referred to in Article 87" inserted after "freedoms" establishes the qualitative identity of these freedoms with those beyond the economic zone, as Article 87 is the basic Article enumerating high seas freedoms[21]

In addition, the basic underlying principles of UNCLOS III have reaffirmed this freedom,[22] which have not caused widespread disagreement among the nations. However, applying the regime of the freedom of navigation to the EEZ proved problematic, because this application had to correlate with the interests of coastal states.

As observed by one legal expert, "the conclusion seems to prevail that on the matter of navigation in *lato sensu* the new law of the sea does not depart from the essential principles of the former."[23] What has transpired in the EEZ is the interchangeability between the traditional dichotomy of the high seas and territorial sea regimes with the new dichotomy of a practical nature that involves and overlaps the interests in navigation with interests in the exploita-

---

[20] See Myres S. McDougal, "The Law of the High Seas in Time of Peace," *DJILP* 3 (1973): 45–58.

[21] Bernard H. Oxman, "The Third United Nations Conference on the Law of the Sea: The 1977 New York Session," *AJIL* 72 (1978): 72; Elliot P. Richardson, "Power, Mobility and the Law of the Sea," *FA* 58 (1980): 916.

[22] Tullio Treves, "La Navigation," in *Traité du Nouveau Droit de la Mer,* ed. René-Jean Dupuy and D. Vignes (Paris: Éditions Economica, 1985), 687–808.

[23] Willem Riphagen, "La Navigation dans le Nouveau Droit de la Mer," *RGDIP* 84 (1980): 174. Translated by the author.

tion of natural resources.[24] This new dichotomy clarifies the restrictions the freedom of navigation may face in the EEZ.[25]

The freedom of navigation given to third states in the EEZ is subject to the relevant provisions of the LOS Convention.[26] Some of these relevant provisions are embodied in Part V on the EEZ whereas others are dispersed through other parts of the LOS Convention. In some cases, these relevant provisions place restrictions on the exercise of freedom of navigation in the EEZ. The first expressed restriction is the general principle of due regard[27] to the interests of other nations in the exercise of high-seas freedoms, stipulated by Article 87(2) and reinforced by Article 58(3). Other states must also, under all circumstances, have due regard under Article 58(3),[28] with *other states,* referencing the coastal state. Second, freedom of navigation in the EEZ is subject to Articles 88 thru 115 of the LOS Convention dealing with navigation on the high seas "in so far as they are not incompatible" with the tenets of part on the EEZ.[29] This suggests that other restrictions exist on the absolute freedom of navigation on the high seas, such as the ship's nationality,[30] prohibition slave trading,[31] piracy,[32] and the right of hot pursuit,[33] all of which are applicable in the EEZ and universally acceptable.[34] Moreover, Article 60(4) stipulates, "The coastal state may, where necessary, establish reasonable safety zones around artificial islands, installations and structures in which it may take appropriate measures to ensure the safety of navigation and of the artificial islands, installations and structures." This provision, similar to that contained in Article 5(2) of the 1958 Convention on the Continental Shelf, expressly grants coastal states the right to regulate navigation of third states in some portions of the EEZ.[35] The lack of definitive

---

24 *Ibid.*, 174–75.

25 Vicuña, "Towards an Effective Management of High Seas Fisheries," 81.

26 "The Law of the Sea Convention," Article 58(1).

27 The concept of "due regard" was derived from the "reasonable regard" provision of Article 2 of the 1958 Convention on the High Seas. See Oxman, "The Third United Nations Conference on the Law of the Sea: The 1976 New York Sessions," 261.

28 Churchill and Lowe, *The Law of the Sea*, 141.

29 "The Law of the Sea Convention," Article 58(2).

30 *Ibid.*, Articles 91–93.

31 *Ibid.*, Article 99.

32 *Ibid.*, Article 100.

33 *Ibid.*, Article 111.

34 Thomas A. Clingan, "Freedom of Navigation in a Post-UNCLOS III Environment," *LCP* 46 (1983): 114.

35 Horace B. Robertson, "Navigation in the Exclusive Economic Zone," VJIL 24, no. 4 (1984), 866.

guidelines in "appropriate measure" give coastal states wide discretion in implementing measures that establish safety zones.

Nevertheless, Article 60(7) prohibits the creation of safety zones "where interference may be caused to the use of recognized sea lanes essential to international navigation." Additionally, paragraph 5 of the same Article states that the size of safety zones should be limited to five hundred meters around artificial islands, installations, and structures, unless the size is authorized by generally accepted international standards or recommended by a competent global organization. These provisions seem to have been taken literally from Article 5(3) of the Convention on the Continental Shelf. They highlight important restrictions on the siting of safety zones as well as geographical size, and on the scope of a coastal state's unilateral regulatory authority, as mentioned above. Regarding these restrictions on the discretionary choices of the coastal state, it is hard to fathom that the siting of artificial islands and installations or rules governing navigation in the surrounding safety zones would have a pertinent effect on the freedom of navigation in the EEZ. However, the coastal state's exclusive right to establish artificial islands and installations and structures for economic purposes in the EEZ likely would, under certain circumstances, limit navigation in the EEZ. This is because, even though such objects may not be constructed when they would likely cause interference with recognized sea lanes that are vital to global navigation, they could be placed in such a manner that coastal states could monitor foreign submarines, which could result in limited use of the EEZ by the naval forces of third states.[36]

Article 73(i), which covers enforcement powers granted to coastal states on fishing in the EEZ, is a provision of the LOS Convention that could have an adverse effect on the freedom of navigation.[37] It states,

> The coastal state may, in the exercise of its sovereign rights to explore, exploit, conserve, and manage the living resources in the exclusive economic zone, take such measures, including boarding, inspection, arrest, and judicial proceedings, as may be necessary to ensure compliance with the laws and regulations adopted by it in conformity with the Convention.

---

[36] Boleslaw A. Boczek, "Peacetime Military Activities in the Exclusive Economic Zone of Third Countries," *ODIL* 19 (1988): 451.

[37] William T. Burke, "Exclusive Fisheries Zones and Freedom of Navigation," *SDLR* 20 (1983): 603.

The coastal state's capability to implement enforcement measures affecting foreign navigation in the EEZ has been a widely disputed issue. One view supports a strict interpretation of this issue.[38] Addressing the problem of balancing coastal states' resource rights with the rights of third states in the EEZ, legal expert Bernard Oxman noted,

> The sovereign rights of the coastal state with respect to fishing do not deprive a fishing vessel of freedom of navigation. Absent specific evidence, it would be manifestly unjustifiable to stop and board a freighter or oil tanker navigating through the zone to ensure that it is not fishing, but it would also be manifestly imprudent to expect the coastal state to refrain from inquiry regarding a large fishing fleet moving slowly with gear in readiness and with no apparent destination through a rich fishing ground far from any known navigation route.[39]

In the narrowest sense, this observation restricts the coastal states' regulatory and enforcement powers over foreign vessels that pass through the EEZ. This statement seems to suggest that the coastal state is legally bound to board and inspect vessels that are actually conducting fishing activities.[40] Other edicts would also be prohibited even if they are reasonable concerning coastal states' interests.

An opposing viewpoint concerning the balance in the LOS Convention is that the right of freedom of navigation is subject to the relevant provisions of the LOS Convention and, therefore, this right is subordinate to a coastal state's competencies in the EEZ. Under this view, any foreign vessels that pass through the EEZ could be stopped and inspected to ensure the vessel was upholding the laws and regulations implemented by the coastal state, as directed by the LOS Convention.[41]

In all consideration, a viable compromise between the two opposing viewpoints seems to be the correct position. The reasons a foreign vessel is in the

---

[38] Elliot P. Richardson, "Law of the Sea: Navigation and Other Traditional National Security Considerations," *SDLR* 19 (1982): 573.

[39] Oxman, "The Third United Nations Conference on the Law of the Sea: The 1976 New York Sessions," 263.

[40] Professor Burke noted that at least Oxman's observation is open to this interpretation. Burke, "The Law of the Sea Convention Provisions," 603–4.

[41] This position is supported by Edward D. Brown, "The Exclusive Economic Zone: Criteria and Machinery for the Resolution of International Conflicts between Different Users of the EEZ," Marit. Pol. Mgmt. 4 (1977): 334: "The balance of principles is weighted heavily in favor of the coastal state."

EEZ should be the determining factor regarding the coastal state's enforcement action. Hence, if a freighter or oil tanker is travelling at a slow rate of speed, this does not mean that a coastal state has the authority to take enforcement action against the vessel. In addition to this, just because the vessel's crew may have a few fishing lines in the water does not give the coastal state the authority to stop, board, and inspect the vessel. However, if the foreign vessel is part of a fishing unit, it is not reasonable for the coastal state to take enforcement measures to ensure that the ships that are merely passing through the EEZ are not, in fact, engaged in illegal fishing.

Also, certain provisions of Part XII of the LOS Convention[42] grant coastal states the power to implement measures with respect to ships navigating their EEZ, to enforce environmental-oriented laws that correlate to international standards and enforce regulations designed to discourage dumping of waste materials. These rights of the coastal state further constitute limitations.[43] However, as one noted commentator observed, this limitation does not affect the *rights* expressed in Article 58; only the *manner* in which these rights are deployed.[44]

Freedom of Overflight

Under customary international law as well as the general principles of international law, coastal states have authority over their territorial sea and the airspace above it.[45] Although foreign ships, excluding warships, enjoy the right of innocent passage in the territorial sea,[46] such rights are denied to foreign aircraft through the airspace above it.[47]

The Convention on the Territorial Sea and the Contiguous Zone[48] refers to control by the coastal state "in a zone of the high seas contiguous to its terri-

---

42 Part XII of the LOS Convention pertains to the protection and preservation of the marine environment. The provisions associated with the coastal state's authority regarding pollution from vessels and dumping are contained in Articles 210; 211, paras. 5 and 6; 220, paras. 3 and 7; and 234.

43 Churchill and Lowe, *The Law of the Sea,* 141.

44 Clingan, "Freedom of Navigation in a Post-UNCLOS III Environment," 115.

45 "Convention on the Territorial Sea and the Contiguous Zone," Articles 1 and 2; "The Law of the Sea Convention," Part II, Article 2 paras. 1 and 2; Malcolm N. Shaw, *International Law* (Cambridge: Grotius, 1991), 350.

46 Brownlie, *Principles of Public International Law,* 203–4. The issue of innocent passage of warships in peacetime is still hotly disputed.

47 Oppenheim, Lassa. *International Law: A Treatise,* vol. 1, ed. H. Lauterpacht. New York: Congmans, Green, 1955), 523.

48 "The Law of the Sea Convention."

torial sea" for designated purposes only. Under the guidelines expressed in Article 24, a coastal state has the authority to exercise certain preventive and punitive powers regarding custom, fiscal, immigration, or sanitary matters.[49] Furthermore, Article 1 of the Convention on the High Seas[50] states that the "high seas" involve "all parts of the sea that are not included in the territorial sea or the internal waters of a state." Thus, a coastal state's rights in such a zone does not come under the umbrella of "sovereignty, which allows other states to exercise rights in the high seas, including the right to overflight."

According to the 1958 Geneva Convention on the Continental Shelf,[51] coastal states are granted authority over the shelf but only to explore and exploit the natural resources of the continental shelf.[52] The Convention definitively states that the rights enjoyed by the coastal state does not affect the status of the superjacent waters as high seas or the airspace above the waters.[53] In exclusive fishing zones, coastal states are granted exclusive rights regarding all fishery matters.[54] The status of the high seas and the rights of coastal states goes beyond the limitations placed on the freedom of the high seas, and must be interpreted in cases where there is conflict in the rights associated with the principle of freedom of the high seas.[55] In essence, similar to the freedom of navigation, freedom of overflight that goes beyond the territorial sea is granted to all nations, subject to the criteria of "reasonable use" and consideration for the rights of other nations in those areas.

Article 58(1) stipulates that all nations are granted the referenced freedoms concerning navigation and overflight. Article 87 of the LOS Convention, which highlights the freedom of the high seas, is noteworthy. It indicates that the freedom of overflight granted to nations is qualitatively the same as the freedoms enjoyed over the high seas.[56] This same paragraph also provides that any freedom of overflight in the EEZ is subject to the relevant provisions of the LOS Convention. Furthermore, paragraph 3 of the same article states that "in exercising their rights and performing their

---

[49] *Ibid.*, Article 24(1)(a) and (b).

[50] *Ibid.*, Article 55. Under the 1958 system the contiguous zone was an integral part of the high seas, while under the LOS Convention it would form a part of the EEZ.

[51] "Convention on the Continental Shelf."

[52] "The Law of the Sea Convention," Articles 2(1) and 77.

[53] *Ibid.*, Articles 3 and 78.

[54] Brown, "The Exclusive Economic Zone," 229.

[55] *Ibid.*

[56] Oxman, "The Third United Nations Conference on the Law of the Sea: The 1977 New York Session," 72.

duties under this Convention in the exclusive economic zone, states shall have due regard to the rights and duties of the coastal state and shall comply with the laws and regulations" implemented by the coastal state. Thus, freedom of overflight is not absolute, and when exercising it, states must comply with the provisions set forth in the LOS Convention.

Similar to the freedom of navigation, the freedom of overflight has definitive limitations placed on it. These restrictions come under the domain of due regard for other states and for Articles 88–115 of the LOS Convention that detail the requirements for navigating the high seas and highlight other rules of international law that must correspond with EEZ provisions.[57] Moreover, the freedom of overflight is expressly subject to additional limitations. First, the EEZ regime gives the coastal state sovereign rights of exploration and exploitation in the EEZ (i.e., production of energy from the winds). This could involve wind-energy apparatuses used by aircraft for exploitation purposes.[58] Second, aircraft are subject to the coastal state's capacity to prevent and regulate the dumping of waste.[59]

Freedom of Laying Submarine Cables and Pipelines

The concept of freedom to lay cables and submarine pipelines has been a generally accepted principle of international law for many years.[60] This authority, granted to all nations, is protected under the law of the continental shelf provision outlined in the 1958 Convention on the Continental Shelf.[61]

The tenets of the LOS Convention endorsed the traditional position. Article 58 assures that this freedom is on par with the freedoms of navigation and overflight, by cross-referencing Article 87, and also by ensuring it is subject to the expressed limitations of due consideration for the interests of other nations and for Articles 88–115 of the LOS Convention. Although many of these Articles do not apply to cables and pipelines, Articles 112–15 specifically address them.[62]

---

57 Churchill and Lowe, *The Law of the Sea*, 142. It is worth mentioning that many of these articles do not apply to aircraft.

58 *Ibid.*

59 "The Law of the Sea Convention," Article 216(1)(a) grants the coastal state the power to enforce laws and regulations for the prevention, reduction, and control of pollution of the marine environment by dumping in its EEZ.

60 "Convention on the High Seas, Geneva," Article 2(3); Georg Schwarzenberger, *International Law as Applied by International Courts and Tribunals*, vol. 1, 3rd ed. (London: Stevens and Sons, 1957), 348.

61 "Convention on the Continental Shelf," Article 4.

62 Churchill and Lowe, *The Law of the Sea*, 142.

These articles are designed to protect cables and pipelines from damage and to compensate vessels for any damages done to their equipment. The 1958 High Seas Convention has provisions that offer similar protections.[63]

Furthermore, Article 79 contains additional limitations. Even though Article 79 is found in Part VI on the continental shelf, it is applicable to the EEZ because the seabed of the EEZ is adjacent to the continental shelf.[64] Article 79(3), contrary to the 1958 Convention on the Continental Shelf,[65] states that "the delineation of the course for the laying of such pipelines" can only be exercised through the consent of the coastal state. In some instances, this could be problematic. Article 58(1) acknowledges that all nations have the freedom to lay pipelines in the EEZ. Thus, an argument could be made that a coastal state's authorization is only required with regard to the continental shelf that lies beyond the EEZ. In contrast, the same Articles provide that the right to lay pipelines is "subject to the relevant provisions of this Convention." Hence, it is plausible to apply the consent requirement contained in Article 79(3), even in the EEZ.[66]

In addition, coastal states, under the auspices of Article 79(4), are empowered to establish conditions for cables and pipelines that enter its territorial sea, and this same provision also allows a coastal state to exercise jurisdiction over cables and pipelines constructed or used during exploration of its continental shelf and its natural resources. This makes sense because the coastal state, according to the tenets of customary and conventional international law, has sovereignty over its territorial sea and authority over the exploitation and exploration of continental-shelf resources. The question remains, how compatible are the provisions of Article 79(3) with the freedom to lay pipelines? As one leading expert has observed, "the term freedom" can be somewhat ambiguous.[67]

Other International Uses of the Sea: Navigation, Overflight, and the Laying of Cables and Pipelines

According to Article 58(1) the rights of third states in the EEZ covers "other internationally lawful uses of the sea" associated with the freedoms of movement and communication, such as those rights addressing "the operation of

---

63 "Convention on the Continental Shelf," Articles 27, 28, and 29.

64 Churchill and Lowe, *The Law of the Sea*, 142.

65 Under the 1958 Convention on the Continental Shelf, no consent is required. "Convention on the Continental Shelf," Articles 3 and 4.

66 Churchill and Lowe, *The Law of the Sea*, 192.

67 *Ibid.*, 143.

ships, aircraft and submarine cables and pipelines, and compatible with the other provisions" of the LOS Convention. This concept was an integral part of Article 46(1) of the Revised Single Negotiating Text (RSNT).[68] The provisions of Article 2(2) of the Convention on the High Seas[69] bear textual similarities to the RSNT. The Convention on the High Seas states that the freedom of navigation, fishing, overflight, and the laying of cables and pipelines cited by paragraph 1 of Article 2 "and others which are recognized by the general principles of international, shall be exercised by all states with reasonable regard to the interests of other states in their exercise of the freedom of the high sea." Adding this specific provision to the Convention of the High Seas highlighted that the list of freedoms contained in paragraph 1 is not exhaustive[70] and that the convention allows for military uses.[71]

However, what is very clear is that incorporating the terms "other internationally lawful uses of the related" to the basic freedoms in Article 58(1) of the LOS Convention was designed to ensure that, although coastal states have certain unspecified rights when it comes to the exploitation of resources, third states have the authority to deployed unspecified rights in the EEZ that align with basic freedoms.[72] Nonetheless, the particular terms used to express the scope of the uses are ambiguous, open to various interpretations, and lack precision, all of which was pointed out by the Peruvian representative.[73] A persuasive justification was not given for the significance of such uses, and their exact meaning and sphere of influence was the main topic of discussion in the Consultative Group and in Informal Negotiating Group No. 1.[74] This

---

68 Revised Single Negotiating Text Part II, UN Doc. A/Conf. 62/WP. 8/Rev. 1/Pt. II, *Official Records* 5 (1976): 51; Paolillo, "The Exclusive Economic Zone in Latin American Practice and Legislation," 106.

69 "Convention on the Continental Shelf."

70 See commentary by the ILC on Article 27 of its final Draft Articles, which was later transformed into Article 2 of the Convention on the High Seas. ILC, "Freedoms of the High Seas," *YILC* 2 (1956): 278.

71 *Ibid.*, also see Pohl, "The Exclusive Economic Zone in the Light of Negotiations," 55.

72 Clingan, "Freedom of Navigation in a Post-UNCLOS III Environment," 116.

73 *Official Records* 3 (1975): 193.

74 Awadh Mohamed Al Mour, "The Legal Status of the Exclusive Zone," *REDI* 33 (1977): 59. Extensive negotiations pertaining to Article 58(1) took place in an informal group of interested states chaired by Ambassador Jorge Castañeda, head of the Mexican Delegation. He was aided in this endeavor by Ambassador Helge Vindenes of Norway. For an interesting analysis on these negotiations, see K. G. Brennan, "Jurisdiction of Coastal States and Other States in the Exclusive Economic Zone," paper presented before the Seventh International Ocean Symposium of the Ocean Association of Japan, Oct. 21–22, 1982, 45–50.

ambiguity has led some supporters of the coastal state's jurisdiction to assert that certain foreign military activities in the EEZ could not be considered related to the freedoms of navigation, overflight, and the laying of cables and pipelines, and could not be embraced as a "lawful use of the sea" expressed under Article 58 of the LOS Convention, nor is it compatible with Article 8 of the LOS Convention, which concerns using the high seas for peaceful purposes. This strict interpretation, which places emphasis on routine navigational operations and military activities in the scope of this article, cannot be deemed associative with the operation of ships and aircrafts.[75]

During the Seventh Session of UNCLOS III, held at Geneva in 1978,[76] Brazil and Peru still tried to elucidate this view in an unsuccessful attempt to reconsider this issue by adding a provision that prevented foreign warships and military aircrafts passing through the EEZ from taking part in any military activities within their two-hundred-mile EEZs without prior authorization.[77] Cape Verde and Uruguay supported this viewpoint, insisting that the provisions of the LOS Convention prohibit third states from carrying out military activities in the EEZ that might unduly harm the rights and interests of the coastal state without that consent of that state.[78] This position suggests that, with the exception of routine navigational activities of warships and military aircrafts, all other military activities come under the authority vested in the coastal state.[79] In contrast, major industrial nations have referenced the internationally lawful uses of the sea associated with the normal operations of ships, aircraft, and submarine cables and pipelines, indicating that third states' navigational rights extend to military

[75] Elmar Rauch, "Military Uses of the Oceans," *GYIL* 28 (1985): 242.

[76] Bernard H. Oxman, "The Third United Nations Conference on the Law of the Sea: The Seventh Session 1978," *AJIL* 73 (1979): 1–41.

[77] See, for example, the Peruvian proposal at Informal Meeting, C.2 Inf. Meeting/9, April 27, 1978.

[78] See the interpretative Declarations of Cape Verde and Uruguay made under Article 310 of the LOS Convention: Office of the Special Representative of the Secretary General for the Law of the Sea, *Law of the Sea: Status of the United Nations Convention on the Law of the Sea* (New York: United Nations, 1985), 12 and 28, respectively. "Declarations" are possible under Article 310 of the LOS Convention, although reservations and exceptions are not allowed [Article 309]. Declarations or statements can be made, with a view, *inter alia*, to the harmonization of the declaring state's laws and regulations with the provisions of the LOS Convention, provided such declarations or statements do not purport to exclude or modify the legal effects of the provisions of the LOS Convention in their application to that state [Article 310].

[79] This is inferred from the Declaration of Cape Verde. It is also noteworthy that major industrial countries opposed this position. See, for instant, Italy's Declaration upon signing of the LOS Convention, *ibid.*, 19.

uses of the EEZ. This supposition includes the conduct of military operations subject only to the obligation to have due regard for the rights of other states exercising their rights on the high seas.[80]

What is certain is that military uses of the EEZ and the airspace above it is authorized under the guidelines of the LOS Convention through the inclusion of a general reference to freedoms of navigation and overflight contained in Article 58 paragraph 1, specifically under the phrase "and other internationally lawful uses of the sea related to these freedoms." However, giving these terms a broad interpretation seems to be a stretch. In the first instance, the military uses of the EEZ must correlate with the relevant provisions of the LOS Convention, including those pertaining to the interests of the coastal state with respect to the living resources.[81] Second, Article 58(1) suggests a legitimate link must exist between internationally lawful uses of the sea and the freedoms with which states' uses align.[82] Although the normal activities of anchoring, patrolling, and other operational activities are necessary to lay cables and pipelines, as specified by the freedom of navigation,[83] and pose no visible incompatibility issues, this is not the case for other military uses. For example, strategically deploying mines in the EEZ has nothing in common with the freedom of the seas and deploying these weapons conflicts with the interests of the coastal state, which would justify their removal or destruction by the coastal state aligned with the right of self-defense under Article 51 of the UN Charter.[84] Along these same lines, military operations involving explosives and weapons testing have no legitimate link with the freedoms expressed in Article 58(1) and completely ignore the coastal state's rights over the EEZ's living resources. Yet, during times of geopolitical tension, naval maneuvers involving the use of weapons in the waters of another country's EEZ may be considered hostile and intimidating *vis-à-vis* that coastal state. The borderline is somewhat nebulous, but under such situations, these exercises could be deemed as an illegal threat of force proscribed by Article 2(4) of the UN Charter, as well as by the guidelines of Article 301 of the LOS Convention. Furthermore, a coastal state could assert that certain devices deployed

---

[80] Tullio Treves, "Military Installations, Structures and Devices on the Seabed," *AJIL* 74 (1980): 833; Oxman, "The Third United Nations Conference on the Law of the Sea: The 1976 New York Sessions."

[81] "The Law of the Sea Convention," Article 58 para. 1.

[82] Al Mour, "The Legal Status of the Exclusive Zone," 59.

[83] John T. Bosma, "The Alternative Futures of Naval Force," *ODIL* 5 (1978): 194; Treves, "Military Installations, Structures and Devices on the Seabed," 843–94.

[84] Treves, *ibid.*, 845.

by a third state are not part of the normal operations of ships and should not be available to third states in the EEZ.

The conclusion one could draw from the above analysis of third state's rights in the EEZ is that freedom granted to these states is qualitatively the same as freedoms of the high seas. However, they are not representative or an extension of the high-seas regime, but originate from the concept of *sui generis* as it relates to the EEZ, subject to specific limitations. On a quantitative level, the traditional high-seas freedoms are more inclusive because, under Article 58 of the LOS Convention, the uses have been limited to a legitimate link with the freedoms of navigation, overflight, and the laying of submarine cables and pipelines.

Unattributed (Residual) Rights

Concerning the exercise of rights in the EEZ, all of the most recognizable economic rights are highlighted in the LOS Convention.[85] Rights specifically addressing scientific research are explicitly addressed.[86] All drilling in the seabed requires the coastal state's authorization.[87] In addition, all of the most obvious communication rights have been granted to third states.[88] Concerning the latter, navigational and overflight freedoms are most important.

Hence, in contrast to the previous functional regimes that affected the high seas, this system created an ambiguity that still exists: which state could retain possible uses that do not fall under the rights of the coastal state or third states in residual rights, including rights that allow unexpected uses of the ocean, brought on by technological advances. The provision of Article 59 of the LOS Convention should be applicable:

> In cases where this Convention does not attribute rights or jurisdiction to the coastal state or to other states within the EEZ, and a conflict arises between the interests of the coastal state and any other state or states, the conflict should be resolved on the basis of equity and in the light of all the relevant circumstances, taking into account the respective importance of the interests involved to the parties as well as to the international community as a whole.

---

[85] "The Law of the Sea Convention," Part V, Article 56(1)(a).

[86] *Ibid.*, Articles 56(1)(b)(ii), and 246.

[87] *Ibid.*, Article 81.

[88] *Ibid.*, Article 58.

This provision was developed from a proposal by Ambassador Castañeda of Mexico at the Second Substantive Session of UNCLOS III, Geneva 1975.[89] It was later incorporated into the ISNT by the chair of the Second Committee of UNCLOS III as a compromise between those states that supported the notion of residual rights for coastal states and the major industrial nations, which believed residual uses should remain subject to the high-seas regime. It became an integral part of subsequent texts.[90]

Various developing states viewed this notion as a presumption that greatly favors coastal states.[91] However, such a view seems problematic. First, this position finds no evidential support in the negotiating history of UNCLOS III.[92] Second, the major industrialized nations rejected such a position after the conclusion of the LOS Convention.[93] This rejection was highlighted by Italy's Declaration made upon the signing of the LOS Convention: "According to the Convention, the coastal state does not enjoy residual rights in the exclusive economic zone."[94] Thus, Article 59 suggests there is no presumption in favor of coastal states or third states in unattributed rights and each case should be decided on its own merits on the basis of the guidelines contained in Article 59.[95]

Nonetheless, the Article made it clear that all relevant circumstances must be considered in addition to the interests of the global community as a

---

[89] Jorge Castañeda, "Negotiations on the Exclusive Economic Zone at the Third United Nations Conference on the Law of the Sea," in *Essays in International Law in Honor of Judge Manfred Lachs,* ed. Jerzy Makarczyck, (The Hague: Martinus Nijhoff, 1984), 615.

[90] The provision established in Article 59 of the LOS Convention was adopted in 1975 in paragraph 3 of Article 47 of the ISNT and has witnessed no material change throughout the Conference's texts, with the exception that it was later added as the separate Article 59.

[91] For a good example see the Declaration made by the Representative of Uruguay at the signing ceremony of the LOS Convention on behalf of his government, Office of the Special Representative of the Secretary General for the Law of the Sea, *Law of the Sea.*

[92] See the statement of Jorge Castañeda before the Fisheries Committee of FAO, Doc. COFI/77/Inf. April 8, 1977, cited by Jean-Pierre Quéneudec, "Les Incertitudes de la Nouvelle Convention Sur le Droit de la Mer," in *Essays on the New Law of the Sea,* ed. Budislav Vukas (Zagreb, Yugoslavia: University of Zagreb, 1985), 53 note 51. See also Treves, supra note 80, 845.

[93] Boczek, "Peacetime Military Activities," 451.

[94] Declaration made upon the signing of the LOS Convention, Office of the Special Representative of the Secretary General for the Law of the Sea, *Law of the Sea,* 19.

[95] Churchill and Lowe, *The Law of the Sea,* 144.

whole.[96] This equity requirement seems to support the notion of the equitable principles that are a part of international law, particularly the rules of interpretation that allow courts deliberate on all relevant circumstances to avoid any sense of injustice or maltreatment. This is not similar to the concept of *ex aequo et bono* expressed under Article 38(2) of the Statute of the ICJ, under which the court may go beyond the rules expressed under the principles of international law if the parties involved agree to it.[97] As far as dispute resolutions goes, the guidelines of Article 59 imply that parties to a dispute must, in good faith, make diplomatic efforts to peacefully resolve their issues in accordance with the provisions of the LOS Convention.[98] If the dispute-resolution methods used by the parties fail to provide a viable resolution, the dispute must be submitted, upon the request of one of the parties involved, to one of the governing judicial authorities listed in Article 287[99] of the LOS Convention unless the issue pertains to military activities and at least one of the parties has, upon signing and ratifying the LOS Convention, made a written statement exempting itself from such dispute-resolution procedures.[100]

The Right of Third States' Access to the Living Resources of the EEZ

Under the tenets of the LOS Convention, coastal states have jurisdiction over the resources of the EEZ and this jurisdiction comes with a duty to manage the living resources and provide access to these resources to foreign nations. For access, Article 62(2) asserts that, if the coastal state's capacity "does not" permit it to harvest the entire allowable catch, it "shall" grant third states access to the surplus. The term "shall" denotes the coastal state's obligation

---

96 The Swiss delegate commented during the informal debates in the Second Committee of the Fifth Session of the Conference that such expressions in Article 59 as "interests of the respective parties," "relevant circumstances," and "equity" were vague and could result in erroneous interpretations. Cited by Extavour, *The Exclusive Economic Zone*, 271, footnote 89.

97 For the World Court's perspective on this issue, see "The Diversion of Water from the Meuse Case, (Netherland v. Belgium)," *PCIJ Report* Series A/B (1937): 70, 76–77; "North Sea Continental Shelf Cases," 46–50; "Fisheries Jurisdiction Case (United Kingdom v. Iceland)," 33.

98 "The Law of the Sea Convention," Articles 279–84; Churchill and Lowe, *The Law of the Sea*, 144.

99 A list of the judicial authorities includes the International Tribunal for the Law of the Sea, established pursuant to Annex VI; the ICJ, an arbitral tribunal created in accordance with Annex VII; and a special arbitral tribunal created in accordance with Annex VIII.

100 "The Law of the Sea Convention," Article 298(1)(b) allows states to do this.

to grant access to the surplus, but what is the scope of the coastal state's obligation to give access to the surplus?

In addition to this overriding question, the foreign state's status as an LLS or GDS should be considered.[101] The LOS Convention highlights the conditions for LLS and GDS access the fishery surplus. However, the Convention has left a number of issues unresolved. One of the most important issues is whether these states have priority in sharing the surplus of the fishery of the coastal state in its EEZ.

Third States' Access to the Surplus Resources of the EEZ

According to the provisions set forth in Article 62(2), if a coastal state proclaims a surplus after taking its share, the coastal state "shall" enter into agreements or similar arrangements that would grant other states access to this surplus. The word "shall" obligates coastal states to give access to the surplus of the allowable catch. Yet, whether or not paragraph 2 of Article 62 compels the coastal state to grant access to third states for the surplus, other calculations should be considered. First, there must be reflection on the provision that references the surplus in the context of the harvesting capacity of the coastal state. In essence, this means the surplus based on the harvesting capacity of the coastal state should not be qualified by the guidelines of objective criterion. Thus, to deny the existence of any surplus and bar third states access to this surplus, a coastal state only must equate its harvesting capacity to the allowable catch that is capable of supporting levels facilitating its economic interests.

Second, third states' access to the surplus is conditional, involving an "agreement or other arrangement," specific terms that a third state that wants access to the surplus may or may not accept. The phrase "shall through agreement or other arrangements" suggests that the coastal state has a duty to enter into negotiations with other states that wish to access the surplus.[102] The mandate to negotiate does not mean an obligation to reach a viable agreement. Regardless, a coastal state is obligated, under the principles of international law and the provisions of the LOS Convention, to negotiate in good faith. In this context, the Permanent Court of International Justice (PCIJ), in its advisory opinion in the *Railway Traffic (Lithuania v. Poland) Case*,[103] stated that the obligation was "not only to enter into negotiations but

[101] "The Law of the Sea Convention," Articles 62(2) and (3), 69(3), and 70(4).

[102] For an opposing viewpoint, see J. C. Philips, "The Exclusive Economic Zone as a Concept in International Law," *ICLQ* 26 (1977): 602–3.

[103] PCIJ Series A/13, No. 42, 1931.

also to pursue them as far as possible with a view to concluding agreements."[104] In essence, it would be in conflict with the provisions of the LOS Convention, which obligates a coastal state to impose conditions to deny access to foreign nations once a surplus is declared. Such action would be inconsistent with Article 300, which asserts that state parties to the LOS Convention should undertake a good-faith duty to enter into conformity with the Convention and to exercise their rights, jurisdiction, and freedoms, recognized in the Convention, in a manner that would not compromise and uphold these rights. Essentially, this means that the incomprehensive list of various regulatory powers contained in Article 62(4), such as fee payments, fixing quotas, setting the fishing season, and establishing the areas to be fished, should be read in light of the provisions established in Article 300 and Article 62(2) of the LOS Convention that granted the access.

Finally, if disputes arise that involve the coastal state's sovereign rights with respect to the living resources in the EEZ or the exercise of these rights, such disagreements may be resolved through various peaceful venues such as negotiations or other practical procedures to which the parties previously agreed. However, a coastal state is not obligated, under Article 297 of the LOS Convention, to submit compulsory dispute-settlement procedures on an issue that develops from the exercise of its sovereign rights to fisheries.[105] This includes the coastal state's discretionary authority to establish the allowable catch ratio, its ability to set its harvesting capacity, and its allocation of the surplus to third states in accordance with the guidelines of the LOS Convention. Hence, a coastal state's refusal to set an allowable catch ratio or harvesting capacity cannot be challenged. Only if the decision on the part of the coastal state is considered arbitrary can it be pursued through compulsory "conciliation." However, the Conciliation Commission cannot replace the coastal state's discretion with its own.[106] Additionally, the report of the Commission, including final analysis and recommendations, are not binding on the parties involved.[107]

In conclusion, the coastal state has the authority, under the auspices of the LOS Convention, to decide the total allowable catch of the living resources in its EEZ as well as its harvesting capacity. Flexibility is an integral part of this important process. In addition, the dispute-settlement mechanism outlined in the LOS Convention prohibits effective review of the coastal state's deci-

---

[104] *Ibid.*, 116.

[105] "The Law of the Sea Convention," Article 297(3); see also Shabtai Rosenne, "Settlement of Fisheries Disputes in the Exclusive Economic Zone," *AJIL* 73 (1979): 98.

[106] "The Law of the Sea Convention," Article 297(3) para. 3(c).

[107] Annex V, Conciliation, Article 7(2), *Official Records* 15 (1981): 235.

sions on these types of issues. In short, the LOS Convention grants the coastal state great latitude in discretionary powers when it comes to deciding whether foreign states are permitted to fish its EEZ.

LLS and GDS Access to the Living Resources of Another State's EEZ

Article 62(2) states that, in granting access for third states to EEZ resources, coastal states shall have due regard for the provisions of Articles 69 and 70, which embody the rights and duties of LLS and GDS. Many of the limitations on the coastal state's authority to allocate their surplus are characterized by the latter articles.

Land-Locked States

The term *land-locked state* was not originally part of UNCLOS III. On the contrary, the origin of the term preceded the convening of UNCLOS III.[108] The UN Convention on Transit Trade of Land Locked States[109] refers to the term almost a decade before the start of UNCLOS III. It described LLS as "any ... state which has no sea coast."[110] This definition originated from the 1958 Geneva Convention on the High Seas.[111] The LOS Convention used the same definition to describe LLS.[112]

Geography is the determining factor as to whether a state is considered land locked. Coastal states, located along the borders of the sea, are excluded from this definition and this includes whether a state displays some of the characteristics associated with LLS such as being useless for international trade or having very short water corridors that branch out into the sea.[113] In contrast, LLS that exhibits certain characteristics of a coastal state by their position on international navigational rivers,[114] and having access to the sea that runs through them, remains part of the definition of an LLS.

---

108 G. E. Toulmin, "The Barcelona Conference on Communications and Transit and the Danube Statute," *BYIL* 23 (1922): 177.

109 Done at New York, July 8, 1965. For text see *ILM* 9 (1965): 957.

110 *Ibid.*, Article 1(a).

111 "Convention on the Continental Shelf," Article 3(1).

112 "The Law of the Sea Convention," Article 124(1)(a).

113 A good example is Iraq and Jordan. For an in-depth analysis, see Martin Ira Glassner, *Access to the Sea for Developing Land-Locked States* (The Hague: Nijhoff, 1970), 2.

114 Various European LLS are crossed by several navigable river systems including the Danube and the Rhine. Many of these rivers were opened to international traffic through treaties established at a very early date. See Singela, *Land-Locked States,* 1.

Until the early 1990s, the number of LLS stabilized at thirty states: fourteen African states, nine European states, five Asian states, and two Latin American states.[115] However, the number of these states has increased dramatically.[116] The majority of LLS belong to Asia or Europe. The number of Asian LLS grew from five to twelve states because of the declared independence of the former Soviet Republics of Central Asia.[117] Regarding European LLS, their numbers have steadily increased. The cause of this increase involves the dissolution of the Soviet Union and the disappearance of the former Yugoslavia, along with the replacement of the former Czechoslovakia with Czech and Slovak Republics.[118]

Geographically Disadvantaged States

The term *geographically disadvantaged states* originated from the notion of *shelf locked states* that were frequently used in legal texts during the early portion of the 1970s.[119] The latter terms refer to states that are "Cut off from the seabed and subsoil beyond national jurisdiction ... the continental shelf of such states have no boundary with the seabed beyond national jurisdiction, the area where no individual sovereignty exists."[120] Such states have "limited possibilities for extending their jurisdiction far offshore because of their geographical situation. This, for example, is the case with states that border on enclosed or semi-enclosed seas."[121]

By the time the UN Seabed Committee[122] had commenced preparatory work for UNCLOS III in the late 1960s, the acceptance and establishment of a two-

---

[115] Jean Monnier, "Le Droit d'Accès a la Mer et la Liberté de Transit Terrestre," in *Traité du Nouveau Droit de la Mer,* ed. René-Jean Dupuy and D. Vignes, (Paris: Economica Bruylant, 1989), 442–47; also Laurent Lucchini and Michel Voelckel, *Droit de la Mer* (Paris: Pédone, 1990), 506, Table 1.

[116] See Appendix C.

[117] For more information see Paul Tavernier, "Les Nouveaux Etats Sans Littoral d'Europe et d'Asie et l'Accès à la Mer," *RGDIP* 97 (1993): 729.

[118] *Ibid.*, 729–30.

[119] Janusz Symonides, "The Concept and Claims of Geographically Disadvantaged States at the Third United Nations Law of the Sea Conference," *RCADI* (1988): 293.

[120] Vladimir Ibler, "The Interests of the Shelf-Locked States and the Proposed Development of the Law of the Sea," *IJIL* 11 (1971): 389–90.

[121] John R. Stevenson and Bernard H. Oxman, "The Preparations for the Law of the Sea Conference," *AJIL* 68 (1974): 18.

[122] The Committee on the Peaceful Uses of the Seabed and Ocean Floor Beyond the Limits of National Jurisdiction. It was established by the UN General Assembly in 1968 via Resolution 2467 A (XXIII) of December 21, 1968. For the text see Oda, *The International Law of the Ocean Development,* Chapter 2 note 55, 40–41.

hundred-mile functional economic zone was well within the realm of possibility. A number of states became aware that, in addition to being shelf-locked, they were also zone-locked, yielding them unable, geographically, to establish a full two hundred-mile zone. These states also discovered that their interests, due to the rapid changes that take place on the high seas, would be compromised. This realization was particularly true because of the potential limits placed on the freedom of fishing. Since the expression *shelf-locked states* did not adequately address the gravity of the situation, a new, more comprehensive concept, *geographically disadvantaged states,* was developed. This new concept engenders wide support,[123] although many nations rarely referred to the new concept during the initial stages of the UN Seabed Committee Sessions.

During the first two substantive sessions of UNCLOS III, numerous proposals used the concept GDS along with a coherent definition of the term.[124] Despite the widespread and consistent use of the term, no key definition was formulated. Various states recommended a definition of the concept build on biological, ecological, and politicoeconomic factors.[125] Disagreement over a coherent definition of the concept seems to be the underlying reason it was not included in the ISNT.

Even during subsequent sessions, a workable definition remained an arduous task. The ICNT initiated in 1977[126] referred in Article 70(1) to "certain developing coastal states in the subregion or region." This caused resentment from the Informal Group of LLS and GDS,[127] which demanded that the term GDS be included in the eventual treaty on the grounds that it was the appropriate term because of its widespread and consistence use in the conference's documents. In contrast, coastal states, fearing a definition that would be am-

---

123 Symonides, "The Concept and Claims of Geographically Disadvantaged States," 295.

124 For example see the Nigerian proposal entitled Draft Articles on the Exclusive Economic Zone, in III Official Records, 1975, 199; and the Haitian and Jamaican proposals entitled Draft Articles on Item 6.1, *ibid.*, 213.

125 Panama, for example, considered itself a disadvantaged state on political grounds, whereas Jamaica regarded the term GDS as referring to developing states that are either LLS or for geographical, biological, or ecological reasons derive no substantial economic advantage from establishing an EEZ, or are adversely affected in their economies by setting up such zones, or had short coastlines. See the statements of their corresponding delegates made at UNCLOS III, Caracas, 1974, *Official Records* 3 (1975): 248–52.

126 "Informal Composite Negotiating Text."

127 The group was formed at the 1976 New York Summer Session. Its main goal was to produce a text on the rights and responsibilities of LLS and GDS that would meet the approval of LLS, GDS, and coastal states. For additional information see Singela, *Land-Locked States*, 299.

biguous, continued to object to its introduction in the provisions pertaining to the EEZ. All subsequent texts, including the Draft Convention,[128] did not use the term GDS but instead used the phrase "states with special geographical characteristics." This specific phrase was developed by the chair of the Informal Group of LLS and GDS, Satya Nandan of Fiji. The representative from Fiji explained that this was the most viable option for conveying the same idea of GDS without encountering problems exactly defining GDS.[129]

The definition that eventually found its way into Article 70(2) of the LOS Convention is not built on a fixed definition of GDS. Rather, refers to this group of states as

> coastal states, including states bordering enclosed or semi-enclosed seas, whose geographical situation makes them dependent upon the exploitation of the living resources of the exclusive economic zones of other states in the subregion or region for adequate supplies of fish for nutritional purposes of their populations or parts thereof, and coastal states which can claim no exclusive economic zones of their own.

In the first instance, the chair of Negotiating Group 4, Ambassador Satya Nandan of Fiji, had proposed this definition on May 15, 1978.[130] The Ambassador's recommendations became influential concerning the right of access of GDS to the living resources of the EEZs of coastal states. Second, the terms "including states bordering enclosed or semi-enclosed seas" was, as noted by Nandan, added to clarify the provisions of Article 70 and not as new guidelines for the identification of the group of states to which Article 70 addressed itself.[131] Article 122 of the LOS Convention has defined the terms "enclosed or semi-enclosed sea" as "a gulf, basin, or sea surrounded by two or more states and connected to another sea or the ocean by a narrow outlet or consisting

---

[128] UN Doc. A/Conf. 62/L. 78, August 28, 1981, *Official Records* 15 (1981): 172–248.

[129] See an explanatory memorandum by the chair of Negotiating Group 4—Ambassador Satya Nandan (Fiji), *Official Records* 10 (1978): 88–92. In its last plenary meeting on September 24, 1982, the conference decided by majority vote to replace the phrase "states with special geographical characteristics" with the expression "geographically disadvantaged states," in Article 70 of the LOS Convention. In addition to this, the term "geographically disadvantaged states" also appears in other parts of the LOS Convention. It was agreed that the characterization of these states contained in Article 70(2) would only apply for purposes of Part V. See Caminos, "The Regime of Fisheries in the Exclusive Economic Zone," 158 note 19.

[130] See UN Doc. NG 4/9/ Rev. 2, 15 May 1978, *Official Records* 10 (1978): 50 para. 16.

[131] Explanatory Memorandum, *Official Records* 10 (1978), 90.

entirely or primarily of the territorial seas and exclusive economic zones of two or more coastal states."[132] Hence, the geographic position of states situated on the Mediterranean, the Black Sea, or the Aegean Sea might, but not necessarily, fit the definition contained in Article 70(2). This definition falls under two categories of states. The first of these states are coastal states that cannot claim an EEZ of their own. The underlying problem associated with the first category of states is whether this means states that cannot assert an EEZ of two hundred miles or states that have no EEZ at all. In all likelihood, the latter states falls under this category because, under Article 57 of the LOS Convention, the two-hundred-mile figure is the maximum breadth of the EEZ and not a mandatory breath.[133] Thus, a state that can assert, say, a 50-mile EEZ, can still claim an EEZ. In the second instance, those states that are geographically challenged and unable to claim a full two-hundred-mile EEZ might fall under the guidelines of the second category. The latter refers to coastal states whose geographical position makes them dependent on the exploitation of the living resources of the exclusive economic zones of states in the same region or subregion. Therefore, for states to fall under the second category, they must meet two conditions: first, proof of a specific geographical characteristic and second, because of this special geographical situation, the state depends on the exploitation of the living resources of the EEZs of other states in the same region or subregion. Upon closer examination, both conditions are problematic.[134] A number of questions connect with these flawed conditions. First, what geographical circumstances make such states dependent on the exploitation of the EEZ of other states in the region or subregion? Second, what is the level of dependence required for this specific purpose?[135]

Concerning the first question, it seems that a feasible answer is that the term *geographical situation* refers to those coastal states that, due to their close proximity to other states in the surrounding area, can only assert small EEZs or those that, because of the geographical position of the adjacent seas, could gain only minimal benefits from exploiting fisheries from an asserted EEZ. Although every state that is a member of the Group of Land-Locked and

---

[132] For additional information regarding enclosed and semienclosed seas, see Lewis M. Alexander, "Regionalism and the Law of the Sea: The Case of Semi-Enclosed Seas," *ODIL* 2 (1974): 151–86; Janusz Symonides, "The Legal Status of the Enclosed and Semi-Enclosed Seas," *GYIL* 27 (1984): 315–33.

[133] Juda, "The Exclusive Economic Zone," 8.

[134] Symonides, "The Concept and Claims of Geographically Disadvantaged States," 307.

[135] Additional questions are "How will the level of nutritional needs of claiming states be determined?" and "Who will determine these nutritional needs?"

GDS[136] may fulfill the requirements of the first condition, only a limited number of them can assert their dependence on the exploitation of the fisheries resources of other states' EEZs for the nutritional needs of their populations. Belgium, the Netherlands, or Sweden might be representative of these types of states, because apart from these states, members of the Group are not involved in fishing activities on a significant level,[137] thereby reducing their level of dependence on fishing. Nevertheless, considering the nutritional needs of developing GDS and the nutritional value these fisheries resources bring to these states, it is reasonable to say that the provisions of Article 70(2) must be understood to mean past and future dependence. This position seems to be supported by the provisions of Article 62(2), which asserts that in giving access to the surplus, coastal states should have due regard to Article 69 and 70, especially in relation to developing LLS and GDS of the same region or subregion. However, the definition expressed in Article 70(2) is unclear and an argument exists about which states are covered by it.[138]

Sharing the Living Resources of EEZs

Although most developing states supported the notion of the creation of the two-hundred-mile EEZ during the formative stages of UNCLOS III negotiations, LLS objected to the establishment of such zones because they did not want to lose their rights in the area, which until then were part of the high seas.[139] Because these states protested loudly, it was realized during the early stages of the debates that some type of compromise was needed to ensure these states supported the concept. An intense struggle took place among the coastal states, the LLS, and the GDS regarding the exact formula to be used for

---

136 The Group was composed of 29 LLS: Afghanistan, Austria, Bhutan, Bolivia, Botswana, Burundi, Byelorussian SSR, Central African Republic, Chad, Czechoslovakia, Hungary, Laos, Lesotho, Liechtenstein, Luxembourg, Malawi, Mali, Magnolia, Niger, Paraguay, Rwanda, San Marino, Swaziland, Switzerland, Uganda, Upper Volta, Zambia, Zimbabwe. The GDS are Algeria, Bahrain, Belgium, Bulgaria, Ethiopia, Federal Republic of Germany, Gambia, German Democratic Republic, Greece, Iraq, Jamaica, Jordan, Kuwait, the Netherlands, Poland, Qatar, Romania, Singapore, Sudan, Sweden, Syria, Turkey, United Arab Emirates, United Republic of Cameroon, and Zaire. See Symonides, "The Concept and Claims of Geographically Disadvantaged States," 299.

137 Lawrence Juda, "World Marine Fish Catch in the Age of Exclusive Economic Zones and Exclusive Fishery Zones," *ODIL* 22, no. 1 (1991): 2–5.

138 Symonides, "The Concept and Claims of Geographically Disadvantaged States," 307; also Antonio Martínez Puñal, "The Rights of Land-Locked and Geographically Disadvantaged States in Exclusive Economic Zones," *JMLC* 23, no. 3 (1992): 430–36.

139 Singela, "Land-Locked States' Rights in the Exclusive Economic Zone," 65.

sharing the living resources of the EEZs.[140] LLS and GDS demanded that all coastal states reserve themselves and to LLS and GDS in its region parts the living resources of its EEZ that would satisfy the needs of all these states, and would enable LLS and GDS to exercise their right to participate in these resources on an "equal and nondiscriminatory basis."[141] Only then would other states have the authority to participate in the resources of the zone.

In essence, they sought to grant to themselves access to the living resources of the EEZ in preference to all states except the coastal state concerned. This proposal was widely rejected by the industrialized states, that conducted distant water fishing and did not want to grant access to LLS above themselves, and by the coastal states that did not want to accept the right of LLS "on an equal and nondiscriminatory basis." The compromise that resulted from this tense debate involved the formula incorporated into the last text of UNCLOS III, which granted LLS and GDS the right "to participate, on an equitable basis, in the exploitation of an appropriate part of the surplus of the living resources of the exclusive economic zones of coastal states of the same subregion or region, taking into account the relevant economic and geographical circumstances of all the states concerned."[142]

Therefore, contrary to the demands put forth by the LLS and GDS, this provision grants these states the right to participate "on an equitable basis," which supports the notion of fair play and justice, but not equality.[143] In addition, it was made very clear that the participation of these states in the EEZ fisheries of coastal states of the same region or subregion is similar to any other third state, limited only to the surplus of the allowable catch of the living resources of the EEZ of the same region or subregion, directed by the coastal state.[144] Thus, if a coastal state does not declare a surplus or finds that the allowable catch is equal to or less than its capacity to harvest, then LLS and GDS have no right to claim access.

Moreover, this provision grants LLS and GDS the right to participate in an "appropriate part of the surplus" of the living resources of coastal states' EEZ located in the region or subregion. However, the LOS Convention does not clari-

---

140 Singela, *Land-Locked States*, 287–311.

141 See Article 2 of a proposal introduced by Land-Locked States to the Caracas Session 1974, known as the Afghan Proposal, UN Doc. A/Conf. 62/C. 2/L. 39, in Platzoder, *Third United Nations Conference on the Law of the Sea*, 124.

142 "The Law of the Sea Convention," Articles 69(1) and 70(1).

143 Puri, "The Legal Regime of Marine Fisheries," 244.

144 Burke, "The Law of the Sea Convention Provisions," 96.

fy exactly what is "appropriate." The lack of a clear definition means coastal states have the discretion to determine exactly what "appropriate" means.

The convention further provided that the specific guidelines of such participation would be established by the states concerned through such venues as bilateral, subregional, or regional agreements.[145] Coastal states demanded that the principle of agreement be included because they vehemently argued against the claim of LLS to the fishery resources of their EEZs as an infringement on their rights.[146] When trying to establish an agreement, the states involved are required to consider the listed factors contained in Articles 69(2) and 70(3).[147] The first factor is "the need to avoid effects detrimental to fishing communities or fishing industries of the coastal state."[148] In this context, LLS and GDS can secure access to the zones of coastal states if they make appropriate arrangements and if they give due regard to any effect, the arrangements may have on the communities and industries of the coastal states.

Since the ICNT limited LLS and GDS rights to the surplus, these states were concerned that coastal states, through bilateral agreements with major industrial fishing nations, would harvest the entire allowable catch, which would result in excluding them from participation in the zone, despite the guidelines of Articles 69 and 70.[149] To remedy such situations, new provisions were amended to Article 69 and 70,[150] also granting the right of participation even when no surplus existed. "When the harvesting capacity of a coastal state approaches a point which would enable it to harvest the entire allowable catch of the resources in its exclusive economic zone," the coastal state and other states concerned shall cooperate to establish "equitable arrangements" on a bilateral, regional, and subregional basis. The objective of such arrangements involves allowing LLS and GDS to participate in the exploitation of the living resources of the EEZ on a level that promotes equity for all parties and in accordance with the tenets set forth in paragraph 2 and 3 of Articles 69 and

---

145 "The Law of the Sea Convention," Articles 69(2) and 70(3).

146 Puri, "The Legal Regime of Marine Fisheries," 244.

147 Article 69(2) and 70(3) set out an open-ended list of factors which states are required to consider when seeking an agreement. See Burke, "The Law of the Sea Convention Provisions," 99.

148 "The Law of the Sea Convention," Articles 69(2)(a) and 70(3)(a).

149 Explanatory Memorandum, *Official Records* 10 (1978), 89–90.

150 Paragraph 3 and 4 was added respectively. UN Doc. A/Conf. 62/WP 10/Rev. 1, April 28, 1979.

70.[151] As noted by the chair of Negotiating Group 4, these additional paragraphs provided a unique and limited situation and not all cases where the coastal state is able to harvest the entire allowable catch. They are not applicable to developed LLS and GDS. In addition, the terms "as may be appropriate in the circumstances" means that emphasis rests on developing LLS and GDS that have actually participated in fishing activities in certain EEZs when the occasion arises.[152]

This obligation is qualified by cooperative efforts to achieve an "equitable arrangement." Although an obligation was placed on coastal states, this duty is not burdensome.[153] Once a coastal state has given consideration to its duty by initiating negotiations in good faith with a developing LLS or developing GDS, it has met its obligation.[154]

Finally, Article 62(2) asserts that, when the coastal state does not have the capacity to harvest the entire allowable catch, it shall grant access to other states, through either agreements or some other procedure and must also have "particular regard to the provisions of Article 69 and 70, especially in relations to the developing states mentioned therein." This provision, along with the expressed provisions contained in Articles 69 and 70 highlighting the rights of LLS and GDS, have been noted by certain commentators as giving a priority or preference to access of these states over third states.[155] In this context, Antonio Puñal stated, "it is reasonable to consider the rights of participation of LL/GDS as being of a different nature ... and enjoying

---

[151] These tenets are: (1) The need to avoid detrimental effects to fishing communities or industries of the coastal state; (2) The extent to which LLS and GDS, as the case may be, are participating in the exploitation or are entitled to participate under existing bilateral, subregional, or regional agreements in the exploitation of the living resources of EEZs of other coastal states; (3) The extent to which other LLS and GDS are participating in the exploitation of the living resources of the EEZ of the coastal state, and the consequent need to avoid a particular burden for any single coastal state or part of it; and the nutritional needs of the population of the respective states.

[152] Explanatory Memorandum, *Official Records* 10 (1978), 90.

[153] For additional information on what constitutes cooperation and what consequences would result from failure to cooperate, see Burke, "The Law of the Sea Convention Provisions," 95–101.

[154] *Ibid.*, 101.

[155] See Lucius Caflish, "The Fishing Rights of Land-Locked and Geographically Disadvantaged States in the Exclusive Economic Zone," in *La Zona Economica Esclusiva*, ed. Benedetto Conforti (Milan: Giuffrè, 1983), 29–38; Mohammed Dahmani, "Access of Land-Locked and Geographically Disadvantaged States to the Fisheries Resources of the Exclusive Economic Zone under the New Convention on the Law of the Sea," *Marit. Pol. Mgmt.* 10 (1983): 268.

preference over those of third-party states."[156] But, it seems somewhat complicated to infer that LLS and GDS have priority or preference because these states have two reasons to have the right to participate in the exploitation of the EEZ's living resources, and they could use the provisions of Articles 69 and 70 to support their claims.

First, the interests of coastal states are among the relevant factors that shall be "taken into account" when the coastal state decides to implement its discretionary powers concerning the repartition of the surplus under Article 62(3). Because this provision references Articles 69 and 70 for relevant considerations, it should be expected that certain allocation under Article 62 will also, in practical terms, suffice to fulfill the requirements of Articles 69 and 70. Second, such a position finds no historical support during any stages of the negotiating stages of UNCLOS III. The terms, "having particular regard to the provisions of Articles 69 and 70, especially in relation to the developing countries mentioned therein" were introduced by Ambassador Nandan, the chair of Negotiating Group 4 in April 1978, as amendments to Article 62 of the ICNT. In explaining the need to create the proposed amendments, Nanda stated[157] he wanted to find a practical balance between the position of the coastal states that repudiated the terms "priority" or "preference," and the position of LLS and GDS that argued to the contrary. According to Nandan, such a compromise was reflected in the amendment to Article 62(2). This, he believed, was the reason the terms "priority" or "preference" were avoided in Articles 69 and 70, simultaneously highlighting the need for special considerations to be given to LLS and GDS, clarifying the relationship between Article 62 and Articles 69 and 70.[158] Thus, Articles 62, 69(3), and 70(4) seem to indicates that, where the states competing for participation in EEZs fisheries are subject to similar terms and conditions, there appears to be a basis to support the superior claims of competing LLS and GDS, but where coastal states can make better arrangements with a state other than an LLS or a GDS, the LOS Convention seems to leave this discretion up to the coastal state.

In its totality, the provisions of Articles 69 and 70 represent a constraint on the coastal state's discretion to allow access, but this constraint is limited. Burke correctly believed that these provisions give the LLS, GDS, or developing LLS and GDS a claim to secure access to the surplus. Nevertheless, the realization of this claim requires negotiating with the coastal state to secure

---

156 Martínez Puñal, "The Rights of Land-Locked and Geographically Disadvantaged States," 430–36.

157 Explanatory Memorandum, *Official Records* 10 (1978), 90.

158 *Ibid.*

satisfactory terms for the coastal state through the medium of bilateral, regional, and subregional agreements.[159] Thus, the duty of the coastal state with regard to LLS and GDS is slightly different from its duty to other third states.

[159] Burke, "The Law of the Sea Convention Provisions," 100; also Wali noted that "although the Convention characterized participation in the EEZ by land-locked states as a right, its status as such is overshadowed by a number of qualifications. In effect all the right amount to is a gratuity that may or may not be granted in any situation." Ibrahim J. Wali, "An Evaluation of the Convention on the Law of the Sea from the Perspective of Landlocked States," *VJIL* 22 (1982): 649.

Chapter 4

State Practice and the Exclusive Economic Zone

State practice, as it relates to coastal states' jurisdiction over natural resources in the EEZ, shows that the majority of coastal states whose geographical features allow for the development of an EEZ have claimed and enforced their rights in the two-hundred-mile EEZ. The rapid expansion of claims in the two-hundred-mile zone, with the objective of controlling fisheries and other resources in this zone, dramatically increased during the latter part of the 1970s.[1] Even states that had vehemently protested against this practice and that tried but failed to convince other states to abandon their goals of developing a two-hundred-mile EEZ, have increased their fishing authority over the coastal zones.[2] When it came to extending fishing rights over coastal zones, the United States, the United Kingdom, and the Federal Republic of Germany led the way.[3] Such extension was important because it represented a general consensus and near agreement concerning coastal zones and fishing rights during the years immediately prior to UNCLOS III.

The Territorial Sea

Prior to convening UNCLOS III, the global community attempted but failed to secure an agreement on a maximum breadth of the territorial sea.[4] During the convening of UNCLOS I, in 1958, the territorial sea limits oscillated between three hundred and two hundred miles. Practically, most of the extended territorial sea claims came from Latin American and African nations. The chief objective of these extensive territorial sea claims involved protecting fisheries

---

[1] Smith, *Exclusive Economic Zone Claims,* 33.

[2] Fitzmaurice-Lachs, "The Legal Regime of the Baltic Sea Fisheries," 230.

[3] *Ibid.* It is worth noting that, through accession of the German Democratic Republic to the Federal Republic of Germany, which went into effect October 3, 1990, the German states have since unified to establish one sovereign state. From the date of unification, the Federal Republic of Germany is designated as "Germany" as a member of the UN. See *Law of the Sea Bulletin,* no. 19 (1991): 2, note 6.

[4] Schwarzenberger and Brown. *A Manual of International Law,* 105; Clingan, "Freedom of Navigation in a Post-UNCLOS III Environment," 108.

resources in adjacent seas, and securing the right to allow nations to exploit these resources.[5] However, most coastal states approved the territorial sea's three-mile limit. The entry into force of UNCLOS III changed this situation. By the early 1990s, no less than 129 nations had developed a territorial sea of twelve miles or less,[6] of which 121 had established a twelve-mile limit, which is also the maximum limit according to the LOS Convention,[7] with the remainder having limits of either three, four, or six miles.[8]

The number of states claiming a twelve-mile territorial sea limit has consistently increased since the development of the LOS Convention. A majority of states that claimed a twelve-mile limit were either independent states or states with previously claimed limits of less than twelve miles. For example, in January of 1972, Gabon asserted a thirty-mile territorial sea limit and within one year, it increased the limit to one hundred miles.[9] Then, in the early 1980s, Gabon changed back to the twelve-mile limit.[10] In 1985, The Netherlands increased its territorial sea from three to twelve miles.[11] In 1987, the United Kingdom enacted legislation that extended the breadth of the territorial sea from three to twelve miles, which correlated with most industrialized states.[12] Virtually all major maritime nations have adhered to the twelve-mile territorial sea limit.[13] In addition, three coastal states developed from the disintegration of the Soviet Union and adopted laws that set the breadth of the territorial sea at twelve miles: Latvia on December 20, 1990, Ukraine on November 4, 1991, and Lithuania on June 25, 1992.[14] Estonia also developed a twelve-mile territorial sea through legislation on March 10, 1992.[15]

---

[5] Hjertonson, *The New Law of the Sea,* 34–36.

[6] See UN Division for Ocean Affairs and the Law of the Sea. *Practice of States,* 203–14, Annex 1.

[7] *Ibid.* It is worth recalling that Article 3 of the LOS Convention states that "every state has the right to establish the breath of the territorial sea up to a limit not exceeding twelve nautical miles, measured from the baselines determined in accordance with this Convention."

[8] *Ibid.*

[9] Smith, *Exclusive Economic Zone Claims,* 20 Annex 2.

[10] *Ibid.*, 23.

[11] "The Netherlands Territorial Sea Act, January 9, 1985," *Law of the Sea Bulletin,* no. 6 (1985): 16.

[12] "The Territorial Sea Act 1987," *Law of the Sea Bulletin,* no. 14 (1989): 1.

[13] Those states include Canada, France, Japan, New Zealand, and the United States. See *Law of the Sea Bulletin,* no. 25 (1994): 2, 3, 5, 6, and 10 respectively.

[14] UN Division for Ocean Affairs and the Law of the Sea. *Practice of States,* 120.

[15] *Ibid.*

However, some developing states still claim a territorial sea of two hundred miles: Benin, Congo, Ecuador, El Salvador, Liberia, Panama, Peru, and Somalia.[16] These claims, without exception, do not offer any provisions clarifying the duties of the coastal state when it comes to conserving and managing the living resources in the asserted two-hundred-mile zone. Moreover, no reference is made concerning the participation of third states in the exploitation of natural resources. In virtually all cases, fishing within the claimed two-hundred-mile territorial sea has been reserved for vessels flying their flags. Additionally, these claims have made it quite clear that vessels of third states only have the right of innocent passage in the asserted two-hundred-mile area. It is important to note that international law has always acknowledged that coastal states have authority over their internal waters and almost exclusive sovereignty over their territorial sea, subject only to the right of innocent passage.[17] It is also worthy of note that each state mentioned above has made an assertion of a two-hundred-mile territorial sea in the strictest sense.

A majority of these comprehensive territorial sea claims existed years before the adoption of the LOS Convention.[18] Some seem to have changed to be more compatible with the LOS Convention. Guinea's claim, which was widened in 1978 to 150 miles[19] and later adjusted to twelve miles in 1980,[20] supports this notion. Similar action was initiated by Cape Verde in 1977,[21] Senegal and Madagascar in 1985,[22] Argentina in 1991,[23] and Brazil in 1993.[24] Although the dates that the reduction of these territorial sea claims took place indicates that the actions taken by these states were a concerted response to the consensus reached at UNCLOS III, many direct legislative actions taken by certain states, notably Cape Verde[25] and Madagascar,[26] serves as solid support for this view.

---

16 Food and Agriculture Organization of the United Nations, "Fisheries and Aquaculture Department," 2017, http://www.fao.org/fishery/index.htm (accessed December 28, 2017).
17 Schwarzenberger and Brown. *A Manual of International Law,* 100.
18 Pfirter, "Straddling Stocks and Highly Migratory Stocks in Latin American Practice and Legislation," 132.
19 Smith, *Exclusive Economic Zone Claims,* 8.
20 *Ibid.*
21 *Ibid.*
22 *Ibid.*
23 See Act No. 23. 968 of August 14, 1991, in UN Division for Ocean Affairs and the Law of the Sea, *The Law of the Sea: National Legislation on the Exclusive Economic Zone* (New York: United Nations, 1993), 17–18.
24 *Ibid.,* 38.
25 Decree Law No. 126 of December 31, 1977, in Smith, *Exclusive Economic Zone Claims,* 8 95.

In essence, the existing practice of states relating to the territorial sea indicates that states claiming rights to a territorial sea of two-hundred miles has historically declined. As mentioned earlier, claims to territorial seas beyond twelve miles, especially those of Latin American states, were predicated on the perceived need of the coastal states to protect their offshore resources from exploitation by major industrialized states in an era when the relevant divisions of the ocean space were simply those of the territorial sea or the high seas. The advent of the EEZ provides new avenues and fulfills the practical requirements for coastal states in protecting their resources without implementing excessive territorial sea claims.

In contemporary times, a large majority of states adheres to the twelve-mile territorial sea limit. State practice indicates that large and small states, industrialized and nonindustrialized states in the international community, are involved in this practice.[27] This is accomplished without disapproval or objections from the global community.[28] Adherence to this practice has rested on the belief that such practices are consistent with the tenets of international law. In this context, the Minister of State, Foreign and Commonwealth Office of the United Kingdom noted, "We believe that such limits are permitted by customary law and I believe that, though it has a three miles limit, the United States now take the same view."[29] Hence, the requirements expressed by the ICJ in the *North Sea Continental Shelf Cases, 1969*[30] for a practice to become a custom seem to have been met. Thus, coastal states are permitted to extend their territorial sea limit of twelve miles and any nation that asserts a territorial sea limit that goes beyond twelve miles would be in violation of international law.

The Exclusive Fishery Zone

The EFZ, as noted in Chapter 1,[31] is a maritime zone that lies beyond the territorial sea limit in which a coastal state can exercise exclusive rights that pertain to fisheries.[32] It must be noted that although the coastal state's authority to establish such a zone was denied at UNCLOS I and at UNCLOS II, the right of coastal states to develop an EFZ was established in the early 1970s.[33] Nev-

---

26 Ordinance of September 16, 1985, in *ibid.*, 254.
27 See UN Division for Ocean Affairs and the Law of the Sea. *Practice of States,* 1–10.
28 Bernhardt, "Custom and Treaty in the Law of the Sea," 289.
29 Parliamentary Debates, Territorial Sea Bill, House of Lords, 3 February 1987, 401.
30 "North Sea Continental Shelf Cases," 43.
31 See Chapter 1, pp. 34–38.
32 Fitzmaurice-Lachs, "The Legal Regime of the Baltic Sea Fisheries," 230.
33 *Ibid.*

ertheless, as noted in the *Fisheries Jurisdiction Case,* international law permitted the creation of such a zone to a maximum limit not exceeding twelve miles. Additionally, the coastal states' authority was confined to fisheries of the water column and did not include jurisdiction over marine scientific research for the preservation of the marine environment. In essence, two-hundred miles could not be regarded as an acceptable limit during the mid-1970s, giving coastal states the right to expand their jurisdiction to protect fisheries.[34] The situation changed greatly between 1976 and 1978. As suggested earlier, during these years a consensus formed at UNCLOS III regarding the new two-hundred-mile maritime zone.[35]

In addition to the two-hundred-mile territorial-sea claims previously mentioned, other states extended their fishery limits to two-hundred miles between 1976 and 1978, including the major industrial powers of the United States, Japan, and the EEC states.[36] One of the most persistent objectors to early Latin American extensive maritime claims, the United States, has asserted control over the living resources of the waters within the two-hundred-mile limit by implementing the Fishery Conservation and Management Act (FCMA),[37] which effectively expanded U.S. fisheries jurisdiction from twelve miles to two-hundred miles from the baseline of the territorial sea. The Act prohibits foreign fishing from the fishing zone, unless an existing treaty permits access or a foreign state has a permit to fish and asserts that the United States has exclusive fisheries-management authority over the fishery resources of the continental shelf and the zone's waters.[38] Aside from eliciting a diplomatic protest from Japan,[39] the FCMA was successfully implemented and enforced with widespread support from the international community.[40]

---

34 Fitzmaurice-Lachs, "The Legal Regime of the Baltic Sea Fisheries," 230.

35 Jean-Pierre Lévy, "Les Nations Unies et la Convention de 1982 sur le Droit de la Mer," *RBDI* 28, no. 1 (1995): 13.

36 Smith, *Exclusive Economic Zone Claims,* 21–22.

37 For the text of the Fishery Conservation and Management Act, see *ILM* 15 (1976): 635.

38 See generally, Burke, "The Law of the Sea Convention Provisions," 24–55; George A. B. Pierce, "Selective Adoption of the New Law of the Sea: The United States Proclaims its Exclusive Economic Zone," *VJIL* 23 (1983): 587.

39 Japan asserted that the unilateral establishment of an exclusive management authority up to the two-hundred-mile limit violated the principles of international law. See note from the Embassy of Japan to the United States Department of State, April 15, 1976, reproduced in Gary H. Knight, *The Law of the Sea: Cases, Documents, and Readings* (Baton Rouge, LA: Claitor's Law Books, 1980), 121.

40 Pierce, "Selective Adoption of the New Law of the Sea," 587.

The states that have asserted a two-hundred-mile EFZ let it be known that they were not in violation of international law. On the contrary, the extension of their exclusive fishery limits up to two-hundred miles was in accordance with the actions taken by nations at UNCLOS III. For example, when the United States developed its two-hundred-mile EFZ in 1976, it asserted that the established zone was "generally consistent with the consensus" among nations at the Conference.[41] Being consistent with the consensus may also imply that it conforms to the standards of international law. In the *Fisheries Jurisdiction Case,*[42] the ICJ addressed, *inter alia,* the concept of preferential fishing rights in the adjacent high seas in favor of nations that depend on coastal fisheries for their economic development or whose populations depend on fishing for their livelihood. This concept was first introduced by Iceland during the convening of UNCLOS I, and had been a central point of discussion at UNCLOS II. The ICJ ruled that the concept had become customary law by the early 1970s.[43] In doing so, the Court reasoned that subsequent to UNCLOS II, "the law evolved through the practice of states on the basis of the debates and near agreements at the Conferences."[44]

Within this context, the Canadian Secretary for External Affairs, in a statement to Parliament, noted that "Our action is based on a growing consensus among nations, a consensus which is increasingly finding its way into state practice and is reflected in the provisions of the Single Negotiating Text that emerged from the 1975 Session and has been confirmed in this year's revised ISNT."[45]

During the latter part of 1976, development in the EEC in organizing a coherent fishing policy took on a new urgency. It became clear that before the end of the year, a more centralized position became apparent when it came to the establishment of a two-hundred-mile EFZ.[46] During September of 1976,

---

[41] See the Statement of the President of the United States upon signing the FCMA into law, in *ILM* 15 (1976): 634.

[42] "Fisheries Jurisdiction Case (United Kingdom v. Iceland)."

[43] *Ibid.*, 195.

[44] *Ibid.*

[45] For the full text, see *CYIL* 15 (1977): 327.

[46] Albert W. Koers, "The External Authority of the EEC in Regard to Marine Fisheries," *CMLR* 14 (1977): 269.

the Commission of the European Communities[47] submitted proposals to the EEC Council of Ministers[48] regarding a common fisheries policy and a regime for negotiations between certain nonmember states and the community. The Council implemented a series of negotiating authorizations and shortly thereafter the Council of the European Community, to add a protective shield around the legitimate interests of the member states and to comply with the emerging trends at UNCLOS III concerning fishery rights, decided that member states would, through cooperative efforts, establish two-hundred-mile EFZs in the North Sea and in the Northeast Atlantic Ocean.[49] Belgium, Denmark, the Federal Republic of Germany, Ireland, the Netherlands, and the United Kingdom quickly complied with this decision.[50]

Other industrial powers took similar steps. The Soviet Union, to protect its interests, issued an Edict of the Presidium of the USSR Supreme Soviet[51] on December 10, 1976. Article 1 of this Edict states, "In marine areas adjacent to the coast of the USSR, of a breadth up to two hundred nautical miles computed from the same baselines as the territorial waters, there shall be introduced

---

[47] The Commission of the European Communities is composed of several members chosen on the grounds of their general competence. The commission generally comprises a mixture of lawyers, economists, former ministers, former members of parliament, and former diplomats. See Dominik Lasok and John William Bridge, *An Introduction to the Law and Institutions of the European Communities,* 5th ed. (Oxford: Butterworth, 1991), 107–17; also Shaw, *International Law,* 766.

[48] It is noteworthy that the Council of Ministers of the European Communities comprises one representative of the government of each member state. The usual minister who represents a member on the council is its foreign minister. But the overall make-up of the council may vary depending on the issues discussed. For additional information see Lasok and Bridge, *An Introduction to the Law and Institutions of the European Communities,* 118–29; also David Freestone, "Some Institutional Implications of the Establishment of Exclusive Economic Zones by EC Member States," *ODIL* 23 (1992): 99.

[49] European Communities, Council Resolution on External Aspects of the Creation of a 200 Miles Fishing Zone, November 3, 1976. For full text, see *ILM* 15 (1976): 1425. It is good to know that member states are called upon to establish fishery zones only off their North Sea and North Atlantic Coasts without prejudice to any future claim in other areas such as the Mediterranean Sea. For an in-depth analysis of the common fisheries policy of the European Community, see Robin Rolf Churchill, *EEC Fisheries Law* (New York: Martinus Nijhoff, 1987), 83–165.

[50] Koers, "The External Authority of the EEC," 299.

[51] Edict on Provisional Measures for the Preservation of Living Resources and the Regulation of Fishing in Marine Areas, December 10, 1976. For the full text, see *ILM* 15 (1976): 1381.

... provisional measures for the preservation of living resources and for the regulations of fishing."

Japan, which had protested the U.S. claim of a two-hundred-mile EFZ,[52] made a similar motion on May 2, 1977.[53] Japan developed a fishery zone that extended up to two-hundred miles but was not applicable beyond Japanese territorial waters in the areas facing China and the Republic of Korea.[54]

As mentioned previously, most of these states relied on the emerging consensus at UNCLOS III when formulating their territorial-sea policy. In this context, a very important question must be asked: Did the emerging consensus at UNCLOS III during 1976 relate to the EFZ or did it involve a more comprehensive analysis of the EEZ? Despite the fact that fishery zones, as they related to fishing activities, served as functional equivalents of EEZs,[55] it is important to ascertain the core element of this consensus because the EEZ provides the coastal state with sovereign and jurisdictional rights to nonliving resources that go beyond those associated with fishery zones. In the EEZ, coastal states, for example, are permitted to exercise jurisdiction over marine scientific research and environmental protection in addition to rights to nonliving resources.[56] In answering the above question, referring to UNCLOS III is a necessity. It must be remembered that the Second Committee of UNCLOS III had the most complete mandate, encompassing virtually all subjects pertaining to the traditional law of the sea such as the territorial sea, straits, archipelagos, the continental shelf, and the high seas.[57] The competence of the Committee also covers the topic of the EEZ, including living and nonliving resources.[58]

Under the rubric "Exclusive Economic Zone," various issues became the central focus of the debates. These issues include the economic rights and obligations of the coastal state within the two-hundred-mile limits, the rights

---

[52] See note from the Embassy of Japan to the United States Department of State, April 15, 1976, Knight, *The Law of the Sea.*

[53] Law No. 31 May 1977 on Provisional Measures Relating to the Fishing Zone as amended by Law No. 83 of 29 November 1977, in ST/LEG/SER. B/19 (1980): 215.

[54] A map that defines the Japanese fishing zone is found in K. Nakauchi, *Japan's Ocean Affairs* (Saitama, Japan: Law of the Sea Institute, 1988), 23.

[55] Lawrence Juda, "The Exclusive Economic Zone: Non-claimant States," *ODIL* 19 (1988): 439.

[56] See Article 56 of the LOS Convention, as well as other pertinent provisions in Parts V, XII, and XIII of that Convention, and Roeland Jansoone, "La Pratique Etatique Belge et la Zone Economique Exclusive," *RBDI* 28 (1995): 93–94.

[57] See Stevenson and Oxman. "The Third United Nations Conference on the Law of the Sea: The 1975 Geneva Session," 12–25.

[58] *Ibid.,* 15–18.

of coastal states as they pertain to noneconomic uses of the zone, and the rights and obligations assigned to third states.

An in-depth analysis of no less than twenty proposals[59] many by various states (developed and developing states), with the objective of defining the rights and obligations of the coastal state within the proposed two-hundred-mile limit, reveals that, with the exception of a few proposals, proposals referred to the sovereign rights of the coastal state as these rights pertain to the natural resources located within the two-hundred-mile limit, and to the coastal state's power over marine scientific research and the protection and preservation over the marine environment.

In addition, all UNCLOS III texts beginning with the ISNT,[60] RSNT,[61] ICNT,[62] Revision 1 and 2,[63] and the Draft Convention[64] had provisions that addressed the fishing rights of coastal states as well as the coastal states' jurisdictional authority over marine scientific research and the protection and preservation of the marine environment within the two-hundred-mile limit. Moreover, all the LOS Convention's provisions pertaining to the two-hundred-mile jurisdictional zone makes reference to the EEZ, not the EFZ. As one noted expert observed, "the concept of the exclusive fishing zone is nowhere referred to in ... the UN Convention."[65]

Based on the evidence presented above, all indication suggests that the consensus that emerged at UNCLOS III between 1976 and 1978 did not restrict

---

[59] Among the proposals examined are Nicaragua's Proposal on the National Zone, A/Conf. 62/C. 2/L. 17, 23 July 1974, in Platzoder, *Third United Nations Conference on the Law of the Sea,* 102–3; Nigeria's Draft Article on the Exclusive Economic Zone, A/Conf. 62/C. 2/L. 21, Rev. 1, August, 1974, in *ibid.,* 111–13; Jamaica Draft Article on the Rights of Developing Geographically Disadvantaged States within the Exclusive Economic Zone, A/Conf. 62/C. 2/L. 35 of August 1, 1974, in *ibid.,* 138–39; the Draft Articles on the Exclusive Economic Zone submitted by Greece, A/Conf. 62/C. 2/L. 32, 31 July 1974, in *ibid.,* 153; the United States Draft Articles for a Chapter on the Economic Zone and the Continental Shelf, A/Conf. 62/L. 47, August 8, 1974, in *ibid.,* 155–62; also Doc. A/Conf. 62/C. 2/ L. 38, August 1974, in *ibid.,* 140; and Doc. A/Conf. 62/C. 2/L. 39, August 5, 1974, in *ibid.,* 144. See also generally Andrés M. Aguilar, "The Patrimonial Sea or Economic Zone Concept," *SDLR* 11 (1974): 579–602.

[60] "Informal Single Negotiating Text."

[61] "Revised Single Negotiating Text," 51.

[62] "Informal Composite Negotiating Text."

[63] *Ibid.*

[64] Draft Convention on the Law of the Sea, UN Doc. A/Conf. 62/L. 78, August 28, 1981, *Official Records* 15 (1981).

[65] Brown, *The International Law of the Sea.*

the rights of coastal states over fisheries within the two-hundred-mile zone, as asserted by Japan and other protesting Western European states, but covered the EEZ, including direct and collateral uses such as marine scientific research and the protection of the environment. Undeniably, as the United Kingdom observed in the *Channel Continental Shelf Arbitration (U.K. v. France)*[66] 1977 case, controversies persisted surrounding the content of the jurisdiction that would be exercised by the coastal state within the two-hundred-mile EEZ.[67] However, those controversies centered on only a few issues: the access of fisheries by LLS and GDS, and the protection of marine mammals and anadromous species.[68] The issue of marine scientific research in the two-hundred-mile EEZ, the continental shelf, and the protection and preservation of the marine environment were pressing issues that fell under the competence of the Third Committee of UNCLOS III.[69] A large majority of declarations and proposals pertaining to marine scientific research supported the notion that coastal states would enjoy jurisdiction over scientific-research activities related to the natural resources found in the EEZ.[70] The main difference between these declarations and proposals involved the extent of the coastal state's jurisdiction with regard to scientific-research activities that have nothing to do with the EEZ's natural resources.[71]

That coastal states can exercise jurisdiction over marine scientific-research activities that take place in the EEZ and involve the resources of the EEZ is a generally accepted proposition. In this framework, one leading commentator noted, "state practice clearly shows that coastal states can claim some exclusive rights in the 200 miles zone," and "there are good reasons for the assumption that customary international law also reserves to the coastal states the other rights mentioned in Article 56 of the Convention" if they decide to exercise such rights.[72] This viewpoint suggests that, under current customary international law, coastal states can claim jurisdiction over marine scientific research in accordance with the guidelines of Article 56 para. 1(b)(ii).

In the seminal work "Marine Scientific Research and the Law of the Sea," Soons observed that "claims to jurisdiction over scientific research in EEZs

66 "Channel Continental Shelf Arbitration (United Kingdom v. France), 1977 XV," *RIAA* 3 (1978): 3.

67 *Ibid.*, 34–37.

68 Oxman, *The Law of the Sea*, 6.

69 See Platzoder, *Third United Nations Conference on the Law of the Sea*, 216.

70 For additional information see Extavour, *The Exclusive Economic Zone*, 205–12.

71 *Ibid.*

72 Bernhardt, "Custom and Treaty in the Law of the Sea," 296.

going beyond the jurisdiction coastal states are entitled to exercise over marine scientific research involving the taking of fish, are not valid under present-day general customary law."[73] What Soons is implying is that coastal states are allowed, under customary law, to exercise authority over marine research activities related to the EEZ's resources, if they desire to do so.

When it comes to the protection and preservation of the marine environment in the EEZ, it must be remembered that before the start of UNCLOS III a number of proposals were submitted to the UN Seabed Committee highlighting the idea that the future EEZ regime would allow coastal states to take some measures to prevent pollution in the EEZ with the goal of protecting the EEZ's economic interests.[74] This idea received widespread support at UNCLOS III. Oxman gives a vivid picture of the developments surrounding the EEZ at the Caracas Session of 1974:

> Over 100 countries spoke in support of an economic zone extending to a limit of 200 nautical miles as part of an overall treaty settlement. With respect to the content of the zone, there is widespread support for the following: (a) coastal states sovereign or exclusive rights for the purpose of exploration and exploitation of living and non-living resources; (b) exclusive coastal state rights over artificial islands and most installations; (c) exclusive coastal state rights over drilling for all purposes; (d) coastal state rights and duties with respect to pollution and scientific research.[75]

Under customary international law that relates to extended jurisdictional zones, coastal states are empowered to claim EEZs, along with exclusive fishery zones. As noted earlier, the EEZ is a much broader concept and exclusive fishing is an integral part of those rights that compose the basis for the EEZ.[76] Although the EEZ is a broader concept, customary international law does not compel coastal state to implement the broader concept.[77] With this in mind, Soons correctly noted that states "are not required by international law to

---

[73] Soons, *Marine Scientific Research and the Law of the Sea,* 305.

[74] See for example, Doc. A/AC. 138/SC. II/L. 10 Draft Articles on the Exclusive Economic Zone Concept, submitted by Kenya, in Oda, *The International Law of the Ocean Development,* 215–16.

[75] See Stevenson and Oxman. "The Third United Nations Conference on the Law of the Sea: The 1975 Geneva Session," 16.

[76] Bernhardt, "Custom and Treaty in the Law of the Sea," 296.

[77] C. A. Fleischer, "Global Situation with Respect to National Legislation, Bilateral Agreements, and Regional Commissions," in Clingan, "Freedom of Navigation in a Post-UNCLOS III Environment," 97–98.

fully exercise all rights (with corresponding duties) they acquire under customary international law."[78] Thus, if a state wishes to restrict its claims to one of the prescribed functions, as in the case of the United Kingdom,[79] Canada,[80] Denmark,[81] Japan,[82] and The Netherlands,[83] its actions comply with the standards of customary international law.

The Evolution of EEZ Claims

The time period between 1975 and the continuation of the Eighth Session of UNCLOS III in New York from July 16 to August 24, 1977, witnessed a tremendous growth in the development of the two-hundred-mile EEZ in state practice. In this concise time frame, a little over forty-six coastal states asserted claims to a two-hundred-mile EEZ.[84] Of these claims, Africa produced fifteen, Asia ten, Latin America seven, the Caribbean Island states five, Western Europe four, and Oceania/Australia a total of six.[85] This rapid development of the two-hundred-mile EEZs in state practice, and the extension of these developments on the international level to every geographical region at a time when at least three years were still needed to close out the work of UNCLOS III, was precipitated by the general consensus and near-agreement that were emerging at UNCLOS III relating to the two-hundred-mile EEZ of this period.

During this same time frame, a small number of states chose to establish an EFZ,[86] in essence asserting a claim that was less than an EEZ. Chief among the states who took this action were the United States, the United Kingdom, the USSR, and Japan.[87] The assertion, by major industrial powers, of an EFZ when they were allowed to assert a full EEZ during the height of UNCLOS III negotiations is quite significant. It indicated that these major maritime powers sought to undermine the EEZ concept that was put forth by the developing

---

[78] See Convention on Fishing and Conservation 1958, Article 2 and Agreement for the Implementation of the Provisions of the United Nations Convention on the Law of the Sea of December 10, 1982, Relating to the Conservation and Management of Straddling Fish Stocks and Highly Migratory Fish Stocks, United Nations, Doc. A/Conf. 164/37, September 8, 1995, Article 5(b).

[79] Churchill and Lowe, *The Law of the Sea*, 145.

[80] *Law of the Sea Bulletin*, June (1993): 2.

[81] *Ibid.*, 3.

[82] *Ibid.*, 5.

[83] *Ibid.*, 6.

[84] Johnston and Gold, "Extended Jurisdiction," 27–49.

[85] *Ibid.*

[86] *Ibid.*

[87] *Ibid.*

states of Latin America and Africa. At the Caracas Sessions in 1974, various major maritime powers voiced their displeasure with the concept of a two-hundred-mile EEZ. The Japanese representative noted that: "His delegation interpreted proposals for an exclusive economic zone as involving a zone in the high seas in which the coastal state had exclusive rights over all resources, living and non-living."[88]

The British representative concurred with this viewpoint when he stated,

> His delegation had, however, made it clear that it regarded the coastal state rights in an economic zone to be rights in relations to the resources of the sea-bed and water column. It had therefore been deeply concerned to note a growing tendency to take for granted those rights to the resources and to make demands for further competencies, not directly related to resources within the zone.[89]

Hence, these two statements highlighted the desire for the content of the two-hundred-mile EEZ concept to be confined to the economic resources of the zone. All other collateral activities that take place in the zone and are not connected with the exploration and exploitation of natural resources, including marine scientific-research activities, would remain outside the competence of the coastal states.

However, by resorting to EFZs at a time when UNCLOS III was still in session, the major industrial powers were attempting to influence the work of UNCLOS III on the EEZ to restrict the rights of coastal states in the zone. Domestic legislation that established these zones and placed emphasis on the provisional nature of the measures that were enacted seems to confirm this hypothesis. The Decree of the Presidium of the Supreme Soviet of the USSR of December 10, 1976, on Provisional Measures to Conserve Living Resources and Regulate Fishing in the Sea Areas Adjacent to the Coast of the USSR supports this viewpoint. The Decree noted that an "increasing number of states, including some adjoining the USSR" have been developing economic fishing zones up to two hundred miles without waiting for the conclusion of UNCLOS

---

[88] *Official Records* 3 (1975): 217.

[89] *Ibid.*, 200. For similar views, see the statement of the Belgium delegate, in *ibid.*, 206, para. 52; the Soviet Union's delegate, in *ibid.*, 221, para. 51; and the Italian delegate, in *ibid.*, 195, paras. 10, 11, 12, and 14.

III, and that "pending the conclusion of a Convention" immediate action must be taken to preserve and protect the interests of the Soviet Union.[90]

But the action of these states failed. In contrast, many other coastal states, some of them developing states, subsequently followed the EEZ model when establishing their own two-hundred-mile EEZ. In essence, in addition to the forty-seven made up to 1978,[91] seven other claims were asserted in 1979, eleven in 1980, and five in 1981.[92]

In 1982, state practice that sought to establish two-hundred-mile EFZs completely failed. This was the result of the EEZ concept being fully retained in the final text of UNCLOS III. Since the adaption of the LOS Convention in 1982, the number of states claiming EEZs increased dramatically. During 1983, five additional EEZ claims were made, with six in 1984, three in 1986, one in 1987,[93] two between the years 1989 and 1990,[94] and at least six EEZ claims between the years 1991 and 1995.[95] During the time period of the 1990s, at least ninety-two coastal states proclaimed EEZs with the two-hundred-mile limit from the baseline from which the breadth of the territorial

[90] Note from the Embassy of Japan to the United States Department of State, April 15, 1976, Knight, *The Law of the Sea.* To some extent, this may be also said of the EEC Resolution on External Aspects of the Creation of a 200-Mile Fishing Zone, November 3, 1976 wherein it is stated that "the present circumstances, and particularly the unilateral steps taken or about to be taken by certain third countries, warrant immediate actions by the community to protect its legitimate interests," Koers, "The External Authority of the EEC," 299.

[91] Johnston and Gold, "Extended Jurisdiction," 82.

[92] Juda, "The Exclusive Economic Zone," 433, Table 1.

[93] *Ibid.*

[94] See "The Territorial Sea and Exclusive Economic Zone Act of Tanzania, 1989," in *Law of the Sea: Current Developments in State Practice,* no. 2 (New York: United Nations, 1989), 76; and "The Claim of Namibia of 1990," in *Law of the Sea: Current Developments in State Practice,* no. 3 (New York: United Nations, 1992), 81.

[95] See, for instance, "Jamaica's Exclusive Economic Zone Act No. 33 December 31, 1991," *Law of the Sea Bulletin,* no. 21 (1992): 28; "Belize Act of January 24, 1992," *ibid.,* 3; "The Estonian Claim," UN Division for Ocean Affairs and the Law of the Sea, *Practice of States,* 120; "The Argentine Claim," UN Division for Ocean Affairs and the Law of the Sea, *The Law of the Sea,* 17–18; "The Brazilian Claim," *ibid.,* 38; "Sweden's Act on Sweden's Economic Zone, December 3, 1992," *Law of the Sea Bulletin,* no. 23 (1993): 24–28; The United Kingdom of Great Britain and Northern Ireland, Pitcairn, Henderson, Ducie and Oeno Islands, Proclamation No. 1 of 1992: "South Georgia and the South Sandwich Islands Proclamation No. 1 of 1993," *Law of the Sea Bulletin,* no. 24 (1993): 46–47.

sea is measured.[96] Indeed, several other coastal states such as Algeria, Bahrain, Cyprus, Israel, Greece, Italy, and Lebanon have not established EEZs.[97] In all likelihood, the reason has more to do with certain practical limitations than the viability of establishing such a zone. A large percentage of states that have not developed an EEZ border one or more semienclosed seas.[98] One of the most conspicuous considerations lies in the notion that such sea delimitation issues become very difficult because they involve boundaries with adjacent and opposites states.[99] For example, the Mediterranean Sea is a semienclosed sea with the furthest point from the shore measuring approximately 229 miles.[100] Virtually the entire Mediterranean would be subject to the national jurisdiction of states of the region that had developed a two-hundred-mile EEZ. As a result, every state would be compelled to delimit its boundaries with not only adjacent states but with opposite states as well.[101] In reality, such claims could also lead to jurisdictional disputes in geographical areas known for political instability. With this in mind, many states have been very cautious when making claims that would extend their zone's jurisdiction.

Of the eighteen states bordering the Mediterranean Sea, only Egypt, France, Morocco, Spain, and Turkey have established EEZs.[102] Upon ratifying the LOS

---

[96] Central Intelligence Agency, *World Factbook*, 2018, https://www.cia.gov/library/publications/the-world-factbook/geos/le.html (accessed January 28, 2018).

[97] *Ibid.*

[98] Semienclosed seas include the Gulf of Aden, Arabian Sea, Andaman Sea, Baltic Sea, Bay of Bengal, Behring Sea, Black Sea, Caribbean Sea, Celebes Sea, East China Yellow Sea, Gulf of Guinea, Sea of Japan, Mediterranean Sea, Gulf of Mexico, North Sea, Sea of Okhotsk, Gulf of Oman, Persian/Arabian Gulf, Red Sea, Solomon Sea, South China Sea, Sulu Sea, and Timor-Arafura Seas. See Lewis M. Alexander, "Regional Arrangement in the Oceans," *AJIL* 71 (1977): 90.

[99] Norman G. Letalik, "Boundary Making in the Mediterranean," in *Ocean Boundary Making: Regional Issues and Developments*, ed. Douglas M. Johnston and P. M. Saunders (London: Croom Helm, 1988), 122; Choon-ho Park, "Offshore Oil Development in the China Seas: Some Legal and Territorial Issues," in *Ocean Yearbook*, vol. 2, ed. E. M. Borgese and N. Ginsburg (Chicago: University of Chicago Press, 1980), 307; Kriangsak Kittichaisaree, *The Law of the Sea and Maritime Boundary Delimitation in South-East Asia* (Singapore: Oxford, 1987), 10; Sun, "Policy of the Republic of China toward the South China Sea," 401. It is worth mentioning that many of these states are located on semienclosed seas and spoke against the concept of the EEZ at UNCLOS III, because they can obtain no significant benefit from it. See Juda, "The Exclusive Economic Zone," 440.

[100] Letalik, *ibid.*

[101] Tullio Scovazzi, "Implications of the New Law of the Sea for the Mediterranean," *MP* 5 (1981): 306.

[102] See Appendix B.

Convention, Egypt announced it would exercise the rights given it in the EEZ by the provisions of Part V of the LOS Convention.[103] In addition, both France and Spain established EEZs in the vicinity of their Atlantic coasts, which resulted in avoiding the creation of such a zone in the Mediterranean.[104] This was also true of Morocco, which promulgated a two-hundred-mile EEZ for its Atlantic waters but not for its Mediterranean waters.[105] In a similar fashion, Turkey developed an EEZ in the Black Sea in 1987, excluding the Mediterranean coast by legislation due to delimitation problems with Greece.[106]

Finally, those states that did assert EFZs did so with the knowledge that international law authorized coastal states to claim more than sovereign rights over living resources. This is supported by the idea that, even though a large majority of states had established EEZs before the conclusion of the LOS Convention, none of the EFZs claimant states objected to such a practice. On the contrary, some of these states showed a willingness to adapt their domestic legislation to the LOS Convention.[107] Although others had already done so, the United States and the former Soviet Union changed their former two-hundred-mile EFZs into EEZs in 1983 and 1984 respectively.[108] These Conventions facilitated the growth of states claiming EEZs. They also lent additional support to the view that the consensus that emerged at UNCLOS III was concerned with issues surrounding the full EEZ, not just the sovereign rights of the coastal state over living resources.

Subsequent conversions of existing two-hundred-mile EFZs into EEZs was implemented by Poland in 1991,[109] Sweden in 1993,[110] and Australia in

---

[103] Declaration (upon ratification of the United Nations Convention on the Law of the Sea of December 10, 1982), in Smith, *Exclusive Economic Zone Claims,* 123–24.

[104] See French Decree No. 77–130 of February 11, 1977, in *ibid.,* 147–49, Article 1; and Spanish Law No. 15-1978 of February 20, 1978, in *ibid.,* 425.

[105] Decree No. 1-81-179 of April 8, 1981, in *ibid.,* 303. For additional information see Juda, "The Exclusive Economic Zone," 434.

[106] On Turkey's development of an EEZ, see *Keesing's Contemporary Archives,* May (1987): 35133.

[107] Juda, "The Exclusive Economic Zone," 440.

[108] See, for example, Presidential Proclamation No. 5030 and Decree of the Presidium of the Supreme Soviet of the USSR on the Economic Zone of the USSR, 28 February 1984, in Smith, *Exclusive Economic Zone Claims,* 467 and 417, respectively.

[109] "Act Concerning the Maritime Areas of the Polish Republic and the Marine Administration, 1991," *Law of the Sea Bulletin,* no. 21 (1991): 66.

[110] "Sweden's Act on Sweden's Economic Zone December 3, 1992"; see also Said Mahmoudi, "Sweden: Sweden's Economic Zone Act," *IJMCL* 28 (1993): 524.

1994.[111] A number of coastal states that had established EFZs in the past have considered exercising their jurisdictional competencies in the North Sea in accordance with the LOS Convention, specifically with regard to Part XII.[112]

Conceptual Framework of EEZ Claims

According to Article 55 of the LOS Convention, the EEZ is an "area beyond and adjacent to the territorial sea, subject to the specific legal regime established in" Part V. This provision implies that the territorial sea and the EEZ are completely two separate geographical and judicial zones in the LOS Convention.

At least seventy of the eighty claims examined included a provision pertaining to this definition of the EEZ. Of these seventy claims, fifty-one had adopted a definition similar to the words expressed in Article 55 and 57 of the LOS Convention. The U.S. Presidential Proclamation No. 5030 of March 10, 1983, for instance, defines the United States' EEZ as a "zone contiguous to the territorial sea ... extending to a distance of 200 nautical miles from the baseline from which the breadth of the territorial sea is measured."[113] Likewise, Thailand's Royal Proclamation of February 23, 1981, provides that the EEZ "of the Kingdom of Thailand is an area beyond and adjacent to the territorial sea whose breadth extends" to two-hundred miles measured from the baselines used for measuring the breadth of the territorial sea.[114] The domestic EEZ legislative acts of Cuba,[115] Costa Rica,[116] Dominican Republic,[117] Guyana,[118] Iceland,[119] India,[120] Indonesia,[121] the Ivory Coast,[122] Kiribati,[123] Madagascar,[124]

---

[111] See Stuart Kaye and Donald R. Rothwell, "Australia's Antarctic Maritime Claims and Boundaries," *ODIL* 26, no. 3 (1995): 209.

[112] Lewis M. Alexander, "Regional Arrangement in the Oceans," 90. Aggregates compiled by NationMaster. http://www.nationmaster.com/country-info/stats/geography/maritime-claims/Exclusive-fishing-zone (accessed January 28, 2018); Soons, "Regulation of Marine Scientific Research," 272.

[113] Smith, *Exclusive Economic Zone Claims*, 467.

[114] *Ibid.*, 437.

[115] Decree Law No. 2 of February 24, 1977, in *ibid.*, 109 Article 2.

[116] Decree No. 56-99 of 1975 amending Article 6 of the constitution, in *ibid.*, 107.

[117] Law No. 573 of 1977, *ibid.*, 119 Article 4.

[118] Act No. 10 of 1977, in *ibid.*, 209 Article 15.

[119] Law No. 41 of June 1979, in *ibid.*, 209, Part II Article 3.

[120] Maritime Zones Act, 1976, in *ibid.*, 213 Article 7(1).

[121] Act No. 5 of 1983, in *ibid.*, 228 chapter II Article 2.

[122] Act No. 77-926, in *ibid.*, 241 Article 2.

[123] Act No. 7 of 1983, in *ibid.*, 245, Part II Article 7(1).

[124] Ordinance No. 85-013 of September 1985, in *ibid.*, 255, Article 1.

Malaysia,[125] Mauritius,[126] Mexico,[127] Morocco,[128] Mozambique,[129] New Zealand,[130] Nigeria,[131] Pakistan,[132] Philippines,[133] Sao Tome and Principe,[134] Seychelles,[135] Solomon Islands,[136] Spain,[137] Sri Lanka,[138] Suriname,[139] Tonga,[140] Trinidad and Tobago,[141] Vanuatu,[142] Venezuela,[143] Vietnam,[144] and Western Samoa[145] contain similar provisions. Thus, like the guidelines of the LOS Convention, domestic legislation of states that pertains to the EEZ indicate that the territorial sea and the EEZ are two distinct doctrines of the law of the sea, subject to two different legal regimes.[146]

Furthermore, although very few states omitted any definition of the EEZ,[147] others selected definitions that are ambiguous at best. For example, Guatemala's Decree No. 20/76 of July 1, 1976 notes in Article 3 that: "The Republic of Guatemala establishes an exclusive economic zone which should extend two hundred nautical miles from the baseline from which the breadth of the

---

125 Exclusive Economic Zone Bill 1984, in *ibid.*, 259 Part II Article 3(1).
126 Act No. 13 of 1977, in *ibid.*, 288 Article 6.
127 Act of February 10, 1976 Regulating the Provisions of Paragraph 8 of Article 27 of the Political Constitution of the United Mexican States Concerning the Exclusive Economic Zone, in *ibid.*, 295 Article 1.
128 Law No. 1-81 of 1981, in *ibid.*, 303 Article 1.
129 Decree No. 31-76, of 1976, in *ibid.*, 307 Article 2.
130 Territorial Sea and Excusive Economic Zone Act, 1977, in *ibid.*, 309 Article 9(1).
131 Decree No. 28 of 1978, in *ibid.*, 347 Article 1(1).
132 Territorial Waters and Maritime Zones Act, 1976, in *ibid.*, 357 Article 6.
133 Presidential Decree No. 1599 of 1979, in *ibid.*, 369 Section 1.
134 Decree Law No. 15-78 of 1978, in *ibid.*, 405 Article 1.
135 Act No. 15 of 1977, in *ibid.*, 407 Article 6(1).
136 Act No. 32 of 1978, in *ibid.*, 413 Article 6(1).
137 Law No. 15-1978, in *ibid.*, 425 Article 1.
138 Maritime Zones Law No. 22 of 1976, in *ibid.*, 427 Article 5(1).
139 Law No. 26 of 1978, in *ibid.*, 433 Article 3.
140 Act No. 32 of 1978, in *ibid.*, 441 Article 9(1).
141 Ministry of Foreign Affairs Notice No. 500 of 1983 of May 27, 1983, in *ibid.*, 456.
142 Maritime Zones Act No. 23 of 1981, in *ibid.*, 471 Article 9(1).
143 Act Establishing an Exclusive Economic Zone Along the Coasts of the Mainland and Island of the Republic of Venezuela, in *ibid.*, 477 Article 1.
144 Statement on Economic Zone of May 12, 1977, in *ibid.*, 481 para. 3.
145 Exclusive Economic Zone Act 1977, in *ibid.*, 483 Article 3(1).
146 Pfirter, "Straddling Stocks and Highly Migratory Stocks in Latin American Practice and Legislation," 132.
147 National EEZ legislations omitting any definition of the EEZ includes Haiti's Decree No. 38 of April 8, 1978 and Maldives Law No. 3076 of December 5, 1976, in Smith, *Exclusive Economic Zone Claims*, 201 and 277, respectively.

territorial sea is measured."[148] In similar fashion, the Portuguese Law No. 33/77 of May 28, 1977 states that: "An economic zone is hereby established, the outer limit of which is a line where each point is at a distance of two hundred nautical miles from the point closest to the baseline from which the breadth of the territorial sea is measured."[149] Such corresponding definitions have been found in EEZ proclamations or legislative acts of other states as well.[150] However, in many cases, the problem seems to be more of a matter of imperfect wording rather than intent to confuse the distinction between the two jurisdictional zones. This is one of the underlying reasons most states have expressly claimed a twelve-mile territorial sea.[151]

The Legal Status of the EEZ

Articles 55 and 56 of the LOS Convention indicate that the EEZ is neither part of the high seas nor the territorial sea. Article 55 defines the legal status of the EEZ only within the framework of the LOS Convention. It is a zone *sui generis.* It is worth mentioning that *generis* formulations' main objective is to resolve conflicts between certain developing coastal states, which supports the territorial-sea characterization of the EEZ,[152] suggesting that the residual competences remain with the coastal states, and the major maritime powers that advocate a high-sea characterization to ensure that the freedom of navigation and other lawful uses of the ocean in the vast areas enclosed by the EEZ would remain with the flag states.[153]

A large number of EEZ claims did not expressly attempt to integrate the EEZ with the high seas. The absence of state practices favorable to the proposition of the EEZ as the high seas is logical because this premise was strongly rejected at UNCLOS III and refuted by the final text of the Convention.

---

[148] *Ibid.,* 185.

[149] *Ibid.,* 371 Article 1(1).

[150] These states include: the Democratic People's Republic of Korea Guinea, Guinea-Bissau, Norway, Oman and Togo.

[151] See, for example, Article 1 of Decree No. 20/76 of Guatemala, Article 1 of Decree No. 336/PRG/80 of Guinea, and Article 2 of Law No. 3/78 of Guinea-Bissau, in Smith, *Exclusive Economic Zone Claims,* 185, 187, and 191, respectively.

[152] Mfodwo, Tsamenyi, and Blay, "The Exclusive Economic Zone," 450.

[153] For the *sui generis* formulation, see Introductory Note to Part II of the "Revised Single Negotiating Text," 151–53. For additional information see Al Mour, "The Legal Status of the Exclusive Zone"; and Alfonso A. Schreiber, "The Exclusive Economic Zone: Its Legal Nature and the Problem of Military Uses," in *The Exclusive Economic Zone: A Latin American Perspective,* ed. Francisco Orrego Vicuña (Boulder, CO: Westview Press, 1984), 123–41.

Likewise, the practice of states that support the territorial proposition is somewhat sporadic. A limited number of developing coastal states, specifically those of Latin America, have asserted a two-hundred-mile zone of national sovereignty,[154] thereby incorporating the asserted zone with a territorial sea claim. Furthermore, the number of states adhering to this practice decreased precipitously because of the need to make national legislation more compatible with the provisions of the LOS Convention.[155]

In addition, Uruguay modified their position by moving from the group that supported the territorial proposition and becoming a party to the LOS Convention,[156] whereas Nicaragua, Panama, and El Salvador signed the LOS Convention, which indicates their strong belief in the principles of the Convention.[157] Out of this group, Nicaragua went a step further by promising, upon signing the Convention, to adjust it national laws "as may be required in order to harmonize it with the Convention."[158]

Because state practice did not support the premise of the territorial sea or high seas, the alternative is, therefore, the *sui generis* nature of the EEZ. This can be seen when states enumerated the rights to be enjoyed by the claimant state in the EEZ and specified the rights of third states. for example, Article 48(1) of Decree No. 77 of January 7, 1987 of the State Council of the People's Republic of Bulgaria on the Exclusive Economic Zone of Bulgaria in the Black Sea[159] states that, in the EEZ, Bulgaria shall exercise "sovereign rights for the purpose of exploring, developing, exploiting, protecting and managing the living, mineral, and energy resources of the sea-bed, its subsoil and the water superjacent to the sea-bed, and with regard to other activities for the exploration and exploitation of the zone." Paragraph 2 further adds that Bulgaria also has the authority to exercise exclusive rights and jurisdiction regarding the construction and use of artificial islands, installations and structures, marine scientific research, and the protection of the marine environment. Article 49, in contrast, provides that in the EEZ, "all states enjoy the freedoms of naviga-

---

154 Food and Agriculture Organization of the United Nations, "Fisheries and Aquaculture Department,"

155 See UN Division for Ocean Affairs and the Law of the Sea, *The Law of the Sea.*

156 Uruguay, Declarations made upon signature (10 December 1982) and confirmed upon ratification (10 December 1982).

157 Paolillo, "The Exclusive Economic Zone in Latin American Practice and Legislation," 106.

158 See *Law of the Sea Bulletin,* no. 5 (1985): 17.

159 For the full text, see United Nations, *The Law of the Sea: Current Developments in State Practice,* no. 2 (New York: United Nations, 1989), 2–18.

tion, overflight, the laying of cable and pipelines and other international lawful procedures related to the use of the sea for such purposes."

Correspondingly, the Territorial Sea and Exclusive Economic Zone Act of 1989[160] of Tanzania states in Article 9(1) states that in the EEZ, the United Republic of Tanzania enjoys "sovereign rights for the purpose of exploring and exploiting, conserving and managing the natural resources, whether living or non-living, of the waters superjacent to the seabed and its subsoil, and with regard to other activities for the economic exploration and exploitation of the zone." The same Article also notes, in para. 2, that the Republic has jurisdiction regarding the establishment and use of artificial islands, installations and structures, as well as over scientific research and the protection and preservation of the marine environment. Furthermore, Article 11 states that the United Republic recognizes in its EEZ "the rights of other states, whether coastal or land-locked, the freedom of navigation and overflight, the laying of cables and pipelines and other uses of the sea relating to navigation and communication." Other coastal states have implemented similar provisions in their domestic and EEZ proclamations.[161] This notion indicates that the EEZ is viewed as a practical maritime area in which coastal states and third states enjoy rights and have certain duties toward each other. Such practice is compatible with the provision contained in Article 55 of the LOS Convention. In essence, the *sui generis* nature of the EEZ is supported by state practice.

Delimitation of the EEZ between Adjacent and Opposite States

The issue of delimitation of the EEZ between states with adjacent or opposite coasts was a central point of discussion at UNCLOS III.[162] Debates centered on whether boundaries should be implemented in accordance with the median or equidistance line or according to the principles of equity and special

160 "The Territorial Sea and Exclusive Economic Zone Act of Tanzania, 1989," Article 9(1).

161 These include the claims of the following states: Antigua, Barbados, Burma, Cambodia, Cape Verde, Comoros, Cuba, Djibouti, Dominica, Dominican Republic, Egypt, Republic of Equatorial Guinea, Fiji, Gabon, Grenada, Guatemala, Guinea Bissau, Guyana, Honduras, India, Indonesia, Ivory Coast, Kenya, Kiribati, The Democratic People's Republic of Korea, Malaysia, Mauritania, Mexico, Morocco, Norway, Oman, Pakistan, Philippines, Portugal, Seychelles, Solomon Islands, Spain, Suriname, Thailand, Trinidad and Tobago, Tuvalu, the United States, Vanuatu, Venezuela, and Western Samoa.

162 See Bernard H. Oxman, "The Third United Nations Conference on the Law of the Sea: The Tenth Session, 1981," *AJIL* 76 (1981): 14–15; Hungdah Chiu, "Some Problems Concerning the Application of the Maritime Boundary Delimitation Provisions of the 1982 United Nations Convention on the Law of the Sea," *Maryland Journal of International Law* 9, no. 1 (1985): 1–19.

circumstances.[163] Because of a lack of resolution to the issue, the Convention's text that relates to this problem is vague and provides very little guidance.[164] The provision contained in Article 74(1) pertaining to the delimitation of the EEZ, which bears a striking resemblance to Article 83(1) provisions on the delimitation of the continental shelf, provides that "The delimitation of the exclusive economic zone between states with opposite or adjacent coasts shall be effected by agreement on the basis of international law, as referred to in Article 38 of the Statute of the International Court of Justice, in order to achieve an equitable solution." In this context, the process of delimitation of the EEZ and the continental shelf involves three important principles: agreement, compatibility with international law, and an equitable resolution.

State practice varies when it comes to the delimitation of the EEZ. Many national legislative acts and EEZ proclamations concerning the issue of adjacent or opposite states and maritime boundaries support the notion that these problems should be remedied by mutual agreement. Although the issue is in the resolution stages, the boundary must not exceed the median or equidistance line from the nearest point from which the width of the territorial sea is measured. This is logical for countries where the sea areas between them are less than four hundred miles. The provision of para. 3 of Article 7 of the Territorial Sea and Exclusive Zone Act of the United Republic of Tanzania of 1989[165] states that, where the median line between the Republic and any adjacent or opposite state is less than two-hundred miles from the baselines, "the outer boundary limit of the zone shall be fixed by agreement between the United Republic and that other of other states, but where there is no such agreement, the outer boundary limit shall be the medium line." An identical provision is included in Icelandic Law No. 41 concerning the Territorial Sea, the Economic Zone, and the continental shelf,[166] the Maritime Boundary Act No. 10 of 1977 of Guyana,[167] and the 1978 Act No. 20 of Grenada.[168] However, such a provision is enumerated in only a few domestic EEZ proclamations.

In some instances, domestic EEZ legislation does not refer to agreements.[169] The LOS Convention mandates delimitation by agreement in accordance with

---

163 Chiu, *ibid.*, 69.

164 Charney, "The Exclusive Economic Zone and Public International Law," 243.

165 "The Territorial Sea and Exclusive Economic Zone Act of Tanzania, 1989," Article 7(3).

166 Maritime Zones Act, 1976, Article 7 (1), in Smith, *Exclusive Economic Zone Claims*, 213.

167 Law No. 41 of June 1979, Part II Article 3, in Smith, *Exclusive Economic Zone Claims*, 209.

168 For the text, see Smith, *Exclusive Economic Zone Claims*, 176.

169 For example, the national legislation of New Zealand, Norway, and Spain.

the principles of international law. Hence, any domestic legislation that does not provide for EEZ boundaries delimitation by agreement or departs from the mandate of the LOS Convention also deviates from the general acceptable principles of international law. In regard to comparable claims, the ICJ has expressed the view that, in accordance with the fundamental guidelines of international law and of *opinion juris,* delimitation of boundaries should be made by agreement between the parties concerned according to the principles of equity and considering all relevant circumstances.[170]

In other cases, only delimitation by agreement is provided in domestic legislation without referring to the median/equidistance-line principle.[171] Yet, the practice of certain states vacillates. The United States, for instance, has not subscribed to the strict rule of boundary delimitation by legislative act or by state practice. Instead, to comply with the principle of equity, it has developed a position based on specific circumstances surrounding boundary issues. Thus, it argued against the application of equidistance in the *Gulf of Maine Area Case* with Canada before the ICJ,[172] but applied equidistance in its agreement to resolve the boundary issue with Mexico.[173] Furthermore, a number of domestic enactments has failed to reference the question of delimitation of boundaries at all.[174] In conclusion, with regard to EEZs delimitation, state practice is neither homogeneous nor stabilized.

The Basic Rights and Jurisdiction of Coastal States in the EEZ

According to the tenets of the LOS Convention, coastal states have sovereign rights over the natural resources of the zone and jurisdiction with respect to the establishment and use of artificial islands, installations and structures,

---

[170] See, for instance, "North Sea Continental Shelf Cases," 47 and 54; "Case Concerning Delimitation of the Maritime Boundary in the Gulf of Maine Area," 299–300; also Dixon, *Textbook on International Law,* 181.

[171] See, for example, Territorial Waters and Maritime Zones Act, 1976, Article 6, in Smith, *Exclusive Economic Zone Claims,* 357.

[172] "Case Concerning Delimitation of the Maritime Boundary in the Gulf of Maine Area"; also Mark B. Feldman and David A. Colson, "The Maritime Boundaries of the United States," *AJIL* 75 (1981): 754–56.

[173] *Ibid.,* 743–45. The United States favored equidistance in the three boundary disputes with Canada on the West Coast and the Arctic, *ibid.,* 750.

[174] For example, Chilean Law No. 18.565 of October 13, 1986 Amending the Civil Code with Regard to Maritime Space, *Law of the Sea Bulletin,* no. 5 (1985): 28; Mauritanian Ordinance 88–120 of August 31, 1988, *ibid.,* 34.

marine research, and the protection and preservation of the marine environment in the EEZ.[175]

The Rights of Coastal States Under Article 56 Paragraph 1(a)

When it comes to rights, Article 56(1)(a) of the LOS Convention states that, in the EEZ, the coastal state enjoys "sovereign rights" for the purpose of exploring and exploiting, conserving and managing the natural resources found in the zone and with regard to other activities for additional economic exploitation and exploration of the zone such as the production of energy from the water, currents, and winds. Concerning the rights contained in Article 56, para. (1)(a), the coastal state's sovereign rights in the EEZ is vividly enumerated and enjoys widespread consensus among the nations of the international community. Virtually all states that claim rights to an EEZ have included this fundamental concept in the text of their national legislation.[176] Indeed, wording in the various domestic legislative acts vary little when they are compared with the corresponding provision of the LOS Convention, but this may be coincidental.[177]

Furthermore, the notion that coastal states have sovereign rights in the EEZ over the natural resources of the zone is contained in various agreements. For example, Article 64 of the Fourth ACP-EEC Convention of Lomé of December 15, 1989, states that the community and the African, Caribbean, and Pacific states recognize the sovereign rights of coastal states for the expressed purpose of exploring, exploiting, conserving, and managing the fishery resources of their respective EEZs.[178] Likewise, the preamble of the Niue Treaty on Cooperation in Fisheries Surveillance and Law Enforcement in the South Pacific Region, which was concluded on July 9, 1992 provides that "in accordance with international law as expressed in the United Nations Convention on the Law of the Sea, coastal states have sovereign rights for the purpose of explor-

---

175 "The Law of the Sea Convention," Article 56 paras. 1(a) and (b).

176 Smith, *Exclusive Economic Zone Claims,* 35–73 Table 7 column titled "Natural Resources."

177 Paolillo, "The Exclusive Economic Zone in Latin American Practice and Legislation," 107. The words used include, among others, *sovereign powers* and *exclusive powers.*

178 "African, Caribbean and Pacific States-European Economic Community: Final Act, Minutes, and Fourth ACP-EEC Convention of Lomé," *ILM* 29 (1990): 783.

ing and exploiting, conserving and managing the fisheries resources of their exclusive economic zones and fisheries zones."[179]

The claim of the Sultanate of Oman is the only state claim that expressly mentions sovereignty. The Royal Decree No. 15/81 of 1981 notes that Oman "shall have all sovereignty of the EEZ for the purposes of exploring and developing its aquatic and other wealth."[180] Sovereignty for a state is defined as "having full and exclusive authority within its jurisdiction" to the exclusion of other states.[181] Hence, that the above provision highlights sovereignty that pertains to specific economic rights means that the range of the claim is limited. In essence, Oman's claims are more of a functional claim than it is a claim of sovereignty over the zone itself.

The Rights of Coastal States Under Article 56(1)(b)

The other rights prescribed by Article 56(1)(b) are strictly jurisdictional rather than sovereign in nature.[182] These jurisdictional rights specifically pertain to artificial islands and installations, and structure, the full regime of which is explained in Article 60; marine scientific research, which is stipulated in Part XIII of the LOS Convention, particularly Articles 246–54; and the preservation of the marine environment, which is expressed in Article 208, 210, 211, 214, 216, and 220 of Part XII.

An analysis of the provisions pertaining to the rights of coastal states as they relate to domestic legislation establishing EEZs indicates that most EEZ claimant states have often asserted certain other jurisdictional rights in the EEZ. In this context, a number of legislative acts has built on specific claims involving the jurisdictional rights of coastal states over artificial islands, installations, and structures in the EEZ, which corresponds with the provision contained in Article 56(1)(b) of the LOS Convention. Almost seventy national legislative acts have

---

179 For the text, see "Niue Treaty on Cooperation in Fisheries Surveillance and Law Enforcement in the South Pacific Region," *ILM* 32 (1993): 136; similar provisions are found in the preamble of "Treaty on Fisheries between the Government of Certain Pacific Island States and the Government of the United States of America, April 2, 1987," *ILM* 26 (1987): 1048; "Convention Relative au Développement Régional des Pêches dans le Golf de Guinée, 2 Juin 1984," *RGDIP* 91 (1987): 1115 Article 2; "Accord Cadre de Coopération en Matière de Pèche entre le Gouvernement de la République Algérienne Démocratique et Populaire et le Gouvernement de la République Islamique de Mauritanie, 1988," *JORADP,* No. 6 (1988): 149 preamble.

180 Smith, *Exclusive Economic Zone Claims,* 355 Article 4.

181 Eelco Nicolaas van Kleffens, "Sovereignty in International Law," *RCADI* 82 (1953): 84.

182 See Dixon, *Textbook on International Law,* note 145.

addressed this type of claim.[183] The states that mandated this type of legislation include Bulgaria,[184] the Dominican Republic,[185] India,[186] Jamaica,[187] Kenya,[188] Malaysia,[189] Mexico,[190] Nigeria,[191] Sweden,[192] Suriname,[193] Tanzania,[194] the United States,[195] and Venezuela.[196] For example, the Bulgaria Decree No. 77 of January 7, 1987 states in Article 2(2) that in the EEZ, the Republic of Bulgaria has jurisdiction over "the establishment and use of artificial islands, installations and structures." Identical provisions have been implemented through the domestic legislation of various other coastal states.[197]

On the other hand, some state legislation has claimed jurisdiction not only over artificial islands, installations, and structures, but also over devices for economic development. These states include Burma, India, Kenya, Mauritania, Pakistan, Sri Lanka, and Vanuatu. It is important to note that, unlike the 1958 Convention on the Continental Shelf,[198] neither Article 56 nor Article 60

---

183 Smith, *Exclusive Economic Zone Claims,* 35–37 Table 7, column titled "Artificial Islands."

184 Decree No. 77 of 1987, *Official Records* 2 (1994).

185 Law on the Territorial Sea, Contiguous Zone, Exclusive Economic Zone, and Continental Shelf, April 1, 1977, in Smith, *Exclusive Economic Zone Claims,* 119.

186 Brown, *The International Law of the Sea,* 229,

187 "Jamaica's Exclusive Economic Zone Act," 28.

188 Presidential Proclamation of February 28, 1979, in Smith, *Exclusive Economic Zone Claims,* 243.

189 Exclusive Economic Zone Bill, 1984, in *ibid.,* 259 part II Article 3(1).

190 "Law Concerning Maritime Zones, December 20, 1985," *ILM,* 25 (1986): 889 Article 6.

191 Exclusive Economic Zone of Nigeria, Decree No. 28 of 5 October 1978, Section 3(1)(a), National Legislations – DOALOS/OLA-United Nations.

192 Sweden's Act on Sweden's Economic Zone, December 31, 1992, Article 5.

193 Act No. 32 of 1978, in Smith, *Exclusive Economic Zone Claims,* 441.

194 "The Territorial Sea and Exclusive Economic Zone Act of Tanzania, 1989."

195 Brown, *The International Law of the Sea,* 229.

196 Act Establishing an Exclusive Economic Zone along the Coasts of the Mainland and Island of the Republic of Venezuela, Smith, *Exclusive Economic Zone Claims,* 477.

197 For instance, the legislation of Antigua and Barbuda, Cambodia, Comoros, Cuba, Dominica, Egypt, Iceland, Indonesia, Morocco, Nigeria, Trinidad and Tobago, the United Arab Emirates, and Venezuela.

198 McDorman, "Stateless Fishing Vessels, International Law and the UN High Seas Fisheries Conference," Article 5.

of the LOS Convention refers to "devices,"[199] a term used in other portions of the LOS Convention.[200] Thus, all domestic legislations listing such objects that fall under the coastal state's authority have exceeded what is allowed by the guidelines of the LOS Convention.

Furthermore, a large majority of states that claim an EEZ have already explicitly or implicitly asserted authority over scientific-research activities in their EEZ. Of those states that made claims of an EEZ, over sixty state legislative measures have made a claim over scientific-research activities.[201] Examples of states that implemented these jurisdictional assertions include Antigua and Barbuda, Barbados, Colombia, Dominica, Fiji, Grenada, Honduras, Iceland, Indonesia, Malaysia, Mexico, Norway, Philippines, Portugal, and Western Samoa,[202] with the United States,[203] France,[204] and Spain[205] being notable exceptions.

A vast majority of these domestic legislative acts claimed only *jurisdiction* regarding this matter, essentially following the provisions of Article 6 of the LOS Convention. However, other states asserted *exclusive jurisdiction* in their domestic legislation rather than merely mentioning the term *jurisdiction*, as provided for in Article 56 and 246 of the LOS Convention.[206] Examples of these types of claims can be found in the legislative acts of Burma, Guatemala, Guy-

---

199 The term "installations" is not new in the domain of the law of the sea. It was incorporated in Article 71 of the ILC Draft Articles and later in Article 5 para. 2 of the 1958 Convention on the Continental Shelf. Additionally, the same article speaks of other "devices" necessary for the exploration and exploitation of the continental shelf. The two terms were not defined in the Convention. However, the introduction of the term "devices" in Article 71 of the ILC Draft Articles was a Dutch proposal, based on the consideration that the term "installations" refers to fixed installations used in the exploration and exploitation of the natural resources of the continental shelf, whereas the term "devices" was deemed to refer to certain other objects like mobile drilling rigs. For more information, see Paul Peters, Alfred H. A. Soons, and Lucie A. Zima, "Removal of Installations in the Exclusive Economic Zone," *NYIL* 15 (1984): 171.

200 "The Law of the Sea Convention," Part XI the Area, Article 145(a); Part XII Protection and Preservation of the Marine Environment, Article 194(3)(c)(d); and Part XIV Development and Transfer of Marine Technology, Article 274(b).

201 Smith, *Exclusive Economic Zone Claims*, 35–37, Table 7, column titled "Scientific Research."

202 Juda, "The Exclusive Economic Zone," 29, Table 7.

203 Presidential Proclamation No. 5030, in Smith, *Exclusive Economic Zone Claims*, 467.

204 See Law No. 76-655 of July 16, 1976 pertaining to the Economic Zone off the Coasts of the Territory of the Republic, in Smith, *Exclusive Economic Zone Claims*, 147.

205 Law no. 15-1978, Article 1, in Smith, *Exclusive Economic Zone Claims*, 425.

206 Juda, "The Exclusive Economic Zone," 29 Table 7(A).

ana, India, Kenya, Mauritius, Pakistan, Sri-Lanka, and Vietnam.[207] Why the term *exclusive jurisdiction* is used is unknown, but such wording likely has meaning that transcends the normal meaning of the terms.[208]

Additionally, in Article 56(1)(b)(iii) of the LOS Convention, the coastal state can exercise jurisdiction, under relevant provisions, when it comes to the protection and preservation of the marine environment in the EEZ. An overview of domestic legislation related to creating EEZs shows that a majority of them contained a specific claim regarding the protection of the marine environment in the zone.[209] Over eighty states asserted these types of claims.[210] Of these eighty claims, at least sixty-nine believed the coastal state has jurisdiction[211] to implement these claims, which corresponds with the principles explicitly defined in the LOS Convention and other instruments.[212] However, very few enacted detailed provisions that would facilitate the implementation of Article 207 through 222 of the LOS Convention, which mandates states to design and enforce appropriate laws and regulations.[213]

Several domestic claims have asserted *exclusive jurisdiction* over the protection of the environment in the EEZ, which exceeds the terminology of the LOS Convention, which grants coastal states *jurisdiction* only with regard to the protection and preservation of the marine environment. For example, Colombian Law No. 10 of August 4, 1978 states in Article 8 that Colombia "shall also exercise exclusive jurisdiction for … the preservation of the marine environment."[214] Similar guidelines were included in the national legislation of Burma,[215] Guyana,[216] India,[217] Mauritius,[218] Seychelles,[219] and Vanuatu.[220]

---

207 *Ibid.*, (B).

208 *Ibid.*, 28–29.

209 Charney, "The Exclusive Economic Zone and Public International Law," 253; Smith, *Exclusive Economic Zone Claims*, 38.

210 Smith, *ibid.*, 35–37, column entitled "Protection of Environment"; also "Jamaica's Exclusive Economic Zone Act," para. 4; the Mexican "Law Concerning Maritime Zones," Article 6; "Sweden's Act on Economic Zone," Article 2; and United Kingdom of Great Britain and Northern Ireland, Pitcairn, Henderson, Ducie and Oeno Island, Proclamation No. 1, 1992, "South Georgia and the South Sandwich Islands Proclamation No. 1 of 1993," Article 3.

211 Smith, *Exclusive Economic Zone Claims*.

212 *Ibid.*, 38.

213 UN Division for Ocean Affairs and the Law of the Sea. *Practice of States*.

214 Law No. 10 August 4, 1978 Establishing Regulation on the Territorial Sea, Exclusive Economic Zone and Continental Shelf, and Other Provisions, in Smith, *Exclusive Economic Zone Claims*, 99 Article 8.

215 Territorial Sea and Maritime Zones Law, April 9, 1977, Article 18(d), in *ibid.*, 85.

However, many of these claims were made during the height of UNCLOS III deliberations, and likely were influenced by an earlier draft of UNCLOS III that grants *exclusive jurisdiction* concerning this matter.[221] The terminology was later changed to reflect the notion that the coastal state and the flag state can share responsibility for enforcing rules that are implemented to reduce and prevent marine pollution in the EEZ.

Furthermore, some European states, which had earlier proclaimed EFZs, made their intention clear that their objective was to increase jurisdiction over environmental protection that corresponds with the LOS Convention. In this context, the Paris Ministerial Declaration on the Coordinated Extension of Jurisdiction in the North Sea, formulated in September 1992, notes that the states concerned should

> undertake to initiate the process either of establishing exclusive economic zones in areas of the North Sea where they do not exist for the purpose of protecting and preserving the marine environment or of increasing coastal state jurisdiction for that purpose, in accordance with international law and without going beyond the scope of the provisions of the United Nations Convention on the Law of the Sea.[222]

An overview of domestic legislation seems to suggest that when EEZ claimant states established EEZs, they generally followed the traditional rights granted to them in Article 56 of the LOS Convention. However, certain domestic laws pertaining to the EEZ involved asserting jurisdictional claims that differ from the text of the LOS Convention. In some instances, those differences may explain why some domestic laws relating to the EEZ were implemented before the texts of UNCLOS III were completely formulated.[223]

Nevertheless, virtually all EEZ domestic legislation emphasized the coastal state's various rights and excluded any mention of the duties placed on them by the provisions of Article 56(2). On this central issue, one noted commenta-

---

216 Act No. 10 of 1977, Article 15, in *ibid.*, 202

217 Maritime Zones Act, 1976, Part II Article 3, in *ibid.*, 209.

218 Act No. 13 of 1977, Article 6, in *ibid.*, 288.

219 Act No. 15 of 1977, Article 6(1), in *ibid.*, 407.

220 Maritime Zones Act No. 23 of 1981, Article 9(1), in *ibid.*, 471.

221 Smith, *Exclusive Economic Zone Claims*, 38.

222 For the full text, see *Law of the Sea Bulletin*, no. 23 (1993): 65–66.

223 Paolillo, "The Exclusive Economic Zone in Latin American Practice and Legislation," 107.

tor stated that there exists "almost universal elimination of reference to 'duties' in the 'catch-all' phrase at the end of the enumeration of coastal states' rights over the EEZ."[224] In addition to this, a Food and Agriculture Organization of the United Nations (FAO) study identified the term *duties* as only being used in the national legislation of Antigua and Barbuda, Djibouti, Dominica, Guatemala, and Kenya.[225]

The Fundamental Rights of States in Foreign EEZs

As acknowledged earlier, under customary international law and under the Convention on the High Seas,[226] the freedom of navigation, overflight, and laying of submarine cables and pipelines in the high seas were available to ships and aircrafts of all nations under the criterion of *reasonable use* and in consideration of the legitimate rights of other high seas users. Article 58 of the LOS Convention recognizes these freedoms in the EEZ. Under Article 56(2), coastal states must have due regard for the rights and duties of third states, treating them in a manner that corresponds to the provisions of the Convention. A complementary due regard obligation *vis-à-vis* the coastal state is imposed on third states under Article 58(3). This due-regard requirement is described by one leading expert as a Latinized version[227] of the reasonable-regard mandate stipulated in Article 2 of the 1958 Convention on the High Seas.

On the national level, the legislative action of a large number of states has expressly acknowledged freedom of navigation and overflight by foreign ships and aircrafts through or over the EEZ. For example, Article 3 of the Royal Proclamation of Thailand[228] states that, in the EEZ, the freedoms of navigation and overflight and of laying of submarine cables and pipelines should be governed according to the standards of international law. Furthermore, in an announcement made in 1993 by the Thai Foreign Minister,[229] Thailand acknowledges that the freedom of navigation in the EEZ of foreign states is apart from customary international law and codified by the LOS Convention, and declared it was not bound by laws and regulations that restrict this freedom. Similarly, the 1978 Act of Venezuela Establishing an Exclusive Economic Zone Along the Coasts of the

---

224 Gerald K. Moore, *Coastal State Requirements for Foreign Fishing,* FAO Legislative Study No. 21, Rev. 2 (Rome: FAO, 1985), 4–6.
225 *Ibid.*
226 See "Convention on the Continental Shelf," Preamble.
227 Clingan, "Freedom of Navigation in Post-UNCLOS III Environment," 116–19.
228 Smith, *Exclusive Economic Zone Claims.*
229 Document A/48/90, cited in UN Division for Ocean Affairs and the Law of the Sea. *Practice of States,* 72.

Mainland and Islands of the Republic notes that "other states, whether coastal or land-locked, shall enjoy, subject to the relevant provisions of the present Act, the freedoms of navigation and overflight ... and other internationally lawful uses of the sea associated with navigation and communication."[230] This provision compares favorably with the guidelines of the LOS Convention. Similar provisions have found their way into the legislative agenda of Barbados,[231] Bulgaria,[232] Burma,[233] Dominican Republic,[234] Grenada,[235] Guatemala,[236] Indonesia,[237] the Ivory Coast,[238] Jamaica, Morocco,[239] Philippines,[240] Sao Tome and Principe,[241] Spain,[242] Suriname,[243] Sweden,[244] Thailand,[245] Trinidad and Tobago,[246] Tanzania,[247] and the United States.[248]

In contrast, various other EEZ claims did not make reference to the freedoms of navigation and overflight. Representative of these claims can be found in the claims of Bangladesh, Cape Verde, Colombia, Comoros, Cooks Islands, France, Guinea Bissau, Haiti, Iceland, Mozambique, New Zealand, Sri Lanka, Togo, and Vietnam.[249] Such omissions have been viewed by some commentators as indi-

---

230 The Act of Venezuela Establishing an Exclusive Economic Zone Along the Coasts of the Mainland and Islands of the Republic, 1978.

231 Maritime Boundaries and Jurisdiction Act, 1978, in Smith, *Exclusive Economic Zone Claims,* 73 Article 7.

232 United Nations, *The Law of the Sea: Current Developments in State Practice,* 2–18.

233 Territorial Sea and Maritime Zones Law, Article 18(d), April 9, 1979, in Smith, *Exclusive Economic Zone Claims,* 85.

234 Law No. 573 of 1977, Article 4, *ibid.*, 119.

235 *Ibid.*, 176.

236 Guatemala's Decree No. 20/76 of July 1, 1976, *ibid.*, 185.

237 Act No. 5 of 1983, chapter II Article 2, *ibid.*, 228.

238 Act No. 77-926, Article 2, *ibid.*, 241.

239 Law No. 1-81 of 1981, Article 1, *ibid.*, 303.

240 Presidential Decree No. 1599 of July 11, 1979, in Smith, *Exclusive Economic Zone Claims,* 369 Section 4.

241 Decree Law No. 15-78 of 1978, Article 1, *ibid.*, 405.

242 Law No. 15-1978, Article 1, *ibid.*, 425.

243 Suriname, Law No. 26 of 1978, in *ibid.*, 433, Article 5.

244 "Sweden's Act on Sweden's Economic Zone, December 3, 1992," Article 10.

245 Thailand's Royal Proclamation of February 23, 1981, Article 3, in Smith, *Exclusive Economic Zone Claims,* 437.

246 Trinidad, Ministry of Foreign Affairs Notice No. 500 of 1983 of May 27, 1983, in *ibid.*, 456.

247 Tanzania, "The Territorial Sea and Exclusive Economic Zone Act of Tanzania, 1989."

248 United States, Presidential Proclamation No. 5030, in Smith, *Exclusive Economic Zone Claims,* 467.

249 Juda, "The Exclusive Economic Zone," 34(B).

cating a refusal to acknowledge such freedoms or recognize such rights as being an integral part of the EEZ regime.[250] However, this view seems to be problematic because all state legislations that do not contain a reference to the freedom of navigation and overflight in the EEZ asserted, at UNCLOS III, that they favor retaining these freedoms in the EEZ. For instance, during the First Substantive Session, Caracas 1974, the Bangladesh delegate stated that the future EEZ regime should include the statement that "All states should enjoy freedom of navigation and overflight and freedoms to lay submarine cables and pipelines subject to the exercise by the coastal state of its rights as provided in the future Convention."[251] Identical statements were made during this Session by the delegates of Haiti,[252] Malaysia,[253] and Sri Lanka.[254]

This omission should not be taken with a negative connotation on the freedom of navigation and overflight,[255] but should be interpreted as a simple omission that does not change the essence of the EEZ. This viewpoint appears to be supported by the notion that a number of states belonging to the groups mentioned above ratified the LOS Convention,[256] thereby supporting acceptance of the basic freedoms enjoyed by third states in the EEZ.

Some EEZ claims from developing states seem to be problematic. The developing states of Guyana, India, Mauritius, and Pakistan made assertions in their respective domestic legislation that allowed them, in designated areas of the EEZ, to regulate foreign passage through the waters and airspace of the EEZ.[257] For example, Article 7(6) of the Indian act on the Maritime Zone specifies that the government may provide for the regulation of entry and passage through designated areas "by establishment of fairways, sealanes, traffic separations schemes or any other mode of ensuring freedom of navigation which

---

250 See, for example, Wolfrum, "The Emerging Customary Law of Marine Zones," 140.

251 *Official Records* 3 (1975): 182.

252 *Ibid.*, 215.

253 *Ibid.*, 198.

254 *Ibid.*, 186.

255 Tullio Scovazzi, "Coastal State Practice in the Exclusive Economic Zone: The Right of Foreign States to Use this Zone," in *New Developments in Marine Science and Technology: Economic, Legal, and Political Aspects of Change, Proceedings of the Twentieth Annual Conference 1988,* ed. Lewis M. Alexander, Scott Allen, and Lynne Carter Hanson (Honolulu: Law of the Sea Institute, University of Hawaii, 1989), 312–13.

256 See Appendix A.

257 Guyana, Maritime Boundaries Act No. 10, Article 18 paras. (a) and (b)(vi); India, Territorial Water, Continental Shelf, Exclusive Economic Zone, and other Maritime Zones Act, Article 7(b); Mauritius, the Maritime Zones Act, 1977, Article 9(a) and (b)(vi); Pakistan Territorial Waters and Maritime Zones Act, 1976, Article, 6(a) and (b)(vi).

is not prejudicial to the interests of India."[258] Comparable provisions grace the legislative texts of Guyana, Mauritius, and Pakistan.[259] Such claims extend beyond the rights granted to coastal states in the territorial sea, in which, under Article 22 of the LOS Convention, traffic separation stratagems may be implemented, but several subjects are to be considered, including consideration of recommendations of the competent global organization and other customary approaches used for international navigation. The domestic legislation of those states that applied to establish an EEZ do not consider these factors, but rather emphasize the state's discretion in these matters. The LOS Convention does not support such assertions.

In addition to the asserted claims mentioned above, three other states asserted rights that significantly impacted navigation. For example, Section 1 of Law No. 32/76 of the Maldives provide that "ships of all states shall enjoy the right of innocent passage through the ... exclusive economic zone of the Republic of the Maldives."[260] Innocent passage is a practice that relates to the territorial sea alone and its use in connection with the EEZ obscures the distinction between these two zones. The same law further provides that Maldives prohibits, without its prior approval, any entry of foreign fishing vessels into its EEZ.[261] The motivating factor that lies behind this provision seems to be the protection of the EEZ fisheries from unauthorized foreign fishing activities. Regardless, the claim has no foundation in the LOS Convention.

A number of domestic laws, in accordance with Article 58 of the LOS Convention, provide for the freedom of laying submarine cables and pipelines.[262] Nonetheless, when it comes to navigation and overflight, the record is not as good. Either the reference to the laying of cables is excluded, even after the freedom of navigation has been agreed,[263] or the national legislation allows for subsequent restriction.[264]

---

258 *Ibid.*

259 *Ibid.*

260 Law No. 32/76 Relating to the Navigation and Passage by Foreign Ships and Aircrafts Through the Airspace, Territorial Waters, and the Economic Zone of the Republic of Maldives, December 5, 1976, in Smith, *Exclusive Economic Zone Claims,* 278, Article 1.

261 *Ibid.*

262 Antigua and Barbuda, the Comoros, Cuba, Djibouti, Dominica, Dominican Republic, Egypt, Fiji, Gabon, Guatemala, Honduras, the Ivory Coast, Kiribati, Mexico, Morocco, Norway, the Philippines, Sao Tome and Principe, the Solomon Islands, Tuvalu, the United States, Venezuela, and Yemen.

263 Portugal, Qatar, Spain, and the United Arab Emirates.

264 Barbados, Cape Verde, St. Lucia, and the Seychelles.

The EEZ Fisheries System in Coastal States Practice

According to the fisheries system provided for in Part V of the LOS Convention, specifically Articles 61 to 73, coastal states are granted sovereign rights over and the responsibility to secure conservation of the living resources in the EEZ and to protect these resources from overexploitation.[265] Management and conservation measures should be implemented to maintain stacks at levels capable of producing maximum sustainable yields predicated on relevant environmental and economic factors, and considering fishing patterns; the interdependence of stocks; and compliance with recommended subregional, regional, and international standards. The coastal state is mandated to promote optimum use of those resources,[266] and in this context, determine the allowable catch of fish species in its EEZ[267] and the harvesting capacity.[268] If the coastal state does not have the capacity to harvest the entire allowable catch, other states must have access to any surplus.[269] In selecting these "other states," the coastal state must consider the significance of the living resources of the zone in assessing its own economy, the rights of LLS, the requirements of the developing nations in the region or subregion, and traditional fishing practices.[270]

The Conservation and Management Responsibilities of Coastal States

According to the tenets of the LOS Convention, coastal states are granted sovereign rights over and the responsibility for the conservation, management, and optimum use of the living resources of the EEZ.[271] Article 61 is the essential article that primarily addresses the regulation of conservation. The objective of conservation is to (1) determine the total allowable catch (TAC),[272] (2) protect against overexploitation of the living resources,[273] (3) maintain or restore harvested species at levels that can produce the maxi-

---

265 "The Law of the Sea Convention," Articles 56 and 61.

266 *Ibid.*, Article 62(1).

267 *Ibid.*, Article 61(1).

268 *Ibid.*, Article 62(2).

269 *Ibid.*

270 *Ibid.*

271 *Ibid.*, Articles 56(1)(a), 61, and 62.

272 *Ibid.*, Article 61(1).

273 *Ibid.*, para. 2.

mum sustainable yield (MSY),[274] and (4) maintain associated or dependent species above levels that facilitate their reproduction.[275]

Analyzing EEZ legislation, proclamations, and fisheries regulations of EFZ claimant states that may be relevant[276] indicates, on the whole, that reference to conservation and management duties of the coastal state with regard to living resources found in the asserted two-hundred-mile zone is a common occurrence in the national legislations of a great number of claimant states.[277] Some legislative acts and proclamations contain detailed guidelines specifying the goals of management and conservation of living resources in terms that correlate with the provisions of UNCLOS III.[278] The Mexican legislation,[279] for example, states that the objective of management and conservation measures is to protect the living resources of the EEZ from overexploitation.[280] The legislation mandates that the Federal Executive Branch implement proper management and conservation measures.[281] The relevant Portuguese law[282] provides that the government shall enact and enforce regulation of fishing in the EEZ, including the TAC and the MSY for fisheries as a whole, and protect, conserve, and restore the living resources of the EEZ.[283]

The EEZ Proclamation[284] of the United States acknowledges the responsibility of the United States to manage and conserve the living resources of the EEZ, but does not go into great detail about conservation measures in the zone. The Fishery Conservative and Management Act of 1976[285] is the seminal measure that covers U.S. actions in the two-hundred-mile zone. Conservation

---

[274] *Ibid.,* para. 3.

[275] *Ibid.,* para. 4.

[276] *Ibid., see* Section II, entitled "Fishing Zones Trends," 176–84.

[277] Barbara Kwiatkowska, "Conservation and Optimum Utilization of Living Resources," in *The Law of the Sea: What Lies Ahead?* ed. Thomas A. Clingan (Honolulu: Law of the Sea Institute, University of Hawaii, 1989), 248.

[278] It is important to remember that the main conservation objectives expressed in Article 61 of the LOS Convention received widespread support at UNCLOS III and was unaltered when they were included in the 1975 ISNT. See Attard, *The Exclusive Economic Zone in International Law,* 154.

[279] Amendment to Article 27 of the Constitution.

[280] *Ibid.,* Article 6(1).

[281] *Ibid.,* (2).

[282] Portuguese Law No. 33/77 of May 28, 1977, Article 1(1), in Smith, *Exclusive Economic Zone Claims,* 371.

[283] *Ibid.,* Article 5.

[284] Presidential Proclamation No. 5030, *ibid.,* 467.

[285] United States, *Fishery Conservation and Management Act,* 1976.

and management legislation, by definition, requires states to restore or maintain fishing resources and protect the marine environment, to ensure a steady supply of food, and to avoid any long-term adverse effects to the resources in the EEZ.[286] The optimum yield ratio is determined by the MSY, qualified by relevant economic and socioecological factors.[287] A large number of EFZ and EEZ claims have implemented the objectives expressed in UNCLOS III.[288]

In contrast, various states, most of them developing states, have referred to the duty to manage and conserve the living resources of the EEZ in their domestic legislation, but such references are considered general in nature and do correspond to the precise language of Article 61 and 62 of the LOS Convention.[289] Bangladesh,[290] Malaysia,[291] and Tuvalu[292] are prominent members of this group.

In many cases, without the aid of a reliable factual basis, it is difficult to establish sound fisheries management and conservation strategies.[293] Authoritative scientific information on fish stocks, technology, and professionally trained personnel are essential for good fishery management and development.[294] Complicated and prompt scientific computations and research to satisfy the requirements provided in Article 61, paras. 1, 2, 3, and 4 are normally beyond the capacity of a vast number of developing coastal states. Thus, the reason a significant number of developing states failed to adopt the LOS Convention's specific objectives in their national legislation may be be-

---

286 *Ibid.*, Section 3(18).

287 *Ibid.*, Section 3(18)(B); also Gerald K. Moore, "National Legislation for the Management of Fisheries under Extended Coastal State Jurisdiction," *JMLC* 11 (1980): 159.

288 For instance, "Australian Fisheries Amendment Act, 1978," in *New Direction in the Law of the Sea: Documents,* ed. Robin Churchill, Myron H. Nordquist, and S. Houston Lay, vol. 10 (Dobbs Ferry, NY: Oceana, 1973), 19, Article 6; Fiji's Marine Space Act, 1978, in Smith, *Exclusive Economic Zone Claims,* 129, Article 2; the Japanese Law No. 31, 1977, Article 2(3); the Pakistan Territorial Waters and Maritime Zones Act, 1976, section 6; Act No. 24 of 1986 of Trinidad and Tobago, in "The Law of the Sea: Current Development in State Practice," in *Law of the Sea: Current Developments in State Practice,* no. 3 (New York: United Nations, 1992), 36–47.

289 See E. E. E. Mtango and Friedl Weiss, "The Exclusive Economic Zone and Tanzania: Considerations of a Developing Country," *ODIL* 14 (1984): 31–30.

290 Territorial Waters and Maritime Zones Act, 1974, in Smith, *Exclusive Economic Zone Claims,* 63, Article 6.

291 Malaysia, Exclusive Economic Zone Bill, 1984, Article 9, in *ibid.*, 259.

292 Marine Zone Ordinance, 1983, in Smith, *Exclusive Economic Zone Claims,* 459, Article 10.

293 H. S. Kibola, "A Note on Africa and the Exclusive Economic Zone," *ODIL,* 16 (1986): 377.

294 *Ibid.*

cause they do not have the technological knowledge to obtain the scientific evidence directed under the provisions of the LOS Convention.[295]

Furthermore, a third group of EEZ laws has remained silent when it comes to the duty to conserve resources and to implement the specific management and conservation goals expressed in Articles 61 and 62 of the LOS Convention. States that reflect these types of claims include Cambodia,[296] Costa Rica,[297] Egypt,[298] Equatorial Guinea,[299] Guatemala,[300] Guinea,[301] Guinea Bissau,[302] Ivory Coast,[303] Mozambique,[304] Oman,[305] and Thailand.[306] However, the omission of any reference in this legislation to conservation responsibilities does not mean that these nations do not accept such duties. This is because, for one, the very development of the two-hundred-mile zones has always been closely connected with the notion of conservation.[307] Second, the duty to conserve and the conservation objectives included in Articles 61 and 62 of the LOS Convention receive widespread support at UNCLOS III and this support remained the same since it first appeared in the 1975 ISNT;[308] and third, these who drafted legislation generally used cautionary language that unnecessarily acknowledges their nation's obligations under international law.[309] These legislative drafters usually are concerned with the coastal state's fisheries rights in the asserted zone. In essence, any problem that arises from this issue seems to be a matter of legislative semantics rather than any intent to ignore management and conservative responsibilities.

---

[295] Mtango and Weiss. "The Exclusive Economic Zone and Tanzania."

[296] Decree on the Limits of PRK's Maritime Zones and Continental Shelf, in Smith, *Exclusive Economic Zone Claims*, 91.

[297] Decree No. 5699 of May 20, 1975, in *ibid.*, 101.

[298] Declaration Concerning the Exercise by Egypt of its Rights in the Exclusive Economic Zone, December 10, 1982, in *ibid.*, 124.

[299] Act No. 15/1984 of 12 November 1984, in *ibid.*, 125.

[300] Guatemala's Decree No. 20/76 of July 1, 1976, in *ibid.*, 185.

[301] Decree No. 336/PRG/80, in *ibid.*, 187.

[302] Law No. 3/78, in *ibid.*, 191.

[303] Ivory Coast, Act. No. 77-926, Article 2, in *ibid.*, 241.

[304] Mozambique, Decree No. 31-76 of 1976, Article 2, in *ibid.*, 307.

[305] Royal Decree No. 15/81 of February 20, 1981, in *ibid.*, 355.

[306] Thailand Royal Proclamation of February 23, 1981, in *ibid.*, 437.

[307] Fleischer, "The Exclusive Economic Zone under the Convention Regime and in State Practice," 261.

[308] Attard, *The Exclusive Economic Zone in International Law*, 154.

[309] Moore, "National Legislation for the Management of Fisheries," 260, note 33.

Optimum Use and Foreign Access

As was discussed in Chapter 2,[310] one of the central obligations placed on coastal states is the duty to promote optimum use of the living resources in their EEZ.[311] However, according to Article 62, any activity should not be prejudicial to the obligatory conservation duties found in Article 61. This intent suggests that whatever the level of "optimum" use of its living resources, the exploitation of the EEZ's living resources must not go beyond the prescribed limits set forth in Article 61 (i.e., going beyond the level of MSY, qualified by relevant economic and environmental factors that ensure that fish stocks are protected from overexploitation).

Specific reference to this duty is found in the EFZ and EEZ claims of various states. Examples of these claims can be found in the national laws of Australia, Cuba, Mexico, Malaysia, New Zealand, Papua New Guinea, Fiji, Sao Tome and Principe, and Venezuela.[312] A prime example is Article 6 of the 1978 Act Establishing an Exclusive Economic Zone Along the Coasts of the Mainland and Islands of the Republic of Venezuela.[313] This measure states that "the Republic shall promote the optimum use of the living resources of the exclusive economic zone without prejudice" to the guidelines related to the conservation of the living resources. This provision is identical to the provision located in Article 62 paragraph 1 of the LOS Convention. Australia's legislation asserting a two-hundred-mile fisheries zone compels the Minister of Fisheries to give particular regard to the goal of optimum use of the living resources of

---

310 Chapter 2, Section 1(B)(1)(3).

311 "The Law of the Sea Convention," Article 62, para. 1. Optimum use literally means use that is "best or more favorable." See Dahmani, *The Fisheries Regime of the Exclusive Economic Zone,* 39.

312 "Australian Fisheries Amendment Act, 1978"; Cuba, Decree Law No. 2 of 1977, in Smith, *Exclusive Economic Zone Claims,* 109; Mexico, Law Regulating the Eighth Paragraph of Article 27 of the Constitution Relating to the Exclusive Economic Zone, in Smith, *Exclusive Economic Zone Claims*; New Zealand, Territorial Sea and Exclusive Economic Zone Act of 1977, Smith, *Exclusive Economic Zone Claim*; Papua New Guinea, Fisheries Act of 1977, in Smith, *Exclusive Economic Zone Claims,* 363; Fiji, Marine Space Act of 1977, Smith, *Exclusive Economic Zone Claims*; Sao Tome and Principe, Decree Law No. 15-78 of 1978, Smith, *Exclusive Economic Zone Claims*; Decree of the Presidium of the Supreme Soviet of the USSR on the Economic Zone of the USSR, Smith, *Exclusive Economic Zone Claims*; Venezuela, Act Establishing an Exclusive Economic Zone Along the Coasts of the Mainland and Islands of the Republic of Venezuela, Smith, *Exclusive Economic Zone Claims*; and Malaysia, Exclusive Economic Zone Bill of 1984, Smith, *Exclusive Economic Zone Claims.*

313 *Ibid.*

the Australian fishing zone and to protect the living resources of this zone from overexploitation.[314] Likewise, the Malaysian Exclusive Economic Zone Bill of 1984 places an obligation on the Director General of Fisheries to prepare and continuously upgrade fishery programs that reflect the latest technological and scientific advancements and to ensure that optimum use of fishery resources are compatible with good management practice.[315]

In contrast, a large majority of national laws are completely silent on optimum use as a key objective that should be promoted by the coastal state. However, this silence does not imply that the states in question completely ignore the optimum-use standard that is required of coastal states. This is because, in the first instance, the historical development of the EFZ and EEZ and the negotiations process that took place at UNCLOS III support the notion that all states wanted to improve the global community's socioeconomic development.[316] Second, although national legislation and proclamations that comes from this group do not mention the provision contained in Article 62 paragraph 2 of the LOS Convention, which obligates coastal states to have a harvesting ratio for the entire allowable catch, direct or implied inference to the objective of optimum use of the living resources of the zone is located in various fishery agreements to which these nations are party. In this context, the preamble to the Fishery Agreement between the United Mexican States and the Republic of Cuba of July 26, 1976, states that "considering that the Government of the United Mexican States plans to promote the optimum utilization."[317] Similar language can be found in the Angola/Spain Fishing Agreement of April 6, 1981 as well as in the Mauritania/Spain Fishing Agree-

314 *Ibid.*, Article 6.

315 Mohd Ibrahim Hj Mohamed, "National Management of Malaysian Fisheries," *MP* 15, no. 1 (1991): 10.

316 The preamble to the LOS Convention particularly refers to the desire to promote, "taking due regard for the sovereignty of all states ... the equitable and efficient utilization of their resources." It further states that "the realization of a just and equitable international economic order which take into account the interests and needs of mankind as a whole."

317 United Nations ST/LEG/SER. B/19 (1980): 425.

ment of 1982;[318] third, the Fourth Lome Convention, a treaty concluded between the EEC and the African, Caribbean, and Pacific states in December 1989, obligate the parties "to promote the optimum utilization of fishery resources," of African, Caribbean, and Pacific coastal states.[319] Unless a coastal state has reasonable justification for refusal to establish conservation measures, it is obligated under the principles of customary international law to give due regard to the interests of third states and promote the goal of optimum use of its EEZ fisheries.

When it comes to the rights of third states to conduct fishing activities in foreign EEZs, the LOS Convention grants the coastal state the authority and obligates those states that are party to it to determine the AC of the living resources of its EEZ and to promote the goal of optimum use of its EEZ fisheries. Once a state has determined the AC, it would be required to set its own capacity to harvest these resources. If the state's capacity does not allow it to harvest the entire allowable catch, other states must be given access to the surplus.[320] Nonetheless, the obligation to accommodate third states is not overwhelming. Coastal states have a high level of flexibility when it comes to harvesting the resources of the EEZ. A decision involving granting foreign states access may consider the coastal state's economy and other direct and collateral interests.[321] Furthermore, the dispute-settlement process established by the provisions of the LOS Convention precludes effective review of the coastal state's decision on these issues.[322] Essentially, the LOS Convention

---

318 Angola/Spain Fishing Agreement April 6, 1981, in Boletín Oficial del Estado, No. 34, February 9, 1981, 2916–19, cited by Mfodwo, Tsamenyi, and Blay, "The Exclusive Economic Zone," 456 note 146; "Mauritania/Spain Fishing Agreement," *Industrias Pesqueras* June 1 (1982): 9; also US/Mexico Fisheries Agreement of November 24, 1976, in ST/LEG/SER. B/19 (1980): 430; Spain/US Fisheries Agreement Concerning Fisheries off the United States Coasts 16 February, 1977, in ST/LEG/SER. B/19 (1980): 228. An implied reference to the same principle is found in some other fishery agreements by the inclusion of the factors mentioned in Article 62, para. 3. See for instance, EEC/Denmark (Faroes) Agreement Concerning Fisheries of March 15, 1977 and Brazil/Trinidad and Tobago Shrimp Agreement of February 28, 1975, cited by Mtango and Weiss. "The Exclusive Economic Zone and Tanzania," 7.

319 "African, Caribbean and Pacific States-European Economic Community," 824, Article 58.

320 "The Law of the Sea Convention," Article 62(2).

321 *Ibid.*, para. 3.

322 *Ibid.*, Article 297, para. 3.

grants the coastal state wide discretion when it comes to determining whether to allow third states to fish in its EEZ.[323]

The treatment of national EEZ and EFZ legislation in the provisions of the LOS Convention differ markedly. Some national legislation mirrors the provisions contained in the LOS Convention. For instance, the legislation of Cape Verde, Cuba, Portugal, Sao Tome and Principe, New Zealand, the Cook Islands, Fiji, Niue, and Tonga is drawn very closely to the Convention's guidelines.[324] The Territorial Sea and Exclusive Economic Zone Act of New Zealand, for example, requires the Minister of Fisheries to set the TAC ratio for every fishery in the EEZ and to determine the harvesting capacity of the national fleet and further specifies that the remaining portion constitutes the allowable catch for foreign fishermen.[325] It also grants the Minister the authority to apportion the allowable catch for foreign fishing vessels among third states and establishes criteria that the Minister must consider when making such apportionment.[326] The qualifications, in their entirety, include support for the interests of the states that have traditionally fished in the zone or cooperated with the research and stock identification, or helped with the conservation and management of the resources and the enforcement of New Zealand's laws pertaining to such resources.[327] The list of criteria is not exhaustive. Similar provisions are part of the fisheries legislation of the Federated States of Micronesia, the Marshall Islands, and Palau.[328]

In contrast, a large number of state claims grant foreign access to EFZ or EEZ fisheries under domestic licenses and official permits but omit any mention of the foreign right to fish for any surplus. States that make these types of claims include Barbados, Grenada, Guinea Bissau, Mauritania, Norway, Spain,

---

[323] Burke, "The Law of the Sea Convention Provisions," 93.

[324] Cape Verde, Decree Law No. 126/77 of 1977, in Smith, *Exclusive Economic Zone Claims*, 95; Cuba, Decree Law No. 2 of February 29, 1977, in *ibid.*, 109; Portugal, Law No. 33/77 of May 28, 1977, in *ibid.*, 371; Sao Tome and Principe, Decree Law No. 15-78 of 1978, in *ibid.*, 405; New Zealand, Territorial Sea and Exclusive Economic Zone Act, 1977, in *ibid.*, 309; the Cook Islands, Act No. 16 of November 14, 1977, in *ibid.*, 325; Fiji, Marine Space Act, 1978, in *ibid.*, 129; Niue Territorial Sea and Exclusive Economic Zone Act of 1979, in *ibid.*, 336; Tonga, Act No. 32 of 1978, in *ibid.*, 441.

[325] New Zealand, Territorial Sea and Exclusive Economic Act, 1977, Articles 11, 12, and 13.

[326] *Ibid.*, Article 13.

[327] *Ibid.*, Article 13(2).

[328] Federated States of Micronesia—Title 52 of the Trust Territory Code, Section 15(3); Marshall Islands, Marine Resources Jurisdiction Act of 1978, S. 406; Palau, Public Law 6-7-14 S. 12(3). See The South Pacific Forum Fisheries Agency, *Regional Compendium of Fisheries Legislation (Western Pacific Region)*, vol. 2 (Rome: FAO, 1984), 1–150.

Togo, and Western Samoa.[329] Some commentators have questioned whether access provided by this type of legislation meant access to the surplus or access in general.[330] However, such uncertainty can be excluded, upon further analysis of the practices of these states. This legislation can be interpreted as meaning that access can be granted to the surplus of fish, as directed by the provisions of the LOS Convention. This is because, first, a number of these legislative acts have sought to adopt the obligation of optimum use of the living resources found in the established zone;[331] second, a large number of bilateral instruments concluded by the states in question have added, in their preamble, a direct reference to the work of UNCLOS III or a specific reference to the guidelines contained in Article 62 of the LOS Convention. These fisheries agreements include agreements concluded during the 1980s by Guinea Bissau with the EEC;[332] third, a number of these instruments have referred either to the concept of surplus[333] or to the optimum use of the fishery zone. The Spanish/Angola Agreement of 1980 and the 1982 Fishery Agreement between Mauritania and Spain, for example, referred to the reasonable management and full use of the living resources in their respective EEZs as well as to optimum exploitation of the biological resources located therein.[334]

Furthermore, when it comes to national legislation on the EEZ, some cases have made no reference at all to third-state access to EEZ fisheries. The national legislation of Bangladesh, Burma, Colombia, Comoros, Dominican

---

329 Barbados, Marine Boundaries and Jurisdiction Act 1978, Article 11, in Smith, *Exclusive Economic Zone Claims,* 73; Grenada, Act No. 20, 1978, Article 6, in *ibid.*, 176; Guinea Bissau, Law No. 3/78, Article 4, in *ibid.*, 191; Mauritania, Law 78-043, Article 186, para. 2, in *ibid.*, 281; Norway, Act No. 91 of 1976 para. 4, in *ibid.*, 303; Spain, Law No. 15/1978, Article 3, in *ibid.*, 427; Tonga, Ordinance No. 24 of 1977, Article 4, in *ibid.*, 439; Western Samoa, Exclusive Economic Zone Act of 1977, Act. 5, in *ibid.*, 483.

330 See Vicuña, *The Exclusive Economic Zone,* 157; Wolfrum, "The Emerging Customary Law of Marine Zones," 135.

331 The Act Establishing an Exclusive Economic Zone Along the Coasts of the Mainland and Islands of the Republic of Venezuela, 1978 is representative of this type of obligation.

332 "Accords Passés avec la Guinée Bissau le 27 Février 1980," *OJEC,* No. L. 226 du 29 Aout 1980, 33; "Avec la Guinée," *OJEC,* No. L. 237 du 28 Aout 1983, 15; "Accord Cadre de Coopération en Matière de Pèche," 149.

333 This is the case of Norway/Portugal, Exchange of Notes on Fishing, December 23, 1980 and Norway/Spain, Fisheries Agreement 21 January 1981 cited by Carroz and Savini. "The Practice of Coastal States Regarding Foreign Access to Fishery Resources," 48.

334 Spanish/Angola Fishing Agreement of 1980, April 6, 1981, in *Boletín Oficial del Estado,* No. 34, February 9, 1981, 2916-19; "Mauritania/Spain Fishing Agreement", *Industrias Pesqueras,* June 1, (1982): 9.

Republic, Iceland, India, Indonesia, Malaysia, Nigeria, and Thailand[335] is representative of these types of legislative acts. However, this does not suggest that the states in question comprehensively limited the access of foreign fishermen to their respective EEZs. This is because, in the first place, none of these states expressly denied foreign access to their zone for fishing purposes,[336] and second, several cooperative fisheries instruments to which these states are party indicate that foreign access to fisheries resources located in the maritime zones under their jurisdiction is explicitly acknowledged.[337] On an evidential level, it can be concluded that a majority of the coastal states that established EFZs or EEZs granted access to foreign fishermen to the living resources of their zones.

Criteria of Access

Article 62(3) of the LOS Convention provides that the coastal state would consider "all relevant factors" when providing access to foreign fishing vessels. The same provision further enumerates a number of contributing factors that are meant to be illustrative. Except for the first one, which pertains to the significance of the EEZ's living resources to the coastal state's economy and other national interests, all other factors provide guidance for selecting the foreign states that would be allowed access.

Reference to the Provisions of Articles 69 and 70 and LLS and GDS

On the national level, the legislative measures of two states have expressly referenced the participation of LLS and GDS in exploiting the living resources in the asserted zone: Moroccan Law No. 1-81-179 and Togo's Ordinance No.

---

335 Bangladesh Territorial Waters and Maritime Zones Act, 1974, in Smith, *Exclusive Economic Zone Claims,* 69; Comoros, Ordinances No. 76-038/CE, in *ibid.*, 197; Dominican Republic, Law on the Territorial Sea, Contiguous Zone, Exclusive Economic Zone, and Continental Shelf, April 1, 1977, in *ibid.*, 119; Iceland, Law No. 41 of June 1979, in *ibid.*, 209; India, Maritime Zones Act, 1976, Article 7(1), in *ibid.*, 213; Indonesia, Act No 5 of 1983, chapter II Article 2, in *ibid.*, 228; Malaysia, Exclusive Economic Zone Bill, 1984, Part II Article 3(1), in *ibid.*, 259; Nigeria, Decree No. 28 of 1978, Article 1(1), in *ibid.*, 347; and Thailand, Thailand's Royal Proclamation of February 23, 1981, in *ibid.*, 437.

336 Juda, "The Exclusive Economic Zone," 23.

337 See, for example, Iceland/Norway Exchange of Notes on Fishing of March 10, 1976, cited by Carroz and Savini. "The Practice of Coastal States Regarding Foreign Access to Fishery Resources," 51; also "African, Caribbean and Pacific States-European Economic Community," Articles 58, 64, and 66.

24/1977.[338] For example, Article 4 of Togolese Ordinance No. 24 of 1977 states that "the Togolese state engages itself to allow neighboring states in the hinterland to participate in the exploration of biological resources in the context of bilateral and regional agreement." Likewise, the Moroccan Law No. 1-81-179 provides that "in particular, in consideration of African solidarity, Morocco will uphold the principle of privileged cooperation concerning biological resources with land-locked neighboring countries under terms and conditions to be established by bilateral, regional, or sub-regional agreements."[339]

The language of the above provisions corresponds to the wording of the 1974 Declaration of the Organization of African Unity on the Issues of the Law of the Sea.[340] This conformity may relate to the notion that African coastal states, from the very beginning of the UNCLOS III proceedings, showed an intense interest in the problems encountered by LLS and GDS and expressed a need to remedy the problems these states faced.[341]

A corresponding nature exists between the Moroccan and Togolese legislative measures and the provisions of UNCLOS III. This is indicated in Article 62 of the LOS Convention and the previous correlating provisions of the ISNT and RSNT. These two provisions, along with Article 62(2) of the LOS Convention, characterize the privilege of a neighboring state fishing in the EEZ, without expressly describing this right. The qualification of such participation is determined by an agreement between the coastal state and the LLS and GDS involved. Thus, access to the zone is not an automatic process but a required duty to negotiate an agreement, subject to the conditional terms of the coastal state.

The Moroccan and Togolese provisions differ very little. Both provisions require precondition for LLS and GDS that use the living resources based on bilateral or regional agreements. However, Togo places a self-imposed duty on itself to grant LLS and GDS access to the living resources of its EEZ. Morocco, in contrast, simply complies with the principle of *privileged cooperation*.

As mentioned previously, most national legislation contains no specific provision relating to the access of LLS and GDS to the living resources of the EEZ

---

338 Morocco, Law No. 1-81-179, Article 1, in *ibid.*, 303; Togo, Ordinance No. 24/1977, Article 4, in *ibid.*, 439.

339 Moroccan Law, No. 1-81-179, *ibid.*, Article 13, para. 2.

340 Oda, *International Law of the Resources of the Sea*,. The Declaration states that "the African countries recognizes in order that the resources of the region may benefit all peoples therein, that the land-locked and other disadvantaged countries are entitled to share in the exploitation of living resources of neighboring economic zones on an equal basis" as expressed by bilateral agreements.

341 See "African States: Conclusions of the Regional Seminar on the Law of the Sea," 210.

including general principles pertaining to foreign fishing, more or less leaving the task of determining intricate rules up to the administrators. For example, establishing the guidelines by which foreign states must adhere to when fishing in foreign zones has been an integral part of several bilateral and regional agreements concerning EEZ claims.

Certain coastal states have translated the above formulation into a more definitive proposition. New Zealand and the United States are representative of these states. The legislative measures of these two states have subscribed to some important considerations—such as whether foreign fishermen who have traditionally fished in the waters that encompass the EEZ and the overall pattern of cooperation of foreign fishermen when it comes to research, conservation, and management efforts in the area[342]—without specifically referring to LLS and GDS. When comparing this legislation with the provisions of Article 62(3) of the LOS Convention, noticeable differences emerge. Not only did the legislation fail to address the use of the living resources in the EEZ by LLS and GDS, but, more importantly, it seems to imply a complete rejection of access to the fisheries resources by LLS and GDS. This is apparent from the above enumeration, which does not mention any type of reference to LLS and GDS. It is noteworthy that, at this stage, most LLS and GDS are developing nations[343] that have no marine fishing industry. It follows that any access that is restricted to those states that have traditionally exercise fishing in the EEZ is an implied refusal on the part of LLS and GDS to participate in the use of the living resources of the zone. The reasoning behind this is that LLS and GDS lacks a marine fishing industry and if they do have one, they might not have been fishing in those areas long enough to qualify as a traditional user of those areas.

On a practical level, fishing in foreign EEZ is governed by the provisions of agreements and other arrangements.[344] The integral details of these access agreements are complex and multiform, which makes identifying specific

---

342 New Zealand, Territorial Sea and Exclusive Economic Zone Act, 1977, in *ibid.*, 309, Article 13, para. 2; United States, Fishery Conservation and Management Act, 1976, Section 201(e).

343 Singela, *Land-Locked States*, 1; also Tavernier, Tavernier, Paul. "Les Nouveaux Etats Sans Littoral d'Europe et d'Asie," 730.

344 William R. Edeson, "Types of Agreements for Exploitation of EEZ Fisheries," in *The UN Convention on the Law of the Sea: Impact and Implementation. Proceedings of the Nineteenth Annual Conference, Cardiff, 1985*, ed. E. D. Brown and R. R. Churchill (Honolulu: Law of the Sea Institute, 1987), 151–77.

patterns or trends all the more difficult.[345] Four distinct arrangements seem to predominate: bilateral agreements, joint venture agreements,[346] charter agreements,[347] and contractual agreements for over-the-side sales.[348] For coastal states, bilateral and joint venture agreements serve as instruments to regulate and secure a wide range of benefits from the granting of access. For foreign fishing states, they operate in a certain framework that defines what concessions are given regarding the two-hundred-mile zone, and what specific technique is used to secure access in times of intense competition.

Regarding Articles 69 and 70 of the LOS Convention that address the rights of LLS and GDS to participate on an equitable basis in the surplus of the living resources of EEZs of coastal states, treaty practice has not been impacted by these provisions. In this context, a study covering over one-hundred bilateral fishing agreements was conducted by Carroz and Savini, who concluded that "none of the bilateral agreements concluded so far make an express reference to the right of these two categories of states."[349] Furthermore, in a subsequent analysis related to fishery agreements concluded by the African coastal states located on the Atlantic Ocean, Carroz and Savini came to the same conclu-

345 See further Jean F. Carroz and Michel Savini, "Les Accords de Pèche Conclus par les Etats Africains Riverains de l'Atlantique," *AFDI* 24 (1983): 674–709; Carroz and Savini. "The Practice of Coastal States Regarding Foreign Access to Fishery Resources," 42–72; Edeson, "Types of Agreements for Exploitation of EEZ Fisheries"; Roniti Teiwaki, "Agreements in the South Pacific: Kiribati and the Distant Water Fishing States," *MP* 11 (1987): 273–84.

346 A joint venture is commonly defined as an association of two or more parties, whether private or governmental, formed to undertake a commercial project and involving an agreement on the sharing of risks and profits. The term covers a multitude of arrangements, many of them entailing the development of a separate joint company in which each of the parties holds a proportion of the capital/shares. In other cases, no independent company is formed and the relationship between the two parties is governed strictly by the contractual terms of the joint venture. When the partners come from different countries, the expression "international joint venture" is often used.

347 The displacement of fishing vessels belonging to developed states from the two-hundred-mile EFZs or EEZs has resulted in a considerable surplus of vessels that are not granted access to the various zones under bilateral agreements. Local companies may therefore hire or charter such vessels to fish in their own EFZ or EEZ, or serve as a floating factory, receiving supplies from artisan fishermen for freezing and subsequent export. Legislation regulating charter exists in Nigeria, Ghana, Senegal, and Mauritania. See Moore, *Coastal State Requirements for Foreign Fishing*, 83–97.

348 Over-the-side sales involve the mooring of a foreign ship, usually a factory ship from the EEC, in an EEZ for a specific period of time, such that local industrial or artisan vessels supply it with fish.

349 Carroz and Savini. "The Practice of Coastal States Regarding Foreign Access to Fishery Resources," 49.

sion: "None of the bilateral agreements concerned so far in the region ... are expressly referred to the law of these two types of states or to confer rights of fishing on land-locked states."[350]

However, since the early 1980s, reference to Articles 69 and 70 of the LOS Convention has gradually emerged in treaty practice. In 1984, the seven-nation members of the Economic Community of West African States, which includes Benin, Burkina Faso, the Ivory Coast, Mali, Mauritania, Niger, and Senegal, decided to create a Higher Fishery Science Institute to train qualified specialists from the region. They discussed the practicability of establishing a joint fishing company with financial aid coming from the African Development Bank.[351] It stands to reason that setting up such joint fishing ventures would enhance the opportunities for three LLS—Burkina Faso, Mali, and Niger—to participate in the exploitation of the living resources in the EEZs of coastal states in the subregion.

Additionally, in 1987, Algeria and Mauritania concluded an agreement relating to cooperation in fishing matters; the preamble expressly refers to the LOS Convention as well as to Article 70 on the rights of GDS to take part in the exploitation of the EEZ's living resources.[352]

Moreover, Bolivia, a party to the LOS Convention, signed an agreement with Peru in January of 1992 that grants Bolivia the free use of its port facilities. This agreement also allowed Bolivia to enter into joint ventures with Peruvian companies that engaged in fishing activities.[353] Such agreements represent the initial steps in implementing Article 69 of the LOS Convention, which grants fishing rights to LLSs that are part of a region or subregion.

State Fishing Activities and the Evolution of the EEZ

Article 62(3) adopted "the need to minimize economic dislocation in states whose nationals have habitually fished in the zone" as one of the chief factors that coastal states must consider when granting access to the surplus of its EEZ. This factor refers to states whose fishing vessels have traditionally engaged in regular fishing activities in the area that were previously the high

---

[350] Carroz and Savini, "Les Accords de Pèche Conclus par les Etats Africains Riverains de l'Atlantique," 682. Translated by author.

[351] UN Department of International Economic and Social Affairs, *Economic Cooperation among Developing Countries in Marine Affairs* (New York: United Nations Publications, 1987), 26.

[352] "Accord Cadre de Coopération en Matière de Pèche," 149.

[353] Text in *Law of the Sea Bulletin*, no. 21 (1992): 87.

seas but evolved to encompassed the EEZ. It is the last mentioned factor that must be considered when allowing access to the surplus. In essence, if there is a legal hierarchy given to these factors, as suggested by some commentators,[354] the factor of economic dislocation in states whose nationals have traditionally fished in the zone together with that of states that have made significant efforts in research and identification of stocks should enjoy the least weight when it comes to the enumeration of these factors. However, as suggested in Chapter 3,[355] the coastal state's choice is largely dependent on the terms and conditions that are most satisfactory, and this means that a state that falls in this last category will be given preference. If there is an order of priority, as suggested by the provision contained in paragraph 3 of Article 62, it seems to be undermined by the discretionary power granted to the coastal state in establishing the conditions and terms of access to the zone.

Thus, under the above provision, coastal states are only obligated to take this factor into consideration along with other corresponding factors. Furthermore, it must be considered only when it applies to minimizing the economic dislocation of the state whose nationals have traditionally fished the waters that are now coming under the jurisdiction of the coastal state. With this in mind, these nationals are not recognized as having automatic access to the allowable catch reserved for foreign states.

Domestic practice involving the criteria for access to the living resources of the EEZ's surplus varies. A small percentage of national legislations reference traditional fishing rights as the main factor to be considered when granting access to the surplus. These states include Fiji, New Zealand, Papua New Guinea, Spain, and the United States.[356] The national legislation of New Zealand, Papua New Guinea, and Fiji assumes control over all fishing resources in the two-hundred-mile EEZ and authorizes the Minister who is responsible for the legislation to grant licenses relating to the terms and conditions, as well as to the payment of fees.[357] In addition, all states implement specific criterion to be applied when granting access to foreign fishing vessels. Although each state's legislative measure refer to the criteria for granting access to states that traditionally fished

---

[354] See, for example, Nguyen Quoc Dinh, Patrick Daillier, and Alain Pellet, *Droit International Public*, 3rd ed. (Paris: Librairie Générale Droit et de Jurisprudence, 1987), 992.

[355] Explanatory Memorandum, *Official Records* 10 (1978): 90.

[356] Fiji, "Australian Fisheries Amendment Act, 1978," Section 11(4)(a); New Zealand, Smith, *Exclusive Economic Zone Claims*, 309, Section 13(2)(a); Papua New Guinea, Fisheries Act of 1977, in *ibid.*, 363 Article 4; Spain, Law No. 15-1978, Article 5(1), in *ibid.*, 427; and the United States, Fishery Conservation and Management Act, 1976.

[357] See Philips, J. C. "The Economic Resources Zone and the South West Pacific," 269.

in the area,[358] none of them refer to LLS and GDS. However, as noted by one commentator, lack of reference to LLS and GDS may be due to the notion that the participation of LLS and GDS is postulated on a regional level.[359]

Spanish Law No. 15/1978 notes that "fishing in the economic zone shall be reserved for Spanish national, and subject to agreements ... to nationals of those countries whose fishing vessels have fished in the zone."[360] This provision did not refer to other factors cited in Article 62 of the LOS Convention but seems to reflect Spain's clear understanding of Articles 62(3), 69, and 70, which give top priority to states that have traditionally fished in the EEZ over LLS and GDS that seeks to fish the zone.[361]

The legislation of the United States includes some interesting details regarding the requirements for access. Section 201(e) of the 1976 Fishery Conservation and Management Act[362] states that the Secretary of State shall determine the allocation among foreign nations of the total allowable level of foreign fishing that is permitted with respect to any fishery, subject to the exclusive fishery management authority of the United States. When making such a determination, the Secretary of State should consider, first, whether and to what extent did foreign nationals traditionally engage in such fishery; second, whether such nations cooperated with the United States and made substantial contributions to fishery research and the identification of fishery resources; and third, whether such nations cooperated with the United States in enforcement and with respect to the conservation and management of fishery resources. Thus, although the U.S. legislation, similar to the LOS Convention, provides for a comprehensive list of factors, it gives top priority to traditional fishing rights. However, this approach by the United States is not readily clear, perhaps due to the position the United States took toward the law of fisheries at this time, which included opposing the concept of an EEZ up to the mid-1970s. Implementing the 1976 Act indicated U.S. support for the traditional law of fisheries reflected in the 1958 Convention and the 1974 *Fisheries Jurisdiction* judgment.

The 1980 amendment to the FCMA formula mentions traditional fishing rights as one of the seminal factors to be considered in granting access to the

---

358 For instance, "Belize Act of January 24, 1992, *Law of the Sea Bulletin*, no. 21 (1992); and Cape Verde, Decree Law No. 126/77 of 1977.

359 Philips, J. C. "The Economic Resources Zone and the South West Pacific," 269

360 Spanish Law No. 15/1978.

361 See its declaration on signature, in Office of the Special Representative of the Secretary General for the Law of the Sea, *Law of the Sea*, 25, para. 5.

362 Fishery Conservation and Management Act of 1976, Section 201.

surplus.[363] But allocation is primarily made on the basis of collaborative trade policies and reciprocity agreements.[364]

With the exception of the abovementioned claims, no other existing national legislation that establishes EFZs or EEZs refers to the notion of traditional fishing rights. All national legislation implemented by African and Latin American states followed this pattern. A feasible explanation for such a pattern seems to be that a great number of these states does not wish to address this issue. Any allusion to traditional fishing rights would signify an open invitation to plunder what is left of the living resources of the sea adjacent to their coasts.

Bilateral fishery agreements have no clear picture of conduct. A majority of bilateral treaties concluded between developed states have often referred to traditional fishing rights.[365] For example, the preamble of the Japan/South African Fishery Agreement of December 6, 1977 states that "considering also the desire of the Government of Japan that nationals and fishing vessels of Japan continue to pursue their traditional interests in the development and utilization of fishery resources off the coast of the Republic of South Africa."[366] Likewise, the framework of the agreements entered by the United States with the EEC, Norway, Portugal, and the USSR stipulated that "in determining the portion of the surplus that may be available to the vessels of the country, the Government of the United States will decide on the basis of the factors identified in the United States law, including whether and to what extent the fishing vessels of such nations have traditionally engaged in fishing in such fishery."[367] Moreover, almost all bilateral instruments concluded by Spain[368] and the EEC[369] contain a preambular reference to this matter.

---

[363] Burke, "The Law of the Sea Convention Provisions," 38.
[364] Pierce, "Selective Adoption of the New Law of the Sea," 594.
[365] Carroz and Savini, "Les Accords de Pèche Conclus par les Etats Africains Riverains de l'Atlantique," 684.
[366] Mfodwo, Tsamenyi, and Blay, "The Exclusive Economic Zone," 482, note 161.
[367] See, for instance, "United States/EEC Agreement Concerning Fisheries off the United States Coasts, February 15, 1977," *ILM* 16 (1977): 257; "United States/Portugal Agreement Concerning Fisheries off the Coasts of the United States with Annexes, October 16, 1980," cited by Carroz and Savini, "Les Accords de Pèche Conclus par les Etats Africains Riverains de l'Atlantique," 684.
[368] See Juan Prat y Coll, "Some Considerations on the Adoptions of National Policy in a Distant Water Fishing Nation to the Recent Evolution of the Law of the Sea," in *Food and Agriculture Organization of the United Nations Fisheries Report No. 293* (Food and Agriculture Organization of the United Nations, Rome, 1983), 89–94.
[369] Courier No. 64 November-December, 1980, 73.

In contrast, various bilateral fishery agreements granting access to fisheries in waters under the jurisdiction of developing nations made no specific reference to traditional fishing and the need to reduce economic dislocation. However, exceptional cases do exist, particularly in the bilateral instruments concluded between the EEC and some developing states. These agreements include the Guinea Bissau/EEC Fisheries Agreement of April 26, 1981, the EEC/Senegal Agreement of January 21, 1982, amending the Agreement on Fishing off the Coast of Senegal signed on June 15, 1979, and the Equatorial Guinea/EEC Fisheries Agreement of 1984. All of these instruments contain the routine EEC clause, "taking into account the fact that vessels flying the flags of member states of the community habitually engaged in fishing activities in that zone."[370]

Finally, the concept of traditional fishing rights was significantly elucidated by the ICJ in the 1974 *Fisheries Jurisdiction Cases.*[371] In these cases, the Court observed that the traditional rights of the United Kingdom should be accommodated with the preferential rights of Iceland. Such accommodation could not be based on the phasing out of the United Kingdom's fishing rights. The Court further noted that "due recognition must be given to the rights of both parties, namely the rights of the United Kingdom to fish in the waters in dispute, and the preferential rights of Iceland. Neither rights is an absolute one."[372] Thus, the Court placed British traditional fishing rights on an equal level with Iceland's.

However, traditional fishing activities in areas that were previously considered high seas but evolved to encompass the two-hundred-mile EFZ or EEZ do not have the same position under the LOS convention and in state practice. As mentioned earlier, traditional fishing rights constitute, according to the guidelines of the LOS Convention, only one of the many requirements that a coastal state may consider in granting access to the living resources that fall within their jurisdiction. In addition, access of third states, including access of states whose fishing fleets have traditionally fished in the area included in the zone, has been limited to the surplus whose determination resides at the coastal state's discretion. Furthermore, the coastal state has no duty to give a portion of what is left of the TAC to states whose fishing fleets have traditionally carried out fishing activities in the asserted two-hundred-mile zone. Rather, the coastal state may exclude them altogether. If they were excluded, no remedy to correct the situation would be available to them be-

---

370 See Mfodwo, Tsamenyi, and Blay, "The Exclusive Economic Zone," 482, note 162.

371 "Fisheries Jurisdiction Case (United Kingdom v. Iceland)."

372 *Ibid.*, 30.

cause the dispute-settlement system established by the LOS Convention prevents effective review of the coastal state's decisions.[373]

The Cooperative Efforts of States during the Research and Identification of Stocks

According to Article 62(3), there are other considerations that coastal states have in granting access to the EEZ. Chief among these considerations involves the efforts surrounding research and identification of stocks located in the coastal state's EEZ. Similar to the preceding criteria, states which have made substantial efforts in research and identification of stocks are, at least when it comes to undeveloped nations, also distant-water fishing states (DWFS).[374]

This criterion has been highlighted in New Zealand's Territorial Sea and Exclusive Economic Zone Act of 1977. The Act states that when making an apportionment of the surplus, the Minister may consider, among other criteria, "whether such countries have cooperated with New Zealand in fisheries research and in the identification of fish stocks within the zone."[375] The U.S. FCMA of 1976, Section 201(e), as amended in 1980, has a similar provision. However, many national legislative acts that established EFZs or EEZs omit any reference to this specific requirement. Furthermore, with the exception of a few bilateral fisheries instruments concluded by some DWFSs, such as Japan and the United States,[376] no other agreement seems to acknowledge it.

The Criterion of Developing States in the Subregion or Region in Harvesting Surplus

This criterion is the third item mentioned in the comprehensive list of factors located in Article 62(3) of the LOS Convention. National legislations have very

---

373 As explained in Chapter 3 in greater detail, as provided by Article 297 of the LOS Convention, the powers of the coastal state pertaining to the determination of the TAC, its harvesting capacity, and access of other states to its EEZ are excluded from the scope of the compulsory settlement procedure.

374 These categories were introduced by the distant water fishing states (DWFSs) in the Seabed Committee. See the Soviet Draft Articles on Fishing (A/AC.138/8C.II/L.6) July 25, 1972, and The United States Draft Articles on the Breadth of the Territorial Sea, Straits, and Fisheries (A/AC.138/SC.II/L.9) July 1972, in Oda, *The International Law of the Ocean Development*, 213–15.

375 New Zealand's Territorial Sea and Exclusive Economic Zone Act of 1977, Section 13(b).

376 For instance, Japan/United States Exchange of Notes Concerning Fisheries off the United States Coasts of 10 February 1977, "United States/EEC Agreement Concerning Fisheries off the United States Coasts, February 15, 1977," 287.

little reference to this requirement. Only two African coastal states, Morocco and Togo, mention this requirement. Article 13 of the Moroccan Decree No. 1/81/79[377] states that "in consideration of African solidarity, Morocco will uphold the principle of privileged cooperation concerning biological resources with landlocked neighboring countries under terms and conditions to be established by bilateral, regional, or sub-regional agreements." In similar fashion, the Togolese Ordinance No. 24 of 1977 provides that "in the spirit of intra-African solidarity, the Togolese State ... allow neighboring states in the hinterland to participate in the exploitation of biological resources in the context of bilateral and regional agreements."[378] In the final analysis, these two states remained faithful to the 1974 Declaration of the Organization of African Unity on the Issues of the Law of the Sea[379] to which they both were party.

Excluding the legislation mentioned above, all other EFZ or EEZ claims omitted any reference to this criterion. Moreover, only very few bilateral fisheries agreements seem to consider the criterion relating to the requirements of developing states in the subregion or region. These agreements include Shrimp Fishing Agreements concluded by Brazil with Barbados, Trinidad and Tobago, and Suriname[380] in 1975.

Conditions Governing Access

Article 62(4) of the LOS Convention states that foreign fishermen must comply with the conservation measures and "other terms and conditions established in the regulations of the coastal state." These "other terms and conditions" may include licensing and payment of fees (which, in developing coastal states, may involve "compensation in the field of financing, equipment, and technology relating to the fishing industry"), management measures, regulation of catch efforts, and conditions relating to surveillance, the conduct of specified research programs, the landing of the catch in the coastal state, joint ventures and other cooperative arrangements, and the training of personnel.[381]

---

377 Moroccan Decree No. 1/81/79, Article 13, in Smith, *Exclusive Economic Zone Claims,* 303.

378 Togolese Ordinance No. 24 of 1977, Article 4., in *ibid.,* 439.

379 "African States Declaration on the Issues of the Law of the Sea, May 1973," *ILM* 12 (1973): 1200.

380 Cited by Carroz and Savini. "The Practice of Coastal States Regarding Foreign Access to Fishery Resources," 49.

381 "The Law of the Sea Convention," Article 64, para. 4(a) to (k).

An analysis of the national claims made by coastal states that pertains to EFZs or EEZs suggests that the conditions attached to foreign fishing are in conformity with the provisions located in Article 62 of the LOS Convention. In a great number of cases, these conditions include the following: licensing and payment of fees, conservation and management measures, reporting requirements and observers, joint ventures, and research and fishery development assistance.

Licensing and Payment of Fees

The participation of third states in the sharing of the two-hundred-mile living resources of coastal states is not allowed automatically, once a surplus of the TAC is declared by coastal states. In fact, most states that have established EFZs of EEZs make such participation qualified by the conclusion of an agreement and the issuance of a fishing license by the competent authorities of the coastal states in which the fishing activities take place.[382] Furthermore, the main condition most fishery agreements impose on the exercise of foreign fishing in the EFZ or EEZ is the possession of a valid license by foreign fishing vessels. In essence, even in cases where there is a fishery between a coastal state and a foreign state, nationals of the foreign state must, as a precondition, obtain a fishing license whose obtainment depends on the completion of the prior conditions attached to it. License prerequisites are usually an integral part of legislative measure,[383] whereas in certain other cases the standards are set by the administrators at a later date.[384]

The payment of fees is a chief requirement for obtaining a fishing license. In establishing licensing fees and other required payments to fish, coastal states face a choice between fees based on actual catch and lump-sum payments.[385] Royalty and residual payments provide a more accurate and equitable method of instituting revenue sharing between coastal states and foreign fishing vessels and also impede the danger of overintensive fishing activities. They

---

382 See, for example, Antigua and Barbuda, the Territorial Water Act No. 18 of 1982, in Smith, *Exclusive Economic Zone Claims,* 61, Article 19(i)(e); Barbados, Maritime Boundaries and Jurisdiction Act, 1978, in *ibid.,* Article 6; Cuba, Decree Law No. 2 February 29, 1977, Article 4, in *ibid.,* 109; Fiji, Marine Space Act, 1978, Article 12(2),in *ibid.,* 129; Grenada, 1978 Act No. 20 of Grenada, in *ibid.,* 176, Article 6; and Guyana, Act No. 10 of 1977, Article 17, in *ibid.,* 209. For more details, see *FAO Legislative Study No. 35,* vol. 2.

383 See, Vanuatu's Maritime Zones act of 1981, Part V.

384 For instance, Tokelau's Territorial and Exclusive Economic Zone Act of 1977 provides that "the Governor-General mar from time to time ... make regulations prescribing conditions that shall be deemed to the implied licenses," in Smith, *Exclusive Economic Zone Claims,* 340, Article 8(1)(p).

385 Moore, *Coastal State Requirements for Foreign Fishing,* 166.

also seem to place the least risks on foreign vessels, which pay for only the fish they catch. In contrast, lump sum payments place the least amount of administrative burden on the coastal state.

In practical terms, license fees that must be paid are specified in fishery agreements or merely referenced the relevant national legislation of the coastal state.[386] States implement various methods to compute the license fees that will be applied, including those based on the tonnage of fishing vessels,[387] a fixed sum per vessel,[388] and a total lump-sum fee that covers fishing activities.[389]

Conservation and Management Measures

A majority of coastal states that license foreign fishing operations provides, at least theoretically, for compliance with management measures as a prerequisite for licenses.[390] The first of two types of these measures includes general management measures such as establishing fishing seasons, minimum mesh usage, or size and age of species caught. These are normally part of the general fisheries law and regulations, and generally are incorporated as a precondition for foreign vessels to obtain a license.[391] The second category involves special measures based partly on conservation principles, but commonly on domestic policies of protecting local artisanal fisheries from competitive foreign fleets. For example, the Solomon Islands Foreign Fishing Vessels Regulations of 1981 states that foreign fishing vessels should not fish in the waters contained in the outermost limits of the territorial sea or other areas that require permission.[392]

---

[386] Mexico/United States Fisheries Agreement of November 24, 1976, in ST/LEG/SER. B/19 (1980).

[387] Mauritania/Greece Agreement for Fishing Cooperation April 1, 1977, cited by Mtango and Weiss, "The Exclusive Economic Zone and Tanzania," 9.

[388] Chile/Spain Agreement on Cooperation in Fishing June 7, 1977. For more details, see Moore, *Coastal State Requirements for Foreign Fishing,* 166–67.

[389] Kiribati/Japan Agreement on Fisheries, 1982, cited by Attard, *The Exclusive Economic Zone in International Law,* 173.

[390] See for example, the legislative acts of Barbados, Maritime Boundaries and Jurisdiction Act, 1978, Article 12, in Smith, *Exclusive Economic Zone Claims,* 73; Fiji Marine Space Act, 1978, Article 14, in *ibid.,* 129; Grenada, 1978 Act No. 20 of Grenada, Article 12, in *ibid.,* 176; Honduras, Decree Law No. 921 of June 13, 1980, in *ibid.,* 205, Article 4; Kenya, Presidential Proclamation of February 28, 1979, in *ibid.,* 243 Section 2; and Tonga, Act No. 32 of 1978, Article 9(1), in *ibid.,* 441.

[391] See, for example, Tonga's Territorial Sea and the Exclusive Economic Zone Act No. 30 of 1978, in *ibid.,* 441.

[392] *FAO Legislative Study No. 35,* 17.

Reporting Requirements and Observers

Various national legislation pertaining to EFZs or EEZs refers to the reporting and the placing of observers on board foreign fishing vessels that are allowed to fish the zone.[393] The requirements of reporting, mandated by legislation, involves entry into the zone, the starting of fishing operations, and when operations should cease and the vessel should depart from the zone.[394] In addition, to facilitate the process of stock assessment, several states require periodical statistics and other data information on their catches and other fishing activities. This requirement complies with Article 62(4)(e) of the LOS Convention.

Moreover, various states make provision for observers to be placed on board foreign vessels with the observers given proper accommodation (i.e., food and other living arrangements) as well as access to the vessels' facilities and other equipment required for them to properly perform their duties.[395] This arrangement also complies with the provisions of Article 62(4)(g) of the LOS Convention. This system is most effective when large foreign fishing vessels are involved.

Joint Ventures

With the exception of the Gambian Fisheries Act No. 17 of 1977,[396] all other national legislation pertaining to EFZs or EEZs does not reference the requirement for foreign fishing vessels' owners to operate in joint ventures with local interests. Some coastal states encourage joint ventures, as specified by Article 62(4)(i) of the LOS Convention in bilateral agreements. Most of those instruments are cloaked in generic terms, calling for cooperative efforts through joint ventures and other means. Good examples of these types of agreements include the 1985 agreement between the EEC and Seychelles[397] and the 1992 agreement between Bolivia and Peru.[398] For instance, the former stipulates that the EEC was to participate in projects connected with fisheries development in the Seychelles. But many of these instruments are more spe-

---

393 See, for example, the Norwegian Royal Decree of December 17, 1976, para. 3, in Smith, *Exclusive Economic Zone Claim*, 303.

394 *Ibid.*

395 See, for example, New Zealand's Territorial Sea and Exclusive Economic Zone Act of 1977, in Smith, *Exclusive Economic Zone Claims*, 309, Section 15(3)(o).

396 ST/LEG/SER. B/19 (1980): 33.

397 See, UN Division for Ocean Affairs and the Law of the Sea. *Practice of States*, 46.

398 Text in *Law of the Sea Bulletin*, No. 21 (192): 82.

cific, in the sense that they reference such joint ventures in catching, buying, processing, and marketing sea fishery products.[399]

Cooperative Assistance in Fishery Research and Development

Under Article 62(4)(i), coastal states are also permitted to request the training of personnel and the transfer of fisheries technology, including improvement of their ability to conduct fisheries research. Various national legislation contains these requirements. For example, the Canadian legislation requires that the captain of the vessel comply with the instructions given by the authorized officials of the flag state regarding observation or research before any license can be issued by the Minister of the flag state.[400] An obligation to conduct specific fisheries research programs is also one of the conditional requirements of foreign fishing vessels provided under the national legislation of Fiji and New Zealand.[401]

This mandate is also found in bilateral fishery agreements. In this context, a number of agreements have been concluded, particularly between developed and developing states, that include provisions that state that the developed state will provide the research vessel and equipment and bear the responsibility for research activities. The agreements that include such provisions are the agreement concluded by the USSR with Gambia in 1975, Guinea Bissau in 1975, Sierra Leone in 1976, Angola in 1977, Mauritania in 1978, Morocco in 1978, and Seychelles in 1978.[402] Furthermore, in other cases, some developed states agree to form an alliance with the developing state and to allow their trainees to enroll in their scientific institutions.[403]

Other Conditions

A number of countries impose a specific number of conditions described above. The Bahamas legislation, for instance, stipulates that license allocations can only be made to third states under a bilateral agreement that specifies, *inter*

---

399 See, for example, Senegal/Poland Convention Concerning Marine Fisheries, March 17, 1976, Mtango and Weiss. "The Exclusive Economic Zone and Tanzania," 47, note 43.

400 Foreign Vessels Fishing Regulations of December 23, 1976, in Lay, Churchill, and Nordquist, *New Directions in the Law of the Sea,* 72.

401 Fiji Marine Space Act 1977, Art. 12 (3); New Zealand, Territorial Sea and Exclusive Economic Zone Act, 1977.

402 Fiji, Marine Space Act 1977, Article 12(3)(i); New Zealand Territorial Sea and Exclusive Economic Zone Act, 1977, Article 15(j).

403 All of these instruments are reproduced in *FAO, Committee on Fisheries, Twelfth Session,* Rome June 6–12, 1978, COFI/78/Inf. 8 May 1978, 43–65.

alia, that access to the markets of the foreign state shall be granted for fishery resources and fishery products harvested by the fishermen of the Bahamas in the EEZ.[404] Some countries—Fiji, New Zealand, and Western Samoa—simply indicate that requirements concerning local landings and processing is a precondition of the issuance of a fishing license.[405] Whether local landings are encouraged or not seems to depend, in large part, on the state of the local fishing effort and market, and the demands of the processing-industry sector. In some cases, too many landings would cause economic depression to the local markets to the detriment of local fishermen. This is one reason certain states impose a prohibition on local landings by foreign vessels.

Surveillance and Enforcement

As noted earlier in Chapter 2, Article 73 of the LOS Convention grants the coastal state the authority to enforce measures in its EEZ, including the boarding, inspection, arrest, and judicial proceedings that may be necessary to ensure compliance with its regulations and laws. Vessels and crew members who are arrested must be released promptly upon the posting of reasonable bond or some other security. In addition, penalties do not include imprisonment unless an agreement expressly permits it or any other form of corporal punishment. Moreover, in instances where vessels are detained and the crew arrested, the coastal state must notify the flag state of the action taken and the penalties imposed.

Similar powers of stopping, boarding, inspecting, seizure, and arrest in the event of suspected violations are contained in virtually all EFZ or EEZ claims, as well as in many formal agreements. For example, Trinidad and Tobago's Act No. 24 of 1986[406] defines the powers to be taken by the competent authorities for any foreign fishing vessels in the country's fisheries zone as follows: (a) Stop and board, inspect, seize, and detain a foreign fishing craft; (b) Seize any fish and equipment found on board the foreign fishing craft; and (c) Arrest the captain and crew members of any foreign fishing craft, along with instituting

---

[404] Also see, for example, the United States/EEC Agreement Concerning Fisheries off the United States Coast, 15 February 1977, in ST/LEG/SER. B/19, Article 3; "Accord Cadre de Coopération en Matière de Pèche," Articles 3, 4, and 5.

[405] Fiji's Marine Space Act, Article 14(3)(p); New Zealand's Territorial Sea and Exclusive Economic Zone Act, article 15 (3)(p); Western Samoa, Exclusive Economic Zone Act, Article 5(p). Also, see Fisheries Resources (Jurisdiction and Conservation), Act No. 13 of June 16, 1977, in ST/LEG/SER. B/19 (1980): 179, Article 10(4).

[406] Trinidad and Tobago's Act No. 24 of 1986.

such criminal proceedings against them as may be necessary to ensure compliance with the Act and the Regulations.[407]

These powers are enforced by the Trinidad and Tobago coast guard, members of the police service, fisheries officers, custom officials, and any other officials authorized by the Minister who is responsible for the fishery zone.[408] Enforcement of these powers and similar ones reflected in the national legislation of some other coastal states is assigned to the fisheries authorities or members of the military force.[409]

National legislation of various states has implemented procedures for reporting fisheries violations and for assessing the offending foreign vessel. A prime example of these procedures can be found in the Senegalese Maritime Fishing Law No. 76-89,[410] which provides for three procedures for reporting violations and arresting foreign vessels, depending on the conditions and reactionary response of the offending vessels. The Senegalese procedures also authorize pursuit when offenders cross jurisdictional boundaries, provided that an agreement is concluded that states this specific requirement.[411] This particular provision raises questions as to whether states are permitted to engage in hot pursuit of foreign vessels that violate their EFZ or EEZ regulations into another country's EFZ or EEZ. As noted earlier, very little information concerns state practices that clarify this situation. In the *United States v. F/V Kaiyō Maru, 1974*[412] case, a Japanese fishing ship, the *Kaiyō Maru*, violated the fishery zone of the United States and was pursued by the U.S. Coast Guard into the high seas and arrested. Regarding this action, a U.S. court held that Article 24 of the Geneva Convention on the Territorial Sea and Contiguous Zone, to which the United States was a signatory, permitted this pursuit, and that the United States could establish a contiguous zone for fishery purposes and that hot pursuit could start from there.

---

407 *Ibid.*

408 *Ibid.*, Section 28(1). Similar powers are contained in the Brazil/Trinidad and Tobago Shrimp fishing Agreement of 28 February 1978, and the Japan/USSR Agreement of 28 February Concerning Fisheries off the Coast of Japan, August 4, 1977.

409 *Ibid.*, Section 28(2).

410 For example, Fiji, the Gambia, New Zealand, the United States, and Poland. On the use of the military forces for the protection of fisheries, see Eugene R. Fidell, "Fisheries Legislation: Naval Enforcement," *JMLC* 7 (1976): 351–63.

411 ST/LEG/SER. B/19 (1980): 377.

412 *Ibid.*, Article 52.

The policy statement[413] of the United Kingdom suggested it would undertake hot pursuit of vessels violating its EFZ rules and regulations into the high seas, but not into the foreign fishing zone. Whether this policy of the United Kingdom is influenced by the fact that Britain relies on its naval forces for enforcement or whether foreign EFZs or EEZs would not be entered even if civilian enforcement units were operational is debatable. However, a legal obstacle does seem to exist governing the hot pursuit of an offending vessel into a foreign EEZ, either in customary international law or under the LOS Convention.[414]

When applying penalties for violating fisheries laws and regulations, the majority of EFZ or EEZ claims impose fines.[415] A number of agreements reflects this practice,[416] but the level of fines varies from one state to another and rests on the seriousness of the violations.[417] For instance, former Soviet national law covered fines for violating fishing regulations as well as for illegal fishing, based on the seriousness of the offense.[418] Fines for injuring specific species, such as the walrus, have been specified in rubles per animal, and

---

[413] Eric Allan Sisco, "Hot Pursuit from a Contiguous Fisheries Zone—An Assault on the Freedom of the High Seas," *SDLR* 14 (1977): 656–80.

[414] Patricia W. Birnie, "Contemporary Maritime Legal Problems," in *The Maritime Dimensions*, ed. Ronald Peter Barston and Patricia W. Birnie (London: George Allen and Unwin, 1980), 172–73.

[415] Article 111(3) states, "the right of hot pursuit ceases as soon as the ship pursued enters the territorial sea of its own state or of a third state."

[416] For example, the Bahamas, Fiji, New Zealand, Seychelles, Trinidad and Tobago, the United Kingdom, and the United States; also see Moore, *Coastal State Requirements for Foreign Fishing*, 214.

[417] For additional information see Dean Robb, "Access Conditions and Compliance Control," in *FAO Fisheries Report No. 295* (Rome: FAO, 1984), 65–79.

[418] For example, in Barbadian law, the amount of the fine is fixed at twenty thousand dollars, Maritime Boundaries and Jurisdiction Act, 178, Section 11(5); Mauritius law fixed it at two hundred thousand rupees, Act No. 13 of 1977, Section 12; and Cape Verde law provides that the violation of the provisions of Article 7(2) shall be punishable by a fine up to twenty thousand escudos, and violations of the provisions of Article 8(2–3) shall be punishable by a fine of up to thirty-five thousand escudos per ton of gross tonnage of the violating vessel, Decree Law No. 126/77 of 1977, Article 13.

fines levied for the black marketing of certain fish and fish products, such as caviar, is specified in terms of fair market value.[419]

In addition to imposing fines, most claims grant courts the power to order forfeiture of fishing equipment and boats.[420] This practice is also an integral part of various bilateral agreements.[421] In some instances, forfeiture of the catch and gear is automatic, even in cases of first offenses.[422]

Although imprisonment or another form of corporal punishment are prohibited by the texts of UNCLOS III, some national claims have included this penalty for the violation of fisheries regulations and illegal unlicensed fishing.[423] The national legislative acts of the Bahamas, for example, not only consider imprisonment penalties for fishing violations, but also provide for summary punishment.[424] Concerning Cape Verde, the penalty is generally a financial penalty, whereas imprisonment only applies in cases of repeated violations.[425] Such claims go beyond the powers granted to coastal states under the LOS Convention. Yet, the few states that previously included imprisonment in their national legislation seemed to gradually move toward bringing their conduct on this issue in line with Article 73 paragraph 3 of the LOS Convention. Evidence indicates that a number of states have either eliminated imprisonment as a course of action in subsequent legislative measures or altogether excluded imprisonment penalties from their practice. For example, Australia eliminated impris-

---

[419] Decree of the Presidium of the Supreme Soviet, in Smith, *Exclusive Economic Zone Claims,* Articles 19, 21; Resolution of the Council of Minister of the USSR on fixing compensation for the damage to living resources of the economic zone of the USSR and to the anadromous stocks, originating in the rivers of the USSR, beyond the limits of the economic zone of the USSR, 1986, cited by Elena N. Nikitina and Peter H. Pearse, "Conservation of Marine Resource in the Former Soviet Union: An Environmental Perspective," *ODIL* 23 (1992): 380, note 22.

[420] *Ibid.,* 376.

[421] For example, Burma, Canada, the Gambia, Ghana, Guyana, Japan, Madagascar, Mauritius, New Zealand, Nigeria, Norway, Papua New Guinea, Portugal, Seychelles, Sri Lanka, and the United States.

[422] See FAO *Committee on Fisheries, Twelfth Session,* 11–12.

[423] For example, Guyana, New Zealand, Papua New Guinea, and Seychelles.

[424] For instance, the Bahamas, supra note 406, Section 19 and 21; Cape Verde, Decree Law no. 126/77 of 1977, Article 13; Guinea, Decree No. 336/PRG/80, in Smith, *Exclusive Economic Zone Claims,* Article 8; Mauritius, Act No. 13 of 1977, Section 12(1); Philippines, Presidential Decree No. 1599 of 1979, in ibid., 369, Section 5(b); Seychelles, Act No. 15 of 1977, Article 12; and Tanzania, Territorial Sea and Exclusive Economic Zone Act of Tanzania, 1989, Section 10(3).

[425] Cape Verde, Decree Law No. 126/77 of 1977.

onment penalties through its 1978 amendments[426] to the 1975 Fisheries Act,[427] whereas the bilateral agreement between the United States and Japan in 1977 stipulates that, in case of the violation of fishery regulation, the U.S. government will recommend that the court refrains from including imprisonment or other forms of corporal punishment.[428]

Similar to the provisions of the LOS Convention, a large number of EFZ and EEZ claims provide for the release of seized fishing vessels and their crews upon the posting of a satisfactory bond or another form of security.[429] The bond acts as a security measure for full payment of any fine or any other penalty ordered by the court.

Effective supervision and enforcement of rules and regulations depends on the availability of physical capabilities and financial means. Thus, in many instances, the burden of ensuring compliance with the laws and regulations of the coastal states rests with the foreign flag state. The legislative measures of the United States, for example, states that entrance of any foreign fishing vessel into the fishery conservation zone of the United States for fishing purposes depends on the conclusion of an agreement under which the foreign flag state must be bound on its own behalf and on behalf of its vessels, and the foreign flag state must comply with the conditions applicable to foreign fishing operations.[430] The national legislative measures of the Bahamas contain similar provisions.[431] Various states require that the flag state's authorities assume responsibility for compliance with certain aspects of coastal state controls, such as ensuring that proper reports are given on authorized fishing operations.[432]

---

426 Australian Fisheries Amendment Act, 1978, in Smith, *Exclusive Economic Zone Claims*, 74.

427 *Ibid*, 45.

428 United States/Japan Agreement on Fisheries off the United States Coasts, February 10, 1977.

429 Canada, Fiji, Guinea, Mauritania, and New Zealand are very good examples.

430 Treaty on Fisheries between Certain Pacific Island States and the United States, 1048 Article 5(3).

431 *Ibid*.

432 The Maritime legislative acts of Fiji, New Zealand, and Western Samoa are prime examples; also see "Treaty on Fisheries between the Government of Certain Pacific Island States and the Government of the United States of America," 1048, Article 5(3); "African, Caribbean and Pacific States-European Economic Community," Article 68; "Niue Treaty on Cooperation in Fisheries Surveillance and Law Enforcement in the South Pacific Region," Article 4(5).

Additionally, foreign fishing vessels could escape punishment for violations due to a lack of evidence, as required by national law.[433] Most coastal states have circumvented such evidentiary requirements by using such rebuttable semantics as "all fish found on bound a fishing vessel that has been discovered committing an offense in waters under the jurisdiction of the coastal state shall be presumed to have been caught in those waters during the commission of the offense."[434] This would exempt a coastal state from proving the origins of the fish caught; a matter that would prove very difficult after the catch, especially when the species caught is mixed with fish caught in other areas.

Resources Located in More than One Zone

Under Article 63, a coast state must cooperate with other states that fish for the shared or straddling stocks associated with its EFZ or EEZ. Concerning shared stocks, the objective is to "seek to agree upon the measures necessary to coordinate and ensure the conservation and development of such stocks," without compromising the provisions contained in Part V concerning fisheries. This means that cooperative efforts do not infringe on the sovereign rights granted to cooperative states.

Furthermore, any cooperative efforts are, according to Article 63(1), flexible. These efforts may be either direct or through appropriate regional or subregional organizations. If efforts to achieve cooperation through these avenues fail, coastal states have the option to exercise their sovereign rights unilaterally.

The Gambian Fisheries Act of 1977,[435] the United States Fishery Conservation and Management Act of 1976 [436] and Venezuela's 1978 EEZ Act[437] adopted provisions similar to the one above. For instance, the Venezuelan Act provides that the "Republic shall seek, either directly or through appropriate sub-regional or region organizations, to agree upon the measures necessary to

---

433 Examples, "Canada, Coastal Fisheries Protection Regulations, December 9, 1979." *ILM* 15 (1976): 1372; "Fisheries Agreement between Iceland and Belgium Relating to the Extension of the Icelandic Fishery limits to 200 Nautical Miles, November 28, 1975," in *New Directions in the Law of the Sea,* ed. Robin Rolf Churchill and Myron H. Nordquist, vol. 5 (Dobbs Ferry, NY: Oceana, 1977), 33; "Niue Treaty on Cooperation in Fisheries Surveillance and Law Enforcement in the South Pacific Region," Article 4(3).

434 Times (London), August 22, 1978. The Master of the Soviet Trawler MPPT 10 was released due to lack of evidence as required by Scottish Law.

435 Gambian Fisheries Act No. 14, 1977, Section 5(1).

436 The United States Fishery Conservation and Management Act of 1976.

437 Venezuela, Territorial Waters and Maritime Zones act, 1976, in Smith, *Exclusive Economic Zone Claims,* 357.

coordinate and enforce the conservation and development of the same stock or stocks of associated species occurring within the EEZ of the Republic and the EEZs of neighboring states."[438] Several other fisheries agreements have similar guidelines. For instance, such guidelines are found in the Canada/European Community Agreement on Fisheries of December 30, 1981,[439] and the Convention Relating to Regional Development of Fisheries in the Gulf of Guinea concluded on June 21, 1984, between Congo, Gabon, Equatorial Guinea, Sao Tome and Principe and Zaire.[440] For example, Article 4 of the former agreement provides, in part, that "the two parties shall cooperate, either bilaterally or through appropriate international organizations, to ensure the proper management and conservation of stocks occurring within the fishery zones of both parties and stocks of associated species."

Furthermore, a "conduct provision" that corresponds with the provision of Article 63(1) of the LOS Convention is contained in the Fisheries Commission of the Northwest Atlantic Fisheries Organization.[441] In all of these instances, cooperation has taken the form of agreeing on TAC for each fish stock, allocating this between the states concerned, and agreeing to some extent, on other conservation measures.

Resources Occurring in the EEZ and the High Seas

Article 63(2) addresses fish stocks that lie across the EEZ/high seas boundary line,[442] similar to the provisions of Article 63(1). However, unlike the case of shared stocks, cooperative efforts with the objective of adopting measures necessary for the conservation of the fish stocks concerned is required between coastal states and states fishing for such stocks in the high sea areas adjacent to

---

[438] *Ibid*,

[439] Canada/European Community Agreement on Fisheries of December 30, 1981.

[440] The Convention Relating to Regional Development of Fisheries in the Gulf of Guinea, June 21, 1984.

[441] "Convention Relative au Développement Régional des Pêches," 1115, Article, 2; see also Edeson, "Types of Agreements for Exploitation of EEZ Fisheries," 162–63.

[442] The Northwest Atlantic Fisheries Organization was set up in 1978 to replace the previous International Commission for the Northwest Atlantic as a result of the establishment by Canada and the United States of their respective two-hundred-mile fishery zones. The text of the convention establishing the new organization is reproduced in the *Official Journal of the European Community,* No. L/378/16 (1978); see also *FAO Circulaire sur les Pêches No. 835,* Rev. 1 (Rome: FAO, 1992), 8; Moritaka Hayashi, "The Management of Transboundary Fish Stocks under the LOS Convention," *IJMCL* 8 (1993): 252–57.

the EEZ. This obligation also appears in Article 4(1) of the Geneva Convention on Fishing and Conservation of the Living Resources of the High Seas.

In addition, the above provision specifies that conservation measures may be adopted directly or collaterally through existing appropriate subregional or regional organizations, or through appropriate organizations established for this particular purpose. Moreover, it explicitly states that the agreed conservation measures pertain only to fishing on the high seas. Thus, if an agreement cannot be reached, the coastal state can exercise the rights granted it under Articles 56, 61, and 62 of the LOS Convention with regard to those fish species when they are found in its EEZ.

An analysis of national claims made by coastal states regarding EEZs indicates that not even a single claim has made an express reference to the provision contained in Article 63(2) of the LOS Convention concerning stocks that straddle the two-hundred-mile zone and the high seas. In fact, some coastal states have indicated their desire to further extend their offshore claims to encompass *El Mar Presencial* or the *Presential Sea.*[443]

Historically, the concept of the *Presential Sea* was first introduced by Chile in the 1991 amendments to its fisheries law. From a geographic standpoint, the *Presential Sea* area of interest for Chile is the high seas area beyond and adjacent to the EEZ, surrounded by the South American continent, Antarctica, and Easter Island, in a broad quadrangle of the South Pacific. The Chilean fisheries law passed in 1991[444] contains a similar definition.

---

[443] For example, cod, whiting, shrimp, and anchovy. These fish species are usually found in the waters above the continental shelf and are therefore largely contained in the two-hundred-mile EEZ, but often mix across the EEZ—high-seas boundary. See Caddy, "Some Considerations Relevant to the Definition of Shared Stocks," 29–30; also, Hannesson, "Fishing on the High Seas," 371, note 1.

[444] See, for instance, the Chilean Law No. 19, 079 of August 12, 1991, amending Act No. 18. 892, in *Official Journal of the Republic of Chile*, September 6, 1991, Article 154; the Peruvian Decree Law No. 25977 of December 7, 1992, cited in Pfirter, "Straddling Stocks and Highly Migratory Stocks in Latin American Practice and Legislation," 137, note 81; Declaración Conjunta Chile—Brasil, made during the visit to Chile by the Minister of Foreign Affairs of Brazil, from March 23 to 27, 1993, cited in Pfirter, "Straddling Stocks and Highly Migratory Stocks in Latin American Practice and Legislation"; also Jane Gililand Dalton, "The Chilean Mar Presencial: A Harmless Concept or a Dangerous Precedent?" *IJMCL* 8 (1993): 398; Francisco Orrego Vicuña, "The 'Presential Sea': Defining Coastal States' Special Interests in High Sea Fisheries and other Activities," *GYIL* 35 (1992): 265–69; Evelyne Meltzer, "Global Overview of Straddling and Highly Migratory Fish Stocks: The Non-sustainable Nature of High Seas Fisheries," *ODIL* 25 (1994): 269–72.

The 1991 Chilean law states that conservation measures may be enacted for fish stocks existing in the EEZ and in the high seas. When straddling stocks are fished in the high seas in violations of conservation measures, Chile can prohibit the fishing vessels that fish these stocks from landing in their ports. Similarly, when evidence indicates that fisheries activities in the high seas severely affect the exploitation of resources by Chile in the EEZ, the landing of catches, the supplying of ships, or the provision of other direct or indirect services in Chilean ports or other areas of the EEZ and the territorial sea may be prohibited.[445]

However, Article 86 of the LOS Convention states that the asserted presential sea is part of the high seas where every state enjoys the freedom of fishing, subject to the duty to maintain the interests of other states, as well as other mandatory obligations imposed by international law.[446] Also, where the same stock of species occurs in an EEZ and in adjacent areas of the high seas frequented by foreign fisherman, the states involved are, under the provisions of Article 63(2) of the LOS Convention and Article 7 9a0 of the 1995 United Nations Agreement for the Implementation of the Provisions of the LOS Convention, obligated to cooperate in enacting appropriate conservation and management measures. Thus, the presential sea claim mentioned earlier is not compatible with the standards of international law.

The straddling-stocks issue has been one of the most highly debated issues to emerge since the adoption of the LOS Convention.[447] Numerous cooperative initiatives pertaining to the conservation and management of these fish species, in a way similar to that contained in the LOS Convention, have been implemented by affected states. Examples of those types of cooperative ventures can be found in the practice of the Fisheries Commission of the Northwest Atlantic Fisheries Organization,[448] the Latin American Organization for Fishery Development, established by the countries of Bolivia, Costa Rica, Ecuador, El Salvador, Guatemala, Peru, Guyana, Haiti, Honduras, Mexico,

---

445 *Ibid.*

446 Pfirter, "Straddling Stocks and Highly Migratory Stocks in Latin American Practice and Legislation," 136.

447 See General Assembly Resolution 44/225 (1989), 45/195 (1990), 46/215 (1991) and General Assembly Decision 47/433 (1992) imposing a moratorium on large scale high seas driftnet fishing; also Grant J. Hewison, "The Legally Binding Nature of the Moratorium on Large-scale High Seas Driftnet Fishing," *JMLC* 25, no. 4 (1994): 557–78.

448 See Francisco Orrego Vicuña, "Trends and Issues in the Law of the Sea of Applied in Latin America," *ODIL* 26, no. 2 (1995): 99.

Nicaragua, and Panama,[449] and the 1991 Convention on Fisheries Cooperation among 22 African States Bordering the Atlantic Ocean.[450]

Marine Mammals

Article 65 of the LOS Convention grants coastal states or competent international organizations the authority to prohibit, limit, or regulate the exploitation of marine mammals more strictly than provided for in the other EEZ fisheries provisions. This article does not apply to the conservation and exploitation of these mammalian species in the EEZ only but, in accordance with Article 120, it also applies to the conservation of marine mammals in the high seas. Thus, it supports the notion of a single and uniform management regime that applies to both the EEZ and the high seas.

States are encouraged to work through appropriate organizations for the conservation and management of whales and other cetaceans. However, Article 65, similar to most of the Articles of the LOS Convention, do not identify which appropriate international organization has the power to prohibit or limit the exploitation of marine mammals. It seems safe to say that the drafters had the International Whaling Commission in mind to perform this task, an international agency that addresses the exploitation of marine mammals.[451]

On the domestic level, only three national claims contain specific provisions pertaining to the conservation and management of marine mammals. Senegal, Guinea, and the United States represent these types of claims.[452] Nevertheless, a trend developed that mirrored the international regulations of marine mammals in a manner similar to the standards reflected in the LOS Convention. This trend is particularly reflected in the practice of International Whaling Commission membership states.[453] This practice had taken the form

---

449 The Latin American Organization for Fishery Development, Article XI (9).

450 *FAO Circulaire sur les Pêches No. 835,* 53. For a detailed examination of this Agreement, see Edeson, William R., and Jean-François Pulvenis, *The Legal Regime of Fisheries in the Caribbean Region.* Berlin: Springer Verlag, 1983), 93.

451 Text in *Law of the Sea Bulletin,* no. 19 (1991): 33.

452 Edeson and Pulvenis, *The Legal Regime of Fisheries in the Caribbean Region,* 52. As a side note, the International Whaling Commission, like most fisheries organizations, does not have the authority to make binding decisions on conservation measures. It can only make recommendations that become binding after a period of 90 days on any member that does not object to its recommendations, *ibid.*

453 Senegal, Law 76-89 of July 1976, Article, 16; Guinea, Marine Fisheries Code, Article 32; the United States, Marine Mammal Protection Act, 1992.

of regulatory measures such as establishing seasons and the areas to be fished, TAC, and the age and size of animals caught.[454]

Anadromous Species

As mentioned earlier, anadromous fish are migratory fish that hatch in fresh water, make their way to the sea to grow, and then return to fresh water to spawn. Regarding anadromous species, the state of origin, namely the state in whose rivers anadromous stocks spawn, has the primary interest in and responsibility for these stocks.[455] The state can establish measures for fishing in waters landwards of the outer limits of its EEZ and, after consulting with other states interested in harvesting these stocks, set a TAC ratio for stocks originating in its rivers.[456] Moreover, as a general rule, enforcement of regulations pertaining to anadromous species that are harvested beyond the EEZ requires an agreement between the coastal states and the other states concerned. Specifically, the state of origin can enforce laws relating to anadromous species harvesting on the high seas against stateless vessels.[457]

Harvesting of anadromous species is allowed only in waters landwards of the outer limits of EEZs. There is an exception in cases where the prohibition to fish on the high seas would "result in economic dislocation for a state other than the state of origin."[458] Additionally, there is no mandate that requires that a coastal state needs the consent of the state of origins before it harvests the species of its own EEZ.

An examination of national EFZ or EEZ claims indicates that only a few domestic legislative measures have implemented specific provisions pertaining to anadromous species. Chief among these types of legislative acts are the United States' Fishery Conservation and Management Act of 1976[459] and the Japanese Law No. 31/77 of 1977.[460] The United States and Japan claimed exclusive management authority over anadromous species through their migratory range, even if this range ventured beyond the two-hundred-mile limit, except concern-

---

454 *FAO Circulaire sur les Pêches No. 835*, 53.

455 *Ibid.*

456 "The Law of the Sea Convention," Article 66(1).

457 *Ibid.*, Article 66(2).

458 For more information see McDorman, "Stateless Fishing Vessels, International Law and the UN High Seas Fisheries Conference," 553.

459 "The Law of the Sea Convention," Article 66(3)(9).

460 Japanese Law No. 31/77 of 1977.

ing zones that are under the jurisdiction of other nations.[461] Essentially, the United States and Japan claimed more than what is allowed under the LOS Convention, which mandates cooperative efforts on the international level regarding such matters. Additional evidence relating to the U.S. claim of jurisdiction over anadromous species beyond the two-hundred-mile limit is located in the 1988 Agreement with the USSR on cooperation in fishery matters.[462]

A review of treaty practices indicates that significant development in cooperative efforts between states on the establishment of effective conservation and management measures defined by Article 66 of the LOS Convention. The United States and Canada manage their anadromous stocks on their west coasts in compliance with the provisions contained in Article 66. Both countries have established joint measures on a bilateral level that helps facilitate management. The two states codified this conformity with Article 66(4) when they concluded the Pacific Salmon Treaty.[463] This instrument addresses the interception, by each state, of salmon originating in the rivers of the other state. It also creates a bilateral commission charged with the responsibility to conduct research on the state of the stocks and implement management plans for the stocks subject to its jurisdiction. For enforcement, each state has agreed to prosecute its own nationals for fishery violations that take place near the other state's two-hundred-mile zone.

In the Pacific Northwest, Japan and the USSR concluded, in 1985, an agreement on cooperation in fisheries that directly refers to the adoption of the LOS Convention.[464] Similar to the provision contained in Article 66(3), this agreement prohibited fisheries for anadromous stocks on the high seas except in cases where any prohibition would result in economic hardship for the fisherman from the state other than the state of origin of such stocks.

---

461 A map that defines the Japanese fishing zone can be located in Nakauchi, *Japan's Ocean Affairs,* 23; also, Chilean Law No. 19. 079 of August 12, 1991, amending Act No. 18 892, in Official Journal of the Republic of Chile" September 6, 1991, article 154.

462 The United States FMCA of 1976, Section 1812(2); Japanese Law No. 31/77, Article 12.

463 Agreement between the United States and the USSR of 31 May 1988 on Mutual Fisheries Relations, cited by Fleischer, "The New Regime of the Maritime Fisheries," 153. The Preamble states that the two parties have sovereign rights in zones they have established, extending two hundred nautical miles from their coasts. It further states that they have "authority for management of anadromous species of their respective origin beyond their respective zones, except when found in the equivalent zone or territorial sea of another state."

464 *FAO Circulaire sur les Pêches No. 807* (Rome: FAO, 1987), 9.

In addition to this, four states that had interests in the Pacific Northwest—Canada, Japan, the Russian Federation, and the United States—concluded the Convention for the Conservation of Anadromous Stocks in the North Pacific Ocean on 11 February 1992.[465] The Convention prohibits "directed fishing for anadromous fish," including the use of large-scale driftnets, and, in effect, prohibits fishing for anadromous species in this area.[466]

Catadromous Species

Catadromous species refers to those species that spend part of their life cycle in fresh water but spawn at sea.[467] The eel is representative of these types of species. According to the LOS Convention, states in whose waters these stocks spend the greater part of their life cycle have a primary interest in and responsibility for these stocks. Additionally, harvesting these species may take place "only in waters landward of the outer limits" of EEZs. Therefore, fishing for catadromous species on the high seas is strictly prohibited.

When fish migrate through the EEZ of another state, the coastal state and the state through whose waters these stocks migrate are, in compliance with Article 67(3), required to cooperate to implement appropriate conservation and management measures by agreement.

A majority of EFZ or EEZ claims omit any specific reference to the LOS Convention's guidelines on catadromous species. Additionally, no clear and convincing evidence indicates that cooperative arrangements pertaining to these species exist. Yet, this paradox may be explained by the notion that, in a comparative analysis of these species with anadromous species, their commercial value is limited in tonnage or importance.[468]

Highly Migratory Species

HMS, largely due to their migratory nature, are given special consideration in Article 64 of the LOS Convention. This provision mandates that coastal states and other countries that fish for HMS implement cooperative methods, either directly or through proper international organizations, to initiate conservation measures and optimum use of these species inside and outside the EEZ. A regional approach is specifically outlined with an obligatory duty placed on

---

[465] For the English text, see *Japanese Annual of International Law* (1985): 297.

[466] Convention for the Conservation of Anadromous Stocks in the North Pacific Ocean, done at Moscow, 11 February 1992, text in *Law of the Sea Bulletin*, no. 22 (1993): 21.

[467] See Hewison, Grant J. "The Legally Binding Nature of the Moratorium," 563.

[468] Ponsonby and Dussart, *The Anatomy of the Sea*, 278.

concerned states to create an international organization where none exists.[469] This provision further states that these species are subject to the entire regime of Part V.[470] The obligation to cooperate does not infringe on the sovereign rights of the coastal state over HMS in its EEZ and, if cooperative efforts fail, the unilateral actions of the coastal state would be allowed.[471]

Domestically, numerous EEZ or EFZ legislative measures simply state that the coastal state's management authority in the EEZ encompasses all living resources of that zone, without reflecting on Article 64 of the LOS Convention on HMS.[472] Other national instruments provide specific guidelines for the management of HMS in the EEZ. For example, New Zealand's Territorial Sea and Exclusive Economic Zone Act of 1977 states that the Governor General may, from time to time, develop regulations to identify specific types of HMS of fish, as well as to regulate fishing for these types of fish in the zone.[473] The legislative acts of the Cooks Islands, Fiji, and Western Samoa have implemented similar provisions. Essentially, these countries have confirmed the positions they took at UNCLOS III on this issue.

Moreover, other coastal states have made identical declarations when they became a signatory of the LOS Convention. Costa Rica and Sao Tome and Principe[474] fall in this group. In this framework, the declaration of Costa Rica notes, "The Government of Costa Rica declares that the provisions of Costa Rican Law under which foreign vessels must pay for licenses to fish in its exclusive economic zone, shall apply also to fishing for HMS, pursuant to the provisions of Articles 62 and 64, paragraph 2, of the Convention." This declaration simply restates Costa Rica's right to regulate HMS in its EEZ.

The United States Proclamation of March 10, 1983[475] asserted jurisdiction with respect to the living resources located in the United States' EEZ, as directed by the LOS Convention, except for the express exclusion of its authority

---

469 See *FAO Yearbook of Fishery Statistics* 50 (1980): 92.

470 "The Law of the Sea Convention," Article 64(1).

471 *Ibid.*, Article 64(2).

472 Burke, "Highly Migratory Species in the New Law of the Sea," 273–314.

473 Examples are Barbados, Marine Boundaries and Jurisdiction Act, 1978, Article 11 Section 5, in Smith, *Exclusive Economic Zone Claims,* 73; Cuba, Decree Law No. 2 of 1977, Article 2, in *ibid.*, 109; Guatemala, in *ibid.*, 185, Article 3; Indonesia, Act No. 5 of 1983, in *ibid.*, 228, Article 4; Mauritius, Act No. 13 of 1977, Section 7.

474 For additional information, see Philips, J. C. "The Economic Resources Zone and the South West Pacific," 270–71.

475 Text in Office of the Special Representative of the Secretary General for the Law of the Sea, *Law of the Sea,* 14 and 24, respectively.

over HMS; it confirmed the U.S. policies concerning "marine mammals and fisheries, including HMS of tuna which does not falls under the jurisdiction of the United States and require an international agreement for effective management." But the United States' position regarding HMS gradually transformed in light of the specific issues that had to be addressed in practical terms.[476] This issue was addressed, indirectly, by the 1987 Treaty of Fisheries between the Pacific Island States and the United States[477] under which the vessels of the U.S. were granted licenses to fish for tuna in the exclusive economic zones of those states, and next, directly, in 1991 when the U.S. amended its national legislation to include highly migratory tuna as species of fish under its jurisdiction throughout the EEZ. The change, indicated by the *aide memoire* dated 3 May 1991 of the Permanent Mission of the United States to the United Nations provides, to "make the United States position consistent with the overwhelming state practice subsequent to the 1982 United Nations Law of the Sea Convention, with regard to highly migratory species."[478]

When it comes to HMS, coastal states and other states whose nationals fish in the zone for such fish species are mandated under Article 64(1) of the LOS Convention to use international organizations as a vehicle to facilitate cooperative efforts when implementing appropriate conservation and management resources. The notion of cooperation between affected states or between coastal states and other concerned states is almost completely absent from coastal state laws governing the EEZ. Furthermore, two pieces of legislation have provided for domestic regulation of HMS in and beyond the EEZ. The 1991 Chilean fisheries law,[479] for instance, allows for the implementation of conservation and management measures pertaining to HMS in the EEZ and high seas, in consultation with the Ministry of Foreign Affairs. Penalties for violations are also expressed in this same context. In identical fashion, Argentina's Act of 1991 does not refer to any cooperative efforts, and asserts the right of the government to extend the application of relevant domestic legislation to the high seas adjacent to the Argentine EEZ.[480] Article 5 of the Act states, "National provisions concerning the conservation of resources shall apply beyond the two hundred (200) nautical miles zone in the case of

---

476 Presidential Proclamation No. 5030, in Smith, *Exclusive Economic Zone Claims*, 467.

477 Burke, "Highly Migratory Species in the New Law of the Sea," 273–314.

478 *Ibid.*

479 Among the very few national instruments that have referred to cooperation are the Portuguese Law No. 33/77, Article 1 (1), of May 28, 1977, in Smith, *Exclusive Economic Zone Claims*, 371, Article 6; and the Act Establishing an Exclusive Economic Zone along the Coast of the Mainland and Islands of the Republic ofVenezuela, *ibid.*, 477, Article 5(2).

480 Argentina's Exclusive Economic Act No. 23.968 of August 1991, Article 154.

migratory species or species which form part of the food chain of species of the exclusive economic zone of Argentina."

In essence, the Chilean and Argentina claims regarding HMS go beyond the rights granted to coastal states by the LOS Convention. But inconsistency between the provisions of Article 64 of the LOS Convention and the 1991 Argentine Law seems to have dissipated since Argentina became a party to the LOS Convention.[481]

Various cooperative measures have been established out of necessity,[482] despite laws pertaining to the EEZ that do not specifically reference the coastal state's duty to cooperate on a regional level to ensure proper conservation of HMS. Such cooperative efforts have been seen regarding tuna in the South Pacific, Atlantic, and Indian Oceans. A prime example of these types of cooperative instruments is the Treaty on Fisheries signed on April 2, 1987, between the United States and Certain Pacific Island States.[483] The preamble of this agreement starts by acknowledging the coastal states' sovereign rights over fishing resources of the EEZ, essentially ending the long-standing dispute that has existed between the U.S. and the South Pacific states. The instrument establishes specific guidelines regarding the payment of licenses, complying with and having due regard for national legislations pertaining to the EEZ, enforcement of the agreement, liability, observers, and other vital issues.[484]

Along similar lines, the countries of Ecuador, El Salvador, Mexico, Nicaragua, and Peru formulated the Agreement Establishing the Eastern Pacific Tuna Fishing Organization[485] on July 21, 1989. This instrument applies to the areas under national jurisdiction and to the high seas and acts as a directive for the establishment of a total allowable catch ratio in the area. Coastal states issue fishing licenses for areas under their jurisdiction, whereas organizations issue fishing licenses for the high seas. The Council of the Organization[486] can

---

481 See Act No. 23, 968 on Maritime Areas of August 14, 1991, in *Law of the Sea Bulletin,* no. 20 (1992): 20.
482 See Appendix A.
483 Fleischer, "The New Regime of the Maritime Fisheries," 256.
484 Burke, "Highly Migratory Species in the New Law of the Sea."
485 *Ibid.,* Articles 3, 4, and 5.
486 For text, see FAO, *Compendium of Basic Texts Concerning International Management and Development of Tuna Fisheries,* Fisheries Circular No. 842 (Rome: FAO, 1992), 113–20; also Jean-François Pulvenis, "Vers une Emprise des États Riverains Sur la Haute Mer au Titre des Grand Migrateurs: Les Régime International de la Pêche au Thon dans le Pacific Oriental," *AFDI* 35 (1989): 784–90.

also adopt conservation measures regarding fishing. After resolving problems related to distant water fishing, this Agreement entered into force in 1989.

Regarding the Indian Ocean, the Second Ministerial Conference on Economic, Scientific, and Technical Cooperation in Marine Affairs in the Indian Ocean, held in Arusha, United Republic of Tanzania in 1990, adopted an Agreement on the Organization for Indian Ocean Marine Affairs Cooperation[487] on September 7, 1990. This objective of this organization centers on facilitating joint efforts between East African states and states located in the vicinity of the Indian Ocean. Importantly, this agreement's guidelines closely resemble those contained in the LOS Convention.[488]

Furthermore, cooperation, particularly when it comes to fishing issues, has been pursued through the Indian Ocean Fishery Commission, developed by the FAO. The Indian Ocean Fishery Commission's detailed examination of the conservation and management of the Indian Ocean's highly migratory tuna species resulted in the adoption of an agreement to establish the Indian Ocean Tuna Commission[489] in the 1993.

Regime Relating Marine Research, Artificial Islands, Installations, and Protection of the Marine Environment

The EEZ provides coastal states with sovereign rights to living resources and certain other jurisdictional rights that extend beyond the fishery zone. Rights pertaining to marine scientific research is enshrined in Part XIII of the LOS Convention, particularly Articles 246–54; rights relating to artificial islands, installations, and structures are stipulated in Article 60, whereas rights concerning the preservation of the EEZ's marine environment are set forth in Article 208, 211, 214, 216, and 220 of Part XII.

---

487 Agreement on the Organization for Indian Ocean Marine Affairs Cooperation, September 7, 1990.

488 Text in *Law of the Sea Bulletin*, no. 16 (1990): 57. The following African states were represented at the Second Ministerial Conference includes: Burundi, Kenya, Malawi, Mozambique, Seychelles, Somalia, Sudan, Uganda, the United Republic of Tanzania, Zambia, and Zimbabwe.

489 *Ibid.*, preamble paragraph 1.

State Practice and the Conduct of Marine Scientific Research (MSR) in the EEZ

A majority of the states that claim an EEZ or EFZ[490] asserts their rights to regulate and control marine scientific-research activities that take place in the two-hundred-mile zone. The MSR regime established by the LOS Convention grants coastal states the right to regulate, authorize, and conduct MSR in their EEZs. Moreover, the carrying out of such research activities by any other state requires the approval of the coastal state concerned. However, pure MSR and MSR conducted for economic purposes differ. Regarding pure MSR, the coastal state shall grant its consent and may implement rules and procedures necessitating such consent without undue delay or unreasonable denial.[491] With respect to the latter, the granting or withholding of permission rests solely with the coastal state. State practice, in some instances, does not reflect these types of safeguards imposed by the LOS Convention on the jurisdictional powers of coastal states. For example, Antigua and Barbuda claim "jurisdiction with regard to marine scientific research,"[492] but do not clarify under what circumstances it would give its consent for research projects performed by foreign states in its EEZ. The claims by such states as Barbados,[493] Burma,[494] Colombia,[495] Grenada,[496] India,[497] Indonesia,[498] Kenya,[499] Malaysia,[500] Mexico,[501] Sao Tome and Principe,[502] and Sri Lanka[503] reflect similar provisions.

---

[490] See the UN Division for Ocean Affairs and the Law of the Sea. *Practice of States,* 78.

[491] Example, the Japanese Law No. 31 of 2 May 1977 on Provisional Measures Relating to the Fisheries Zone as amended by Law No. 83 of 29 November 1977, Article 9; Nauru, Marine Resources Act No. 8 of 1978, Act. 13; also Alfred H. A. Soons, "The Developing Regime of Marine Scientific Research: Recent European Experience and State Practice," in *New Developments in Marine Science and Technology: Economic, Legal, and Political Aspects of Change, Proceedings of the Twentieth Annual Conference 1988,* ed. Lewis M. Alexander, Scott Allen, and Lynne Carter Hanson (Honolulu: Law of the Sea Institute, University of Hawaii, 1989), 293–307; Wolf Plesman and Volker Röben, "Marine Scientific Research: State Practice versus Law of the Sea?" in *Law of the Sea at the Crossroads: The Continuing Search for a Universally Accepted Regime,* ed. Rüdiger Wolfrum (Berlin: Duncker and Humblot, 1991), 273–392; Soons, "Regulation of Marine Scientific Research," 268–72.

[492] "The Law of the Sea Convention," Article 246(3).

[493] The Territorial Waters Act No. 18 of 1982, in Smith, *Exclusive Economic Zone Claims,* 62 Article 15(f).

[494] Burma's Territorial Sea and Maritime Zone Law, April 9, 1977, Section 5(a)(iii).

[495] Columbia's Law No. 10 August 4, 1978 Establishing Regulation on the Territorial Sea, Exclusive Economic Zone, Continental Shelf and Other Provisions, Section 18(c).

[496] Grenada's Act No. 20, 1978, Article 8.

[497] Maritime Zones Act, 1976, Article 5(a)(ii).

Many states simply do not refer to MSR in their claims.[504] However, mechanisms in place permit coastal state authorities to assume control over research in the zone. For example, the Territorial Water and Maritime Zones Act of 1974 of Bangladesh authorizes the government to initiate rules regulating the conduct of any person in the EEZ.[505] Maybe these states believe that the authority to control MSR inside the zone, at least when it comes to developing resources, is implied in their assertions to control the zone's resources.[506] In some instances, the issue is addressed in separate regulations.[507]

Furthermore, some national laws, such as the legislative measures of Iceland and Venezuela,[508] contain intricate rules that determine the conduct of MSR in the EEZ. In this context, the 1978 EEZ Act of Venezuela mandates that prior consent be given before research is performed in the EEZ.[509] In addition, the Act states that the "Republic will not withhold it consent to the conduct of a marine scientific research project" unless the latter relates to circumstances similar to those contained in Article 246(5)(a), (b), and (c), of the LOS Convention.[510] Thus, this regime is compatible with the standards expressed in the LOS Convention. Moreover, very few national laws contain no rules of conduct regarding MSR in the EEZ, but do mention the principles of international law. Making a direct reference to international law suggests that these states pay particular attention to the regime on MSR, as required by the LOS Convention.

---

498 Indonesia's Act No. 5 of 1983, Section 7(4)(c).

499 Kenya Maritime Zones Act, No. 6 of 1989, Part III, Exclusive Economic Zone, Section 5(d).

500 Malaysia's Exclusive Economic Zone Bill, 1984, Section 1(c)(ii).

501 Act of February 10, 1976 Regulating the Provisions of Paragraph 8 of Article 27 of the Political Constitution of the United Mexican States Concerning the Exclusive Economic Zone, in Smith, *Exclusive Economic Zone Claims,* 295.

502 Sao Tome and Principe's Decree Law No. 15-78, Article 4(IV)(b), of 1978, in *ibid.*, 405.

503 Sri Lanka's Maritime Zones Law No. 2 of 1978, Article 4(4)(b), in *ibid.*, 427.

504 Suriname, Law No. 26 of 1978, in *ibid.*, 433, Section 5(3)(b).

505 For instance, Bangladesh, Territorial Waters and Maritime Zones Act, 1974, in *ibid.*, 69; France, Law No. 76-655 of July 16, 1976, Pertaining to the Economic Zone off the Coast of the Territory of the Republic, in *ibid.*, 147; Mozambique, Decree No. 31-76 of 1976, in *ibid.*, 307.

506 For instance, the implied actions of Bangladesh, France, and Mozambique.

507 Wesley S. Schulz, "Oceanic Research: International Law and National Legislation," *MP* 4 (1980): 116.

508 For a review of the regulations of specific states, see *ibid.*, 117.

509 Act Establishing an Exclusive Economic Zone along the Coasts of the Mainland and Island of the Republic of Venezuela, in Smith, *Exclusive Economic Zone Claims,* 477.

510 *Ibid.*, Article 9(1).

The United States' position regarding the conduct of marine scientific research in the EEZ is particularly interesting. The President's Proclamation on the United States EEZ does not refer to jurisdiction over the MSR in the EEZ.[511] It emphasizes that it was in the best interest of the United States to encourage MSR and to avoid any unnecessary jurisdictional impediments.[512] However, President Reagan's statement immediately following the Proclamation affirmed that the United States recognized the right of other states to exercise jurisdiction over MSR if done in a "reasonable manner" and compatible with the tenets of "international law."[513] Although the practice of the U.S. deviates from the norm of the LOS Convention, it does so only on a permissive level, merely declining to assert certain rights but not challenging the validity of those rights if asserted by other coastal states.

More important are the views of the United States made through the policy statement that accompanied the EEZ Proclamation creating the U.S. EFZ, and through additional statements by the U. S. State Department recognizing MSR provisions contained in the LOS Convention as reflecting the principles of customary law regarding MSR in foreign EEZs. In this connection, the Assistant Secretary of State for Oceans and International Environmental and Scientific Affairs, James Malone, stated, "The United States believes that most of the provisions of the treaty, apart from the seabed mining text in Part XI, fairly balance the interests of all states and are fully consistent with norms of customary international law."[514]

This statement suggests that the integral details pertaining to MSR found in the LOS Convention are similar to the principles of customary international law. However, this position has its shortcoming because, although it may be true that existing state practice pertaining to the EEZ of coastal states entitles coastal states to exercise some measure of control over the conduct of MSR in their EEZs, insufficient evidence in state practice supports the notion that customary international law contains the specific elements of the Convention's detailed regime relating to the conduct of MSR in the EEZ. In essence, as noted by one leading expert, although customary international law recognizes that a coastal state has authority and control over MSR in its EEZ, the actual safety mechanisms, conditions, and obligations spelled out in the treaty have not been fully tested and cannot be considered a key part of custom-

---

[511] Presidential Proclamation No. 5030, in *ibid.*, 467.

[512] *Ibid.*

[513] Statement by the president, March 10, 1983, in Smith, *Exclusive Economic Zone Claims*, 468.

[514] *Ibid.*

ary international law.[515] Thus, even with a correct interpretation of a provision, it would be very difficult at best for the U.S. or any other state to assert the notion that states that will not become party to the LOS Convention will uphold the provisions concerning MSR.

Artificial Islands, Installations, and Structures in State Practice

As mentioned previously, more than sixty-five domestic laws, decrees, and official proclamations refer to the concept of the coastal state's authority relating to the development and use of artificial islands, installations, and structures.[516] However, some legislative measures do not refer to the jurisdiction of the coastal state in this matter, as directed by Article 56(1)(b).[517] This omission should not be interpreted as indicating that certain states do not acknowledge the coastal state's jurisdiction pertaining to this issue, but should be regarded as a simple lack of reference because many states became signatories to the LOS Convention,[518] which recognizes the coastal state's jurisdiction in question.

Some EEZ claimant states have been cautious when adopting the detailed rules relating to the rights and duties of the coastal state reflected in Article 60 of the LOS Convention. In fact, various states have worded their national legislative measures to go beyond the powers granted to them under Article 56(1)(b) and in connection with Article 60 of the LOS Convention. Article 60 addresses the issue of artificial islands, installations, and structures in the EEZ by giving coastal states exclusive rights to establish artificial islands and to authorize and regulate the construction, operation, and use of such objects without impediment. However, when it comes to installations and structures, coastal states enjoy exclusive jurisdiction and the right to construct, authorize, and regulate the construction, operation, and use of such objects only if they pertain to the purposes expressed in Article 56(1)(b), such as economic purposes, marine scientific research, environmental protection,[519] or if such

[515] Cited by McLaughlin, "Confidential Classification of Multi-Beam Bathymetric Mapping of the U.S. EEZ," 12; see also the explanation made by the successor of Mr. Malone, John Negroponte, at the State Department, in *ibid.*, 13.

[516] William T. Burke, "Scientific Research," in *The United States without the Law of the Sea Treaty: Opportunities and Costs,* ed. Lawrence Juda (Kingston: University of Rhode Island, Center for Ocean Management Studies, 1983), 113–15; also Soons, "Regulation of Marine Scientific Research," 262.

[517] For example, Bulgaria's Decree No. 77 of 1987, *Official Records 2* (1994).

[518] For instance, Colombia Law No. 10 of 1978, in Smith, *Exclusive Economic Zone Claims,* 99; Comoros, Ordinance No. 16-038/CE of 1976, in *ibid.*, 103. And France, Law No. 76-655 of 1976, in *ibid.*, 147.

[519] For example, Comoros.

objects interfere with the coastal state's authority in the zone.[520] In essence, due to the semantics of the LOS Convention's text, not all types of installations and structures (i.e., those used for military purposes) come under the jurisdiction of the coastal state. Examples of such practices are found in the legislative measures of Antigua and Barbuda, Barbados, Belize, Djibouti, Dominica, Egypt, Saint Kitts and Nevis, Saint Lucia, the United States, and Venezuela.[521] In short, the ambiguities of the LOS Convention have been transported to the national laws.

In the national legislation of various states, the enumeration of the rights of the coastal state to establish and use artificial islands, installations, and structures in the EEZ differs from that of the LOS Convention. This difference is expressed in a manner that suggests that the power of coastal states concerning this issue is wider than those that the LOS Convention intend it to be. For instance, the legislative acts of the Dominican Republic, Guatemala, Guyana, Honduras, the Ivory Coast, and Sao Tome' and Principe refer to the "exclusive rights and jurisdiction" of the coastal state rather than to "jurisdiction."[522] In this connection, Law No. 573 of 1977 of the Dominican Republic states that the Republic "shall exercise exclusive rights and jurisdiction with regard to the establishment and utilization of artificial islands, installations and structures within the zones."[523] Similar language is used in the Honduran Decree No. 921 of June 13, 1980.[524]

---

520 "The Law of the Sea Convention," Article 60(1)(b).

521 *Ibid.*, Article 60(1)(c).

522 Antigua and Barbuda, "The Law of the Sea Convention," Article 246(3); Barbados, Maritime Boundaries and Jurisdiction Act, 1978, in Smith, *Exclusive Economic Zone Claims*, 73; Belize, "Belize Act of January 24, 1992," 3; Djibouti, Law 52/An/78 of 1979, in Smith, *Exclusive Economic Zone Claims*, 11; Egypt, Declaration Concerning the Exercise by Egypt of its Rights in the Exclusive Economic Zone, December 10, 1982, in *ibid.*, 124; Saint Christopher and Nevis, Maritime Areas Act of 1984, in *ibid.*, 381; Saint Lucia, Maritime Areas Acts of 1984, in *ibid.*, 383; United States, Presidential Proclamation No. 5030, in *ibid.*, 467; Venezuela, Act Establishing an Exclusive Economic Zone Along the Coasts of the Mainland and Island of the Republic of Venezuela, in *ibid.*, 477.

523 The Dominican Republic, Law on the Territorial Sea, Contiguous Zone, Exclusive Economic Zone, and Continental Shelf, April 1, 1977, in *ibid.*, 119, Article 5; Guatemala, in *ibid.*, 185, Article 3(b); Guyana, Act No. 10 of 1977, in *ibid.*, 209, Article 16(b); Honduras, Decree Law No. 921 of June 13, 1980, in *ibid.*, 205, Article 2(b); the Ivory Coast, Act No. 77-926, in *ibid.*, 241, Article 3(3); Sao Tome and Principe, Decree Law No. 15-78 of 1978, in *ibid.*, 405, Article 4(2).

524 Honduras, Decree Law No. 921 of June 13, 1980, in *ibid.*, 205.

However, these differences likely can be explained by the notion that most of this legislation was developed in the 1970s when the expansion of the texts of Article 56 and 60 of the LOS Convention was still in the developmental stage and no final draft had taken definitive form or had reached consensus.

Furthermore, the laws of some other countries have directly claimed jurisdiction not only over artificial islands, installations, and structures, but also over the use of all devices in the EEZ regardless of their intended use. The national legislation of Argentina, Burma, India, Kenya, Mauritania, Mauritius, Pakistan, Seychelles, Sri Lanka, and Vanuatu falls under this category.[525] For example, according to the Indian Maritime Zones Act of 28 May 1976, India would exercise "exclusive rights and jurisdiction for the construction, maintenance, or operation of artificial islands, off-shore terminals, installations and other structures and devices necessary for the exploration and exploitation of the resources of the zone for the convenience of shipping or for any other purpose."[526]

From the analysis of the above state practice, it seems clear that a majority of all EEZ claimant states have asserted exclusive jurisdiction over the construction, operation, use, and regulation of all types of artificial islands in the zone. The LOS Convention and state practice are consistent on this issue and the provision contained in Article 60(1)(a) of the LOS Convention is compatible with the standards of customary international law.

The EEZ, State Practice, and the Preservation and Protection of the Marine Environment

One of the most important objectives of EEZ claimant states involves the protection and preservation of the marine environment. The national legislation agenda of over eighty states have made provisions for jurisdiction concerning the maintenance and preservation of the marine environment in their respective EEZ.[527] But, only a few of them implement provisions designed to facilitate Article 207 through 222 of the LOS Convention. Additionally, the scope of jurisdictional claims varies. Some countries developed legislative measures to protect the marine environment without placing limitations

---

[525] Argentina's Exclusive Economic Act No. 23.968 of August, 1991, Article 154; Burma, Territorial Sea and Maritime Zone Law, in April 9, 1977, Article 18(d), in *ibid.*, 85; India, Maritime Zones Act, 1976, Article 3, in *ibid.*, 209; Mauritius, Act No. 13 of 1977, Article 6, in *ibid.*, 288; Pakistan, Territorial Waters and Maritime Zones Act, 1976, Article 6, in *ibid.*, 357; Seychelles, Act No. 15 of 1977, in *ibid.*, 407; Sri Lanka, Maritime Zones Law No. 2 of 1978, in *ibid.*, 427; Vanuatu, Maritime Zones Act No. 23 of 1981, in *ibid.*, 471.

[526] Indian Maritime Zones Act of 28 May 1976, in *ibid.*, 213.

[527] See UN Division for Ocean Affairs and the Law of the Sea. *Practice of States*, 17.

on their powers. The countries of Bangladesh, Guyana, India, the Ivory Coast, Malaysia, Mauritius, Pakistan, Seychelles, Spain, and Sri Lanka[528] assert their EEZs with far-reaching authority to protect and preserve the environment. Spain, in accordance with Spanish Law No. 15/1978, has "the authority to enact regulations concerning the preservation of, exploration for and exploitation of [the EEZ] resources with a view to the protection of the marine environment,"[529] and "exclusive jurisdiction to enforce all relevant measures."[530]

Although the coastal state has the authority to enact laws and regulations relating to pollution that comes from vessels, this power is by no means absolute. In fact, the rules and regulations developed by coastal states should be compatible with the generally accepted standards of international law and the standards established through competent international organizations or diplomatic conferences.[531] Where such international rules and standards are deficient in resolving issues, the coastal state may develop special mandatory measures for the prevention of pollution from vessels in the EEZ, provided they have prior approval from a competent international organization.[532] Furthermore, in the EEZ, coastal states' rules and regulations may be enforced only when a foreign vessel is voluntarily docked in a port[533] or when a violation has resulted in a discharge that caused serious damage or threatened eminent harm to the coastline and resource interests of the coastal state's EEZ.[534]

Several other coastal states that claimed jurisdiction in the protection of the marine environment follow the guidelines expressed in Article 56(1)(b)(iii) of the LOS Convention. The countries of Comoros, Egypt, Ghana, Guatemala, Kenya, Madagascar, Mexico, Sao Tome' and Principe, the United Republic of

---

528 Bangladesh, Territorial Waters and Maritime Zones Act, 1974, in Smith, *Exclusive Economic Zone Claims,* 69; Guyana, Act No. 10 of 1977, in *ibid.,* 209; India, Indian Maritime Zones Act of 28 May 1976, in *ibid.,* 213; the Ivory Coast, Act No. 77-926, in *ibid.,* 241, Article 3(3); Malaysia, Malaysia's Exclusive Economic Zone Bill, 1984, Section 1(c)(ii); Mauritius, Act No. 13 of 1977, Article 6, in *ibid.,* 288; Pakistan, Territorial Waters and Maritime Zones Act, 1976, Article 6, in *ibid.,* 357; Seychelles, Act No. 15 of 1977, in *ibid.,* 407; and Spain, Law No. 15-1978, in *ibid.,* 427.

529 Spanish Law No. 15-1978, *ibid.*

530 *Ibid.,* Article 1(2)(b).

531 *Ibid.,* Article 1(2)(c).

532 "The Law of the Sea Convention," Article 211(5).

533 *Ibid.,* Article 211(6).

534 *Ibid.,* Article 220(1).

Tanzania, and Venezuela[535] are part of this category. However, the national laws of these states do not contain explicit rules on their competence to address pollution issues that emanate from various sources. Hence, the exact extent of jurisdiction claimed by these states is cloaked in ambiguity.

The Bulgarian[536] and Soviet legislation[537] gives a much clearer picture and mirrors the provisions of Part XII of the LOS Convention. However, in some instances, they deviate from these provisions. For example, the Soviet decree on the EEZ of February 28, 1984 expressly refers to the prevention, reduction, and control of pollution in the EEZ but does not refer to the "generally accepted internationally rules and standards established through the competent international organization or general diplomatic conference" mentioned in Article 211(5) of the LOS Convention. In like fashion, Article 13 of the same decree, which grants the authority to establish "special areas," does not provide for the involvement of the "competent international organization" referred to in Article 211(6) of the LOS Convention. Furthermore, neither the Soviet decree nor the Russian Environmental Law of March 1992[538] that followed it contains a provision that correlates with Article 228(1) of the LOS Convention, or provides for the suspension of proceedings concerning pollution from ships that started in the coastal state or port state when such proceedings are initiated in the flag state. This last statement also applies to the Romanian Decree No. 142 of April 25, 1986,[539] and to the Bulgarian Law of July

---

535 Comoros, Ordinance 76—038/CE of 1976, in Smith, *Exclusive Economic Zone Claims,* 104 Article 7(b); Egypt, Declaration Concerning the Exercise by Egypt of its Rights in the Exclusive Economic Zone, December 10, 1982, in *ibid.*, 124; Ghana, Maritime Zones Law of 1986, "The Law of the Sea: Current Development in State Practice," 33, Section 5(2)(b)(iii); Guatemala, in *ibid.*, 185, Article 3(d); Mexico, Mexican Act of February 10, 1976, Article 4(IV)(a), in *ibid*, 295; Sao Tome and Principe, Decree Law No. 15-78 of 1978, in *ibid.*, 405, Article 4(4)(a); The United Republic of Tanzania, Territorial Sea and Exclusive Economic Zone Act of Tanzania, 1989, Section 9(2)(iii); and Venezuela, Act Establishing an Exclusive Economic Zone Along the Coasts of the Mainland and Island of the Republic of Venezuela, in *ibid.*, 477, Article 3(b)(iii).

536 Bulgarian Sea Law Decree No. 77 of 1987, *Official Records 2* (1994).

537 The Presidium of the Supreme Soviet of the USSR on the Economic Zone of the USSR, 28 February 1984, in Smith, *Exclusive Economic Zone Claims,* 417.

538 Russian Environmental Law of March 1992, Russian Federation, State Committee for the Protection of Nature. It is important to note that this legislation only makes general statements about the environmental duty to protect the environment without setting specific goals.

539 Romanian Decree No. 142 of April 25, 1986, text in *Law of the Sea Bulletin,* no. 8 (1986): 17.

8, 1987.[540] Article 58(2) of Bulgaria's Law provides for the prohibition "to pollute the marine environment in the exclusive economic zone in a way that interferes with the interests of the People's Republic of Bulgaria," a requirement that extends far beyond the tenets of the LOS Convention.

A fourth category claims explicitly acknowledgment of the competence of coastal states regarding environmental protection in the EEZ and its execution in accordance with international law. French Law No. 76/655 of July 1976, for example, provides that "within the economic zone ... the French authorities shall exercise the powers recognized by international law regarding the protection of the marine environment."[541] Similar provisions are included in the legislative measures of Cape Verde, Fiji, Norway, Portugal, and the United States.[542] Referring to the rules of international law by these state claims suggest that the specific limitations imposed by the guidelines of the LOS Convention are duly acknowledged. However, these claims also represent more the exception than the rule.

---

540 Bulgarian Sea Law Decree No. 77 of 1987, Article 58(2).

541 French Law No. 76/655 of July 1976, Article 4.

542 Cape Verde, Decree Law No. 126/77 of 1977, Article 12(a); Fiji, Marine Space Act, 1978, Section 11(c); Norway, Act No. 91 of December 17, 1976, Relating to the Economic Zone of Norway, in Smith, *Exclusive Economic Zone Claims,* 351, para. 7; Portugal, Decree Law No. 33/77 of May 28, 1977, Article 7(a); the United States, Presidential Proclamation No. 5030, in Smith, *Exclusive Economic Zone Claims,* 467.

Chapter 5

The Development of Customary International Law and the Two-Hundred-Mile EEZ

The precise relationship between state practice and the formation of customary international law has been a highly debated issue among various commentators. Authors and legal experts disagree on the relative importance of the particular elements needed to forge the relationship between state practice and customary international law, and debates also surround the specific elements regarding this relationship.[1] However, Manley O. Hudson,[2] along with the decisions rendered by the ICJ, has identified the rubrics of customary international law as (a) widespread and consistent state practice;[3] (b) repetition of the practice over a considerable time period;[4] (c) the practice performed out of a sense of obligation;[5] and (d) the

---

1 For instance, Kelsen states that "custom by which a norm of general international law is created" is a "long established practice of state." Hans Kelsen, *Principles of International Law* (New York: Rinehart, 1952), 445; Cheng commented, "not only it unnecessary that the usage should be prolonged but there need also be no usage at all in the sense of repeated practice, provided that opinio juris of the states concerned can be clearly established. Consequently, international customary law has in reality only one constitutive element, the opinio juris. Where there is opinio juris, there is a rule of customary international law." Bing Cheng, "United Nations Resolutions on Outer Space 'Instant' International Customary Law," *IJIL* 5 (1965): 23–45.

2 See Manley O. Hudson, "Article 24 of the Statute of the International Law Commission," *Yearbook of the International Law Commission* 2 (1950), UN Doc. A/CN.4/16/Add.1, 5.

3 This element is also identified by the ICJ "Asylum Case (Colombia v. Peru)," *ICJ Rep.* (1950): 266; and "Anglo-Norwegian Fisheries Case (United Kingdom v. Norway)," *ICJ Rep.* (1951): 116.

4 The element is noted in the "North Sea Continental Shelf Cases," 74.

5 In the Lotus Case, the Permanent Court noted that, in determining the motivation of a state abstaining from action, "only if such abstentions were based on their being conscious of a duty to abstain would it be possible to speak of an international custom," "Case of the *S. S. Lotus* (France v. Turkey)," *PCIJ* (1927): Series A. No. 10, 28; see also "North Sea Continental Shelf Cases," 41–44.

practice must be taken by a significant number of states and not rejected by a significant number of states.[6]

Widespread and Consistent State Practice

In the *North Sea Continental Shelf Cases,* the ICJ insisted on "a very widespread and representative participation ... state practice, including that of states whose interests are especially affected, should have been extensive and virtually uniform."[7] Judge Lachs, in a dissenting statement, gave clarity to the terms widespread and representative, and noted that "states with different political, economic, and legal systems, states of all continents should participate in this process."[8] Judge D'Arechaga, giving a separate opinion in the *Continental Shelf (Tunisia v. Libya) Case* noted that "the proclamation by 86 coastal states of economic zones, fishery zones, or fishery conservation zones ... constitutes a widespread practice of states."[9] According to one leading commentator, "the practice must be general not universal... the practice must have been applied by the overwhelming majority of states which hitherto has an opportunity of applying it."[10] Corbett noted that there has to be a sense of "general approval"[11] among the states, whereas Tunkin believes that general practice itself does not necessarily mean the practice of all states.[12] The ICJ supported the notion that universality is not a key requirement.[13]

The most important element is uniformity and consistency.[14] In this context, the ICJ said in the *Asylum Case* that "the Colombian Government must prove that the rule invoked by it is in accordance with a constant and uniform usage practice by the states in question."[15] Lauterpacht echoed this sentiment by

---

[6] See "Temple of Preah Vihear Case, (Cambodia v. Thailand)," *ICJ Rep.* (1962): 25–27 and 29–30.

[7] "North Sea Continental Shelf Cases," 42–43.

[8] *Ibid.*, 227.

[9] D'Arechaga, "Case Concerning the Continental Shelf," 115 para. 54.

[10] Josef L. Kunz, "The Nature of Customary International Law," *AJIL* 47 (1953): 666.

[11] P. E. Corbett, "The Consent of States and the Sources of the Law of Nations," *BYIL* 6 (1925): 24–25.

[12] G. I. Tunkin, *Theory of International Law* (Cambridge: Harvard University Press, 1974), 124.

[13] In the "Anglo-Norwegian Fisheries Case," the ICJ observed that it is not necessary for the customary norm to pass the test of "universal acceptance."

[14] Brownlie, *Principles of Public International Law,* 6–7.

[15] "Asylum Case (Colombia v. Peru)," 276. The Court reaffirmed this view in "Rights of Nationals of the United States in Morocco Case (United States v. France)," *ICJ Rep.* (1952): 200.

stating there should be "concordant international practice."[16] The central point is that there should not be much "uncertainty and contradiction, so much fluctuation and discrepancy" in state practice.[17] Minor inconsistency in state practice does not prevent the creation of a customary rule. In this context, the ICJ, in the *Nicaragua v. United States Case*,[18] emphasized that the practice in question did not have to be "in absolute rigorous conformity" with the purported customary rule. The Court further stated that "In order to deduce the existence of customary rules, the Court deems it sufficient that the conduct of states should, in general, be consistent with such rules, and that instances of state conduct inconsistent with a given rule should generally have been treated as breaches of that rule, not as indications of the recognition of a new rule."[19]

As mentioned in Chapter four, during the time period between 1975 and 1978, over forty coastal states established their own two-hundred-mile jurisdictional zones that related to fisheries and certain other issues such as MSR and the preservation of the marine environment.[20] An additional sixteen EEZ claims were made between 1978 and 1981.[21] This same time period also saw other coastal states establish their own two-hundred-mile EFZ rather than establishing a full EEZ.[22]

It must be remembered that legal scholars who have argued against the biding nature of the EEZ under the general principles of customary international law have mainly relied on two central arguments: (1) the partial and provisional nature of certain two-hundred-mile EEZ claims; (2) the complete "package deal" analogy that ruled out any selective application of the provisions of the LOS Convention.

For the first argument, some asserted that some coastal states have implemented claims to a two-hundred-mile EFZ only when these claims promoted a

---

16 Hersch Lauterpacht, *The Development of International Law by the International Court* (Cambridge: Cambridge University Press, 2011), 378. The Court referred to "consistent international practice" in the "Wimbledon Case (France, Italy, Japan, and the United Kingdom v. Germany)," *PCIJ* Ser. A, No. 1, (1923): 26–28.

17 "Asylum Case (Colombia v. Peru)," 15.

18 "Case Concerning Military and Paramilitary Activities in and Against Nicaragua (Nicaragua v. United States), Merits, June 27th, 1986," *ICJ Rep.* (1986): 14; also "Anglo-Norwegian Fisheries Case," 128.

19 *Ibid.*, 98.

20 Johnston and Gold, "Extended Jurisdiction," 27–49.

21 *Ibid.*, note 93.

22 *Ibid.*, note 37.

provisional element of the state's practice, which ultimately resulted in the non-uniformity of the jurisdictional zone. In this context, one legal scholar stated:

> If we ... look at state practice and we try to analyze the acts adopted by governments, we must come to the conclusion that all of them differ greatly. For example, if we look at the act of the USSR, adopted in 1976, we note that this act will be in force until the date of the entry into force of the convention, and that it said nothing about establishing the exclusive economic zone. So if we analyze all the acts adopted by different states, we find that there is no reason to say that we have a generally recognized practice. For this reason, we cannot say that the exclusive economic zone is a norm of customary law.[23]

But this argument can be countered by simply acknowledging that the fishery regime is a vital element of the EEZ concept and that the exploitation and conservation of fisheries resources located in adjacent seas has been the central basis for the establishment of the two-hundred-mile EEZ since the 1940s. In essence, any claim based primarily on the exclusive fishery zone strengthens the concept of the EEZ.[24]

In addition, it is reasonable to add to the argument of gradual implementation of the EEZ concept into state practice as evidenced, for example, by the approach coastal states take to proclaim exclusive fishery zones. In far sight, the EEZ may well replace all exclusive fishery zones. This appears to be confirmed by the transformation of an existing two-hundred-mile EFZ into an EEZ, which was implemented by the United States in 1983,[25] the Soviet Union in 1984,[26] Poland in 1991,[27] Sweden in 1993,[28] and Australia in 1994.[29]

---

[23] A. J. Zakharov, "Comment to Article by C. A. Fleischer, the Exclusive Economic Zone under the Convention Regime and in State Practice," in *The 1982 Convention on the Law of the Sea, Proceedings of the Seventeenth Annual Conference, July 12–16, 1983,* ed. Albert W. Koers and Bernard H. Oxman (Honolulu: Law of the Sea Institute, University of Hawaii, 1984, 364; also the comments of I. Kolosovski, in *The 1982 Convention on the Law of the Sea, Proceedings of the Seventeenth Annual Conference, July 12–16, 1983,* ed. Albert W. Koers and Bernard H. Oxman (Honolulu: Law of the Sea Institute, University of Hawaii, 1984, 367; A. Kolodkin and A. Zakharov, "Some Aspects of Soviet State Practice on the Development of Ocean Resources," in *Consensus and Confrontation: The United States and the Law of the Sea Convention,* ed. John M. Van Dyke (Honolulu: Law of the Sea Institute, University of Hawaii, 1985), 214.

[24] P. Sreenivasa Rao, "Public Order of Oceans: Problems and Prospects," *IJIL* 17 (1977): 222.

[25] See Presidential Proclamation No. 5030, in Smith, *Exclusive Economic Zone Claims,* 467.

[26] *Ibid.,* 417.

Regarding the package deal dynamics, certain states, such as the former Soviet Union,[30] argued that UNCLOS III resolved all the issues of the sea (under the regimes of the territorial sea, EEZ, international straits, the high seas, continental shelf, and the international seabed area), by combining these problems under one complete package, dramatically improving the effectiveness of the LOS Convention's rules and principles.[31] Thus, the result of this premise is that acceptance of the LOS Convention as a binding instrument that forms a package deal may be considered a source of customary international law only in its totality and not with respect to any selective element of its provisions, such as the concept of the EEZ. Various commentators have supported this argument, particularly following the early years of the LOS Convention, as an essential argument against the global binding nature of the EEZ.[32]

Although the package deal seems to be a viable argument from the standpoint of legal debates and conventional norms, the argument itself is still questionable, mainly because it fails to appreciate the effective role that state practice has when it comes to establishing customary international law, which is a focal point of the formation of the basic principles of international law.[33] This could result in nullifying the legal force of customary international law by way of conventional exclusiveness, which in turn would destabilize international law itself.[34]

---

27 "Act Concerning the Maritime Areas of the Polish Republic and the Marine Administration, 1991," 66.
28 "Sweden's Act on Sweden's Economic Zone, December 3, 1992."
29 Kaye and Rothwell, "Australia's Antarctic Maritime Claims and Boundaries," 209.
30 Barbara Kwiatkowska, "Exclusive Economic Zone: General Evaluation," in *Essays on the New Law of the Sea*, ed. Budislav Vukas (Zagreb: Birotehnika, 1985), 110.
31 See M. Lazarev, "The Sea Economic Zone: An Important Problem of the 'Package,'" *IJIL* 17 (1977): 209–15.
32 See, for example, Zakharov, "Comment to Article by C. A. Fleischer"; Kolosovski, *The 1982 Convention on the Law of the Sea.*
33 Takeo Iguchi, "The Law of the Sea: Conventional Rules and Customary Norms," paper presented at the Annual Meeting of the American Society of International Law, Boston, MA, April 9, 1987 (mimeograph), 5.
34 *Ibid.*, 5–6.

Eastern European, Western, and developing states do not subscribe to the package-deal argument, which emphasizes the nature of the EEZ.[35] In fact, most Western legal publicists consider the package deal something of a procedural mechanism designed specifically to further the achievement of consensus, as expressed by UNCLOS III, which has questionable merits at best.[36] Furthermore, they regard state practice as the primary test of whether third states may enjoy rights that are stipulated in treaties. In this connection, Lee observed,

> Even if the intent of the negotiations of the law of the sea Convention was to limit the benefits of all its provisions to the signatories as parties to a so-called package deal, non-party states may enjoy the same benefits if the particular provision of the Convention ... has since acquired the status of customary rule through widespread acceptance as law and confirmation by state practice.[37]

Additionally, a chamber of the ICJ, in the *Gulf of Maine Case*, reasoned that

> The Chamber notes in the first place that the Convention ... has not yet come into force and that a number of states does not appear inclined to ratify it. This, however, in no way detracts from the consensus reached on large portions of the instrument and, above all, cannot invalidate the observation that certain provisions of the Convention, concerning the... exclusive economic zone ... were adopted without any objections. ... In the Chamber's opinion, those provisions, even if in some respects they bear the mark of the compromise surrounding

---

35 For contrasting views of writers from developing states, see Anand, "The Politics of a New Legal Order for Fisheries," 282–83. For the views expressed by Western authors, see Albert W. Koers, "The United Nations Convention on the Law of the Sea: An Overview," in *The International Law of the Sea, Issues of Implementation in Indonesia, Proceedings of a Seminar at Jakarta on 22–27 August, 1983*, ed. Ellen Hey and Albert W. Koers, (Honolulu: Law of the Sea Institute, 1984), 23–25; Luke T. Lee, "The Law of the Sea Convention and Third States," *AJIL* 77 (1983): 566–67; James L. Malone, "Freedom and Opportunity: Foundation for a Dynamic Ocean Policy," *Department of State Bulletin* 84, no. 2093 (1984): 77.

36 James L. Malone, "Freedom and Opportunity: Foundation for a Dynamic Ocean Policy"; Lee, "The Law of the Sea Convention and Third States."

37 Lee, "The Law of the Sea Convention and Third States," 568; also Koers, "The United Nations Convention on the Law of the Sea," 23; Guy de Lacharrière, "La Reforme du Droit de la Mer et le Rôle de la Conférence des Nations Unies," in *Le Nouveau Droit International de la Mer*, ed. D. Bardonnet and M. Virally (Paris: Editions A. Pédone, 1983), 27–32.

> their adoption, may nevertheless be regarded as consonant at present with general international law on that question.[38]

Hence, considering the number of states that have implemented unilateral legislation creating EEZs and EFZs up to a breadth of two hundred miles, *prima facie* state practice is extensive and uniform.[39] Moreover, coastal states whose interests are severely affected generally have incorporated the formulation of the concept into the texts of their negotiating instruments.

Repetition of the Practice over a Considerable Time Period

Hans Kelsen, in his seminal work *Principles of International Law,* stated that "custom by which a norm of general international law is created" is a "long-established practice of states."[40] Brian Lepard seemed to concur with this assessment when he wrote that "widespread and contiguous state practice will usually be necessary evidence of" customary international law.[41] However, in some instances, this requirement is less stringent. In this connection, in the *North Sea Continental Shelf Cases,* the ICJ made a point that it is not necessary to prove that a specific practice had to be followed for a certain length of time.[42] Thus, the notion of a "long-established" practice is considered a chief requirement because it would negate the possibility of creating new customary norms, even when state actions are "uniform and universal" in practice.[43]

State practice concerning the two-hundred-mile EEZ has grown exorbitantly. This rapid growth prompted Shigeru Oda to comment that "throughout the history of international law, scarcely any other major concept have ever stood at the threshold of acceptance within such a short period."[44]

Opinio Juris

The requirement for the *opinio juris* element is referenced as the "psychological and recognition component" needed to create the formation of a cus-

---

[38] "Case Concerning Delimitation of the Maritime Boundary in the Gulf of Maine Area."

[39] Kwiatkowska, "New Soviet Legislation in the Economic Zone," 43.

[40] Kelsen, *Principles of International Law,* 445.

[41] Brian D. Lepard, *Customary International Law: A New Theory with Practical Applications* (Cambridge: Cambridge University Press, 2010), 122–39.

[42] Opinion of B. Cheng, Kelsen, *Principles of International Law.*

[43] R. R. Baxter, "Treaties and Custom," *RCADI* 129 (1970): 61–62.

[44] D'Arechaga, "Case Concerning the Continental Shelf," 228 para. 120.

tom.[45] In essence, the actions by the state correlate with internationally accepted principles of law.[46] Declarations, draft proposals, and official statements made at UNCLOS III are the main forum from which the *opinio juris* element evolved. During this Conference, particularly at the 1974 Caracas Session, virtually all the states supported the notion of a two-hundred-mile EEZ.[47] Other instances in which the *opinio juris* element can be inferred or identified include proclamations of national legislation, ratification of the LOS Convention, fishery and delimitation instruments regarding the two-hundred-mile EEZ, and legal opinions.[48] All these areas represent states' intent in recognizing the legal nature of their practices.

Rejection and Acceptance

Protest and acquiescence are key elements that need to be acknowledged when determining whether a practice is a customary norm.[49] These two elements also are important when determining whether a state practice is uniform and extensive.[50] Hence, when a pattern of state practice is emerging, some states may choose to stage a persistent objection to such practice, preventing it from becoming a general customary rule. A state's persistent objection is one way a state can protest a particular practice.[51] With this in mind, several judges in the Fisheries Jurisdiction Case noted that EFZs exceeding twelve miles did not create norms because of persistent objections from other states.[52]

But in some instances, states do nothing *vis-à-vis* a known practice but stay silent on the issue. In these cases, the issue that must be confronted is wheth-

---

[45] "International legal doctrine of other countries, with rare exceptions, considers, recognition or opinio juris a necessary and decisive element for the creation of a customary norm of international law." Tunkin, *Theory of International Law,* 119.

[46] Hudson, "Fishery and Economic Zones as Customary International Law." 682.

[47] Extavour, *The Exclusive Economic Zone,* 171–76.

[48] See "Convention Relative au Développement Régional des Pêches," 1115; "Preamble to the Niue Treaty on Cooperation in Fisheries Surveillance and Law Enforcement in the South Pacific Region, June 9, 1992," *ILM* 32 (1993): 136; also "Procureur de la République v. J. Crujeiras Tome, 1981," *RGDIP* (1983): 465.

[49] Attard, *The Exclusive Economic Zone in International Law,* 19.

[50] I. C. MacGibbon, "The Scope of Acquiescence in International Law," *BYIL* 31 (1954): 143.

[51] The dissenting state can also show its dissent by means of an express statement or vote against a particular rule. See Mark E. Villiger, *Customary International Law and Treaties: A Study of Their Interactions and Interrelations, with Special Considerations of the 1969 Vienna Convention on the Law of Treaties* (Boston: Martinus Nijhoff, 1985), 15.

[52] See discussion in chapter 1, note 169. Judge Dillard also emphasized the absence of protests against assertions that did not exceed 12 miles, *ibid.*, 58.

er such a silence should indicate complete dissatisfaction with an emerging state practice, or does the silence indicate that the state agreed with the practice. The ICJ was forced to consider a similar problem in *The Temple of Preah Vihear Case*. In this case, the Court reasoned that long-continued silence on the part of Thailand over a drawn boundary line prepared for Cambodia indicated that Thailand agreed with the drawn boundary line.[53] The Court stated that acquiescence can be assumed if there is "a failure to react ... on an occasion that called for a reaction in order to affirm or preserve [the claim] in the face of an obvious rival claim."[54]

Pertinent to the rapid growth of the EEZ concept, more than seventy states developed EEZs or EFZs between the years 1974 and 1981.[55] Protests were required from other interested states when Mexico first implemented a law based on the RSNT when the enforcement date was set for June 6, 1976,[56] only a month after the Fifth Session of UNCLOS III had ended in New York. Neither the GDS, LLS, nor major industrial states objected to the EEZ concept. In fact, the GDS and LLS sought to preserve some rights for themselves regarding this concept,[57] and the major maritime states were open to the concept, provided they could exercise non-economic rights in the zone.

Acceptance of a practice cannot be presumed unless a state has knowledge that a claim is being made. Regarding the circumstances involving Mexico, it does not seem plausible that participating states in the Fifth Session of UNCLOS III knew nothing about the claims that Mexico put forth. In fact, Mexico's action was followed by various other coastal states. In addition, during the early seventies, protests primarily came from the states of Japan, the United Kingdom, and West Germany. These states eventually developed their own two-hundred-mile EFZs. In essence, desistence from the protest by these states, combined with the notion that these states eventually developed their own EFZ, suggests not only that these states modified their position, but also

---

53 "Temple of Preah Vihear Case, (Cambodia v. Thailand)"; Presidential Proclamation No. 5030, in Smith, *Exclusive Economic Zone Claims*, 467; "Act Concerning the Maritime Areas of the Polish Republic and the Marine Administration, 1991"; Kaye and Rothwell, "Australia's Antarctic Maritime Claims and Boundaries"; Kwiatkowska, "Exclusive Economic Zone: General Evaluation."

54 *Ibid.*, 29.

55 Johnston and Gold, "Extended Jurisdiction", 27-49.

56 Mexico, Act of February 10, 1976 Regulating the Provisions of Paragraph 8 of Article 27 of the Political Constitution of the United Mexican States Concerning the Exclusive Economic Zone, in Smith, *Exclusive Economic Zone Claims*, 295, Article 1.

57 L. D. M. Nelson, "The Emerging New Law of the Sea," *Mod LR* 42 (1979): 54.

provides evidence that they were willing to accept new customary rules regarding the two-hundred-mile EFZ.

As the above analysis indicates, claims to the two-hundred-mile EEZ have satisfied the requirements set by international law for state practice regarding the establishment of customary norms. Thus, as noted in several judicial decisions rendered by the ICJ and arbitration panels[58] and expressed by various international legal experts,[59] the two-hundred-mile EEZ is an integral part of customary international law. As a result, the assertions made by Iguchi[60] and Zakharov,[61] as well as by other noted commentators concerning the nonbinding nature of the EEZ under the rubric of customary law, seems to be problematic.

The Scope of the EEZ Concept in Customary International Law

The importance of the analysis of the main components of the EEZ concept as it relates to customary international law is a central focus of a number of legal experts, especially those from Western Europe. The school of thought these legal experts support involves doubts as to whether the rights of coastal states other than those with interest in the living resources are part of the customary law rule concerning the two-hundred-mile EEZ.[62] In this context, Fleischer stated, "In state practice, it is the right to 200 miles for fisheries which commands the largest measure of general international acceptance, while the right to a full EEZ under contemporary customary law may be more questionable."[63] Thus, under

---

58 For example, D'Arechaga, "Case Concerning the Continental Shelf," 70 para. 100; "Case Concerning Delimitation of the Maritime Boundary in the Gulf of Maine Area," 265, para. 19; "Case Concerning the Delimitation of Marine Areas between Canada and the French Republic," *ILM* 31, no. 1145 (1992): 175, para. 88.

59 See Robert Y. Jenning, "What Is International Law, and How Do We Tell It When We See it," *Swiss YIL* 37 (1981): 82; Charney, "The Exclusive Economic Zone and Public International Law," 283–85.

60 Iguchi, "The Law of the Sea," 7.

61 Zakharov, "Comment to Article"; see also Kolodkin and Zakharov, "Some Aspects of Soviet State Practice on the Development of Ocean Resources," 214; Giulio Pontecorvo, "The Taking of Living Resources: Expectations and Reality," in *The 1982 Convention on the Law of the Sea, Proceedings of the Seventeenth Annual Conference, July 12–16, 1983,* ed. Albert W. Koers and Bernard H. Oxman (Honolulu: Law of the Sea Institute, University of Hawaii, 1984), 364.

62 See Michael Akehurst, *A Modern Introduction to International Law* (London: Routledge, 1982), 270–72; Jesper Grolin, "The Future of the Law of the Sea: Consequences of a Non Treaty or Non-Universal Treaty Situation," *ODIL* 13 (1983): 8–9.

63 Fleischer, "The Exclusive Economic Zone under the Convention Regime and in State Practice," 250.

customary international law, the right to assert a two-hundred-mile zone for fisheries involves a more comprehensive view of the EEZ concept.

National Practice

Many key concepts expressed at UNCLOS III played a considerable role in the implementation of such national instruments as official proclamations, decrees, and legislative measures. These acts became a defining force in state practice. Hence, when EEZ national claims are closely analyzed, it is easy to see the significance of the EEZ concept expressed in Article 56 of the LOS Convention or some of the negotiating texts that led to the development of the Convention.

Germane to the assertion of sovereign rights in exploring and exploiting the living and non-living resources of the EEZ and regarding the direct and collateral economic activities pertaining to the EEZ expressed in Article 56(1)(a) of the LOS Convention, there exists a near-absolute consensus on the national level. Essentially, with the exception of a very few EEZ claims that fail to refer to sovereign rights regarding activities that pertain to other economic uses of the EEZ, all other EEZ claims mirror the general principles of coastal states' sovereign rights reflected in Article 56(1)(a).[64]

Furthermore, except for a small percentage of EFZ claims[65] and fewer EEZ claims, all other EEZ claims include a provision that pertains to coastal states' jurisdiction over artificial islands, installations, and structures, and also includes provisions relating to the marine environment. In this context, of the 87 claims to the EEZ, 57 states claimed jurisdiction over artificial islands, installations, and structures in the EEZ;[66] 63 of these states asserted jurisdiction over MSR;[67] and over 80 states claimed jurisdiction over environmental safety issues.[68] Although these claims of jurisdiction vary according to the circumstances involved, varia-

---

[64] See UN Division for Ocean Affairs and the Law of the Sea. *Practice of States*, 10.

[65] It is noteworthy that, in practical terms, several EFZ claimant states exercise some type of jurisdiction over MSR in their own EFZs. See, for instance, Note from the Permanent Mission of Japan to the United Nations on Provisional Procedures for a Request to Conduct Marine Scientific Research by Foreign Research Vessels in the Territorial Sea, on the Continental Shelf or in the Fishing Zone of Japan, 28 July 1988, in UN Division for Ocean Affairs and the Law of the Sea, *The Law of the Sea*, 143; and Note to the United Nations on Regulations Governing Scientific Research in Waters under Belgian Jurisdiction, November 1, 1988, in *ibid.*, 33. For additional details, also see Soons, "Regulation of Marine Scientific Research," 267–71.

[66] Smith, *Exclusive Economic Zone Claims*, 34.

[67] *Ibid.*, 38.

[68] *Ibid.*, 35–37 Table 7.

tions do not represent a significant change in the basic components of the EEZ concept outlined in Article 56(1)(b) of the LOS Convention mostly because they relate to the specific regimes governing the activities that pertain to the fundamental component of the EEZ concept. Moreover, the EEZ is a package-deal network that comprises the rights of coastal states, as well as their duties and rights and the duties of third states. The rights and duties of each of these groups of states corresponds to the concept of the EEZ.

As mentioned earlier in Chapter four, a majority of EEZ claims have explicitly or implicitly acknowledged the basic rights contained in Article 58(1) of the LOS Convention, which belongs to third states and involves the freedom of navigation, overflight, and laying of submarine cables and pipelines. One legal expert highlighted the magnitude of national practice in this field by noting, "As a general rule, the freedom of navigation, overflight, and the laying of submarine cables and pipelines as well as other associated freedoms, are recognized at the conceptual level."[69]

Additionally, in its decision of June 10, 1992 in the Case Concerning the Delimitation of the Maritime Areas between Canada and the French Republic, the Arbitral Tribunal reasoned that "the principle of freedom of navigation through the 200 mile zone is guaranteed by Article 58 of the 1982 Convention, a provision that undoubtedly represents customary international law as much as the institution of the 200 mile zone itself."[70]

Recent Jurisprudence of the ICJ

Five decades have passed since the four Geneva Conventions on the LOS were implemented,[71] but their acceptance was not as widely accepted as UNCLOS III.[72] However, some states with major maritime interests are not signatories to one or more of these instruments.[73]

---

[69] Vicuña, *The Exclusive Economic Zone,* 149.

[70] UN Division for Ocean Affairs and the Law of the Sea, *Practice of States,* 14.

[71] "Convention on the Continental Shelf."

[72] "The Law of the Sea Convention."

[73] Of the thirty states that are not party to the LOS Convention, fifteen are coastal states and fifteen are landlocked states. The coastal states that are not a party to the convention include Colombia, Iran, Israel, Peru, Turkey, the United States, and Venezuela. The number of states party to the 1958 Geneva Convention on the LOS is relatively small: Convention on the Territorial Sea and the Contiguous Zone, 52 parties; Convention on the Continental Shelf, 58 parties; and Convention on the High Seas, 63 parties, "Convention on the Continental Shelf."

Over the past five decades, various international agreements have made formal reference to the relationship between customary international law and the LOS Convention.[74] This raises the issue of which provisions in these instruments are considered binding on all states under the principles of customary international law. A second and equally important question is which rules of customary international law that do not have a counterpart in LOS treaties are applicable to the principles of the LOS. The judicial decisions of the ICJ and other tribunals provides the answer to the first question. The answer to the second question can be found in the decisions and opinions of the International Tribunal for the Law of the Sea (ITLOS) and arbitration organizations.[75] Table 1 provides a comprehensive list of the cases in which the ICJ and other tribunals have addressed the relationship between customary international law and the provisions of UNCLOS III. Table 2 provides a list of the cases that have identified rules of customary norms that are not a part of LOS treaties, but are applicable in the context of the LOS.

Table 1

Corfu Channel Case (United Kingdom v. Albania), 1949 ICJ Rep. 4 (9 April) (straits used for international navigation)
Anglo-Norwegian Fisheries Case, 1951, ICJ Rep. 116, 128–43 (18 December) (Articles 7(1), 7(3), 7(5) (straight baselines)
North Sea Continental Shelf Cases (Federated Republic of Germany v. Denmark; Federal Republic of Germany v. Netherlands), 1969 ICJ Rep. 3, 22, 25, 27, 29, 32–33, 38–40, 45 (20 February) (1958 Continental Shelf Convention Articles 1–5; 1958 High Seas Convention Preamble)
Case Concerning Delimitation of the Maritime Boundary in the Gulf of Maine Area (Canada v. United States), 1984 ICJ Rep. 246, 294 (12 October) (exclusive economic zone regime)

[74] Examples include Articles 16 of the Agreement on Cooperation on Marine Oil Pollution Preparedness and Response in the Artic, 15 May 2013; Article 16 of the International Convention for the Control and Management of Ships' Ballast Water and Sediments, 2004, 13 February 2004; and Article 15 of the International Convention on the Control of Harmful Anti-Fouling Systems on Ships, 2001, October 5, 2001.

[75] Decisions of institutions that are created by the LOS Convention, supra note 72, such as the International Tribunal for the Law of the Sea (ITLOS), and Annexes VII and VIII arbitral tribunals are not likely to address the first question since only parties to the Convention may invoke their jurisdictional powers. However, Article 293(1) of the LOS Convention requires tribunals to apply "other rules of international law not incompatible with" the LOS convention where the convention did not refer to those rules.

Case Concerning the Continental Shelf (Libya v. Malta), 1985 ICJ Rep. 13, 33 (3 June) (Articles 57 breadth of the EEZ, 76(1) definition of the continental shelf, 83(1) delimitation)
Case Concerning Military and Paramilitary Activities in and Against Nicaragua (Nicaragua v. United States), 1986 ICJ Rep. 14, 111–12 (27 June) (Articles 18 meaning of passage, and 58 rights and duties of other states in the EEZ)
Case Concerning the Land, Island, and Maritime Frontier Dispute (El Salvador v. Honduras; Nicaragua intervening), 1992 ICJ Rep. 351, 588 (11 September) (Article 10 bays)
Case Concerning Maritime Delimitation in the Area Between Greenland and Jan Mayen (Denmark v. Norway), 1993 ICJ Rep. 38, 58, 59, 62 (14 June) (1958 Continental Shelf Convention Article 6 on delimitation)
Maritime Delimitation and Territorial Question Between Qatar and Bahrain (Qatar v. Bahrain), 2001 ICJ Rep. 40, 93, 94, 97, 101, 110, 111 (16 March) (Articles 2(1) legal status of territorial sea, 7(4) straight baselines, 13(1) low-tide elevations, 15 delimitation, 17 right of innocent passage, 74(1) and 83(1) delimitation, 12(2) islands; Articles 4(3), 11(1), 12(1), 14 of the 1958 Territorial Sea Convention)
The MOX Plant Case (Ireland v. United Kingdom), Provisional Measures, ITLOS Order, para. 82 (December 3, 2001) (duty to cooperate in Part XII)
Case Concerning Land Reclamation by Singapore in and around the Straits of Johor (Malaysia v. Singapore), Provisional Measures, ITLOS Order, para. 92 (October 8, 2003) (duty to cooperate Part XII)
Territorial and Maritime Dispute (Nicaragua v. Colombia), 2012 ICJ Rep. 1, 43, 50, 51, 66, 111 (19 November) (Articles 2(1) legal status of territorial sea, 3 breadth of territorial sea, 5 normal baseline, 74(1) delimitation, 76(1) definition of continental shelf, 83(1) delimitation, 121 regime of islands; Articles 1(1) and 2 (sovereign over territorial sea) Territorial Sea Convention)
Maritime Dispute (Peru v. Chile), 2014 ICJ Rep. para. 179 (27 January) (Articles 74(1) and 83(1) delimitation)

Table 2

Case Concerning Military and Paramilitary Activities in and Against Nicaragua (Nicaragua v. United States), 1986 ICJ Rep. 14, paras. 190–91 (27 June) (use of force)
The M/V "SAIGA" (No. 2) Case (Saint Vincent and the Grenadines v. Guinea), ITLOS judgment, para. 155 (1 July 1999) (use of force in maritime law enforcement)
Southern Bluefin Tuna Cases (New Zealand v. Japan; Australia v. Japan), Provisional Measures, ITLOS, sep. op. Judge Laing, para, 16 and note 6 (August 27, 1999) (precautionary principle not customary international law)
Guyana v. Suriname, Decision of Annex VII Arbitral Panel, paras. 405–6, 445 (September 17, 2007) (use of force)
Pulp Mills on the River Uruguay (Argentina v. Uruguay), Judgment, 2010, ICJ Rep. 14, 83, para. 204 (20 April) (environmental assessment required)

The ARA Libertad Case (Argentina v. Ghana), ITLOS Order on request for provisional measures, para. 95 (Case No. 20, December 15, 2012) (sovereign immunity of warships)
The M/V "Virginia G" Case (Panama v. Guinea Bissau), ITLOS Judgment, 49, para. 153 (Case No. 19, April 14, 2014) (exhaustion of local remedies as a prerequisite for diplomatic protect)

Various commentators and legal experts as well as states have voiced their opinion on these questions. For instance, the United States addressed the first question by stating, "The Convention contains provisions with respect to traditional uses of the oceans [such as navigation and overflight] which generally confirm existing maritime law and practice."[76] In the late 1980s, the United States and the Soviet Union declared that the LOS Convention "with respect to the traditional uses of the oceans, generally constitutes international law and practice."[77] The International Law Association (ILA) and the International Law Commission (ILC) have examined various aspects of customary international law. In 2000 at its 60th Conference that took place in London, the ILA implemented a "Statement of Principles Applicable to the Formation of General Customary International Law."[78] The ILC analyzed the subject "Identification of Customary International Law" and its impact on states.[79]

The ICJ, recently, has had to confront the relationship between customary international law and the law of the sea because, in a number of highly publicized cases, some states had not consented to be bound by the relevant instrument. The Court was compelled to choose what provisions of the 1958 or 1982 Conventions were considered customary international law and therefore binding on states that could declare themselves persistent objectors.[80]

---

[76] United States, "President's Ocean Policy Statement, March 10, 1983," The Division of Ocean Affairs and the Law of the Sea.

[77] Joint Statement by the United States and Soviet Union, with Uniform Interpretation of Rules of International Law Governing Innocent Passage. September 2, 1989. *Law of the Sea Bulletin* 14 (1989): 12–13; *ILM* 28 (1989): 1444–47; and *AJIL* 84 (1990): 239–42.

[78] International Law Association, "Final Report of the Committee on Formation of Customary (General) International Law: Statement of Principles Applicable to the Formation of General Customary International Law (as amended at the London Conference)," *Report of the Sixty-Ninth Conference* (London, International Law Association, 2000), 712–77.

[79] International Law Commission (ILC), "Formation and Evidence of Customary International Law and Identification of Customary International Law." To identify elements of the ILC's previous work on this issue, see UN Doc. A/CN.4/659 (March 14, 2013), and the Special Rapporteur's introductory Report, UN Doc. A/CN.4/663 (17 May 2013).

[80] Yoshifumi Tanaka, *The International Law of the Sea* (Cambridge: Cambridge University Press, 2012), 12.

Regarding the persistent objection to the Convention, Turkey and Venezuela are notable examples. Each state regularly voted against the annual UN General Assembly resolution concerning oceans and the law of the sea. Turkey's explanation of its objection reads in part:

> In our opinion, the Convention does not provide sufficient safeguards for special geographical situations, and, as a consequence, does not take into consideration conflicting interesting and sensitivities arising from special circumstances. Furthermore, the Convention does not allow states to register reservations to its articles. Although we agree with the Convention in its general intent and with most of its provisions, we are unable to become a party to it owing to those prominent shortcomings. That being the case, we cannot support a resolution that calls on states to become parties to the United Nations Convention on the Law of the Sea and to harmonize their national legislation with its provisions.[81]

In *Qatar v. Bahrain*[82] and *Nicaragua v. Colombia*,[83] Qatar and Colombia were not party to UNCLOS III whereas Bahrain and Nicaragua were. Neither Qatar or Bahrain were party to the 1958 Conventions whereas Nicaragua did not become a signatory of any of the 1958 Conventions and Colombia only signed the Convention on the Continental Shelf.

It is noteworthy that, except for the North Sea Continental Shelf Cases,[84] 1969, the ICJ has not explained why certain specific provisions of UNCLOS III meet the standards for customary international law: "international custom, as evidenced by a practice generally accepted as law."[85] As will be seen below,

---

[81] UN Doc. A/67/PV. 52 (December 12, 2012), 28. Venezuela objects to assertions of the universality of the LOS Convention for similar reasons, *ibid.*, 27.

[82] "Maritime Delimitation and Territorial Questions Between Qatar and Bahrain (Qatar v. Bahrain)," Judgment, *ICJ Rep.* (2001): 91, para. 167.

[83] "Territorial and Maritime Dispute (Nicaragua v. Colombia)," Judgment, *ICJ Rep.* (2012): 666, para. 114.

[84] "North Sea Continental Shelf Cases," 28–29, paras. 37–38, and 37–45, paras. 60–81.

[85] See "Case Concerning Military and Paramilitary Activities in and Against Nicaragua," 97–98, paras. 184–86, for an examination of the Court's methodology in determining customary international rules. Churchill and Lowe, *The Law of the Sea*, 7, explain that "international custom" means "a general and consistent practice adopted by States," particularly the practice of states mostly directly concerned; and "evidence of a practice generally accepted as law, also known as *opinio juris*, means "the conviction that the practice is one which is either required or allowed by customary international law, or more generally that the practice concerns a matter which is the subject of legal regulation and is consistent with international law."

the Court has acknowledged that only certain treaty provisions may be customary international law or they may not be.

The Exclusive Economic Zone

In the 1980s, a Chamber of the ICJ ruled that the EEZ concept was, indeed, customary international law.[86] Later, in the *Libya v. Malta Case,*[87] the full Court made a similar ruling. In the *Libya* case, the Court further held that Article 57 is also customary international law.[88] The ICJ, in the 1986 *Nicaragua v. United States* case, ruled that high seas navigational freedoms apply to the EEZ, as determined by Article 58.[89] In 2012, a decision by the ICJ held that the delimitation provisions of Article 74(1) represented customary international law.[90] The U.S. supports the notion that military survey activities in the EEZ are compatible with customary international law as a high seas freedom of navigation.[91]

James Crawford asserts that in 2012, "the EEZ forms part of customary law. ... The customary law version of the concept closely relates to the version that emerged in UNCLOS III. Under UNCLOS and customary law, the zone is optional and its existence depends on an actual claim."[92] Crawford observed that "many high seas freedoms are applicable in the EEZ (Articles 58, 86), and this is also the position in customary international law."[93]

---

86 "Case Concerning Delimitation of the Maritime Boundary in the Gulf of Maine Area," 294, para. 94.

87 "Case Concerning the Continental Shelf (Libyan Arab Jamahiriya v. Malta)," 33, para. 34. "The institution of the exclusive economic zone, with its rule on entitlement by reason of distance, is shown by the practice of states to have become part of customary law."

88 *Ibid.*

89 "Case Concerning Military and Paramilitary Activities in and Against Nicaragua," 111, para. 214.

90 "Territorial and Maritime Dispute (Nicaragua v. Colombia)," 674, para. 139. The Court reaffirmed this conclusion in "Maritime Dispute (Peru v. Chile)," ICJ Rep. (2014): para. 179.

91 Views the U.S. expressed to the Republic of Korea in 2001 regarding *USNS Bowditch,* excerpted in *Digest of U.S. Practice in International Law* (Washington, DC: Government Printing Office, 2001), 698.

92 James Crawford, *Brownlie's Principles of Public International Law* (Oxford: Oxford University Press, 2012), 265. Crawford states that "foreign ships have a right of innocent passage through the territorial sea in customary law"; Brownlie, *Principles of Public International Law,* 187, stated that the predecessor of Article 17 and 18 of the LOS Convention and article 14 of the Territorial Sea Convention, "in substance corresponds to the customary law, but it is more specific in certain respects."

93 Crawford, *Brownlie's Principles,* 297, referring to the Nicaragua v. United States Case.

Concerning the EEZ and as expressed in Part V of the LOS Convention, Churchill and Lowe observed that:

> What is part of customary international law are the broad rights of coastal and other states enumerated in article 56 and 58 of the Convention. It is much more doubtful whether the detailed obligations in the articles relating to the exercise of coastal state jurisdiction over fisheries, pollution, and research have passed or are likely to quickly pass into customary international law, partly because of a lack of claims embodying the duties of the Convention, partly because there is some divergence between state practice and the Convention, and partly because some of the conventional rules would not seem to have the 'fundamentally norm-creating character' necessary for the creation of a rule of customary international law.[94]

When it comes to fisheries, the same authors note that,

> What is much less certain is whether the coastal state's fishery management duties set out in article 61 and 62 have become part of customary law.[95]

> Most of the twenty or so states which still claim or in the past have claimed a 200-mile exclusive fishing zone claim the jurisdiction to control fisheries research in the zone where it involves the taking of fish. ... It is likely that in general such claims now represents a rule of customary international law, first because there have been no protests to such claims (so far as we are aware), and secondly, because similar claims made in respect of twelve-mile exclusive fishing zones were ... generally accepted.[96]

Crawford asserted that "the concept of preferential fishing rights seems to have survived in customary law" regardless of its absence from UNCLOS III.[97]

---

94 Churchill and Lowe, *The Law of the Sea*, 161–62.

95 *Ibid.*, 290. See also 291 for a discussion expressing doubts of a possible customary law rule requiring foreign fishing vessels be given access to any surplus in the EEZ.

96 *Ibid.*, 409–10.

97 Crawford, *Brownlie's Principles*, 275–76.

The U.S. asserted that salmon fishing on the high seas, as expressed in Article 66(3), represents the core principles of customary international law.[98]

Concerning the rights of GDS and LLS to exploit the living resources of the EEZ, one commentator observed that "in light of the paucity of state practice on this subject, it remains uncertain whether and to what extent Articles 69–72 of LOSC have become customary international law."[99]

The High Seas

The ICJ has not examined the issue of the status of customary international law as it pertains to the provisions of Part VII "The High Seas" of UNCLOS III. However, the Second Preambular paragraph of the 1958 High Seas Convention provides that its guidelines correlate with the "established principles of international law."[100] The Court has concluded that Article 2 regarding the freedoms of the seas represent customary international law.[101]

The guidelines of the High Seas Convention are reflected in Section 1 of Part VII, Articles 86–115, of the LOS Convention:

1. Article 87—freedom of the high seas (the High Seas Convention, Article 2);[102]
2. Article 89—invalidity of sovereignty claims over the high seas (Article 2, first sentence of the High Seas Convention);[103]

---

98 United States Letter of Submittal on the Convention for the Conservation of Anadromous Stocks in the Northern Pacific, 14 May 1992, S. Treaty Doc. 102-30, excerpted in *Digest of U.S. Practice in International Law, 1991–1999*, 1703–4.
99 Tanaka, *The International Law of the Sea*, 385.
100 "Convention on the High Seas, Geneva."
101 Tanaka, *The International Law of the Sea*, 23. Concurred regarding Article 2.2.
102 Churchill and Lowe, *The Law of the Sea*, 204, stated that Articles 87 and 89 are customary international law. In a submission to the IMO's Marine Environment Protect Committee, the United States, Liberia, the Marshall Islands, Singapore, the International Association of Independent Tankers Owners, the International Chamber of Shipping, and the Oil Companies International Marine Forum stated: "The historical principles of the high seas freedoms of navigation are founded in customary international law and memorialized in Articles 58 and 87 of the United Nations Convention on the Law of the Sea, 1982 (UNCLOS)." IMO doc. MEPC 58/10/7, August 15, 2008, 2, para. 10.
103 Donald R. Rothwell and Tim Stephens, *The International Law of the Sea* (Oxford: Hart, 2010), 155. These authors noted that Article 89 "is consistent with customary international law on this matter."

3. Article 90—right of navigation (Article 4 of the High Seas Convention);
4. Article 91—nationality of ships (Article 5 of the High Sea Convention);[104]
5. Article 92—status of ships (Article 6 of the High Seas Convention);[105]
6. Article 93—ships flying the UN flag (Article 7 of the High Seas Convention);
7. Article 94—duties of the flag state (Article 5(1) and 10 of the High Seas Convention);[106]
8. Article 95—immunity of warships on the high seas (Article 8 of the High Seas Convention);[107]
9. Article 96—immunity of ships used only on government non-commercial service (Article 9 of the High Seas Convention);
10. Article 97—penal jurisdiction in collisions (Article 11 of the High Seas Convention);
11. Article 98—duty to render assistance (Article 12 of High Seas Convention);
12. Article 99—prohibition of transport of slaves (Article 13 of the High Seas Convention);
13. Articles 100–107—piracy (Article 14–20 of the High Seas Convention);[108]

---

[104] Churchill and Lowe, *The Law of the Sea,* 258, expressed doubt that the genuine link requirement in Article 5(1) of the High Seas Convention represents customary international law.

[105] Tanaka, *The International Law of the Sea,* 152 and 155 stated that the principle of the exclusive jurisdiction of the flag state (Article 92(1) first sentence) is well established in customary international law.

[106] See the discussion of the *travaux préparatoires* of Article 10 of the High Seas Conventions, in Bernard Oxman, "The Duty to Respect Generally Accepted International Standards," *New York University Journal of International Law and Politics* 26 (1991): 109, 122–29.

[107] Rothwell and Stephens, *The International Law of the Sea,* 161, surmised that Article 95, 96, and 236 "reflect existing customary international law with respect to sovereign immunity of states which itself is founded upon extensive jurisprudence by domestic courts and relevant municipal legislation."

14. Article 110—right of visit (Article 22 of the High Seas Convention);[109]

15. Article 111—right of pursuit (Article 23 of the High Seas Convention);[110] and

16. Articles 112–15—submarine cables and pipelines (Articles 26–29 of the High Seas Convention).

The United States stated that Article 92 of the LOS Convention, along with Article 6 of the High Seas Conventions, codifies customary international law.[111] The United States noted that the semantics of Article 110 is customary international law.[112]

The ITLOS, in the M/V "SAIGA" Case, provided that:

> Although the Convention does not contain express provisions on the use of force in the arrest of ships, international law, which is applicable by virtue of Article 293 of the Convention, requires that the use of force must be avoided as far as possible and, where force is unavoidable, it must not go beyond what is reasonable and necessary in the circumstances.[113]

---

108 Brownlie, *Principles of Public International Law,* 229, stated that the definition of piracy in Article 15 of the High Seas Convention is thought to represent the existing customary law. Tanaka, *The International Law of the Sea,* 160 noted, "Under customary law and Article 105 of the LOSC, every State may seize a pirate ship or aircraft and arrest suspect pirate."

109 Churchill and Lowe, *The Law of the Sea,* 212, noted that Article 22 of the High Seas Convention and Article 110 of the LOS Convention "are generally regarded as codifying customary international law." Brownlie, *Principles of Public International Law,* believed that the right of approach in time of peace is recognized by customary law. Tanaka, *The International Law of the Sea,* 161, stated, "One can say that the right of visit to a ship that is engaged in the slave trade represents customary law."

110 Churchill and Lowe, *The Law of the Sea,* 214–15, acknowledged that the right of hot pursuit is recognized under customary international law.

111 Statement of the U.S. Representative to the UN Security Council, February 9, 1990, UN Doc. S/PV.2907 (February 9, 1990) 26–37, excerpted in *Digest of U.S. Practice in International Law, 1989–1990,* 454–55.

112 U.S. Department of State telegram to U.S. Embassy Muscat, December 6, 1989, excerpted in, *ibid.,* 468–69.

113 "The M/V *SAIGA* (No. 2) Case (St. Vincent and the Grenadian v. Guinea)," Judgment, (July 1, 1999).

One author noted that "insofar as jurisdiction is concerned, UNCLOS Part VII generally reflects customary international law," commenting specifically on Articles 88–90, 92(1), and 94.[114] This same author observed that "custom has come to reflect" piracy as defined by Article 101,[115] and that the right of approach, although not mentioned in UNCLOS Part VII, is considered customary international law.[116]

Other commenters support the notion that the right of "ships to enter the territorial sea on a temporary basis to provide assistance to vessels in distress or persons in jeopardy at sea" exists under customary international law, in Articles 18(2) and 98 of the LOS Convention and the Safety of Life at Sea Convention.[117] Crawford provides that the "freedom of fishing on the high seas was well established in customary international law," but is qualified by the conditions put forth in the LOS Convention Part VII, Section 2.[118]

Submarine Cables

The ICJ declared, in the *North Sea Continental Shelf Cases,* that Article 4 of the 1958 Continental Shelf Convention was customary international law.[119] The Court also ruled that the Preamble to the High Seas Convention is compatible with the standards of international law.[120] The issue of submarine cables is addressed in Articles 26–29 of the High Seas Convention. The provisions of the LOS Convention that pertain to submarine cables, Articles 21(1)(c), 51(2), 58(1), 79, 87(1)(c), 112–15, and 297(1)(a), have not been examined by the international courts to determine if they correlate to customary norms. In the book *Submarine Cables: the Handbook of Law and Policy,* the authors asserted that "most of the provisions of UNCLOS (including the provisions on submarine cables) can be said to bind non-parties as they are the best evidence of customary law."[121]

---

114 Crawford, *Brownlie's Principles,* 301.
115 *Ibid.,* 303.
116 *Ibid.,* 307.
117 Rothwell and Stephens, *The International Law of the Sea,* 77.
118 Crawford, *Brownlie's Principles,* 321.
119 "Case Concerning the Continental Shelf (Libyan Arab Jamahiriya v. Malta)," 39–40, para. 65.
120 *Ibid.,* 40, para. 65.
121 Douglas R. Burnett, Tara Davenport, and Robert C. Beckman, "Overview of the International Legal Regime Governing Submarine Cables," in *Submarine Cables: The Handbook of Law and Policy,* ed. D. R. Burnett, Robert C. Beckman, and Tara Davenport (Leiden: Martinus Nijhoff, 2014), 65.

The Regime of Islands

In the *Nicaragua v. Colombia* Case, the ICJ reasoned that the three paragraphs of Article 121 pertaining to the regime of the islands are customary norms.[122]

Landlocked and Geographically Disadvantaged States

The customary international status of various provisions relating to LLS and GDS contained in the LOS Convention has not been analyzed by the courts and tribunals. One author noted that navigational freedom relating to the navigational rights of LLS "can reasonably be considered as part of customary international law."[123]

Marine Pollution

The ICJ has noted that the "general obligation of states to ensure that activities under their jurisdiction and control respect the environment or other states or of areas beyond national control is now apart of the corpus of international law relating to the environment."[124] The rule mirrors Article 194(2) of the LOS Convention, which is considered customary international law.[125]

ITLOS has stated that "the duty to cooperate is a fundamental principle in the prevention of pollution of the marine environment under Part XII of the Convention and general international law and that rights arise therefrom which the Tribunal may consider appropriate to preserve under 290 of the Convention."[126]

The ICJ has ruled that "it may now be considered a requirement under general international law to undertake an environmental assessment where there is a risk that the proposed industrial activity may have a significantly adverse impact in a transboundary context, in particular, on a shared resource."[127] This obligation is reflected in Article 206, Assessment of potential effects of activities of the

---

122 "Territorial and Maritime Dispute (Nicaragua v. Colombia)," 674, para. 139.

123 Tanaka, *The International Law of the Sea*, 387 and 382–85.

124 "Pulp Mills on the River Uruguay (Argentina v. Uruguay)," Judgment, *ICJ Rep.* (2010, April 20): 14, 78, para. 193, quoting "Legality of the Threat or Use of Nuclear Weapons," Advisory Opinion, *ICJ Rep.* (1996): 241–42, para. 29.

125 "The MOX Plant Case (Ireland v. United Kingdom)," Provisional Measures, ITLOS sep. op. Judge Wolfrum *ICJ Rep.* (2001, December 3): 3.

126 "Case Concerning Land Reclamation by Singapore in and around the Straits of Johor (Malaysia v. Singapore)," Provisional Measures, ITLOS order, *ICJ Rep.* (2003, October 8): para. 92, quoting the *MOX Plant Case*, Order of December 3, 2001, para. 82. The duty to cooperate is stated in Article 197 of the LOS Convention.

127 "Pulp Mills on the River Uruguay (Argentina v. Uruguay)," 14, 83, para. 204 (20 April).

LOS Convention. Judges Laing and Wolfrum believe that the precautionary principle is not representative of customary international law.[128]

Churchill and Lowe note that the following provisions in Part XII of the LOS Convention reflect customary international law:

1. Article 210(5)—dumping within the territorial sea, EEZ, and onto the shelf;[129]
2. Article 221—intervention beyond the territorial sea;[130] and
3. Article 236—sovereign immunity.[131]

These two authors further observed, "In light of this limited and somewhat divergent practice, it must be doubtful whether those provisions of the Law of the Sea Convention relating to coastal and port state jurisdiction in respect of ships which go beyond the traditional law have become part of customary international law."[132]

Tanaka studied the relationship between customary international law and marine environmental protection prior to 1982[133] and under the LOS Convention.[134] Concerning the LOS Convention, Tanaka said, "there maybe room for the view that obligations for the protection of the marine environment embodied in the LOSC have become part of customary law."[135] He further asserted that the duty to notify that is a part of Article 198 may already fit the requirements of customary international law.[136] The final report of the ILA's Committee on Coastal State Jurisdiction Relating to Marine Pollution states that the terms "generally accepted international rules and standards [located

[128] Judge Laing, "Southern Bluefin Tuna Cases (New Zealand v. Japan; Australia v. Japan)," Provisional Measures, ITLOS, sep. op. *ICJ Rep.* (1999, August 27): para. 16 and note 6; "The MOX Plant Case (Ireland v. United Kingdom)."

[129] Churchill and Lowe, *The Law of the Sea*, 369.

[130] *Ibid.*, 355.

[131] *Ibid.*, 351.

[132] *Ibid.*, 352–53.

[133] Tanaka, *The International Law of the Sea*, 260–61.

[134] *Ibid.*, 264 and 266.

[135] *Ibid.*, 264.

[136] *Ibid.*, 266.

within Articles 21(4), 211(2), 211(5), 211(6)(c), and 226(1)(a)] cannot be equated with customary international law."[137]

Marine Scientific Research

Although the various international courts and tribunals have not address the customary international law status of the provisions on MSR contained in Part XIII of the LOS Convention, the U.S. supports the notion that the right to regulate MSR in the territorial sea contained in Article 21(1)(g) of the LOS Convention is customary international law.[138]

Churchill and Lowe commented upon this issue by observing,

The principle of coastal state consent for research in the EEZ and on the continental shelf is now part of customary international law. However, many of the details of the Convention regime, such as the period of notice and implied consent, are not now, and are probably incapable of becoming part of customary international law because of the paucity of state practice and because they do not seem to have the fundamentally norm-creating character necessary an emergent rule of customary law.[139]

---

137 "Final Report of the ILA Committee on Coastal State Jurisdiction Relating to Marine Pollution," Conclusion No. 2, in International Law Association, "Final Report of the Committee," 475 and 478–81.

138 U. S. State Department telegram, 28 February 1989, excerpted in *Digest of U. S. Practice in International Law, 1989–1990,* 478.

139 Churchill and Lowe, *The Law of the Sea,* 409.

Conclusion

Coastal states could not make any claim to the seabed lying beneath the high seas or to the living resources found in the high seas waters column during the years prior to World War II. This dramatically changed for coastal states during the years that followed the Second World War. During these years, various state acts and assertions led to the development of continental-shelf theory, which facilitated the development of the EEZ. The 1952 Santiago Declaration on the two-hundred-mile Maritime Zone made by Chile, Ecuador, and Peru not only led the way in such developments, but also became instrumental in states controlling all resources off the coast up to two hundred nautical miles, a feature that became the focal point of the EEZ doctrine.

UNCLOS I initiated the attempt to regulate shelf jurisdiction and in many ways was successful, despite its partial failure to set a definitive outer limit to coastal states' jurisdiction over the continental shelf's resources. UNCLOS II took a step further, moving the process to superjacent waters. However, although the two-hundred-mile resource zone figured in the final conclusion of UNCLOS II, the Conference did not have the widespread support it needed to make it a practical reality. In fact, the Conference did not agree on the right of coastal states to have contiguous fishing zones that extended beyond six miles in width when the territorial sea limit was set at six miles, essentially leaving the issue of a contiguous fishery zone in the domain of customary international law.

In the time intervening between UNCLOS II and UNCLOS III, countries realized a need to recognize the two-hundred-mile contiguous zone partly due to political and technological developments that defined this period. Nevertheless, until the start of UNCLOS III proceedings, the two-hundred-mile resources zone was a peculiarity that was germane to the law of the sea practice of Latin American and African nations. Hence, although various Latin American and African states had made claims to extend and had effectively extended their two-hundred-mile fisheries jurisdiction, many independent maritime states—developed and developing nations—confined their fishery jurisdiction to a limit of no more than twelve miles. Thus, by the mid-1970s, the concept of the two-hundred-mile resources zone had not developed into a customary norm because it was not uniform in practice and had not satisfied the element of generality needed to become customary international law.

However, the dramatic depletion of fishing resources that became prevalent during the early 1970s, coupled with the desire of developing states to gain access to new economic resources allocated to them by the global community, helped facilitate a need for a two-hundred-mile EEZ. UNCLOS III, whose objective involved codifying the developments of the law of the sea, provided the platform wherein the conceptual content of the two-hundred-mile EEZ could take form and be clarified.

The results of this Conference were detailed in UNCLOS negotiating texts, particularly the 1977 ICNT. The rules and principles of agreement in the latter text illuminated the conventional legal regime that would govern the future EEZ. These rules and principles remained virtually intact until their inclusion in the LOS Conclusion. The security they offered and the emerging consensus relating to the two-hundred-mile EEZ helped encourage many coastal states to establish EEZs based on the agreed rules, thereby providing a framework for the two-hundred-mile EEZ to become a practical reality and an established rule of customary international law before the final adoption of the LOS Convention.

Regarding the scope of the EEZ concept as it pertains to customary international law, importantly, during the developmental stages of the EEZ concept at UNCLOS III, the EEZ concept to which various states adhered, especially the major industrial states, had competed with the broader EEZ concept. But, as the work of UNCLOS III came into focus and national legislations pertaining to the two-hundred-mile zone were implemented, the fundamental approach of the EEZ outlined in Article 56(1) of the LOS Convention, composed of a series of separate types of jurisdictions, prevailed in state practice. One legal expert commented on this development by stating:

> Owing to widespread acceptance, within a few years the 200 miles fishery zone acquired the status of a customary rule of international law and many coastal states, great maritime powers included, completed their shift towards extended marine jurisdiction by proclaiming exclusive economic zones. Such proclamations were made easier by the fact that the concept of the exclusive economic zone, at least as it appears from Part V of the Montego Bay Convention, does not encroach upon the traditional freedom of navigation.[1]

In essence, contemporary state practice suggests that the right to claim a practical jurisdiction up to a two-hundred-mile limit from the baselines from which the breadth of the territorial sea is measured is considered part of customary international law. Even if a coastal state decides to assert an EEZ of less than two-hundred miles, its actions are still compatible with the princi-

---

[1] Tullio Scovazzi, "Explaining Exclusive Fishery Jurisdiction," *MP* 9 (1985): 125.

ples of international law as the precise width under customary international law and under the LOS Convention is discretionary.

In addition, the right in question is applicable to all parts of the coasts of a state. It is not restricted to states where special circumstances call for a need to implement measures that protect the resource interests of the fishery population, nor to such parts of a coastal state's coastline where specific evidence exists of such needs.

State practice also indicates that within the asserted two-hundred mile EEZ, the claimant state can call on the jurisdictional rights specified in Article 56(1) and (b) of the LOS Convention. A state that was party to the LOS Convention can implement such jurisdictional rights against another party to the Convention under the international norm *pacta sunt servanda,*[2] and against non-parties in accordance with the general principles of customary international law. As noted in Article 38 of the 1969 Vienna Convention on the Law of Treaties: "Nothing in Article 34 to 37 [dealing with the problem of *pacta tertis*] precludes a rule set forth in a treaty from becoming binding upon a third state as a customary rule of international law, recognized as such."

It must be remembered that if a coastal state decides to assert only one of these fundamental rights, its actions remain within the domain of public international law because, as noted by one leading commentator, states they "are not required by international law to fully exercise all rights ... they acquire under customary international law."[3] However, other states retain the option they had before the new customary rule relating to the two-hundred-mile EEZ became a reality because under the LOS Convention and state practice, the EEZ does not exist *ipso facto* as does the shelf, but must be asserted.

Additionally, state practice seems to confirm that the basic conventional rights of third states to have freedom of overflight, laying cables and pipelines, and of navigation, are part of Article 58(1) of the LOS Convention and are viewed as an international norm relating to the two-hundred-mile EEZ, which confirms the *sui generis* nature of the zone agreed at UNCLOS III. In short, the EEZ has been kept as part of customary international law subject to the same rules, specifically those whose main features are *sui generis* in character.

Regarding the status of the EEZ regime in its relationship with customary international law, general compliance with the EEZ's basic provisions of the LOS Convention, coupled with international courts and tribunal judicial ac-

---

[2] Vienna Convention on the Law of Treaties opened for Signature May 23, 1969, Article 26, Text in *ILM* 8 (1969): 679.

[3] Soons, *Marine Scientific Research and the Law of the Sea*, 272.

tions regarding the EEZ customary international law relationship, supports the notion that the two concepts interrelate. For instance, state practice confirms that the conservation objective of Article 61 and the use mandate expressed in Article 62 are considered customary international law, whereas courts and tribunals have identified and substantiated provisions of the law of the sea as customary international law. In essence, these courts and tribunals used an exhaustive analysis to conclude that a substantial number of provisions are customary norms rather than a *tour d'horizon* of the most important decisions related to the law of the sea issues to reach their decisions.

Bibliography

"Accord Cadre de Coopération en Matière de Pèche entre le Gouvernement de la République Algérienne Démocratique et Populaire et le Gouvernement de la République Islamique de Mauritanie, 1988," *Journal Officiel de la République Algérienne Démocratique et Populaire,* No. 6 (1988): 149.

"Accords Passés avec la Guinée Bissau le 27 Février 1980," *Official Journal of the European Community,* No. L. 226 du 29 Aout 1980, 33.

"Act Concerning the Maritime Areas of the Polish Republic and the Marine Administration, 1991." *Law of the Sea Bulletin,* no. 21 (1991): 66.

"African, Caribbean and Pacific States-European Economic Community: Final Act, Minutes, and Fourth ACP-EEC Convention of Lomé." *International Legal Materials* 29 (1990): 783–87.

"African States: Conclusions of the Regional Seminar on the Law of the Sea." *International Legal Materials* 12 (1973): 210–13.

"African States Declaration on the Issues of the Law of the Sea, May 1973." *International Legal Materials* 12 (1973): 1200.

Aguilar, Andrés M. "The Patrimonial Sea or Economic Zone Concept." *San Diego Law Review* 11 (1974): 579–602.

Akehurst, Michael. "Custom as a Source of International Law." *British Yearbook of International Law* 42 (1975): 1–53.

Akehurst, Michael. *A Modern Introduction to International Law.* London: Routledge, 1982.

Alam, Shah. "The Problem of the Legal Status of the Exclusive Economic Zone." *Indian Journal of International Law* 24 (1984): 468–88.

Alexander, Bruce E. "The Territorial Sea of the United States: Is it Twelve Miles or Not?" *Journal of Maritime Law and Commerce* 20 (1989): 449–87.

Alexander, Lewis M. "Breath of Territorial Sea and Other Offshore Zone." In *The Law of the Sea: Offshore Boundaries and Zones,* edited by L. M. Alexander. Columbus: Ohio State University Press, 1967.

Alexander, Lewis M. "Regional Arrangement in the Oceans." *American Journal of International Law* 71 (1977): 84-109.

Alexander, Lewis M. "Regionalism and the Law of the Sea: The Case of Semi-Enclosed Seas." *Ocean Development and International Law* 2 (1974): 151–86.

Al Mour, Awadh Mohamed. "The Legal Status of the Exclusive Zone." *Revue Egyptienne de Droit International* 33 (1977): 35–69.

Amador, F. V. García. *The Exploitation and Conservation of the Resources of the Sea.* Leiden, Netherlands: A. W. Sijthoff, 1973.

Amador, F. V. García. "The Latin American Contribution to the Development of the Law of the Sea." Law of the Sea Institute, Occasional Paper No. 14. July 1972.

Anand, Ram P. *Legal Regime of the Seabed and the Developing Countries.* Delhi, India: Thomson Press, 1975.

Anand, Ram P. "The Politics of a New Legal Order for Fisheries." *Ocean Development and International Law* 11 (1982): 265–95.

"Anglo-Norwegian Fisheries Case (United Kingdom v. Norway)." *International Court of Justice Reports* (1951): 116.

Annex V, Conciliation, Article 7(2). *Official Records* 15 (1981): 235.

Arbour, Jean Maurice. "L'Affaire du Chalutier-Usine 'La Bretagne' ou les Droits de l'État Côtier dans sa Zone Économique Exclusive." *Canadian Yearbook of International Law* 24 (1986): 61–89.

"Asylum Case (Colombia v. Peru)." *International Court of Justice Reports* (1950): 266.

Attard, D. J. *The Exclusive Economic Zone in International Law.* Oxford: Clarendon Press, 1987.

"Australian Fisheries Amendment Act, 1978." In *New Direction in the Law of the Sea: Documents,* edited by Robin Churchill, Myron H. Nordquist, and S. Houston Lay, vol. 10. Dobbs Ferry, NY: Oceana, 1973.

"Avec la Guinée," *Official Journal of the European Community,* No. L. 237 du 28 Aout 1983, 15.

The Bahamas Fisheries Resources Act, 1977, in ST/LEG/SER. B/19 (1980): 18–19.

Balasubramanian, S. P. "Fisheries Provisions of the ICNT—Part II." *Marine Policy* 6 (1982): 27–42.

Baxter, R. R. "Treaties and Custom." *Recueil des Cours de l'Académie de Droit International* 129 (1970): 25–105.

Beale, Joseph H. "Jurisdiction of a Sovereign State." *Harvard Law Review* 36 (1923): 241–262.

"Behring Sea Fur Seals Arbitration (Great Britain v. United States of America), 1893." *Moore Digest* 1 (1898): 755.

"Belize Act of January 24, 1992." *Law of the Sea Bulletin,* no. 21 (1992): 3.

Bernhardt, Rudolf. "Custom and Treaty in the Law of the Sea." *Recueil des Cours de l'Académie de Droit International* 205 (1987): 251–329.

Birnie, Patricia W. "Contemporary Maritime Legal Problems." In *The Maritime Dimensions,* edited by Ronald Peter Barston and Patricia W. Birnie, 169–189. London: George Allen and Unwin, 1980.

Birnie, Patricia W. "The Law of the Sea before and after UNCLOS I and UNCLOS II." In *The Maritime Dimensions,* edited by Ronald Peter Barston and Patricia W. Birnie, 8–26. London: George Allen and Unwin, 1980.

Bishop, W. W. "The 1958 Geneva Convention on Fishing and Conservation of the Living Resources of the High Seas." *Cornell Law Review* 62 (1982): 1206–29.

Black, Henry Campbell, Joseph R. Nolan, and Jacqueline M. Nolan-Haley, *Black's Law Dictionary,* 6th ed. St. Paul, MN; West, 1990.

Boczek, Boleslaw A. "Peacetime Military Activities in the Exclusive Economic Zone of Third Countries." *Ocean Development and International Law* 19 (1988): 445–68.

Bosma, John T. "The Alternative Futures of Naval Force." *Ocean Development and International Law* 5 (1978): 181–249.

Bouchez, L., G. Jaenicke, and R. Y. Jennings. "Feasibility Study on the Development of Industrial Islands in the North Sea." *International Law Aspects* 4 (1974): 2.

Bowett, Derek W. *The Law of the Sea.* Manchester: Manchester University Press, 1967.

Boyle, Alan E. "Marine Pollution under the Law of the Sea Convention." *American Journal of International Law* 79 (1985): 347–72.

"Brazil: Decree-Law Extending Territorial Sea to 200 Miles No. 1098 of May 15, 1970." *International Legal Materials* 10 (1971): 1224–25.

Brennan, K. G. "Jurisdiction of Coastal States and Other States in the Exclusive Economic Zone." Paper presented before the Seventh International Ocean Symposium of the Ocean Association of Japan, Oct. 21–22, 1982, 45–50.

Brown, Edward D. "The Continental Shelf and the Exclusive Economic Zone: The Problem of Delimitation at UNCLOS III." *Maritime Policy and Management* 4 (1976): 377–408.

Brown, Edward D. "The Exclusive Economic Zone: Criteria and Machinery for the Resolution of International Conflicts between Different Users of the EEZ." *Maritime Policy and Management* 4 (1977): 325–50.

Brown, Edward D. *The International Law of the Sea: Introductory Manual.* Brookfield, VT: Dartmouth, 1994.

Brown, Edward D. "The Significance of a Possible EC EEZ for the Law Relating to Artificial Islands, Installations and Structures, and to Cables and Pipelines, in the Exclusive Economic Zone." *Ocean Development and International Law* 23 (1992): 115–44.

Brownlie, Ian. *Principles of Public International Law.* 4th ed. Oxford: Clarendon Press, 1990.

Burke, William T. "Exclusive Fisheries Zones and Freedom of Navigation." *San Diego Law Review* 20 (1983): 595-624.

Burke, William T. "Highly Migratory Species in the New Law of the Sea." *Ocean Development and International Law* 14 (1983): 273–314.

Burke, William T. "The Law of the Sea Convention Provisions on Conditions of Access to Fisheries Subject to National Jurisdiction." *Oregon Law Review* 63 (1984): 73–119.

Burke, William T. "Scientific Research." In *The United States without the Law of the Sea Treaty: Opportunities and Costs,* edited by Lawrence Juda, 113–15. Kingston: University of Rhode Island, Center for Ocean Management Studies, 1983.

Burke, William T. "U.S. Fishery Management and the New Law of the Sea." *American Journal of International Law* 76 (1982): 24–55.

Burke, William T., Richard Legatski, and William W. Woodhead. *National and International Enforcement in the Ocean.* Seattle, WA: University of Washington Press, 1975.

Burnett, Douglas R., Tara Davenport, and Robert C. Beckman, "Overview of the International Legal Regime Governing Submarine Cables." In *Submarine Cables: The Handbook of Law and Policy,* edited by D. R. Burnett, Robert C. Beckman, and Tara Davenport. Leiden: Martinus Nijhoff, 2014.

Caddy, J. F. "Some Considerations Relevant to the Definition of Shared Stocks and their Allocation between Adjacent Economic Zones." In Food and Agriculture Organization of the United Nations Fisheries Circular No. 1749. July 1982.

Caflish, Lucius. "The Fishing Rights of Land-Locked and Geographically Disadvantaged States in the Exclusive Economic Zone." In *La Zona Economica Esclusiva,* edited by Benedetto Conforti, 29–48. Milan: Giuffrè, 1983.

Caminos, Hugo. "The Regime of Fisheries in the Exclusive Economic Zone." In *The Exclusive Economic Zone: A Latin American Perspective,* edited by Francisco Orrego Vicuña, 143–58. Boulder, CO: Westview Press, 1984.

"Canada, Coastal Fisheries Protection Regulations, December 9, 1979." *International Legal Materials* 15 (1976): 1372.

Canadian Yearbook of International Law 15 (1977).

Carlson, Cynthia E. "The International Regulation of Small Cetaceans." *San Diego Law Review* 21 (1984): 577–623.

Carroz, Jean F. "Le Nouveau Droit des Pêches et la Notion d'Excédent." *Annuaire Français de Droit International* 24 (1978): 851–65.

Carroz, Jean F. "Les Problèmes de la Pêche a la Conférence sur le Droit de la Mer et dans la Pratique des Etats." *Revue Générale de Droit International Public* 84 (1980): 705–51.

Carroz, Jean F., and Michel Savini. "Les Accords de Pèche Conclus par les Etats Africains Riverains de l'Atlantique." *Annuaire Français de Droit International* 24 (1983): 674–709.

Carroz, Jean F., and Michel Savini. "The Practice of Coastal States Regarding Foreign Access to Fishery Resources: An Analysis of the Bilateral Agreements." In *Food and Agriculture Organization of the United Nations Fisheries Report No. 293,* 43–72. Rome: Food and Agriculture Organization of the United Nations, 1983.

"Case Concerning the Continental Shelf (Libyan Arab Jamahiriya v. Malta)." *International Court of Justice Reports* (1985): 33.

"Case Concerning Delimitation of the Maritime Boundary in the Gulf of Maine Area (Canada v. United States)." *International Court of Justice Reports* (1984): 299–300.

"Case Concerning Maritime Delimitation in the Area between Greenland and Jan Mayen (Denmark v. Norway)." *International Court of Justice Reports* (1993): 73–74.

"Case Concerning Military and Paramilitary Activities in and Against Nicaragua (Nicaragua v. United States), Merits, June 27th, 1986." *International Court of Justice Reports* (1986): 14.

"Case Concerning the Delimitation of Marine Areas between Canada and the French Republic." *International Legal Materials* 31, no. 1145 (1992): 175.

"Case Concerning Land Reclamation by Singapore in and around the Straits of Johor (Malaysia v. Singapore)." Provisional Measures. ITLOS order. *ICJ Rep.* (2003, October 8): para. 92.

"Case of the *S. S. Lotus* (France v. Turkey)," *Permanent Court of International Justice* (1927): Series A. No. 10, 28.

Cass, Deborah. "The Quiet Revolution: The Development of the Exclusive Economic Zone and Implications for Foreign Fishing Access in the Pacific." *Melbourne University Law Review* 16 (1987): 83–102.

Castañeda, Jorge. "Negotiations on the Exclusive Economic Zone at the Third United Nations Conference on the Law of the Sea." In *Essays in International Law in Honor of Judge Manfred Lachs,* edited by Jerzy Makarczyck, 605–23. The Hague: Martinus Nijhoff, 1984.

Castañeda, Jorge. "The Concept of the Patrimonial Sea in International Law." *Indian Journal of International Law* 12 (1972): 535–42.

Central Intelligence Agency. *World Factbook.* 2018. https://www.cia.gov/library/publications/the-world-factbook/geos/le.html (accessed January 28, 2018).

"Channel Continental Shelf Arbitration (United Kingdom v. France), 1977 XV." *UN Reports of International Arbitral Awards* 3 (1978): 3.

Chapman, Wilbert M. "Fishery Resources in Offshore Waters." In *The Law of the Sea: Offshore Boundaries and Zones,* edited by Louis M. Alexander, 87–105. Columbus: Ohio State University Press, 1967.

Charney, Jonathan I. "Entry into Force of the 1982 Convention on the Law of the Sea," *Virginia Journal of International Law* 35 (1995): 381–404.

Charney, Jonathan I. "The Exclusive Economic Zone and Public International Law." *Ocean Development & International Law* 15 (1985): 233–88.

"Charter of Economic Rights and Duties of States, GA. Res. 3281." *United Nations General Assembly Official Records* 29 Suppl. No. 31, 50, UN Document. A/9631 (1974).

Cheng, Bing. "United Nations Resolutions on Outer Space 'Instant' International Customary Law," *Indian Journal of International Law* 5 (1965): 23–45.

Chilean Presidential Declaration Concerning the Continental Shelf, in UN Legislative Series. *Laws and Regulations on the Regime of the High Seas* 1 (1951): 6.

Chiu, Hungdah. "Some Problems Concerning the Application of the Maritime Boundary Delimitation Provisions of the 1982 United Nations Convention on the Law of the Sea." *Chinese Yearbook of International Law and Affairs* 4 (1984): 68–69.

Churchill, Robin Rolf. *EEC Fisheries Law.* New York: Martinus Nijhoff, 1987.

Churchill, Robin Rolf. "The Fisheries Jurisdiction Cases: The Contribution of the International Court of Justice to the Debate of Coastal State's Fisheries Rights." *International and Comparative Law Quarterly* 24 (1975): 87–88.

Churchill, Robin Rolf, and Alan Vaughan Lowe. *The Law of the Sea,* 3rd ed. Manchester, England: Manchester University Press, 1988.

"The Claim of Namibia of 1990." In *Law of the Sea: Current Developments in State Practice,* no. 3. New York: United Nations, 1992.

Clingan, Thomas A. "Freedom of Navigation in a Post-UNCLOS III Environment." *Law and Contemporary Problems* 46 (1983): 107–23.

"Conservation and Management of Living Resources of the High Seas: Proposal Submitted to the Third Session of the Preparatory Committee for the

United Nations Conference on the Environment and Development, Geneva, August 12–September 4, 1991." *Law of the Sea Bulletin*, no. 19 (1991): 42–44.

"Convention for the Conservation of Anadromous Stocks in the North Pacific Ocean of 1992." *Law of the Sea Bulletin*, No. 22 (1993): 21.

"Convention for the Conservation of Salmon in the North Atlantic Ocean, 1982." *Official Journal of the European Union* L378 (1982): 24.

"Convention on the Continental Shelf." *United Nations Treaty Series* 499 (1964): 311–20.

"Convention on Fishing and Conservation of Living Resources of the High Seas." *United Nations Treaty Series* 599 (1966): 286–300.

"Convention on the High Seas, Geneva, April 29, 1958." *United Nations Treaty Series* 450 (1963): 82–102.

"Convention on the Territorial Sea and the Contiguous Zone." *United Nations Treaty Series* 516 (1964): 205–24.

"Convention Relative au Développement Régional des Pêches dans le Golf de Guinée, 2 Juin 1984," *Revue Générale de Droit International Public* 91 (1987): 1115.

Corbett, P. E. "The Consent of States and the Sources of the Law of Nations." *British Yearbook of International Law* 6 (1925): 20–30.

Courier No. 64 November-December, 1980, 73.

Crawford, James. *Brownlie's Principles of Public International Law.* Oxford: Oxford University Press, 2012.

Dahmani, Mohammed. "Access of Land-Locked and Geographically Disadvantaged States to the Fisheries Resources of the Exclusive Economic Zone under the New Convention on the Law of the Sea." *Maritime Policy and Management* 10 (1983): 265–73.

Dahmani, Mohamed. *The Fisheries Regime of the Exclusive Economic Zone.* Boston: Martinus Nijhoff, 1987.

Dalton, Jane Gililand. "The Chilean Mar Presencial: A Harmless Concept or a Dangerous Precedent?" *International Journal of Marine and Coastal Law* 8 (1993): 397–418.

D'Arechaga, Jimeneze. "Case Concerning the Continental Shelf (Tunisia v. Libyan Arab Jamahiriya)." *International Court of Justice Reports* Sep. Op. (1982): 100–42.

Dean, A. H. "The Geneva Conference on the Law of the Sea: What Was Accomplished." *American Journal of International Law* 52 (1958) 607–28.

De Brencker, Jean. "La Convention de Londres sur la Pêche du a Mars 1964," *Revue Belge de Droit International* 1 (1966): 143–66.

"Declaration on the Establishment of a New International Economic Order, Adopted by the UN General Assembly at its Sixth Special Session. GA. Res. 3201." *United Nations General Assembly Official Records,* Suppl. No. 1 UN. Doc. A/9559, 1974.

"The Declaration of Montevideo on Law of the Sea." *International Legal Materials* 9 (1970): 1081–83.

"The Declaration on the Maritime Zone. August 18, 1952," in UN Legislative Series, *Laws and Regulations on the Regime of the Territorial Sea* (1957): 723–24.

Decree Concerning the Limits of the Territorial Sea. November 6, 1950, and Legislative Decree of February 21, 1951, in UN Legislative Series, *Supplement to Laws and Regulations on the Regime of the High Seas and Laws Concerning the Nationality of Ships* (1959): 9.

Decree No. 1542 on November 10, 1966. In ST/LEG/SER. B/15 (1970): 78.

Decree No. 190 Concerning Fishing and Hunting. September 28, 1949, in UN Legislative Series, *Laws and Regulations on the Regime of the High Seas* 1 (1951): 6–7.

"Delimitation of Maritime Areas between Canada and the French Republic, Decision of Arbitration dated 10 June 1992." *International Legal Materials* 31 (1992): 1145–1219.

De Lacharrière, Guy. "La Reforme du Droit de la Mer et le Rôle de la Conférence des Nations Unies," in *Le Nouveau Droit International de la Mer*, edited by D. Bardonnet and M. Virally, 1–33. Paris: Editions A. Pedone, 1983.

De Vattel, Emmerich. *The Law of Nations or the Principles of Natural Law*, vol. 1. Translated by C. G. Fenwild. Washington: Carnegie Institution, 1916.

Digest of U.S. Practice in International Law. Washington, DC: Government Printing Office, 2001.

Dinh, Nguyen Quoc, Patrick Daillier, and Alain Pellet. *Droit International Public*, 3rd ed. Paris: Librairie Générale Droit et de Jurisprudence, 1987.

"The Diversion of Water from the Meuse Case, (Netherland v. Belgium)." *Permanent Court of International Justice Report* Series A/B (1937): 70, 76–77.

Dixon, Martin. *Textbook on International Law.* London: Blackstone Press, 1995.

Douay, Claude. "Le Droit de la Mer et la Préservation du Milieu Marin." *Revue Générale de Droit International Public* 84 (1980): 178–215.

"Draft Articles on the Economic Zone." UN Document. A/Conf. 62/C. 2/L. 38, August 5, 1974. *Official Records* 3 (1975): 214–15.

"Draft Articles on the Exclusive Economic Zone Concept," in *International Legal Materials* 12 (1973): 210.

"Draft Convention on the Law of the Sea." UN Document. A/Conf. 62/L. 78, August 28, 1981. http://legal.un.org/diplomaticconferences/1973_los/vol14.shtml

Edeson, William R. "Types of Agreements for Exploitation of EEZ Fisheries." In *The UN Convention on the Law of the Sea: Impact and Implementation. Proceedings of the Nineteenth Annual Conference, Cardiff, 1985*, edited by E. D. Brown and R. R. Churchill, 151–77. Law of the Sea Institute, 1987.

Edeson, William R., and Jean-François Pulvenis, *The Legal Regime of Fisheries in the Caribbean Region.* Berlin: Springer Verlag, 1983.

"European Fisheries Convention, and Agreements on Transitional Rights (Fishing Limits; Settlement of Disputes)," *International Legal Materials* 3 (1964): 469–95.

Extavour, Winston Conrad. *The Exclusive Economic Zone: A Study of the Evolution and Progressive Development of International Law of the Sea*. Geneva: Institut Universitaire de Haute Etudes Internationales, 1979.

Feldman, Mark B., and David A. Colson, "The Maritime Boundaries of the United States." *American Journal of International Law* 75 (1981): 729–63.

Ferrero, Eduardo. "El Nuevo Derecho del Mar: El Perú y las 200 Millas." Peruvian Decree No. 781, August 1, 1947.

Fidell, Eugene R. "Fisheries Legislation: Naval Enforcement." *Journal of Maritime Law and Commerce* 7 (1976): 351–63.

Fiji, Marine Space Act 1977, Article 12(3)(i).

"Fisheries Agreement between Iceland and Belgium Relating to the Extension of the Icelandic Fishery limits to 200 Nautical Miles, November 28, 1975." In *New Directions in the Law of the Sea,* edited by Robin Rolf Churchill and Myron H. Nordquist, vol. 5. Dobbs Ferry, NY: Oceana, 1977.

"Fisheries Jurisdiction Case (Federal Republic of Germany v. Iceland), Merits, Judgment of July 25, 1974." *International Court of Justice Reports* (1974): 175.

"Fisheries Jurisdiction Case (United Kingdom v. Iceland), Merits, Judgment July 25, 1974." *International Court of Justice Reports* (1974): 23.

Fisheries Resources (Jurisdiction and Conservation), Act No. 13 of June 16, 1977, in ST/LEG/SER. B/19 (1980): 179, Article 10(4).

Fitzmaurice-Lachs, Malgorzata. "The Legal Regime of the Baltic Sea Fisheries." *Netherlands International Law Review* 29, No. 2 (1982): 174–251.

Fleischer, Carl August. "The Exclusive Economic Zone under the Convention Regime and in State Practice," in *The 1982 Convention on the Law of the Sea, Proceedings of the Seventeenth Annual Conference, July 12–16, 1983,* edited by Albert W. Koers and Bernard H. Oxman, 241–285. Honolulu: Law of the Sea Institute, University of Hawaii, 1984.

Fleischer, Carl August. "The New Regime of the Maritime Fisheries." *Recueil des Cours de l'Académie de Droit International* (1988/2), 122–23.

Fleischer, Carl August. "The Right to a 200 Miles Exclusive Economic Zone or a Special Fishery Zone." *San Diego Law Review* 14 (1977): 548–83.

Food and Agriculture Organization of the United Nations. "Fisheries and Aquaculture Department." 2017. http://www.fao.org/fishery/index.htm (accessed December 28, 2017).

Food and Agriculture Organization of the United Nations Report of the Technical Consultation on High Seas Fishing. Doc. A/Conf. 164/INF/2, 1993.

Freestone, David. "Some Institutional Implications of the Establishment of Exclusive Economic Zones by EC Member States." *Ocean Development and International Law* 23 (1992): 97–114.

Fulton, Thomas Wemyss. *The Sovereignty of the Seas.* London: William Blackwood and Sons, 1911.

Gambian Fisheries Act No. 14, 1977.

Garaioca, Theodore A. "The Continental Shelf and the Extension of the Territorial Sea." *University of Miami Law Review* 10 (1956): 490–98.

Glassner, Martin Ira. *Access to the Sea for Developing Land-Locked States.* The Hague: Nijhoff, 1970.

González-Videla, Gabriel. "Chilean Presidential Declaration Concerning the Continental Shelf." June 23, 1947.

Gotlieb, A. E. "The Canadian Contribution to the Concept of a Fishing Zone in International Law." *Canadian Yearbook of Public & Private International Law* 2 (1964): 55–76.

Grolin, Jesper. "The Future of the Law of the Sea: Consequences of a Non Treaty or Non-Universal Treaty Situation." *Ocean Development and International Law* 13 (1983): 1–31.

Grotius, Hugo. *The Freedom of the Seas, or the Right Which Belongs to the Dutch to Take Part in the Eastern Indian Trade.* Indianapolis, IN: Library Fund, 2004.

Guinea, Marine Fisheries Code, Article 32.

Gulland, J. A. "Conditions of Access to Fisheries: Some Resource Considerations." In *Food and Agriculture Organization of the United Nations Fisheries Report No. 293,* 143–51. Rome: Food and Agriculture Organization of the United Nations, 1983.

Guyana, Maritime Boundaries Act No. 10.

Hannesson, Rögnvaldur. "Fishing on the High Seas: Cooperation or Competition." *Maritime Policy* 19, no. 5 (1995): 371–77.

Harville, John P. "Multidisciplinary Aspects of Optimum Sustainable Yield," in *Optimum Sustainable Yield as a Concept in Fisheries Management,* edited by P. M. Roedel, 59–64. Lawrence, TX: Allen Press, 1975.

Hayashi, Moritaka. "The Management of Transboundary Fish Stocks under the LOS Convention." *International Journal of Marine and Coastal Law* 8 (1993): 245–61.

Healey, Christopher J. "United States Tuna Management Policy." *American Society of International Law* 5 (1981): 67–100.

Henkin, Louis. "Old Politics and New Directions," in *New Directions in the Law of the Sea,* vol. 1, edited by S. Houston Lay, Robin Rolf Churchill, and Myron H. Nordquist, 3–11. Dobbs Ferry, NY: Oceana, 1973.

Hewison, Grant J. "The Legally Binding Nature of the Moratorium on Large-scale High Seas Driftnet Fishing." *Journal of Maritime Law and Commerce* 25, no. 4 (1994): 557–78.

Hey, Ellen. *The Regime for the Exploitation of Transboundary Marine Fisheries Resources.* Dordrecht: Martinus Nijhoff, 1989.

Hjertonson, K. *The New Law of the Sea: Influence of the Latin American States on Recent Development of the Law of the Sea.* Leiden, Netherlands: A. W. Sijthoff, 1973.

Hollick, Ann L. "The Origins of the 200-mile Offshore Zones." *American Journal of International Law* 71 (1977): 435–96.

Hudson, Carolyn. "Fishery and Economic Zones as Customary International Law." *South Dakota Law Review* 17, no. 3 (1980): 661–89.

Hudson, Manley O. "Article 24 of the Statute of the International Law Commission." *Yearbook of the International Law Commission* 2 (1950), UN Doc. A/CN.4/16/Add.1, 5.

Ibler, Vladimir. "The Interests of the Shelf-Locked States and the Proposed Development of the Law of the Sea." *Indian Journal of International Law* 11 (1971): 389–410.

"Iceland-Federal Republic of Germany Exchange of Notes Constituting an Agreement Concerning the Fishery Zone Around Iceland, Reykjavik, July 19, 1961." *United Nations Treaty Series* 409, 47.

Iguchi, Takeo. "The Law of the Sea: Conventional Rules and Customary Norms." Paper presented at the Annual Meeting of the American Society of International Law, Boston, MA, April 9, 1987 (mimeograph).

IMO doc. MEPC 58/10/7, August 15, 2008, 2, para. 10.

India, Territorial Water, Continental Shelf, Exclusive Economic Zone, and other Maritime Zones Act.

"Informal Composite Negotiating Text." UN Document. A/Conf. 62/WP.10. July 10, 1977. http://legal.un.org/docs/?path=../diplomaticconferences/1973_los/docs/english/vol_8/a_conf62_wp10.pdf&lang=E

"Informal Single Negotiating Text." UN Document. A/Conf. 62/WP. 8/pt. II. *Official Records* 4 (1975): 152.

International Conference of American States in Panama. "Declaration of Panama." *American Journal of International Law* 34, Suppl. 1 (1940): 17–18.

International Law Association. "Final Report of the Committee on Formation of Customary (General) International Law: Statement of Principles Applicable to the Formation of General Customary International Law (as amended at the London Conference)." *Report of the Sixty-Ninth Conference* (London, International Law Association, 2000), 712–77.

International Law Commission. "Freedoms of the High Seas," *Yearbook of the International Law Commission* 2 (1956): 278.

International Legal Materials 8 (1969).

International Legal Materials 9 (1965).

International Legal Materials 15 (1976).

"Jamaica's Exclusive Economic Zone Act No. 33 December 31, 1991." *Law of the Sea Bulletin*, no. 21 (1992): 28.

Jansoone, Roeland. "La Pratique Etatique Belge et la Zone Economique Exclusive." *Revue Belge de Droit International* 28 (1995): 93–107.

Japanese Annual of International Law (1985): 297.

Jenning, Robert Y. "What Is International Law, and How Do We Tell It When We See it," *Swiss Yearbook of International Law* 37 (1981): 59–88.

Johnston, Douglas M. *The International Law of Fisheries: A Framework for Policy-Oriented Inquiries.* New Haven, CT: Yale University Press, 1965.

Johnston, Douglas M., and Edgar Gold. "Extended Jurisdiction: The Impact of UNCLOS III on Coastal State Practice." In *The Law of the Sea: State Practice in Zones of Special Jurisdiction, Proceedings of the Thirteenth Annual Conference October 15–18, 1979,* edited by Thomas A. Clingan, 27–49. Honolulu: Law of the Sea Institute, University of Hawaii, 1982.

Juda, Lawrence. "The Exclusive Economic Zone: Compatibility of National Claims and the UN Convention on the Law of the Sea." *Ocean Development and International Law* 16 (1986): 1–58.

Juda, Lawrence. "The Exclusive Economic Zone: Non-claimant States." *Ocean Development and International Law* 19 (1988): 431–44.

Juda, Lawrence. "IMCO and the Control of Pollution from Ships." *International and Comparative Law Quarterly* 26 (1977): 558–84.

Juda, Lawrence. "World Marine Fish Catch in the Age of Exclusive Economic Zones and Exclusive Fishery Zones." *Ocean Development and International Law* 22, no. 1 (1991): 1–32.

Katz, Stephen R. "Consequences of the Economic Zone for Catch Opportunities of Fishing Nations." *Maritime Studies and Management* 2 (1975): 144–53.

Kaye, Stuart, and Donald R. Rothwell, "Australia's Antarctic Maritime Claims and Boundaries." *Ocean Development and International Law* 26, no. 3 (1995): 195–26.

Keesing's Contemporary Archives. May (1987): 35133.

Kelsen, Hans. *Principles of International Law.* New York: Rinehart, 1952.

Kibola, H. S. "A Note on Africa and the Exclusive Economic Zone." *Ocean Development and International Law,* 16 (1986): 369–80.

Kittichaisaree, Kriangsak. *The Law of the Sea and Maritime Boundary Delimitation in South-East Asia.* Singapore: Oxford, 1987.

Knight, Gary H. "Effect of a Law of the Sea Treaty on the Fishery Conservation and Management Act of 1976." In *Report to the Gulf of Mexico Fishery Management Council.* Tampa: Gulf of Mexico Fishery Management Council, 1977.

Knight, Gary H. *The Law of the Sea: Cases, Documents, and Readings.* Baton Rouge, LA: Claitor's Law Books, 1980.

Koers, Albert W. *International Regulation of Marine Fisheries: A Study of Regional Fisheries Organizations.* London: Eyre & Spottiswoode, 1973.

Koers, Albert W. "Enforcement of Fisheries Agreements in the High Seas: A Comparative Analysis of International State Practice." Law of the Sea Institute, University of Rhode Island, Occasional Paper No. 6, June 1970.

Koers, Albert W. "The External Authority of the EEC in Regard to Marine Fisheries." *Common Market Law Review* 14 (1977): 269–301.

Koers, Albert W. "The United Nations Convention on the Law of the Sea: An Overview." In *The International Law of the Sea, Issues of Implementation in Indonesia, Proceedings of a Seminar at Jakarta on 22–27 August, 1983,* edited by Ellen Hey and Albert W. Koers, 19–27. Honolulu: Law of the Sea Institute, 1984.

Kolodkin, A., and A. Zakharov. "Some Aspects of Soviet State Practice on the Development of Ocean Resources." In *Consensus and Confrontation: The United States and the Law of the Sea Convention,* edited by John M. Van Dyke. Honolulu: Law of the Sea Institute, University of Hawaii, 1985.

Kolosovski, I. *The 1982 Convention on the Law of the Sea, Proceedings of the Seventeenth Annual Conference, July 12–16, 1983,* edited by Albert W. Koers and Bernard H. Oxman. Honolulu: Law of the Sea Institute, University of Hawaii, 1984.

Krueger, Robert B., and Myron H. Nordquist. "The Evolution of the 200 Mile Exclusive Economic Zone: State Practice in the Pacific Basin." *Virginia Journal of International Law* 19, no. 2 (1979): 321–400.

Kunz, Josef L. "The Nature of Customary International Law." *American Journal of International Law* 47 (1953): 662–669.

Kwiatkowska, Barbara. "Conservation and Optimum Utilization of Living Resources." In *The Law of the Sea: What Lies Ahead?*, edited by Thomas A. Clingan. Honolulu: Law of the Sea Institute, University of Hawaii, 1989.

Kwiatkowska, Barbara. "Exclusive Economic Zone: General Evaluation." In *Essays on the New Law of the Sea*, edited by Budislav Vukas, 99–117. Zagreb: Birotehnika, 1985.

Kwiatkowska, Barbara. "New Soviet Legislation on the 200-Mile Economic Zone and Certain Problems of Evolution of Customary Law." *Netherlands International Law Review* 33 (1986): 24–50.

Lahlou, Abdelkader. *Le Maroc et le Droit des Pêches Maritimes*. Paris: Librairie Générale de Droit et de Jurisprudence, 1983.

Larkin, P. A. "An Epitaph for the Concept of Maximum Sustainable Yield." *Transactions of the American Fisheries Society* 1 (1977): 1–11.

Lasok, Dominik, and John William Bridge. *An Introduction to the Law and Institutions of the European Communities*, 5th ed. Oxford: Butterworth, 1991.

Lauterpacht, Hersch. *The Development of International Law by the International Court*. Cambridge: Cambridge University Press, 2011.

"Law Concerning Maritime Zone, December 20, 1985." *International Legal Materials* 25 (1986): 889–907.

Law No. 31 May 1977 on Provisional Measures Relating to the Fishing Zone as amended by Law No. 83 of 29 November 1977, in ST/LEG/SER. B/19 (1980): 215.

Law of the Sea Bulletin, no. 5 (1985): 17.

Law of the Sea Bulletin, no. 8 (1986): 17.

Law of the Sea Bulletin, no. 16 (1990): 57.

Law of the Sea Bulletin, no. 19 (1991): 2.

Law of the Sea Bulletin, no. 20 (1992): 20.

Law of the Sea Bulletin, no. 21 (1992): 87.

Law of the Sea Bulletin, no. 22 (1993): 21.

Law of the Sea Bulletin, June (1993): 2.

Law of the Sea Bulletin, no. 23 (1993): 65–66.

Law of the Sea Bulletin, no. 25 (1994): 2, 3, 5, 6, and 10.

"The Law of the Sea Convention." *International Legal Materials* 21 (1982): 1261–1354.

"The Law of the Sea: Current Development in State Practice." In *Law of the Sea: Current Developments in State Practice*, no. 3. New York: United Nations, 1992.

Lay, S. Houston, Robin Rolf Churchill, and Myron H. Nordquist, (eds.). *New Directions in the Law of the Sea*, vol. 1. Dobbs Ferry, NY: Oceana, 1973.

Lazarev, M. "The Sea Economic Zone: An Important Problem of the 'Package.'" *Indian Journal of International Law* 17 (1977): 209–15.

Lee, Luke T. "The Law of the Sea Convention and Third States." *American Journal of International Law* 77 (1983): 541–68.

"Legal Information Relevant to the United Nations Convention on the Law of the Sea." *Law of the Sea Bulletin,* no. 19, 1991, 9–41.

"Le Louis." *Dodson's Admiralty Reports (Great Britain)* 2 (1817).

Lepard, Brian D. *Customary International Law: A New Theory with Practical Applications.* Cambridge: Cambridge University Press, 2010.

Letalik, Norman G. "Boundary Making in the Mediterranean." In *Ocean Boundary Making: Regional Issues and Developments,* edited by Douglas M. Johnston and P. M. Saunders, 109–41. London: Croom Helm, 1988.

Lévy, Jean-Pierre. "Les Nations Unies et la Convention de 1982 sur le Droit de la Mer." *Revue Belge de Droit International* 28, no. 1 (1995): 11–35.

Lucchini, Laurent, and Michel Voelckel. *Droit de la Mer.* Paris: Pédone, 1990.

MacDonald, John M. "Appreciating the Precautionary Principle as an Ethical Evolution in Ocean Management." *Ocean Development & International Law* 26, no. 3 (1995): 255–86.

MacGibbon, I. C. "The Scope of Acquiescence in International Law," *British Yearbook of International Law* 31 (1954): 143–186.

MacRae, Leslie M. "Customary International Law and the United Nations Law of the Sea Treaty." *California Western International Law Journal* 13 (1983): 181–222.

Mahmoudi, Said. "Sweden: Sweden's Economic Zone Act." *International Journal of Marine and Coastal Law* 28 (1993): 524–29.

Malone, James L. "Freedom and Opportunity: Foundation for a Dynamic Ocean Policy." *Department of State Bulletin* 84, no. 2093 (1984): 76–79.

Malone, Linda A. *International Law.* New York: Aspen, 1995.

"Maritime Delimitation and Territorial Questions Between Qatar and Bahrain (Qatar v. Bahrain)." Judgment, *International Court of Justice Reports* (2001): 91, para. 167.

"Maritime Dispute (Peru v. Chile)." ICJ Rep. (2014): para. 179.

The Maritime Zones Act, 1977.

Martínez Puñal, Antonio. "The Rights of Land-Locked and Geographically Disadvantaged States in Exclusive Economic Zones." *Journal of Maritime Law and Commerce* 23, no. 3 (1992): 430–60.

"Mauritania/Spain Fishing Agreement." *Industrias Pesqueras* June 1 (1982): 9.

McDorman, Ted L. "Stateless Fishing Vessels, International Law and the UN High Seas Fisheries Conference." *Journal of Maritime Law and Commerce* 25 (1994): 531–55.

McDougal, Myres S. "The Law of the High Seas in Time of Peace." *Denver Journal of International Law and Policy* 3 (1973): 45–58.

McDougal, Myres S., and William T. Burke. *The Public Order of the Oceans.* New Haven, CT: Yale University Press, 1987.

McLaughlin, Richard J. "Confidential Classification of Multi-Beam Bathymetric Mapping of the U.S. EEZ: Is a New U.S. Marine Scientific Research Policy in Order?" *Ocean Development and International Law* 19 (1988), 1–33.

Meltzer, Evelyne. "Global Overview of Straddling and Highly Migratory Fish Stocks: The Non-sustainable Nature of High Seas Fisheries." *Ocean Development and International Law* 25 (1994): 255–328.

Mfodwo, S. Kwame B., Ben Martine Tsamenyi, and Sam K. N. Blay. "The Exclusive Economic Zone: State Practice in the African Atlantic Region." *Ocean Development and International Law* 20 (1989): 445–99.

Milić, Milenko. "The Third United Nations Conference on the Law of the Sea." *Case Western Reserve Journal of International Law* 8, no. 1 (1976): 168–87.

Mohamed, Mohd Ibrahim Hj. "National Management of Malaysian Fisheries." *Marine Policy* 15, no. 1 (1991): 2–14.

Monnier, Jean. "Le Droit d'Accès a la Mer et la Liberté de Transit Terrestre." In *Traité du Nouveau Droit de la Mer,* edited by René-Jean Dupuy and D. Vignes, 441–62 Paris: Economica Bruylant, 1989.

Moore, Gerald K. *Coastal State Requirements for Foreign Fishing.* FAO Legislative Study No. 21, Rev. 2. Rome: Food and Agriculture Organization of the United Nations, 1985.

Moore, Gerald K. "National Legislation for the Management of Fisheries under Extended Coastal State Jurisdiction." *Journal of Maritime Law and Commerce* 11 (1980): 153–82.

Morin, Jacques-Yvan. "La Zone de Pêche Exclusive du Canada." *Canadian Yearbook of Public & Private International Law* 2 (1964): 77–106.

Mouton, Martinus Willem. *The Continental Shelf.* The Hague: Martinus Nijhoff, 1952.

"The MOX Plant Case (Ireland v. United Kingdom)." Provisional Measures. ITLOS sep. op. Judge Wolfrum *ICJ Rep.* (2001, December 3): 3.

Mtango, E. E. E., and Friedl Weiss. "The Exclusive Economic Zone and Tanzania: Considerations of a Developing Country." *Ocean Development and International Law* 14 (1984): 1–54.

"The M/V *SAIGA* (No. 2) Case (St. Vincent and the Grenadian v. Guinea)." Judgment, (July 1, 1999).

Nakauchi, K. *Japan's Ocean Affairs.* Saitama, Japan: Law of the Sea Institute, 1988.

Narokobi, Camillus. "International Management of Highly Migratory Species." In *Consensus and Confrontation: The United States and the Law of the Sea Convention,* edited by John M. Van Dyke. Honolulu: Law of the Sea Institute, University of Hawaii, 1985.

Nauru, Marine Resources Act No. 8 of 1978.

Nelson, L. D. M. "The Emerging New Law of the Sea." *Modern Law Review* 42 (1979): 42–65.

Nelson, L. D. M. "The Patrimonial Sea." *International & Comparative Law Quarterly* 22 (1973): 668–686.

"The Netherlands Territorial Sea Act, January 9, 1985." *Law of the Sea Bulletin,* no. 6 (1985): 16.

New Zealand Territorial Sea and Exclusive Economic Zone Act, 1977, 309, Article 15(j).

Nikitina, Elena N., and Peter H. Pearse, "Conservation of Marine Resource in the Former Soviet Union: An Environmental Perspective." *Ocean Development and International Law* 23 (1992): 380, note 22.

"Niue Treaty on Cooperation in Fisheries Surveillance and Law Enforcement in the South Pacific Region." *International Legal Materials* 32 (1993): 136–36.

"North Sea Continental Shelf Cases (*Federal Republic of Germany v. Denmark; Federal Republic of Germany v. Netherlands*)." *International Court of Justice Reports* (1969): 3–258.

O'Connell, D. P. *The International Law of the Sea,* vols. 1 and 2, edited by I. A. Shearer. Oxford: Clarendon Press, 1982.

Oda, Shigeru. "Fisheries under the United Nations Convention on the Law of the Sea." *American Journal of International Law* 77 (1983): 739–55.

Oda, Shigeru. *The International Law of the Ocean Development: Basic Documents.* Leiden, Netherlands: Sijthoff, 1972.

Oda, Shigeru. *International Law of the Resources of the Sea.* Germantown, MD: Sijthoff and Noordhoff, 1979.

Oda, Shigeru. "International Law of the Resources of the Sea." *Recueil des Cours de l'Académie de Droit International* (1986): 394–95.

Oda, Shigeru. *The Law of the Sea in Our Time—II: The United Nations Seabed Committee, 1969–1973.* The Hague, Netherlands: Sijthoff Publications on Ocean Development, 1977.

Office of the Special Representative of the Secretary General for the Law of the Sea. *Law of the Sea: Status of the United Nations Convention on the Law of the Sea.* New York: United Nations, 1985.

Official Records 2 (1974).

Official Records 3 (1975).

Official Records 10 (1978).

Okere, B. Obinna. "Nigeria's Exclusive Economic Zone." *Nigerian Law Journal* 12 (1984): 65–78.

Oppenheim, Lassa. *International Law: A Treatise,* vol. 1, edited by H. Lauterpacht. New York: Congmans, Green, 1955.

"Organization of African Unity: Declaration on African Cooperation, Development, and Economic Independence." *International Legal Materials* 12 (1973): 996–1013.

Osicke, Ebere. "The Contribution of States from the Third World to the Development of the Law on the Continental Shelf and the Concept of the Economic Zone." *Indian Journal of International Law* 15 (1975): 313–33.

Oxman, Bernard H. "An Analysis of the EEZ as Formulated in the Informal Composite Negotiating Text." In *The Law of the Sea: State Practice in Zones of Special Jurisdiction, Proceedings of the Thirteenth Annual Conference, October 15–18, 1979,* edited by Thomas A. Clingan. Honolulu: Law of the Sea Institute, University of Hawaii, 1982.

Oxman, Bernard. "The Duty to Respect Generally Accepted International Standards." *New York University Journal of International Law and Politics* 26 (1991): 109, 122–29.

Oxman, Bernard H. "The Third United Nations Conference on the Law of the Sea: The 1976 New York Sessions." *American Journal of International Law* 71, no. 2 (1977): 247–69.

Oxman, Bernard H. "The Third United Nations Conference on the Law of the Sea: The 1977 New York Session." *American Journal of International Law* 72 (1978): 57–83.

Oxman, Bernard H. "The Third United Nations Conference on the Law of the Sea: The Seventh Session 1978." *American Journal of International Law* 73 (1979): 1–41.

Oxman, Bernard H. "The Third United Nations Conference on the Law of the Sea: The Tenth Session, 1981." *American Journal of International Law* 76 (1981): 1–23.

Pakistan Territorial Waters and Maritime Zones Act, 1976.

Paolillo, Felipe H. "The Exclusive Economic Zone in Latin American Practice and Legislation." *Ocean Development and International Law* 26, no. 2 (1995): 105–25.

Park, Choon-ho. "Offshore Oil Development in the China Seas: Some Legal and Territorial Issues." In *Ocean Yearbook*, vol. 2, edited by E. M. Borgese and N. Ginsburg, 302–16. Chicago: University of Chicago Press, 1980.

Parry, Clive, John P. Grant, Anthony Perry, and Arthur D. Watts, eds. *Encyclopedic Dictionary of International Law.* New York: Oceana, 1986.

Permanent Court of International Justice Series A/13, No. 42 (1931).

Peters, Paul, Alfred H. A. Soons, and Lucie A. Zima, "Removal of Installations in the Exclusive Economic Zone," *Netherland Yearbook of International Law* 15 (1984): 167–207.

Pfirter, Frida María Armas. "Straddling Stocks and Highly Migratory Stocks in Latin American Practice and Legislation: New Perspectives in Light of Current International Negotiations." *Ocean Development and International Law* 26 (1995): 127–50.

Pierce, George A. B. "Selective Adoption of the New Law of the Sea: The United States Proclaims its Exclusive Economic Zone." *Virginia Journal of International Law* 23 (1983): 581–601.

Philips, J. C. "The Economic Resources Zone and the South West Pacific." *International Lawyer* 16 (1982): 265–78.

Philips, J. C. "The Exclusive Economic Zone as a Concept in International Law." *International and Comparative Law Quarterly* 26 (1977): 585–619.

Platzoder, R. (ed.). *Third United Nations Conference on the Law of the Sea: Documents of the Caracas Session.* Hamburg: United Nations, 1975.

Plesman, Wolf, and Volker Röben. "Marine Scientific Research: State Practice versus Law of the Sea?" In *Law of the Sea at the Crossroads: The Continuing Search for a Universally Accepted Regime,* edited by Rüdiger Wolfrum, 273–392. Berlin: Duncker and Humblot, 1991.

Pohl, R. Galindo. "The Exclusive Economic Zone in the Light of Negotiations of the Third United Nations Conference on the Law of the Sea." In *The Ex-*

clusive Economic Zone: A Latin American Perspective, edited by Francisco Orrego Vicuña, 31–59. Boulder, CO: Westview Press, 1984.

"Poland and United Kingdom: Fisheries Agreement." *International Legal Materials* 4 (1965): 168–69.

Political Constitution of Panama. March 1, 1946, in UN Legislative Series, *Laws and Regulations on the Regime of the High Seas* 1 (1951): 15 Article 209.

Ponsonby, David, and Georges Dussart. *The Anatomy of the Sea.* San Francisco: Chronicle Books, 2005.

Pontecorvo, Giulio. "The Taking of Living Resources: Expectations and Reality." In *The 1982 Convention on the Law of the Sea, Proceedings of the Seventeenth Annual Conference, July 12–16, 1983,* edited by Albert W. Koers and Bernard H. Oxman, 286–308. Honolulu: Law of the Sea Institute, University of Hawaii, 1984.

Prat y Coll, Juan. "Some Considerations on the Adoptions of National Policy in a Distant Water Fishing Nation to the Recent Evolution of the Law of the Sea." In *Food and Agriculture Organization of the United Nations Fisheries Report No. 293,* 89–94. Food and Agriculture Organization of the United Nations, Rome, 1983.

"Preamble to the Niue Treaty on Cooperation in Fisheries Surveillance and Law Enforcement in the South Pacific Region, June 9, 1992." *International Legal Materials* 32 (1993): 136.

Prescott, J. R. V. "Maritime Boundaries and Issues in the Southwest Pacific Ocean." In *Ocean Boundary Making: Regional Issues and Developments,* edited by Douglas M. Johnston and P. M. Saunders. London: Croom Helm, 1988.

Presidential Declaration with Respect to the Continental Shelf. October 29, 1945 in UN Legislative Series, *Laws and Regulations on the Regime of the High Seas* 1 (1951): 13.

Presidential Proclamation, June 6, 1969, in ST/LEG/SER. B/15 (1970): 95–96.

Presidential Proclamation No. 2667, Concerning the Policy of the United States with Respect to the Natural Resources of the Subsoil and Seabed of the Continental Shelf, September 28, 1945, in UN Legislative Series, *Laws and Regulations on the Regime of the High Seas* 1 (1951): 38.

Presidential Proclamation No. 2668, Concerning the Policy of the United States with Respect to Coastal Fisheries in Certain Areas of the High Seas, September 28, 1945.

Presidential Proclamation of 29 November 1956. In ST/LEG/SER. B/15 (1970): 49.

"President Reagan's Statement on the Two-Hundred-Mile EEZ." *Virginia Journal of International Law* 23 (1983): 598–601.

Proclamation of Governor-General of December 20, 1957. In ST/LEG/SER. B/15 (1970): 107.

"Procureur de la Rėpublique v. J. Crujeiras Tome, 1981." *Revue Gėnėrale de Droit International Public* (1983): 465.

"Program of Action on the Establishment of a New International Economic Order, Adopted by the UN General Assembly at its Sixth Special Session, GA.

Res. 3202." *United Nations General Assembly Official Records*, Suppl. No. 1, UN Document. A/9559, 1974.

"Pulp Mills on the River Uruguay (Argentina v. Uruguay)." Judgment. *International Court of Justice Reports* (2010, April 20): 14, 78, para. 193.

Pulvenis, Jean-François. "Vers une Emprise des États Riverains Sur la Haute Mer au Titre des Grand Migrateurs: Les Régime International de la Pêche au Thon dans le Pacific Oriental." *Annuaire Français de Droit International* 35 (1989): 774–806.

Pulvenis, Jean-François. "Zone Économique et Plateau Continental: Unité ou Dualité." *Revue Iranienne des Relations Internationales* 12 (1978): 103–20.

Puri, Rama. "The Legal Regime of Marine Fisheries." *Indian Journal of International Law* 22 (1982): 240–50.

Quéneudec, Jean-Pierre. "Les Incertitudes de la Nouvelle Convention Sur le Droit de la Mer." In *Essays on the New Law of the Sea*, edited by Budislav Vukas, 47–57. Zagreb, Yugoslavia: University of Zagreb, 1985.

Quince, C. *The Persistent Objector and Customary International Law.* Denver, CO: Outskirts Press, 2010.

Rao, P. Sreenivasa. "Public Order of Oceans: Problems and Prospects." *Indian Journal of International Law* 17 (1977): 216–26.

Rauch, Elmar. "Military Uses of the Oceans." *German Yearbook of International Law* 28 (1985): 229–67.

Reeves, Jesse S. "The Codification of the Law of Territorial Waters," *American Journal of International Law* 24, no. 3 (1930): 486-499.

Rembe, Nasila S. *Africa and the International Law of the Sea: A Study of the Constitution of the African States to the Third United Conference on the Law of the Sea.* Leiden, Netherlands: Sijthoff and Noordhoff, 1980.

Report of the Committee on Land-Locked States, Belgrade Conference, 1980. London: International Law Association, 1980.

"Report of the Committee on the Peaceful Uses of the Seabed and Ocean Floor beyond the Limits of National Jurisdiction." *United Nations General Assembly Official Records* 28th Sess., Suppl. No. 21, UN Document. A/9021 (1969).

Revised Single Negotiating Text Part II, UN Doc. A/Conf. 62/WP. 8/Rev. 1/Pt. II. *Official Records* 5 (1976): 51.

Richardson, Elliot P. "Law of the Sea: Navigation and Other Traditional National Security Considerations." *San Diego Law Review* 19 (1982): 553–76.

Richardson, Elliot P. "Power, Mobility and the Law of the Sea." *Foreign Affairs* 58 (1980): 902–19.

"Rights of Nationals of the United States in Morocco Case (United States v. France)." *International Court of Justice Reports* (1952): 200.

Riphagen, Willem. "La Navigation dans le Nouveau Droit de la Mer." *Revue Générale de Droit International Public* 84 (1980): 141–75.

Robb, Dean. "Access Conditions and Compliance Control." In *Food and Agriculture Organization of the United Nations Fisheries Report No. 295.* Rome: Food and Agriculture Organization of the United Nations, 1984.

Robertson, Horace B. "Navigation in the Exclusive Economic Zone." *Virginia Journal of International Law* 24, no. 4 (1984), 865–915.

Rosenne, Shabtai. "Settlement of Fisheries Disputes in the Exclusive Economic Zone." *American Journal of International Law* 73 (1979): 89–104.

Rothwell, Donald R., and Tim Stephens. *The International Law of the Sea.* Oxford: Hart, 2010.

Schneider, Jan. "Prevention and Control of Marine Pollution: Pollution from Vessels." in *The Environmental Law of the Sea,* edited by Douglas M. Johnston, 203–17. Gland, Switzerland: International Union for Conservation of Nature and Natural Resources, 1981.

Schulz, Wesley S. "Oceanic Research: International Law and National Legislation." *Marine Policy* 4 (1980): 91–127.

Schreiber, Alfonso A. "The Exclusive Economic Zone: Its Legal Nature and the Problem of Military Uses." In *The Exclusive Economic Zone: A Latin American Perspective,* edited by Francisco Orrego Vicuña, 123–41. Boulder, CO: Westview Press, 1984.

Schwarzenberger, Georg. *International Law as Applied by International Courts and Tribunals,* vol. 1, 3rd ed. London: Stevens and Sons, 1957.

Schwarzenberger, Georg, and Edward D. Brown. *A Manual of International Law.* Milton, Oxon, England: Professional Books, 1976.

Scovazzi, Tullio. "Explaining Exclusive Fishery Jurisdiction." *Marine Policy* 9 (1985): 125.

Scovazzi, Tullio. "Implications of the New Law of the Sea for the Mediterranean." *Marine Policy* 5 (1981): 302–12.

Scovazzi, Tullio. "Coastal State Practice in the Exclusive Economic Zone: The Right of Foreign States to Use this Zone." In *New Developments in Marine Science and Technology: Economic, Legal, and Political Aspects of Change, Proceedings of the Twentieth Annual Conference 1988,* edited by Lewis M. Alexander, Scott Allen, and Lynne Carter Hanson. Honolulu: Law of the Sea Institute, University of Hawaii, 1989.

Selden, John. *Of the Dominion or Ownership of the Sea.* Translated by Marchamont Nedham. 1652. Reprint, New York: Arno, 1972.

Senegal, Law 76-89 of July 1976.

Shaw, Malcolm N. *International Law.* Cambridge: Grotius, 1991.

Shearer, Ivan Anthony, ed. *Starke's International Law.* 11th ed. Boston: Butterworths, 1994.

Singela, A. Mpazi. *Land-Locked States and the UNCLOS Regime.* New York: Ocean, 1983.

Singela, A. Mpazi. "Land-Locked States' Rights in the Exclusive Economic Zone from the Perspective of the UN Convention on the Law of the Sea: An Historical Evaluation," *Ocean Development and International Law* 20, no. 1 (1989): 65.

Sisco, Eric Allan. "Hot Pursuit from a Contiguous Fisheries Zone—An Assault on the Freedom of the High Seas." *San Diego Law Review* 14 (1977): 656–80.

Smith, Robert W. (ed.). *Exclusive Economic Zone Claims: An Analysis and Primary Documents.* Boston: Martinus Nijhoff, 1986.

Sohn, Louis B., and Kristen Gustafson. *The Law of the Sea in a Nutshell.* St. Paul, MN: West Group, 1984.

Soons, Alfred H. A. "The Developing Regime of Marine Scientific Research: Recent European Experience and State Practice." In *New Developments in Marine Science and Technology: Economic, Legal, and Political Aspects of Change, Proceedings of the Twentieth Annual Conference 1988,* edited by Lewis M. Alexander, Scott Allen, and Lynne Carter Hanson, 293–315. Honolulu: Law of the Sea Institute, University of Hawaii, 1989.

Soons, Alfred H. A. "Regulation of Marine Scientific Research by the European Community and Its Member States." *Ocean Development and International Law* 23 (1992): 259–77.

Soons, Alfred H. A. *Marine Scientific Research and the Law of the Sea.* Deventer: Kluwer Law and Taxation, 1982.

"South Georgia and the South Sandwich Islands Proclamation No. 1 of 1993." *Law of the Sea Bulletin,* no. 24 (1993): 46–47.

The South Pacific Forum Fisheries Agency. *Regional Compendium of Fisheries Legislation (Western Pacific Region),* vol. 2. Rome: Food and Agriculture Organization of the United Nations, 1984.

"Southern Bluefin Tuna Cases (New Zealand v. Japan; Australia v. Japan)." Provisional Measures. ITLOS, sep. op. *ICJ Rep.* (1999, August 27): para. 16 and note 6.

Spain/US Fisheries Agreement Concerning Fisheries off the United States Coasts 16 February, 1977, in ST/LEG/SER. B/19 (1980): 228.

"Specialized Conference on the Caribbean Countries on the Problems of the Law of the Sea: Declaration of Santo Domingo." *American Journal of International Law* 66 (1972), 918–20.

"Status of the United Nations Convention on the Law of the Sea." *Law of the Sea Bulletin,* no. 19 (1991): 1, note d.

Stevenson, John R., and Bernard H. Oxman, "The Preparations for the Law of the Sea Conference." *American Journal of International Law* 68 (1974): 1–32.

Stevenson, John R., and Bernard H. Oxman. "The Third United Nations Conference on the Law of the Sea: The 1974 Caracas Session," *American Journal of International Law* 69 (1975): 1–30.

Stevenson, John R., and Bernard H. Oxman. "The Third United Nations Conference on the Law of the Sea: The 1975 Geneva Session." *American Journal of International Law* 69, no. 4 (1975): 763–97.

ST/LEG/SER. B/19 (1980): 377.

Straburzyński, Andrzej. "Exclusive Fishery Zones: International and Polish Practice." *Polish Yearbook of International Law* 29 (1970): 257–272.

Sun, Kuan-Ming. "Policy of the Republic of China toward the South China Sea." *Marine Policy* 19 (1995): 401–9.

"Sweden's Act on Sweden's Economic Zone, December 3, 1992." *Law of the Sea Bulletin,* no. 23 (1993): 24–28.

Symonides, Janusz. "The Concept and Claims of Geographically Disadvantaged States at the Third United Nations Law of the Sea Conference." *Recueil des Cours de l'Académie de Droit International* (1988): 293.

Symonides, Janusz. "Delimitation of Maritime Areas between the States with Opposite or Adjacent Coasts." *Polish Yearbook of International Law* 13 (1984): 19–46.

Symonides, Janusz "The Legal Status of the Enclosed and Semi-Enclosed Seas." *German Yearbook of International Law* 27 (1984): 315–33.

Szekely, A. *Latin America and the Development of the Law of the Sea.* Dobbs Ferry, NY: Oceana, 1979.

Taitt, Branford M. "The Exclusive Economic Zone: A Caribbean Community Perspective, Part I, Evolution of a Concept." *West Indian Law Journal* 7 (1983): 36–55.

Tanaka, Yoshifumi. *The International Law of the Sea.* Cambridge: Cambridge University Press, 2012.

Tavernier, Paul. "Les Nouveaux Etats Sans Littoral d'Europe et d'Asie et l'Accès à la Mer." *Revue Générale de Droit International Public* 97 (1993): 727–44.

Teiwaki, Roniti. "Agreements in the South Pacific: Kiribati and the Distant Water Fishing States." *Marine Policy* 11 (1987): 273–84.

"Temple of Preah Vihear Case, (Cambodia v. Thailand)," *International Court of Justice Reports* (1962): 25–27 and 29–30.

"Territorial and Maritime Dispute (Nicaragua v. Colombia)." Judgment. *International Court of Justice Reports* (2012): 666, para. 114.

"The Territorial Sea Act 1987." *Law of the Sea Bulletin,* no. 14 (1989): 1.

"The Territorial Sea and Exclusive Economic Zone Act of Tanzania, 1989." In *Law of the Sea: Current Developments in State Practice,* no. 2. New York: United Nations, 1989.

Toulmin, G. E. "The Barcelona Conference on Communications and Transit and the Danube Statute." *British Yearbook of International Law* 23 (1922): 167–78.

"Treaty on Fisheries between the Government of Certain Pacific Island States and the Government of the United States of America, April 2, 1987." *International Legal Materials* 26 (1987): 1048–50.

Treves, Tullio. "Codification du Droit International et Pratique des Etats dans le Droit de la Mer," Recueil des Cours de l'Académie de Droit International 223 (1990/4): 85.

Treves, Tullio. "Military Installations, Structures and Devices on the Seabed." *American Journal of International Law* 74 (1980): 808–57.

Treves, Tullio. "La Navigation." In *Traité du Nouveau Droit de la Mer,* edited by René-Jean Dupuy and D. Vignes, 687–808 (Paris: Éditions Economica, 1985).

Tunkin, G. I. *Theory of International Law.* Cambridge: Harvard University Press, 1974.

"UN Convention on Transit Trade of Land Locked States." *International Court of Justice Reports* (1984).

UN Department of International Economic and Social Affairs. *Economic Cooperation among Developing Countries in Marine Affairs.* New York: United Nations Publications, 1987.

UN Division for Ocean Affairs and the Law of the Sea. *The Law of the Sea: National Legislation on the Exclusive Economic Zone.* New York: United Nations, 1993.

UN Division for Ocean Affairs and the Law of the Sea. *Law of the Sea Bulletin,* no. 23 (1993): 15.

UN Division for Ocean Affairs and the Law of the Sea. *Practice of States at the Time of Entry into Force of the United Nations Convention on the Law of the Sea.* New York, United Nations, 1994.

UN Doc. A/67/PV. 52 (December 12, 2012).

UN Document. A/AC. 138/SR. *Official Records* 78 (1972): 11.

UN Document. A/CN.4/659 (March 14, 2013).

UN Document. A/CN.4/663 (17 May 2013).

UN Document. A/Conf. 13/C. 1/L. 159. *Official Records* 3 (1958): 253.

UN Document. A/Conf. 13/C. 1/L. 77, Rev. 1, 2, 3. *Official Records* 3 (1958): 232.

UN Document. A/Conf. 13/C. 1/L. 131. *Official Records* 3 (1958): 269.

UN Document. A/Conf. 151/4 (Part II). *Official Records* (1992): chap. 17 paras. 17–52.

UN Document. A/Conf. 62/L. 78, August 28, 1981. *Official Records* 15 (1981): 172–248.

UN Document. A/Conf. 62/WP 10/Rev. 1, April 28, 1979.

UN Document. A/Conf. 164/37. *Official Records* (1995): Article 37.

UN Document. NG 4/9/ Rev. 2, 15 May 1978. *Official Records* 10 (1978): 50.

UN Food and Agriculture Organization. *Compendium of Basic Texts Concerning International Management and Development of Tuna Fisheries.* Fisheries Circular No. 842. Rome: UN Food and Agriculture Organization, 1992.

UN Food and Agriculture Organization Circulaire sur les Pêches No. 807, Rev. 1. Rome: UN Food and Agriculture Organization, 1992.

UN Food and Agriculture Organization Circulaire sur les Pêches No. 835, Rev. 1. Rome: UN Food and Agriculture Organization, 1992.

UN Food and Agriculture Organization, Committee on Fisheries, Twelfth Session. Rome, June 6–12, 1978, COFI/78/Inf. 8 May 1978, 43–65.

UN Food and Agriculture Organization Legislative Study No. 35. Rome: UN Food and Agriculture Organization, 1984.

UN Food and Agriculture Organization Yearbook of Fishery Statistics 50 (1980): 92.

UN Legislative Series. *Laws and Regulations on the Regime of the High Seas* 1 (1951).

UN Legislative Series. *National Legislation and Treaties Relating to the Law of the Sea* (1974).

"United Kingdom and Denmark Agreement Regarding the Fisheries Zone Around the Faroe Islands, 1959." *Revue Générale de Droit International Public* (1963): 621.

"United Kingdom and Denmark Agreement Regarding the Fisheries Zone Around the Faroe Islands, 1959." *Revue Générale de Droit International Public* 67 (1963): 621.

United Nations. *The Law of the Sea: Current Developments in State Practice*, no. 2. New York: United Nations, 1989.

United States. "President's Ocean Policy Statement, March 10, 1983." The Division of Ocean Affairs and the Law of the Sea.

United States Department of State, Bureau of Intelligence and Research, Geographer. *International Boundary Study, Series A: Limits in the Seas, National Claims to Maritime Jurisdiction* No. 36 (1973).

"United States/EEC Agreement Concerning Fisheries off the United States Coasts, February 15, 1977." *International Legal Materials* 16 (1977): 257.

United States FMCA of 1976.

United States, Marine Mammal Protection Act, 1992.

"Uruguay: Decree Extending Territorial Waters." *International Legal Materials* 8 (1969): 1067-72.

US/Mexico Fisheries Agreement of November 24, 1976, in ST/LEG/SER. B/19 (1980): 430.

"U.S.S.R. and United Kingdom: Fisheries Agreement." *International Legal Materials* 4 (1965): 174–75.

Vallarta, Jose Luis. "Protection and Preservation of the Maritime Environment and Marine Scientific Research at the Third United Nations Conference on the Law of the Sea." *Law and Contemporary Problems* 46, no. 2 (1983): 147–154.

Van Kleffens, Eelco Nicolaas. "Sovereignty in International Law." *Recueil des Cours de l'Académie de Droit International* 82 (1953): 84–106.

Vanuatu's Maritime Zones act of 1981, Part V.

Vicuña, Francisco Orrego. *The Exclusive Economic Zone: Regime and Legal Nature under International Law.* Cambridge: Cambridge University Press, 1989.

Vicuña, Francisco Orrego. "The 'Presential Sea': Defining Coastal States' Special Interests in High Sea Fisheries and other Activities." *German Yearbook of International Law* 35 (1992): 264–92.

Vicuña, Francisco Orrego. "Towards an Effective Management of High Seas Fisheries and the Settlement of the Pending Issues of the Law of the Sea." *Ocean Development and International Law* 24 (1993): 81–92.

Vicuña, Francisco Orrego. "Trends and Issues in the Law of the Sea of Applied in Latin America." *Ocean Development and International Law* 26, no. 2 (1995): 93–103.

Villiger, Mark E. *Customary International Law and Treaties: A Study of Their Interactions and Interrelations, with Special Considerations of the 1969 Vienna Convention on the Law of Treaties.* Boston: Martinus Nijhoff, 1985.

Wali, Ibrahim J. "An Evaluation of the Convention on the Law of the Sea from the Perspective of Landlocked States." *Virginia Journal of International Law* 22 (1982): 627–66.

"Wimbledon Case (France, Italy, Japan, and the United Kingdom v. Germany)." *Permanent Court of International Judgment* Ser. A, No. 1, (1923): 26–28.

Wolfrum, Rüdiger. "The Emerging Customary Law of Marine Zones: State Practice and the Convention on the Law of the Sea." *Netherlands Yearbook of International Law* 18 (1987): 121–44.

"World Review of Highly Migratory Species and Straddling Stocks." *Food and Agriculture Organization of the United Nations Fisheries Technical Paper No 337*, 50–63. Rome: Food and Agriculture Organization of the United Nations, 1994.

Yusuf, Abdulqawi A. "Towards a New Legal Framework for Marine Research: Coastal State Consent and International Coordination," *Virginia Journal of International Law* 19 (1979): 411–27.

Zakharov, A. J. "Comment to Article by C. A. Fleischer, the Exclusive Economic Zone under the Convention Regime and in State Practice." In *The 1982 Convention on the Law of the Sea, Proceedings of the Seventeenth Annual Conference, July 12–16, 1983,* edited by Albert W. Koers and Bernard H. Oxman. Honolulu: Law of the Sea Institute, University of Hawaii, 1984.

Abbreviations

AALCC	Asian-African Legal Consultative Committee
AC	Allowable Catch
ACP	African Caribbean and Pacific Coastal States
AFDI	*Annuaire Français de Droit International*
AJICL	*American Journal of International and Comparative Law*
AJIL	*American Journal of International Law*
ASIL	*American Society of International Law*
BYIL	*British Yearbook of International Law*
Colum JWB	*Columbia Journal of World Business*
Colum LR	*Columbia Law Review*
CMLR	*Common Market Law Review*
Courier	*The Courier* (Africa-Caribbean-Pacific-European Community)
CYILA	*Chinese Yearbook of International Law and Affairs*
CYIL	*Canadian Yearbook of International Law*
DJILP	*Denver Journal of International Law and Policy*
DLJ	*Dalhousie Law Journal*
Dods	*Dodson's Admiralty Reports* (Great Britain)
DWFS	Distant Water Fishing States
ECR	*European Court Reports*
EEC	European Economic Community
EFC	European Fisheries Convention
EEZ	Exclusive Economic Zone
EFZ	Exclusive Fishing Zone
FA	*Foreign Affairs*
FAO	Food and Agriculture Organization
FRG	Federal Republic of Germany
GA Res	United Nations General Assembly Resolutions
GDR	German Democratic Republic

GDS (s)	Geographically disadvantaged states
Grotius Trans	*Transactions of the Grotius Society,* 1915–1958/59
GYIL	*German Yearbook of International Law*
Harvard LR	*Harvard Law Review*
HC	Harvesting Capacity
HMS	Highly Migratory Species
ICJ	International Court of Justice
ICJ Rep	*International Court of Justice Reports*
ICLQ	*International and Comparative Law Quarterly*
ICNT	Informal Composite Negotiating Text
IJ	*International Journal*
IJIL	*Indian Journal of International Law*
IJMCL	*International Journal of Marine and Coastal Law*
ILA	International Law Association
ILC	International Law Commission
ILM	*International Legal Materials*
Int. L.	*International Lawyer*
ISNT	Informal Single Negotiating Text
ITLOS	International Tribunal for the Law of the Sea
It. YIL	*Italian Yearbook of International Law*
IUHEI	Institut Universitaire de Hautes Etudes Internationales
JAIL	*Japanese Annual of International Law*
JDI	*Journal de Droit International*
JMLC	*Journal of Maritime Law and Commerce*
JORADP	*Journal Officiel de la République Algérienne Démocratique et Populaire*
Keesing's	*Keesing's Contemporary Archives*
LCP	*Law and Contemporary Problems*
LLS (s)	Land-Locked State(s)
LNTS	*League of Nations Treaty Series*
LOS	UN Convention on the Law of the Sea
Marit. Pol. Mgmt.	*Maritime Policy and Management*
Marit. Stud. Mgmt.	*Maritime Studies and Management*

Mod LR	*Modern Law Review*
Moore	International Arbitrations. Moore, J. B. *History and Digest of International Arbitrations to which the U. S. has been a Party*, 1898
Moore, Digest	J. B. Moore, *Digest of International Law* 8 vols., 1906
MP	*Marine Policy*
MULR	*Melbourne University Law Review*
NAFO	North Atlantic Fisheries Organization
NILR	*Netherlands International Law Review*
NLJ	*Nigerian Law Journal*
NYIL	*Netherland Yearbook of International Law*
OAU	Organization of African Unity
ODIL	*Ocean Development and International Law*
Official Records 1958	*Official Records of the First UN Conference on the Law of the Sea*
Official Records 1960	*Official Records of the Second UN Conference on the Law of the Sea*
Official Records 1973–1982	*Official Records of the Third UN Conference on the Law of the Sea*
OJEC	*Official Journal of the European Community*
OLR	*Oregon Law Review*
OPN	*Ocean Policy News*
Para (s)	Paragraph(s)
PCIJ	Permanent Court of International Justice
Phil LJ	*Philadelphia Law Journal*
PYIL	*Polish Yearbook of International Law*
RBDI	*Revue Belge de Droit International*
RCADI	*Recueil des Cours de l'Académie de Droit International*
REDI	*Revue Egyptienne de Droit International*
RGDIP	*Revue Générale de Droit International Public*
RHDI	*Revue Hellénique de Droit International*
RIAA	*UN Reports of International Arbitral Awards*
RICNT	Revised Informal Composite Negotiating Text
RIRI	*Revue Iranienne des Relations Internationales*

RSNT	Revised Single Negotiating Text
SAYIL	*South African Yearbook of International Law*
SDLR	*San Diego Law Review*
SEP OP	Separate Opinion
ST/LEG/SER. B/1	UN Legislative Series, *Laws and Regulations on the Regime of the High Seas* 1 (1951).
ST/LEG/SER. B/2	UN Legislative Series, *Laws and Regulations on the Regime of the High Seas* 2 (1952).
ST/LEG/SER. B/6	UN Legislative Series, *Laws and Regulations on the Regime of the Territorial Sea* (1957).
ST/LEG/SER. B/8	UN Legislative Series, *Supplement to Laws and Regulations on the Regime of the High Seas and Laws Concerning the Nationality of Ships* (1959).
ST/LEG/SER. B/15	UN Legislative Series, *National Legislation and Treaties Relating to the Territorial Sea, the Contiguous Zone, and the Continental Shelf, the High Seas and to Fishing and Conservation of Living Resources of the Sea* (1970).
ST/LEG/SER. B/16	UN Legislative Series, *National Legislation and Treaties Relating to the Law of the Sea* (1974).
ST/LEG/SER. B/18	UN Legislative Series, *National Legislation and Treaties Relating to the Law of the Sea* (1976).
ST/LEG/SER. B/19	UN Legislative Series, *National Legislation and Treaties Relating to the Law of the Sea* (1980).
Swiss YIL	*Swiss Yearbook of International Law*
SYIL	*Spanish Yearbook of International Law*
Texas ILJ	*Texas International Law Journal*
Trans AFS	*Transactions of the American Fisheries Society*
UK	United Kingdom
UN	United Nations
UNCLOS I	First United Nations Conference on the Law of the Sea (Geneva 1958)
UNCLOS II	Second United Nations Conference on the Law of the Sea (Geneva 1960)
UNCLOS III	Third United Nations Conference on the Law of the Sea (1973–1982)

UN Doc	United Nations Documents
UNGAOR	United Nations General Assembly Official Records
UNTS	*United Nations Treaty Series*
US	United States
USSR	Union of Soviet Socialist Republics
VCT	Vienna Convention on the Law of Treaties
VJIL	*Virginia Journal of International Law*
WILJ	*West Indian Law Journal*
YILC	*Yearbook of the International Law Commission*
YUN	*Yearbook of the United Nations*
YWA	*Yearbook of the World Affairs*

Table of Cases

Anglo-Norwegian Fisheries Case, ICJ Reports, 1951.

Asylum Case (Columbia v. Peru), ICJ Reports, 1950.

Behring Sea Fur Seals Arbitration (Great Britain v. United States), 1893, in Moore, Digest vol. 1 1898, p. 755.

Channel Continental Shelf Arbitration (United Kingdom v. France), 17 UNRIAA, 1978.

Case Concerning the Continental Shelf (Tunisia v. Libyan Arab Jamahiriya), ICJ Reports, 1982.

Case Concerning the Continental Shelf (Libyan Arab Jamahiriya v. Malta), ICJ Reports, 1985.

Case Concerning Delimitation of the Maritime Boundary in the Gulf of Maine Area (Canada v. United States), ICJ, Reports, 1984.

Case Concerning the Delimitation of Marine Areas between Canada and the French Republic, Decision of the Court of Arbitration dated 10 June 1992, in ILM, 1992.

Case Concerning Maritime Delimitation in the Area between Greenland and Jan Mayen (Denmark v. Norway), ICJ Reports, 1993.

Case Concerning the Diversion of Water from the Meuse (Netherlands v. Belgium), 1937, PCIJ Reports, Series A/B N 70.

Case Concerning the Land, Island, and Maritime Frontier Dispute, (El Salvador v. Honduras; Nicaragua intervening), 1992, ICJ Reports, 1992.

Case Concerning Land Reclamation by Singapore in and around the Straits of Johor (Malaysia v. Singapore), 2003, ITLOS, 2003.

Case Concerning Military and Paramilitary Activities in and Against Nicaragua (Nicaragua v. United States), Merits, June 27, 1986, ICJ Reports, 1986.

Corfu Channel Case (United Kingdom v. Albania), 1949 ICJ Reports, 1949.

Fisheries Jurisdiction Case (United Kingdom v. Iceland), Merits, 1974, ICJ Reports, 1974.

Guyana v. Suriname, Decision of Annex VII Arbitral Panel, 2007.

Le Louis, The 2 Dods, 1817.

Maritime Delimitation and Territorial Question Between Qatar and Bahrain (Qatar v. Bahrain), 2001 ICJ Reports, 2001.

Maritime Dispute (Peru v. Chile), 2014, ICJ Report 2014.

The M/V "SAIGA" (No. 2) Case (Saint Vincent and the Grenadines v. Guinea), 1999, ITLOS, 1999.

The M/V "Virginia G" Case (Panama v. Guinea Bissau), 2014, ITLOS, 2014.

North Continental Shelf Cases (West Germany v. Denmark; West Germany v. Netherland), ICJ Reports, 1969.

Pulp Mills on the River Uruguay (Argentina v. Uruguay), 2010, ICJ Reports, 2010.

Railroad Traffic (Lithuania v. Poland) Case (Advisory Opinion), PCIJ Reports Series A/B, No. 42, 1931.

Southern Bluefin Tuna Cases (New Zealand v. Japan; Australia v. Japan), 1999, ITLOS 1999.

Territorial and Maritime Dispute (Nicaragua v. Colombia), 2012, ICJ Reports, 2012.

The ARA Libertad Case (Argentina v. Ghana), 2012, ITLOS, 2012.

The MOX Plant Case (Ireland v. United Kingdom), 2001, ITLOS 2001.

The Rights of Nationals of the United States in Morocco (United States v. France) Case, ICJ Reports, 1952.

The Rights of Passage over Indian Territory (Portugal v. India), Merits, ICJ Reports, 1960.

The Temple of Preah Vihear Case (Cambodia v. Thailand), ICJ Reports, 1962.

Countries with the Largest and Smallest Exclusive Economic Zones

Rank	Area (km^2)	Country
1	11,351,000	United States
2	11,035,000	France
3	8,505,348	Australia
4	7,566,673	Russia
5	6,805,586	United Kingdom
6	6,159,032	Indonesia
7	5,599,077	Canada
8	4,479,388	Japan
9	4,083,744	New Zealand
10	3,879,666	China
11	3,681,989	Chile
12	3,660,955	Brazil
13	3,441,810	Kiribati
14	3,177,593	Mexico
15	2,996,419	Federated States of Micronesia
⋮	⋮	⋮
137	10,503	Syria
138	10,225	Bahrain
139	10,090	Brunei
140	9,974	Saint Kitts and Nevis
141	7,745	Montenegro
142	7,459	Djibouti
143	7,031	Lithuania
144	3,447	Belgium
145	1,606	Democratic Republic of the Congo
146	1,067	Singapore
147	771	Iraq
148	288	Monaco
149	220	Slovenia
150	166	Jordan
151	50	Bosnia and Herzegovina

Source: Food and Agriculture Organization of the United Nations.

Index

A

B

C

E

F

G

J

N

Q

R

T

U

V

W

Y

Z

www.ingramcontent.com/pod-product-compliance
Lightning Source LLC
LaVergne TN
LVHW010722210926
848485LV00007B/1416/J